BOOMS AND BUSTS

Volume 1

BOOMS
AND BUSTS

An Encyclopedia of Economic History
from Tulipmania of the 1630s to the
Global Financial Crisis of the 21st Century

Volume 1

James Ciment, Editor

SHARPE REFERENCE
an imprint of M.E. Sharpe, Inc.

SHARPE REFERENCE

Sharpe Reference is an imprint of M.E. Sharpe, Inc.

M.E. Sharpe, Inc.
80 Business Park Drive
Armonk, NY 10504

Cover photos (background; left to right) provided by Getty Images and the following: Mario Tama; Popperfoto; Yoshikazu Tsuno/AFP; Kean Collection/Hulton Archive; Melanie Einzig.

Library of Congress Cataloging-in-Publication Data

Booms and busts : an encyclopedia of economic history from Tulipmania of the 1630s to the global financial crisis of the 21st century / James Ciment, editor.
  v. ; cm.
Includes bibliographical references and index.
ISBN 978-0-7656-8224-6 (hardcover : alk. paper)
1. Financial crises—Encyclopedias. 2. Finance—Encyclopedias. I. Ciment, James.

HB3722.B67 2010
330.03—dc22   2010021272

Printed and bound in the United States

The paper used in this publication meets the minimum requirements of American National Standard for Information Sciences—Permanence of Paper for Printed Library Materials, ANSI Z 39.48.1984.

CW (c) 10 9 8 7 6 5 4 3 2 1

Publisher: Myron E. Sharpe
Vice President and Director of New Product Development: Donna Sanzone
Vice President and Production Director: Carmen Chetti
Executive Development Editor: Jeff Hacker
Project Manager: Angela Piliouras
Program Coordinator: Cathleen Prisco
Assistant Editor: Alison Morretta
Text Design and Cover Design: Jesse Sanchez
Typesetter: Nancy Connick

Contents

VOLUME 3

Topic Finder

Banks, Brokerage Houses, Financial Firms
  AIG
  Bank of America
  Banks, Commercial
  Banks, Investment
  Bear Stearns
  Capital One
  Citigroup
  Countrywide Financial
  Depository Institutions
  Fannie Mae and Freddie Mac
  Goldman Sachs
  IndyMac Bancorp
  JPMorgan Chase
  Lehman Brothers
  Long-Term Capital
    Management
  Luminent Mortgage Capital
  Merrill Lynch
  Money Store, The
  Morgan Stanley
  Northern Rock
  PNC Financial Services
  Shadow Banking System
  UBS
  Wachovia
  Washington Mutual

Booms and Busts, Historical
  Asian Financial Crisis (1997)
  Boom, Economic (1920s)
  Boom, Economic (1960s)
  Dot.com Bubble
    (1990s–2000)
  Florida Real-Estate Boom
    (1920s)
  Great Depression (1929–1933)

  Housing Booms and Busts
  Mississippi Bubble
    (1717–1720)
  Oil Shocks (1973–1974,
    1979–1980)
  Panic of 1901
  Panic of 1907
  Panics and Runs, Bank
  Ponzi Scheme (1919–1920)
  Poseidon Bubble (1969–1970)
  Recession and Financial Crisis
    (2007–)
  Recession, Reagan
    (1981–1982)
  Recession, Roosevelt
    (1937–1939)
  Recession, Stagflation (1970s)
  Savings and Loan Crises
    (1980s–1990s)
  Souk al-Manakh (Kuwait)
    Stock Market Crash (1982)
  South Sea Bubble (1720)
  Stock Market Crash (1929)
  Stock Market Crash (1987)
  Tequila Effect
  Tulipmania (1636–1637)

Bubbles, Crises, and Cycles, Types
  Asset-Price Bubble
  Bank Cycles
  Business Cycles, International
  Credit Cycle
  Demographic Cycle
  Echo Bubble
  Growth Cycles
  Kondratieff Cycles
  Panics and Runs, Bank

  Production Cycles
  Seasonal Cycles
  Slow-Growth Recovery
  Systemic Financial Crises

Corporations (Nonfinancial) and Corporate Affairs
  Bethlehem Steel
  Chrysler
  Circuit City Stores
  Corporate Corruption
  Corporate Finance
  Enron
  Fleetwood Enterprises
  General Motors
  Linens 'n Things
  Penn Central
  Tribune Company
  Tropicana Entertainment
  VeraSun Energy
  WorldCom

Economic Terms and Concepts
  Balance of Payments
  Behavioral Economics
  Capital Account
  Confidence, Consumer and
    Business
  Consumption
  Creative Destruction
  Current Account
  Debt
  Deflation
  Effective Demand
  Employment and
    Unemployment
  Financial Development/
    Deepening

xi

Editor

James Ciment

Editorial Board

Contributors

Omar J. Khan
University of Maine, Orono

Robert Koehn
Independent Scholar

Teresa A. Koncick
Florida State University

Andrea Krogstad
Augustana College

Bill Kte'pi
Independent Scholar

M.V. Lakshmi
GITAM University

Alexander V. Laskin
Quinnipiac University

Marc Lenglet
European Business School, Paris

Priscilla Liang
*California State University,
Channel Islands*

John Lodewijks
University of Western Sydney

Lyudmila Lugovskaya
University of Cambridge

William J. Luther
George Mason University

D.W. MacKenzie
United States Coast Guard Academy

A.D. Madhavi
Independent Scholar

Nuno Luis Madureira
University of Lisbon

Jerry W. Markham
Florida International University

Wesley C. Marshall
*Universidad Autónoma
Metropolitana, Iztapalapa*

John F. McDonald
Roosevelt University

Elliott McNamee
Dechert, LLP

Asli Yuksel Mermod
Marmara University

Andrew P. Morriss
*University of Alabama School
of Law*

Maria Nathan
Lynchburg College

Roy Nersesian
Monmouth University

Yeva Nersisyan
University of Missouri, Kansas City

Reynold F. Nesiba
Augustana College

John J. Neumann
St. John's University

Andre R. Neveu
Skidmore College

Mehmet Odekon
Skidmore College

Kepa Ormazabal
University of the Basque Country

Laura Peressin
MIB School of Management

Steven Pressman
Monmouth University

Bing Ran
*Pennsylvania State University,
Harrisburg*

William Rapp
New Jersey Institute of Technology

Michael Rawdan
Nova Southeastern University

Felipe C. Rezende
*University of Missouri,
Kansas City*

Charles Richardson
Clark Atlanta University

Louis-Phillipe Rochon
Laurentian University

Justin Ross
Indiana University, Bloomington

Chris Rowley
City University, London

Abhijit Roy
University of Scranton

Manjula S. Salimath
University of North Texas

Marisa Scigliano
Trent University

Mario Seccareccia
University of Ottawa

Sharmistha Self
Missouri State University

Željko Šević
Glasgow Caledonian University

Robert N. Stacy
Independent Scholar

Charles A. Stone
*City University of New York,
Brooklyn College*

Rick Szostak
University of Alberta

Mark Thornton
Ludwig von Mises Institute

Giorgio Valentinuz
MIB School of Management

Hendrik Van den Berg
University of Nebraska, Lincoln

Antonella Viola
European University Institute

Brenda Spotton Visano
York University

Tiia Vissak
University of Tartu

Andrew J. Waskey
Dalton State College

Tim J. Watts
Kansas State University

Cameron M. Weber
New School for Social Research

Frank L. Winfrey
Lyon College

Andrew L. Yarrow
American University

Jamie Shuk Ki Yuen
*California State Polytechnic
University, Pomona*

Ulku Yuksel
University of Sydney

Jesus M. Zaratiegui
University of Navarra

Christina Zenker
Salem College

Introduction

To people whose jobs, lifestyles, families, and futures depend upon the ups and downs of capitalist markets—in other words, just about all of us—economic booms and busts may seem like elemental forces of nature. For every action, it would appear, there is an equal and opposite reaction. What goes up must come down. The cycle of good times and hard times, finally, is beyond human control.

Once upon a time, there was some truth to this view. Prior to the industrial age, when human endeavor was largely confined to agriculture, natural forces largely determined economic feast or famine. Indeed, one of the first intellectual efforts to understand the rhythms of market economies was known as the "sunspot theory." According to its author, the nineteenth-century British economist William Stanley Jevons, the eleven-year cycle of sunspot activity, identified by astronomers of the day, influenced the earth's climate, which affected crops, causing economies to expand and contract.

Subsequent to Jevons's cosmological explanation of the boom-bust cycle, other economists pointed to causes more firmly rooted on Earth and, specifically, in the doings of the planet's most enterprising species: humans. Economic cycles, they said, were the result of credit (John Stuart Mill), of fixed capital investment (Clément Juglar), and of technological innovation (Nikolai Kondratieff). What all of these theories shared was the notion that there are predictable rules and principles, akin to the laws of nature, that explain economic cycles. These rules abide because human beings,

in their role as *homo economicus*, or economic man, act rationally. According to this view, people act as efficient cogs in a great economic machine, their behavior following immutable laws and principles. This mechanistic view of human economic behavior—the British neoclassical paradigm, as it were—was very much in sync with the nineteenth-century Newtonian view of how nature itself works: logically and predictably.

Far from British shores, meanwhile, in the central European city of Vienna, Austria, an alternative paradigm emerged. For the thinkers of the Austrian school, economics is not driven by natural law but by human psychology; value is not determined mechanistically by adding up all the costs of making a product but by how much people want that product. Economic growth and contraction, according to this view, are not determined by natural law but by the ambitions, insights, daring, and, yes, error of very human entrepreneurs. Despite these fundamentally different understandings of what determines the rhythms of an economy, the British neoclassical and Austrian psychological/entrepreneurial schools of thought did share at least one important assumption and conclusion about economic cycles. The assumption was that booms and busts, while obviously having beneficial or deleterious effects on people's lives, are not central to how economies function but are instead self-correcting anomalies. On the basis of this assumption, these very different economic schools both concluded that there is very little governments can or should do to counteract boom-and-bust cycles or even to ease the want and suffering they cause.

The Keynesian revolution of the middle third of the twentieth century changed both the assumption and conclusion of the neoclassical and Austrian schools of thought and put the business cycle and efforts to manage it at the heart of economic theory and practice. Whatever causes booms and busts, argued the British economist John Maynard Keynes, economic forces can produce a situation in which the price equilibrium set by supply and demand—that is, the equilibrium that determines the utilization of economic resources, including both capital and labor—can become stuck well below an economy's full capacity to produce, leaving both factories and labor idle. Thus, the Great Depression formed a backdrop to Keynes's greatest work, *The General Theory of Employment, Interest and Money* (1936). In it, Keynes argued that only government has the power to reinvigorate demand—through fiscal and monetary means—and thus lift an economy out of economic stagnation.

Keynes offered a series of tools governments can use to smooth out economic cycles and the hardships they cause—tools that were eagerly taken up throughout the industrialized capitalist West in the decades following World War II. And so successful were these tools—or so they appeared to be, amid the greatest economic boom in world history—that economists and policy makers spoke of capitalism as having put the economic cycle itself behind it for good.

That illusion was shattered by the repeated economic contractions of the 1970s and early 1980s, accompanied, seemingly in violation of basic economic principles, by large doses of inflation. While Keynes's heirs argued for wage and price controls to rein in inflation, policy makers largely ignored these ideas in favor of a purely monetarist approach—making sure that the money supply was kept in sync with economic growth. Once again, two decades of solid economic growth, with a minimum of economic contractions, led economic thinkers and tinkerers to believe they had found the economic Holy

Grail—a way to avoid or at least minimize the boom-and-bust cycle.

Contributing to this thinking were key technological and financial innovations of the late twentieth and early twenty-first centuries. The information revolution created by the personal computer and the Internet offered better and more easily accessible information to market participants, promising to minimize economic inefficiencies and market errors. And the securitization of debt—whereby the inherent risk of lending could be minimized through the marketplace—meant that more credit was available to drive economic growth.

Of course, as the financial crisis and recession of the late 2000s proved, neither technological innovation nor debt securitization could permanently keep the wolf from the door. Indeed, debt securitization, proving to be the wolf itself, encouraged the kind of reckless financial leveraging that had caused so many booms to turn to busts in the "dark ages"—that is, before economists and policy makers hubristically came to believe they could banish the economic cycle itself.

Conceived and created in the midst of the worst economic recession since the 1930s, this encyclopedia attempts to explain what the boom-and-bust cycle is all about—in theory, in history, and in real-life implications. Before describing the content and organization of this work, a brief explanation of its key concepts is in order. A boom is a period of rising economic expectation and activity triggered by any number of factors—population expansion, a new technology, the discovery of natural resources, the emergence of new industries, an increase in productivity, and the like. Booms go through a series of stages, beginning with a period in which investor confidence is matched by real economic growth. This is followed by a second phase, in which investor euphoria leads to outsized expectations, speculation, and increasing financial leveraging. At some point, when the savviest investors begin to recognize the frothiness of the expansion and start to pull out of the market, a decline in prices follows, which then triggers a mass sell-off and a rapid drop in prices. The bust that follows is marked by a precipitous decline in financial activity, production, and sales, all of which lead to a broad contraction in business, rising unemployment, and a proliferation of bankruptcies—until the cycle is repeated.

Contents of *Booms and Busts*

The contents of this encyclopedia—three volumes, containing more than 360 articles—takes it from there, offering the whys, hows, whats, whens, wheres, and whos of economic booms and busts. Historically, the work begins with the first great episode in modern speculation, the Dutch tulip boom of the 1630s, and concludes with the Great Recession of the late 2000s, encompassing nearly 400 years of economic history. Geographically, it includes articles on all the major economies of the world, but with an emphasis on U.S. economic history. It extensively covers the housing and securities boom of the mid-2000s and the financial crisis and global recession that followed. Readers will also find biographical entries on the important thinkers in the field (most of these are *not* American, a reflection of the history of the discipline) and the theories they advanced, with the emphasis on those economists whose work has focused on business and trade cycles In addition, a number of biographies highlight recent and current economic policy makers and the decisions they have made. There are also profiles of economic and financial institutions, both private sector and government (most of these *are* American). In no small measure, this work also presents more abstract and technical aspects of economics and business-cycle theory, with entries, written in laymen's terms, on essential ideas, terms, and schools of thought.

Finally, a word on what this encyclopedia is not. *Booms and Busts* is not a general economics text. As its title implies, it focuses on one critical aspect of economic history and theory—the economic cycle. At the same time, because the theory and reality of economic cycles are so inter-connected, a close reading of the encyclopedia's contents will provide readers with a general understanding of the last 400 years of both. Within these three volumes, readers are also likely to find articles of varying degrees of difficulty. Many entries, particularly those pertaining to economic history, can be easily understood by readers with a passing knowledge of the field. Other entries, particularly those on theoretical subjects, may be elucidated with the help of the extensive glossary at the back of Volume 3.

Aids for navigating the content of this encyclopedia are provided at the beginning of Volume 1 in the form of two tables of contents—alphabetical and topical—and at the end of each article, where cross-references to related entries in the book are given. A general chronology of booms and busts through history, also contained in Volume 3, orients readers in time. And a Selected Bibliography of books, articles, and Web sites—in addition to a Further Reading list at the end of each article—directs users to a wealth of recommended resources for expanded research. The book concludes with an exhaustive index of names, events, terms, concepts, and so forth.

An encyclopedia of this scope could not have been completed without an amazing team of contributors, editors, and production people. First and foremost are the contributing authors, whose expertise and writing skills make these articles so informative and readable. Our outstanding editorial board of economists—Maureen Burton, Mark Maier, Mehmet Odekon, and Ashish Vaidya—reviewed articles and provided valuable guidance, advice, and useful suggestions and corrections beyond count.

Having worked with them so many times before, I knew the editorial and production staff at M.E. Sharpe publishing would do their usual superb job. Once again, I was not disappointed. Thanks to Jeff Hacker, executive development editor, for his exacting editorial pen; assistant editor Alison Morretta and project manager Angela Piliouras for keeping things organized and moving forward; copyeditor Susanna Sharpe for smoothing out the prose and pointing out the inconsistencies; executive editor Lynn Taylor for all her helpful advice and consultation and for finding experienced and knowledgeable contributors for critical articles. Donna Sanzone, vice president and director of new product development, was an invaluable aide throughout the process, offering suggestions and corrections whose absence would have made this work a much weaker effort. And, lastly, thanks to publisher Mike Sharpe—the man with the last and, uncannily, right word.

Finally, I would like to dedicate these volumes to my children, Bibi and Bruno—may their booms be many and their busts few.

Booms and Busts
Pre-Twentieth Century

Human society has always been subject to the rise and fall of fortunes. For the tens of thousands of years of pre-history, most human communities lived on the edge of survival. If adequate rains fell at the right time, there was wild food to gather and animals to hunt. If not, there was famine. The rise of agriculture during the late Neolithic Period, or New Stone Age, mitigated the vagaries of nature by allowing for a greater abundance and predictability of food supplies and for the provisioning of larders in times of plenty against times of want. Still, climate could undo the best-laid plans. Prolonged drought could disrupt even advanced civilizations, as appears to have been the fate of the Anasazi in the American Southwest. The Anasazi built complex societies and sophisticated architecture around the turn of the second millennium CE, only to disappear two centuries later as the result of an extended drought and the social unrest it triggered.

Rise of Civilization

The development of large-scale irrigation also helped remove human society from the immediate effects of climate, though this did not seem to help the Anasazi. By ensuring a steady source of water, civilizations that mastered the complex engineering of irrigation could further shield themselves from fluctuations in food supplies. But the development of large-scale irrigation was premised on the existence of a centralized government authority that could build and maintain such projects through forced labor and taxes. As civilizations grew more complex, they became more interdependent, with urban dwellers depending on the surplus produced by farmers and rural folk depending on the central government to ensure social peace and infrastructure maintenance.

But even civilizations that had largely overcome climatic uncertainty could experience rises and falls based on environmental factors. In cases as diverse as the Maya of Mesoamerica and the ancient inhabitants of Easter Island (Rapa Nui) in Polynesia, the archaeological consensus is that these civilizations went into periods of prolonged decline when they had grown beyond their local environment's capacity to support them or had caused their local ecosystems to collapse. In addition, with increasing complexity came greater fragility of the social authority. When central authority became weak, the social structure often frayed, leading to civil unrest, anarchy, and disruptions of internal trade. Chinese history, to take one example, was marked for thousands of years by alternating periods of effective government and economic prosperity followed by weakened central government, social chaos, and economic want.

In the West, the rise of Roman authority led to an unprecedented period of economic expansion and prosperity throughout the Mediterranean world and much of Western Europe from the late first millennium BCE to the middle of the first millennium CE. The collapse of the Roman Empire in the fifth century, however, plunged much of the region into what is known as the Dark Ages, a roughly 500-year period marked by a near cessation of trade, a decline in manufacturing, the collapse of cities, and the loss of critical technical skills.

"External Shocks"

Scholars refer to events that arise from outside the existing economic order as external shocks. For Europeans, two external shocks ushered in the modern era. Each resulted in the rise and fall of fortunes for all social classes. The first was the so-called Black Death of the mid-fourteenth century, in which about one-third of the continent's population succumbed to the bubonic plague. While the immediate impact on the people of Europe was devastating, most historians have since concluded that the episode had beneficial long-term economic effects.

Much of Europe was overpopulated when the plague hit, which limited the productivity of land, kept laborers in poverty and subjugation to lords, and perpetuated an unequal distribution of wealth. Those who owned preciously scarce land—a class of people invested in the economic status quo—retained the lion's share of economic power. The reduction in population as a result of the plague shifted power and wealth from the landlords to laboring and trading classes, resulting in higher wages, greater mobility, more freedom of movement, greater demand, and more internal trade. Some economic historians have even argued that the Black Death was a contributing factor to the advent of the capitalist economic system in early modern Europe.

The second great external event of the middle centuries of the second millennium BCE was the European "discovery" of the Americas. For Spain, the nation that conquered most of the New World in the first century after Columbus, the influx of vast quantities of precious metals from mines in Mexico and South America created new wealth, which led to a steady increase in population. But this expansion led to increased demand for products that the economy—hurt by the crown's decision to expel Jews and Moors, key businessmen and craftsmen, respectively—could not provide, leading to inflation. With costs rising, Spanish goods could not compete with those from other parts of Europe, leading to an eventual decline of the Spanish economy and its eclipse by those of Northern Europe.

Even in the latter areas, however, inflation eroded the wealth of those who lived off fixed rent income, such as landlords. For those who borrowed money, particularly middle-class merchants and craftspeople, the effects of inflation were positive, since they could pay back their loans in depreciated currency. As with the Black Death, many economic historians believe that the inflation caused by the influx of precious metals from the Americas had an immediate devastating impact—particularly on the poor—but offered long-term economic benefits in that it undermined the power of conservative landlords in favor of more enterprising and innovative merchants and artisans.

Early Modern Capitalism and Speculation

Natural catastrophes, environmental degradation, the collapse of central authorities, shocks like the Black Death and the conquest of the Americas—all of these factors came from outside the existing economic order. It is only with the modern capitalist order, which began to emerge in Europe early in the second half of the second millennium CE, that can one speak of a business cycle of expansion and contraction primarily driven not by the external factors of natural forces and governance issues—though both would continue to

Speculation in tulips became so frenzied in Holland during the mid-1630s that buyers were paying tens of thousands of florins—or storehouses of food and grain—for a single exotic bulb. A purely market-driven bubble, tulipmania burst suddenly in 1637. *(The Granger Collection, New York)*

play a critical role in such cycles, the latter into the present era—but by economic forces inherent in capitalism itself.

Still, until the late eighteenth and early nineteenth centuries, the dynamic forces of capitalism—the "creative destruction," as Austrian school economist Joseph Schumpeter later put it—had yet to have a major impact on the economic lives of most people. Economic trends were long-term and often little felt beyond those classes with money to invest. Most people earned their livelihood through agriculture—consuming most of what they produced—and participated only tangentially in the larger commercial economy. This norm for much of the world, even into the nineteenth and twentieth centuries, was also true for residents of Europe prior to the industrial and commercial revolutions of the late eighteenth and early nineteenth centuries, despite its being the most economically advanced continent in the early modern era.

Not surprisingly, then, the earliest episodes of boom and bust in Western history were confined to speculators. These included the Mississippi and South Sea bubbles of early eighteenth-century France and England, respectively, and, the most infamous of all, the tulipmania episode of early seventeenth-century Holland, all highly speculative episodes that made and destroyed great fortunes in a matter of a few years and even months. While tulipmania, involving speculation in exotic tulip bulbs and tulip bulb fortunes, was driven by market forces alone, the Mississippi and South Sea bubbles involved quasi-governmental enterprises—one dealing in North American lands and the other South American trade—indicating the large role government played in these mercantilist, early capitalist economies. And, as with the tulip episode, the financial impacts of the South Sea and Mississippi bubbles were largely confined to the upper reaches of society, barely affecting the overall national economy and causing no more than a ripple in the lives of ordinary farmers and workers.

Commercial and Industrial Revolutions

It is only with the advent of the commercial and industrial revolutions in the late eighteenth and early nineteenth centuries that one can speak of the modern business cycle. A complicated phenomenon occurring over centuries, the commercial revolution essentially involved the integration of larger and larger sectors of the populace into the cash economy, selling their labor or crops on the open market in exchange for money that could be used to purchase food in the case of urban dwellers, and manufactured goods and imports and commercially grown foodstuffs such as sugar and tea in the case of both urban and rural households.

The industrial revolution, of course, involved the harnessing of new forms of energy and technology—along with new methods of organizing production—to mass-produce goods for the capital and consumer markets. Both the commercial and the industrial revolutions depended on innovation in the agricultural sector, new forms of transportation, new sources of capital—much of it generated by colonies and slaves abroad—and ever more sophisticated financial markets to make that capital available where it was needed.

But while these twin economic revolutions created ever-greater prosperity—particularly for a rising middle class—they also produced more short-term economic volatility. In pursuit of growth, entrepreneurs competed more intensively with one another, driving down profits and eventually wages, leading to a fall in demand that further eroded revenues and profits. Ultimately, economies would fall into recession, until new demand stimulated new growth, leading to a period of economic expansion.

Arguably the first instance of a modern boom-and-bust cycle in U.S. history came with the economic expansion that followed the end of the Napoleonic Wars in Europe and the War of 1812 in North America, with the subsequent Panic of 1819. Economic historians disagree over the causes of this cycle, with the more Keynesian-minded calling it a classic example of falling profits leading to a decline in wages and falling demand. These forces, in turn, are said to have produced the economic downturn that began in 1819, although Keynesian economists do note that the expansionary monetary policies of the nation's nascent credit markets played a role in creating speculative excesses—particularly in the real-estate market—that resulted in the panic. In contrast, monetarists put the lion's share of blame for the speculative boom, and the bust that inevitably followed, on

the heads of central and commercial bankers who pumped too much money into the economy.

Increasing Financial Integration and Economic Volatility

Ultimately, the Panic of 1819 was short-lived and did not greatly affect those who had not participated in the speculative excesses of the preceding four years, although higher rates of unemployment could be felt among urban workers and declining agricultural prices had an impact on the farm households. For the next seventeen years, however, the U.S. economy prospered, buoyed by investment in transportation, the beginnings of industrialization, and the great expansion of commercial crop production, particularly of slave-grown cotton. By the 1830s, the nation's economy was far more integrated, both internally and to markets in Europe. This was especially the case with financial markets, as U.S. economic growth and prosperity had come to depend on large infusions of foreign capital—especially from Britain—much in the way that emerging markets depend on flows of capital from the developed world in today's global economy.

With greater integration came increasing vulnerability to economic shocks from abroad. In addition, as ever more Americans entered the commercial economy—as farmers producing crops for sale on the national market and urban laborers and artisans selling their skills, brain, and brawn for wages—they became more dependent on the smooth running of financial markets. When the Bank of England decided to curtail investment due to worries that the American economy was becoming overheated (as evidenced in a massive real-estate bubble in Western lands) the U.S. financial markets seized up, leading to a tightening of credit that set off a wave of bankruptcies, layoffs, falling agricultural prices, and collapsed real-estate values. The resulting downturn would drag on for about six years, in the worst depression experienced by the U.S. economy prior to the Civil War. By comparison, the Panic of 1857—triggered by a flight of British capital from U.S. banks—was relatively mild and short-lived. In both cases, there were indigenous causes as well, including the bubble in real-estate prices and prices for agricultural and manufactured goods.

Laissez-Faire Economics and Late-Nineteenth-Century Capitalism

By the post–Civil War era, the United States—while still heavily dependent on foreign sources of capital—had developed large-scale financial markets of its own. Both the Civil War and the boom that followed the cataclysm resulted in the creation of great fortunes and the rise of large-scale enterprises and corporations, particularly in the railroad sector. While much of this expansion was based on real economic need—the nation was expanding westward, rapidly industrializ-

ing and urbanizing, and once again drawing in millions of new immigrants—a great deal of the investment was speculative in nature, much of it the result of a rapidly expanding money supply. When a number of major financiers became overleveraged in their efforts to create a second transcontinental railroad—causing a collapse of their banking house in 1873—it triggered a financial panic that once again saw credit markets dry up, bankruptcies spread, agricultural prices fall, and unemployment among urban workers soar.

The 1873 financial crisis and the multiyear depression that followed began a period of extreme volatility in the history of American and global capitalism—one that would culminate in the worst economic downturn of pre-twentieth-century history, the depression of the 1890s. (There was a milder panic in 1884 as well, which also triggered

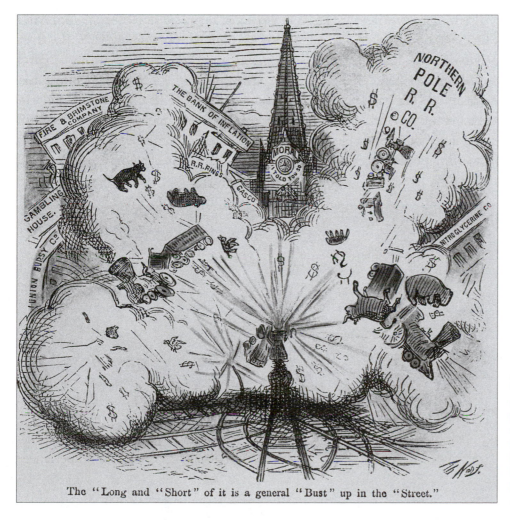

The "Long and "Short" of it is a general "Bust" up in the "Street."

A Thomas Nast cartoon titled "The 'Long' and 'Short' of It" comments on the U.S. bank panic of 1873. A result of overspeculation in the railroad industry, the crisis marked the beginning of a long period of instability and, eventually, depression. *(The Granger Collection, New York)*

a recession in the middle years of that decade.) Like the financial crisis of 1873, the Panic of 1893 was triggered by overinvestment and speculative financing in the railroad industry, which in turn set off a crisis in the credit markets and a prolonged recession that gripped the nation for several years. Economists grappled with the cause of the volatility in late-nineteenth-century capitalism, with some citing too much production and others too little consumption, though most agreed that lax credit and investment practices played a key role. Whatever the reason, business leaders responded to the volatility by attempting to insulate their businesses through the creation of trusts, holding companies, pools, and other organizational structures that reduced cutthroat competition.

While such efforts might have achieved stability within a specific company or even a whole industry, they could not address the overall problem of economic volatility. As events of the twentieth century would prove, only the central government had the means to smooth out the business cycle. But accepting that idea meant dispensing with the extreme laissez-faire thinking at the heart of late-nineteenth-century American capitalism. At the dawn of the twentieth century would arise a movement ready to do just that and begin a new economic era, one in which government played an ever more active—and, to detractors, intrusive—role in the economy.

James Ciment

See also: Mississippi Bubble (1717–1720); Panics and Runs, Bank; South Sea Bubble (1720); Tulipmania (1636–1637).

Further Reading

Appleby, Joyce. *The Relentless Revolution: A History of Capitalism.* New York: W.W. Norton, 2010.

Beaud, Michel. *A History of Capitalism, 1500–2000,* trans. Tom Dickman and Anny Lefebvre. New York: Monthly Review Press, 2001.

Bernstein, William J. *The Birth of Plenty: How the Prosperity of the Modern World Was Created.* New York: McGraw-Hill, 2004.

Cameron, Rondo, and Larry Neal. *A Concise Economic History of the World: From Paleolithic Times to the Present.* 4th ed. New York: Oxford University Press, 2003.

Ferguson, Niall. *The Ascent of Money: A Financial History of the World.* New York: Penguin, 2008.

Gamble, Andrew. *The Spectre at the Feast: Capitalist Crisis and the Politics of Recession.* New York: Palgrave Macmillan, 2009.

Gills, Barry K., and William R. Thompson, eds. *Globalization and Global History.* New York: Routledge, 2006.

Heilbroner, Robert L., and William Milberg. *The Making of Economic Society.* 12th ed. Upper Saddle River, NJ: Pearson Prentice Hall, 2008.

Landes, David S. *The Wealth and Poverty of Nations: Why Some Are So Rich and Some So Poor.* New York: W.W. Norton, 1999.

Maddison, Angus. *Contours of the World Economy, 1–2030 AD: Essays in Macro-Economic History.* New York: Oxford University Press, 2007.

McCraw, Thomas K., ed. *Creating Modern Capitalism: How Entrepreneurs, Companies, and Countries Triumphed in Three Industrial Revolutions.* Cambridge, MA: Harvard University Press, 1997.

Moore, Karl, and David Lewis. *The Origins of Globalization.* New York: Routledge, 2009.

Polanyi, Karl. *The Great Transformation: The Political and Economic Origins of Our Time.* 2nd ed. Boston: Beacon Press, 2001.

Pomeranz, Kenneth, and Steven Topik. *The World That Trade Created: Society, Culture, and the World Economy, 1400 to the Present.* Armonk, NY: M.E. Sharpe, 2006.

Stearns, Peter N. *Globalization in World History.* New York: Routledge, 2009.

———. *The Industrial Revolution in World History.* Boulder, CO: Westview, 2007.

Booms and Busts
The Twentieth and Twenty-First Centuries

The advent of capitalism in the early modern era, and the industrial and commercial revolutions, which transformed the economies of Europe and North America from the late eighteenth through the late nineteenth centuries, created a material abundance for the masses unknown in previous human history. At the same time, these developments brought the economic volatility of the business cycle, the booms and busts that lifted and broke individual and business fortunes on a recurring basis. Throughout the nineteenth century and particularly in its last few decades, the economies of the United States and Europe were periodically rocked by financial panics and recessions, some of them, such as those of the 1870s and 1890s, deep and lasting.

For the most part, economists, business leaders, and government policy makers of the day believed that the volatility of the business cycle, while regrettable, was an inevitable part of capitalism and long-term growth. Proponents of the classical school of economics argued that such booms and busts are, in fact, anomalies and that capitalist economies tend toward equilibriums of low unemployment and inflation. Any actions on the part of the government to smooth out the business cycle or to ease the effects of recession through fiscal or monetary means, they argued, are only likely to distort the natural workings of the marketplace, thereby prolonging recessions or blunting recoveries. Instead, business leaders moved to insulate their industries from the boom-and-bust cycle through consolidation and coordination, whether in the form of pools, holding companies, or trusts.

But while the economic history of the nineteenth century was marked by the full flowering of laissez-faire thinking and practice—and all of the economic dynamism and volatility that brought—that of the twentieth and twenty-first centuries would be one in which governments—backed by new economic thinking—would increasingly intervene in the marketplace in an effort to smooth out the business cycle and to ensure maximum sustainable growth along with low unemployment and inflation.

Progressivism and the Federal Reserve

In the United States, the first pivotal event in this process was the Panic of 1907. Like several late-nineteenth-century episodes of chaos in the credit markets, this first major financial panic of the twentieth century was triggered by the activities of speculators. These activities caused key financial institutions to fail, which in turn set off a credit crunch and stock market crisis that threatened to drag the economy into recession. To counteract the panic, an ad hoc consortium of major New York banks, led by financier J.P. Morgan, moved to shore up securities prices and the credit markets with an infusion of $100 million, an extraordinary sum for the day.

While the effort succeeded in averting a serious economic downturn, the episode concerned policy makers and leading financiers. The credit market was simply growing too big for any one private financial institution, or even group of financial institutions, to effectively deal with large-scale crises; the government, even many bankers had concluded, must play a role in stabilizing the financial markets. At the same time, a new political movement had emerged in the country in the early twentieth century—Progressivism, which argued in favor of an increasing role for government in resisting the economic power of corporations and ensuring competitiveness in the marketplace. While coming from very different ideological origins, both schools of thought held that not only did the government have a useful role to play in the marketplace but that it was the only institution with the power and resources to assure the smooth running of the economy.

Out of this new economic thinking came the Federal Reserve System—the central bank of the United States—created in 1913 by Progressive-minded President Woodrow Wilson and a Progressive-dominated Congress. Like the central banks of other countries, the Fed, as it came to be called, was given broad power over two facets of the economy—regulating banks and setting monetary policy. The Fed, of course, was not the first of its kind. Several European countries—most notably, Great Britain with its Bank of England—had had central banks for centuries. The United States itself had had a version of a central bank—the Bank of the United States—for several decades in the early nineteenth century, until the institution was killed by populist politicians and free financial market advocates. Nearly a century later, there was still a great deal of hostility to the idea of a central bank, particularly in less-developed areas of the country

that depended on easy credit for their growth. The fear there was that a central bank would serve the anti-inflationary, tight money interests of northeastern financial interests. Such fears forced a compromise—the Fed would be a decentralized central bank, with great power residing in the directors and presidents of the twelve local branches.

World War I and the Roaring Twenties

While such decentralization assured that the Fed would be more responsive to interests beyond those of New York bankers, it also contributed to the institution's less-than-effective record during the first several decades of its existence, contributing both to the speculative excesses in the real-estate and securities markets of the 1920s and to the economic contraction of the early 1930s.

But there were other factors beyond Fed policy that contributed to the economic volatility of the roughly two decades between World Wars I and II, both in the United States and globally. The first of these great conflicts had a transformative effect on the economies of both Europe and the United States. Remaining out of the war for its first three years and enjoying great prosperity supplying the Allies with food, materiel, and armaments, the United States became the leading creditor nation in the world as a result of the conflict, with allied countries such as France and Britain going deep into debt to U.S. financial institutions. With the Allied victory in 1918, both London and Paris imposed heavy reparations payments on Germany, because they blamed it for starting the war. An unstable international financial order fell into place, as German reparations payments helped France and Britain pay their debts to the United States, which then bolstered the German economy with loans after the latter had tried to get out of its reparations payments by devaluing its currency through hyperinflation.

Meanwhile, the United States, flush with capital, went on a speculative binge in the 1920s, first in the overheated real-estate market and, more spectacularly, in the latter years of the decade, in a soaring stock market. While some of the increases in securities prices were justified by improvements in productivity and rising corporate profits, much was the result of new forms of financing, in which stock purchasers could buy shares on the margin (paying only a fraction of what the stock cost and borrowing the rest), using the stock as collateral. As long as stock prices were rising, the system worked. But when prices began to fall in 1929, the whole system came crashing down, with shareholders unable to meet their margin calls. The stocks were then sold because the margin calls were not met, causing stock prices to fall even further. Brokers were not able to pay off their credit lines to banks, thus further jeopardizing the solvency of the affected banks.

The Great Depression and Rise of Keynesian Economics

While the Great Wall Street Crash of 1929 is associated with the start of the Great Depression—the worst economic downturn in the history of capitalism—there were other reasons why falling securities prices, which affected the portfolios of only one in ten Americans, soon brought the U.S. and global economies to their knees. In the United States, there were deeper economic problems, hidden behind the façade of 1920s prosperity. These included weaknesses in such key economic sectors as agriculture, coal mining, railroads, and textiles, and increasing household and corporate indebtedness, the former caused in part by rising inequalities in wealth and income, and the latter by a wave of business consolidation in the 1920s. With the collapse of credit on Wall Street came widespread bank failures and a dramatic tightening of the credit markets. With much of the world dependent on American capital and investment, the crisis quickly spread to Europe and other industrialized economies.

The sheer enormity of the economic catastrophe of the 1930s forced economists and economic policy makers to rethink both their analyses of the business cycles and their prescriptions for responding to economic downturns. In Britain, economist John Maynard Keynes challenged the classical notion that economies naturally return to a supply-and-demand equilibrium that ensures low inflation and unemployment. Keynes argued that the stickiness of prices and wages could create a supply-and-demand equilibrium marked by profound under-utilization of capital, productive capacity, and labor.

As a prescription for the crisis, Keynes focused on raising aggregate demand. With businesses and households either unwilling or unable to do so, this left only the government. Thus, Keynes emphasized both expansive monetary stimulus (increasing the money supply) and fiscal stimulus (cutting taxes and spending on infrastructure) measures to jump-start aggregate demand, even if this meant that governments ran large deficits. Such advice ran counter to the conventional economic thinking of the day, which held that government borrowing in an economic slowdown soaks up capital that might otherwise be used for private sector investment, thereby prolonging the slump.

Without necessarily adopting all of Keynes's ideas, governments throughout the industrialized world began to employ monetary and fiscal stimulus policies to "prime the pump," as the contemporary American expression went. In the United States, the Federal Reserve shifted to a loose monetary policy, while the Franklin Roosevelt administration, through a series of New Deal programs, pumped billions of dollars into the economy to build infrastructure and subsidize agriculture, among other things. Still, old orthodoxies died hard. Believing that deficit spending might yet cripple the economy, the Roosevelt administration cut back on its stimulus programs dramatically in 1937, causing a second dip in economic performance that historians have come to call the Roosevelt Recession.

Triumph of Keynes and the Post–World War II Economic Boom

According to most economic historians, New Deal programs only half-lifted the American economy. While corporate revenues and overall economic growth returned, unemployment remained stubbornly high through the end of the decade. Ultimately, however, Keynes was proven right. With enough stimulus, an economy could be lifted out of a high-unemployment, under-capacity equilibrium. The proof came with the massive defense spending accompanying America's preparation for—and entry into—World War II, though putting 16 million Americans into the armed forces certainly helped lower unemployment as well.

While many economists and policy makers feared that the end of World War II and the contraction in defense-related stimulus spending would trigger a new period of economic instability and recession, the opposite proved true. While the first global conflict of the twentieth century ushered in a period of global economic instability, the second brought about the longest and most dramatic period of economic growth in the history of the world—some thirty years of sustained, high growth in industrialized economies from Western Europe to Japan to North America, as well as more modest growth in the developing world that supplied those economies their raw materials.

There were several reasons for this development. First was the massive economic stimulus of rebuilding war-ravaged infrastructures in Japan and Europe. Second was the huge pent-up demand in the United States and elsewhere after nearly a generation of privation in the Great Depression and rationing during World War II. Third was the massive military spending that accompanied the cold war. Fourth was the American-led structuring of an international economic order that ensured monetary stability and free trade. And finally, virtually all industrialized economies adopted the Keynesian paradigm of fiscal and monetary stimulus to smooth out the business cycle, stimulating demand during economic downturns through expansive fiscal and increasingly monetary measures and pulling back on the monetary reins when inflation threatened.

British economist John Maynard Keynes (right), meeting here with U.S. Treasury Secretary Henry Morgenthau, Jr., in 1944, overthrew classical economic theory by advocating massive government stimulus to raise demand in a depressed economy. *(Time & Life Pictures/Getty Images)*

"Stagflation" and the Undoing of the Keynesian Consensus

The Keynesian consensus would finally come undone in the 1970s as the era of stable and sustained economic growth came to an end. As with the onset of the great global expansion, there were a number of contributing factors to the series of recessions that rocked the industrialized world in the 1970s and early 1980s. In Europe, there was the end of postwar reconstruction; in the United States, there was the inflation triggered in part by spending on the war in Vietnam. In addition, there was a slowdown in productivity gains, since new postwar technologies and managerial stratagems, and the productivity-enhancing benefits they brought with them, had already become fully assimilated into the economy. Most devastating of all was the sudden and dramatic run-up in energy and commodity prices, the former triggered by unrest in the petroleum-rich Middle East. The latter was a form of cost-push inflation that led to a wage-price spiral.

All of this contributed to "stagflation"—a phenomenon that complicated traditional Keynesian stimulus solutions. A combination of the words "stagnation" (low or negative growth) and "inflation," stagflation seemed to defy economic theory. Rapidly rising wages and prices were only supposed to occur during times of economic expansion, as a near full-employment economy was unable to meet the demand of businesses and consumers. But in the 1970s, inflation accompanied recession, and Keynes's prescriptions for deficit spending to lift economies out of recession became untenable in the face of high inflation.

Many Post Keynesians argue that a Keynesian approach to stagflation—that is, putting a cap on wage and salary increases—was never tried. Nevertheless, the problems associated with Keynesian economics helped trigger both a dramatic rethinking of what governments should do to respond to economic crises and a significant political realignment, as voters rejected the largely liberal, Keynesian-influenced regimes that had presided over both the boom of the 1950s and 1960s and the bust of the 1970s. Especially in the United States and Great Britain, new conservative governments moved away from the Keynesian emphasis on stimulus measures that would create broad-based demand to policies that would spur investment, including large tax cuts for wealthy individuals and corporations and deregulation of the financial sector. At the same time, to wring inflation out of the economy, the U.S. Fed pursued tight monetary policies. The result of these steps was a dramatic recession in the early 1980s—the worst since the 1930s—followed by a buoyant recovery, albeit one accompanied by increasing inequality in income and wealth.

Speculation and a Second Post–World War II Boom

Some economists argued that the policies pursued by the conservative administrations of Ronald Reagan in the United States and Margaret Thatcher in Great Britain contained many Keynesian elements. In the United States, for instance, the large tax cuts and massive defense spending—both driving government deficits to record levels—provided a kind of Keynesian fiscal stimulus. Conservatives were loathe to call such policies Keynesian but, however, they were labeled, they seemed to work. Barring sharp but short recessions in the early 1990s and again in the early years of the new millennium, the U.S. economy experienced sustained growth from the mid-1980s through the middle of the new millennium's first decade, even if that growth was fueled largely by dramatic productivity gains resulting from the personal computer, mobile telephone, and Internet revolutions.

The period of sustained growth differed significantly from that of the 1950s and 1960s in several key aspects. One was that the immediate postwar boom saw a narrowing of income and wealth inequality, while the boom of the late twentieth and early twenty-first centuries brought a trend toward greater inequality. This contributed to other differences, including much higher rates of household debt and the need for women to enter the workforce to sustain the lifestyles of middle-

The financial crisis of the early twenty-first century touched off the world's worst economic downturn since the Great Depression and recriminations over speculation, deregulation, gimmicky investment instruments, and sheer greed. *(Bloomberg/ Getty Images)*

class families. And finally, there was the matter of regulation. Under the regime of New Deal laws and agencies, financial institutions were unable to engage in many highly speculative activities.

Among the initiatives of the new conservative consensus in many countries was a lifting of such regulations. That, combined with the large amounts of capital in the pockets of the wealthy, contributed to repeated episodes of speculation— the savings and loan–inspired commercial real-estate boom of the early and mid-1980s, the dot .com boom of the late 1990s, and, most spectacularly, the housing bubble of 2003–2006. Admittedly, the dot.com boom was also caused by the introduction of a new technology, but the bubble was inflated by large infusions of venture capital. Ultimately, all of these periods of speculation inevitably led to busts: the recession of the early 1990s in the case of the commercial real-estate collapse (though diminished defense spending in the wake of the cold war was a contributing factor); the recession of 2001–2002 (though the

terrorist attacks of September 11, 2001, played a role); and the "great recession" of 2007–2009, the worst economic downturn to hit the industrialized world since the Great Depression.

Just as the repeated recessions of the 1970s caused both economists and government officials to rethink their reliance on the Keynesian theoretical and policy-making paradigm, so too the financial crisis of 2008–2009 and the subsequent contraction caused many in the economic community and more liberal government administrations (the latter put in place by voters fed up with the failures of conservative policy makers) to question the financial deregulation and supply-side economics that had dominated both since the 1980s. Indeed, the massive stimulus packages instituted by a number of governments in both the industrialized and developing worlds in the early twenty-first century seem to hearken back to the old Progressive-Era ideas and Keynesian paradigm first put into action in the first half of the twentieth century.

James Ciment

See also: Asian Financial Crisis (1997); Boom, Economic (1920s); Boom, Economic (1960s); Dot.com Bubble (1990s–2000); Florida Real-Estate Boom (1920s); Great Depression (1929–1933); Oil Shocks (1973–1974, 1979–1980); Panics and Runs, Bank; Panic of 1901; Panic of 1907; Poseidon Bubble (1969–1970); Recession and Financial Crisis (2007–); Recession, Reagan (1981–1982); Recession, Roosevelt (1937–1939); Recession, Stagflation (1970s); Souk al-Manakh (Kuwait) Stock Market Crash (1982); Stock Market Crash (1929); Stock Market Crash (1987).

Further Reading

Aldcroft, Derek H. *The European Economy 1914–2000.* London: Routledge, 2001.

Barsky, Robert B., and Lutz Kilian. "Oil and the Macroeconomy Since the 1970s." *Journal of Economic Perspectives* 18:4 (2004): 115–134.

Clarke, Peter. *The Keynesian Revolution in the Making, 1924–1936.* New York: Oxford University Press, 1988.

Gran, Peter. *The Rise of the Rich: A New View of Modern World History.* Syracuse, NY: Syracuse University Press, 2009.

Hetzel, Robert L. *The Monetary Policy of the Federal Reserve.* New York: Cambridge University Press, 2008.

Karier, Thomas. *Great Experiments in American Economic Policy: From Kennedy to Reagan.* Westport, CT: Praeger, 1997.

Kindleberger, Charles P. *The World in Depression, 1929–1939.* Berkeley: University of California Press, 1973.

Leuchtenberg, William E. *The Perils of Prosperity, 1914–1932.* Chicago: University of Chicago Press, 1958.

Sawyer, James E. *Why Reagonomics and Keynesian Economics Failed.* New York: St. Martin's, 1987.

Shiller, Robert J. *Irrational Exuberance.* New York: Currency/Doubleday, 2005.

Temin, Peter. *Lessons from the Great Depression.* Cambridge, MA: MIT Press, 1989.

Wilber, Charles K., and Kenneth P. Jameson. *Beyond Reagonimcs: A Further Inquiry into the Poverty of Economics.* Notre Dame, IN: University of Notre Dame Press, 1990.

Booms and Busts
Causes and Consequences

The historical record reveals certain regularities in alternating periods of widespread economic prosperity and poverty, expansion and recession, and boom and bust. But economists—and everybody else affected by the ups and downs of the economy—have long wondered what explains this phenomenon. More recently, since the financial crisis of 2008–2009 and recession of 2007–2009, economists and policy makers have been grappling with the question of whether the crisis and recession were the natural consequences of the previous economic expansion or whether they were simply the result of some bad business decisions.

Consideration of the causes and consequences of booms and busts demands a clear definition of just when these booms and busts occur and what they look like, for it is the "stylized facts" or interpretations about sinusoidal, or wavelike, deviations from trend measures of output, employment, wages, interest rates, and the like that provide the focus of what is to be explained. To complicate matters, according to the twentieth-century American economist Victor Zarnowitz, while "business expansions and contractions consist of patterns of recurrent serially correlated and cross-correlated movements in many economic . . . activities," these alternations in business conditions are not really "cycles"

since they involve no unique periodicities—their amplitude, scope, and duration vary considerably over time. So the question of whether booms are even related to busts is an open one.

Agricultural Versus Industrial Economies

Traditionally, and today, in predominantly agrarian-based market economies, fluctuations in income and employment were and are directly linked to nature's rhythm. Indeed, one of the earliest theories of booms and busts traced an average eleven-year cycle of feast and famine of the harvest back to sunspots and solar flares, which presumably affected climate and hence agricultural output.

In an industrially based capitalist market economy, one finds no such agreement on the cause of fluctuations. Economists have long struggled to define, characterize, explain, and model the causes of booms and busts. There is consensus only insofar as economists are agreed that profits, investment in inventories, plant and equipment, and financial conditions—such as the availability of credit to support loans to businesses—are central to the phenomenon.

But which causes which? Are booms caused by credit surpluses, and busts by credit crunches—that is, are these surpluses and crunches the impulses that in turn cause volatile business investment to propagate the problems? Or are credit conditions merely responding to and spreading the problems arising from the impulse of volatile private investment?

Meanwhile, can government policies counteract this instability, or are government policies themselves a source of the boom-and-bust phenomenon? To what extent are economists even observing objective movements in business activity and not merely artifacts artificially induced by data measurement techniques? Does a boom contain the seeds of the subsequent bust and vice versa, or is the boom and bust independent of the preceding bust and boom, each the result of some other, independent cause?

Beyond the question of measurement, the challenge of understanding causes and consequences of economic booms and busts is taken up by examining the relationship among profits, investment, and financial conditions, and in turn, their relationship(s) to output, employment, and income. To sort it all out, theories attempt to tear apart the impulse or precipitating cause that lies at the root of the boom and bust, from the propagation mechanism that explains how it spreads to other parts of the economy, and from the factors that explain persistence and the tendency for the boom and bust to drag on.

Theories of the business cycle that seek to explain the causes of booms and busts may be categorized into (1) monetary (credit) theories that see financial problems disturbing the entire economy; (2) theories of real disturbances that unbalance specific major sectors (such as oil shocks that affect the energy sector and consequently the rest of an energy-dependent economy); and (3) the Keynesian theory of aggregate demand, which attributes booms (and inflation) to excessive demand, and busts (depression or recession) to a collapse in aggregate demand.

Monetary Theories

Monetary theories of the boom and bust see a change in financial conditions as the impulse or precipitating factor, and view the resulting real economic adjustments as propagating these ef-

fects throughout the economy. Theories of the business cycle that focus on real disturbances unbalancing specific sectors often start, conversely, by assuming that the impulse stems from changes in investment in a major sector of the economy or from technological change, and that it is the financial system that transmits and spreads this disturbance.

In the early 1800s, it was recognized that the credit from which to finance investment played a central role in the state of the economy. In a critical 1826 study, British economist and philosopher John Stuart Mill offered a theory of "commercial crises" that tied the phenomenon of recession and crises to the contraction of credit in the United Kingdom. It was not until the turn of the next century that credit theories of crises evolved into monetary theories of the business cycle with endogenous or self-reinforcing components explaining movements in output, income, and prices. In his 1913 book *Good and Bad Trade*, British economist Ralph Hawtrey explored the possibility that expansions of bank loans lowered the cost of loans, which in turn stimulated the demand for, and then the supply of, capital goods (plant and equipment) that businesses typically borrowed money to buy. Since the expansion process would be restricted by a limit on the ability of banks to increase loans, eventually the expansion process of the boom would reverse itself and cause a bust. In credit theories, then, the cause of the boom lies in an expansion of credit available for loans; the cause of the bust lies in the exhaustion of that credit and is ensured by the limits imposed by the availability of monetary reserves.

The Post Keynesian American economist Hyman Minsky, basing his analysis on changes in aggregate demand, believed that bank credit used to finance investment was the source of business fluctuations, but he focused attention explicitly on the growing mismatch of investment income and related debt obligations over the course of the boom as the source of an inherent fragility. Minsky described how a prolonged economic expansion encourages investors to replace their expectations of a normal business cycle (incorporating an expected recession) with the expectation of perpetual expansion. The new and (unreasonably) confident expectations of continuing profits in turn encourage businesses to take on greater debt loads, which over time decrease financial stability. While funds borrowed are often fixed in nominal, or non-inflation-adjusted terms, profits fluctuate. In a boom, profits are high and rising; in a downturn, profits fall. If businesses borrow so much that they are unable to make the payments on their debt when profits weaken, businesses go bankrupt and the economy descends into recession and possibly crisis.

In addition to the increasingly optimistic expectations of Minsky's investors, there is the vexing problem of liquidity (where the easiness of selling/buying an asset can be a good thing for encouraging investment but can cause greater instability in asset prices) and asset pyramiding (where the capital gains from an asset price increase provide the base from which to demand more assets and drive the price up even further). In combination, these financial market factors serve to increase the fragility of the boom and risk a more severe bust.

When economists complicate matters further by considering the possibility that investors often get caught up in waves of optimism, they look at a market "bubble" as the explanation of the boom. A bubble is said to occur when investors are so optimistic that they bid asset prices up on the enthusiasm of getting rich by buying low and selling high, and forget to pay attention to the real economic prospects of what they are buying. But such a situation cannot go on forever. At some point, the bubble bursts and investors react by becoming pessimistic. At this point, the economy may go bust. This scenario is most likely to occur when the changes in the underlying real economy are new (as when a technological innovation results in restructuring large parts of the economy). While such changes played a role in the collapse of technology stocks in 2000, the primary reason for the failure was over-investment in the sector.

Asset values generally and bubbles specifically are often the product of emotion as much as anything else, as economists and pioneering investment analysts Benjamin Graham, David Dodd, and Sidney Cottle noted in their influential 1962 analysis of securities values. Brenda Spotton Visano later demonstrated how what others think and do influences investor behavior in periods when investors are particularly uncertain about the future. In works from the early 2000s, she also explored the role of emotions in creating the panic that emerges when the bubble bursts.

In short, financial panics appear when investors, fearing a loss in the value of their investments, dump their assets and in so doing cause the collapse of a bank or stock market. Fear that a bank will fail can cause depositors to rush to withdraw their funds. Fear that a stock market will crash can cause investors to sell their shares. And then, in a self-fulfilling way, the large and sudden withdrawal of cash and sale of shares can, by themselves, cause the very collapse that was feared. A bank run or a stock market crash increases the risk of an economic crisis. The breakdown of a market or the credit crunch caused by the failure of a bank can adversely affect the day-to-day operations of business in other sectors of the economy. As American monetary economists Milton Friedman and Anna Schwartz suggest in their explanation of the Great Depression, financial panics can precede and cause economic crises in employment, production, and trade.

Disturbances as Causes

Theories that take instead real economic disturbances as the precipitating factor mostly focus on investment-related disturbances as the root cause of booms and subsequent busts. Whether the predominant investment variable is inventory, fixed investment, or technological change, however, relates closely to the "typical" cycle one is looking at. In a 1923 study, British statistician Joseph Kitchin, for example, identified a 3-to-5-year business cycle corresponding to the observed fluctuations in business inventories. Clément

Juglar's 7-to-11-year cycle, developed in the late nineteenth century, corresponded closely with theories related to fixed investment, while Soviet economist Nikolai Kondratieff identified a 45-to-60-year cycle corresponding to a long technological wave in his pathbreaking 1928 study. Meanwhile, in his 1939 theory of business cycles, Austrian school economist Joseph Schumpeter developed a notion that there are interrelated cycles with credit conditions layered on top of a boom caused ultimately by overinvestment in an original technological innovation.

Whereas Schumpeter developed a theory focused on explaining the booms by investment and technological advancement, John Maynard Keynes of Great Britain, the dominant economist of the first half of the twentieth century, and others focused on developing a theory that would attribute the cause of the bust to deficient consumption demand. While Keynes and Schumpeter shared a belief in the importance of the investment stimulus to explain the boom, Keynes in particular emphasized an aggregate demand deficiency combined with complicated labor and capital market problems as the cause of protracted periods of labor unemployment prevalent in a bust.

There is some debate over whether Keynes's theory of general (un)employment was adequate as a theory of the business or trade cycle. Keynes himself saw his theory of employment as adequate to explain business fluctuations. In his landmark work, *The General Theory of Employment, Interest and Money* (1936), he wrote, "Since we claim to have shown in the preceding chapters what determines the volume of employment at any time, it follows, if we are right, that our theory must be capable of explaining the phenomena of the Trade Cycle."

John Hicks, a follower of Keynes, disputed the relevance of the latter's theory for such a purpose. "Keynesian economics, in spite of all that it has done for our understanding of business fluctuations," wrote Hicks in *A Contribution to the Theory of the Trade Cycle* (1950), "has beyond all doubt left at least one major thing quite unexplained; and that thing is nothing less than the business cycle

itself. . . . For Keynes did not show us, and did not attempt to show us, save by a few hints, why it is that in the past the level of activity has fluctuated according to so definite a pattern."

The multiplier mechanism of Keynes and others, whereby changes in investment having a multiplicative effect on output and income, paired with French economist Albert Aftalion's accelerator principle, whereby an expectation of future demand serves as an independent investment stimulus, formed the basis of "multiplier-accelerator" models of business cycles, as American economist Paul Samuelson noted. Multiplier-accelerator models made explicit in a simple way the idea that Keynes had in mind.

Subsequent developments of Keynesian-type theories of the causes and consequences of booms and busts spread out in a few different directions. "Old" Keynesians such as American James Tobin focused on an investment impulse stemming from the relationship between the cost of new capital and the stock market's valuation of the firm: as the share price of the firm rises relative to the cost of investing in plant and equipment, firms expand and that spending contributes to the boom. "New" and "neo" Keynesians seek to explain nominal frictions and real rigidities by exploring the microfoundations of slow-to-adjust labor markets, for example. When the demand for investment goods and consumer durables fluctuates, firms adjust only slowly and imperfectly, which then explains alternating periods of high and low employment. Post Keynesians examine the role of money in economic decision-making, the cost of making economic decisions in a world where future economic conditions cannot be predicted, and the reality that a degree of nonstructural unemployment and inequitable distributions of income are an intrinsic part of modern entrepreneurial economic systems.

Benefits and Costs

All of these theories, however, address only the economic causes and consequences of the boom and bust. During a boom period, one sees higher incomes, more employment, and possibly higher prices; during a bust, one sees lower national income, higher unemployment, and lower prices. Thus, accordingly, the Great Depression can be viewed as a sharp downturn on a graph. What all of these theories omit are the considerable human benefits and costs of both booms and busts. The consequences of a low income or job loss can be socially and personally devastating. Such consequences are not measured by typical economic data and so escape consideration when economists talk about booms and busts.

Yet these consequences are very real in human terms and in many ways more important than the abstract issues discussed by economists. If the consequences were clearly separate and apart from all economic considerations, then one could argue that theorists and policy makers need only solve the economic problem. If society could find a way to avoid extreme busts, at least, the social and human damage would be avoided. While many economists are confident that this is indeed the case, others believe that attention to those who suffer and how much they suffer should be the impetus for policies designed to lessen the dire effects of the bust. It is not enough to say that the government should step in to bail out a failing business; if a government cannot bail out all of them, how should it decide which ones will benefit from its largesse?

A fundamentally different approach to causes and consequences of booms and busts has its roots in the 1930s work of the Norwegian Ragnar Frisch and the Russian Eugen Slutsky, who demonstrated the possibility of inducing "cycles" by the filtering process used to de-trend random observations. This statistical artifact paved the way for viewing booms and busts as the result of random real shocks to productivity originating from technology (such as innovations in information and communications brought on by computing technology) or from the energy and environment (such as an oil price shock).

The real business-cycle theories of economist and Federal Reserve Bank president Charles Plosser and others effectively challenged previously held views that booms and busts were the manifestation of cyclical phenomena to be explained by theories with endogenous, self-perpetuating components. In Plosser's view, the financial system—having much in common with earlier classical models of the business cycle—is, like money, merely a veil on the real economy. Booms and busts are real economic phenomena that occur independently of the financial sector and are manifestations of the market economy adjusting to a new real economy. Government policies designed to stabilize the economy actually produce detrimental effects, so the proponents argue, since the policies are too imprecise and difficult to implement.

Like the 1930s bust in the European and American economies, the global financial crisis of 2008–2009 challenges this extreme new classical view most profoundly. It may be that those who adhere to real shocks as the root cause of booms and busts remain unconvinced that the source of the latest problem was anything but another real shock. At a minimum, however, it will now be difficult to deny that the financial system plays a critical role in the propagation of those shocks, as evidenced by the economic devastation measured in terms of output and jobs lost, together with the commensurate increases in social hardship.

Brenda Spotton Visano

See also: Austrian School; Behavioral Economics; Catastrophe Theory; Classical Theories and Models; Fisher's Debt-Deflation Theory; German Historical School; Institutional Economics; Keynesian Business Model; Kondratieff Cycles; Marxist Cycle Model; Minsky's Financial Instability Hypothesis; Monetary Theories and Models; Neoclassical Theories and Models; Neo-Keynesian Theories and Models; Over-Savings and Over-Investment Theories of the Business Cycle; Political Theories and Models; Post Keynesian Theories and Models; Real Business Cycle Models; Seasonal Cycles; Sunspot Theories.

Further Reading

Friedman, Milton, and Anna Jacobson Schwartz. *A Monetary History of the United States, 1867–1960.* Princeton, NJ: Princeton University Press, 1963.
Frisch, Ragnar. "Propagation Problems and Impulse Problems

in Dynamic Economics." In *Economic Essays in Honor of Gustav Cassel.* London: George Allen & Unwin, 1933.

Graham, Benjamin, David Dodd, Sidney Cottle, and Charles Tathum. *Security Analysis: Principles and Technique.* 4th ed. New York: McGraw-Hill, 1962.

Hawtrey, Ralph G. *Good and Bad Trade: An Inquiry into the Causes of Trade Fluctuations* London: Constable, 1913.

Hicks, John R. *A Contribution to the Theory of the Trade Cycle.* Oxford, UK: Clarendon Press, 1950.

Keynes, John Maynard. *The General Theory of Employment, Interest and Money.* London: Macmillan, 1936.

Kindleberger, Charles P. *Manias, Panics, and Crashes: A History of Financial Crises.* New York: Basic Books, 1978.

Kitchin, Joseph. "Cycles and Trends in Economic Factors." *Review of Economic Statistics* 5 (1923): 10–16.

Kondratieff, Nikolai D. *The Long Wave Cycle*, trans. Guy Daniels. New York: Richardson and Snyder, 1984.

Mill, John Stuart. "Paper Currency and Commercial Distress." In *The Collected Works of John Stuart Mill. Vol. 4. Essays of Economics and Society, Part I,* ed. John M. Robson. Introduction by Lord Robbins. Toronto: University of Toronto Press, 1967.

Minsky, Hyman. *Can "It" Happen Again? Essays on Instability and Finance.* Armonk, NY: M.E. Sharpe, 1982.

Samuelson, Paul A. "Interactions Between the Multiplier Analysis and the Principle of Acceleration." *Review of Economics and Statistics* 21:2 (May 1939): 75–78.

Schumpeter, Joseph A. *Business Cycles: A Theoretical, Historical, and Statistical Analysis of the Capitalist Process.* 2 vols. New York: McGraw-Hill, 1939.

Slutzky, Eugen. "The Summation of Random Causes as the Source of Cyclic Processes." *Econometrica* 5:2 (April 1937): 105–146.

Tobin, James. "A Dynamic Aggregative Model." *Journal of Political Economy* 63:2 (April 1955): 103–115.

Zarnowitz, Victor. "Recent Work on Business Cycles in Historical Perspective: A Review of Theories and Evidence." *Journal of Economic Literature* 23:2 (June 1985): 523–580.

Africa, Sub-Saharan

The second-largest continent by landmass and population—after Asia, in both cases—Africa is a land of contrasts. (All references in this article to "Africa" refer to sub-Saharan Africa; for a discussion of North Africa, see the article "Middle East and North Africa.") On the one hand, its vast mineral wealth and abundant supply of arable land make it potentially one of the richest regions of the world. But centuries of exploitation—including the slave trade and European colonization—along with corruption, mismanagement, and a lack of political stability since independence came to most of the continent in the 1960s have left it with the lowest per capita income of any major region in the world.

Aside from South Africa, the continent is not heavily industrialized and it accounts for a miniscule percentage of global trade. Only its mineral sector—including a growing oil industry—has garnered significant foreign investment since independence. But reliance on the export of minerals has also left it vulnerable to global price swings in that notoriously volatile sector.

Still, by modern globalization standards, Africa's economy is relatively unintegrated with that of the rest of the world. That isolation, along with Africa's growing trade with Asia, has led some economists to argue that Africa may have become less dependent on the West and less vulnerable to economic fluctuations originating there, though the global financial crisis and subsequent recession of the late 2000s has tested that assumption.

Colonial Legacy

Africa is where humankind first evolved, though for much of human history the continent remained largely isolated from the civilizations of Asia, the Middle East, and Europe, separated by vast oceans and the daunting expanses of the Sahara Desert. By the European Middle Ages, however, significant parts of the continent had begun to be integrated into global trading networks, with Arab traders engaging in seaborne commerce along the eastern coast of the continent and in trans-Saharan commerce with West and Central Africa. Such commerce included trade in precious metals, exotic tropical goods, and slaves, connecting the African urban centers of Zimbabwe and Timbuktu.

With the rise of European seaborne commerce in the middle of the second millennium CE, the people of Africa—particularly those in its coastal regions—found new trading partners interested in the same goods that Arab traders had been. In particular, Europeans were interested in exporting human beings—in the form of chattel slaves—to colonies in the Western Hemisphere. Between 1500 and the late nineteenth century, when the international trade in slaves was effectively banned, tens of millions of Africans were shipped overseas. The negative impact of the slave trade on Africa's economic development was huge. Not only did European slavers—aided by African allies—remove millions of the continent's most productive residents—persons in the prime of life were obviously more valuable than children and the elderly—but the trade itself created endemic political instability that hampered economic development and internal trade.

And just as Europeans abandoned the slave trade, they found a new way to exploit the region. While sizable European settlements had existed on the continent since the sixteenth century, particularly in southern Africa, it was not until the latter half of the nineteenth century that new weaponry and public health measures, which allowed outsiders to overcome African resistance and disease, led to the continent's colonial subjugation. By 1900, all of sub-Saharan Africa—aside from Ethiopia and Liberia—was controlled by various European powers.

Governance varied widely in quality among the various European colonizers. While Britain and France made some efforts to build modern infrastructure and train administrators in their holdings, smaller powers, such as Belgium and Portugal, provided little of either. And even in model colonies, such as France's Senegal and Britain's Gold Coast (later Ghana), much of the infrastructure was built to serve European interests. In particular, transportation systems were built to bring raw materials to coastal ports rather than to integrate the continent's economy. Perhaps even more destructive were the unnatural borders Europe imposed on Africa, dividing ethnic groups among different nations and throwing sometimes mutually antagonistic groups into single political entities. Thus, when independence came, the

dozens of new African states were nations in name only. Moreover, they were nations with little infrastructure and few trained administrators.

Post-Independence Politics and Economics

In the days immediately following independence there was much optimism, on the continent and abroad, that Africa could leapfrog over the centuries it took Europe to emerge as a modern industrialized region. After all, the continent was blessed with enormous natural resources, abundant fertile land, and a youthful, vibrant population. Many of the newly independent states—often led by the charismatic men who had liberated them from European rule—embraced a statist, even socialist approach to economic development, with the government investing in heavy industry and infrastructure. The idea was to create self-sufficient economies, where local needs for everything from steel to consumer goods would be met by manufacturing goods internally, freeing Africa from what was viewed as capitalist, neocolonial exploitation.

It did not turn out that way for several reasons. First, the internal markets of most African countries were too small and too poor to sustain much industry and the lack of continent-wide transportation systems made it difficult for one country to trade with another. Second, there was a lack of trained technicians and managers to run these new industries. Finally, many of the new leaders and officials proved either incompetent or corrupt or both, pocketing much of the foreign capital that came into the country for their own personal use.

Continued poverty and corruption contributed to political instability. Beginning with Togo in 1963 and continuing into the early twenty-first century, African countries have been rocked by violent coups and bloody and destructive civil conflicts, the latter often inflamed by tribal divisions. Such strife and corruption were often exacerbated from the 1960s through the 1980s by cold war tensions, as the United States and the Soviet Union propped up authoritarian and repressive regimes as long as they sided with Washington or Moscow in the superpowers' global struggle for political dominance.

With a few exceptions, African economies stagnated in the late twentieth century as well, many actually shrinking from where they had been at independence. Adding to the continent's woes, many European countries pursued agricultural and import policies—including subsidies to domestic farmers and high tariffs on certain goods—that made it difficult for Africans to export their goods to their former colonizers. Finally, many African countries experienced rapid population growth—particularly in urban areas—that strained various governments' ability to provide sufficient services and overwhelmed the job-creating capacities of underdeveloped economies. Africa, in the second half of the twentieth century, became highly dependent on foreign aid. All told, nearly one-half of all Africans subsist on the equivalent of less than $1 per day per person, making it the most impoverished major region in the world. By comparison, in South Asia—the second poorest region in the world—about one-third of the population lives on a dollar a day or less, while in Latin America the figure is between 10 and 20 percent.

Promise and Peril in the Twenty-First Century

As the twenty-first century has dawned, much of Africa continues to struggle with the same economic problems that plagued it in the latter half of the twentieth century, including the AIDS pandemic, which, like the slave trade centuries before, has decimated the ranks of Africa's most productive age cohorts. Despite being a major oil-producing region, Africa has experienced acute energy shortages, undermining efforts to industrialize. And while the number of coups has gone down and the number of democracies has gone up, Africa's reputation for political instability and its endemic corruption continue to

discourage foreign investment. Moreover, despite numerous efforts to create transnational political organizations, the continent's various national economies operate largely independently of one another.

But while such problems have discouraged Western investment in Africa, the continent has found a new and important trading partner in East Asia. Led by China, a number of rapidly growing East Asian economies have begun investing heavily in the continent. China, in particular, sees Africa as a strategically important region and has struck deals with various governments there for long-term access to mineral resources, oil, and timber. Other East Asian and oil-rich Middle Eastern countries have also obtained long-term leases for agricultural land. In exchange, many of these new trading partners have committed to infrastructure development even as they pursue a policy of non-interference in domestic political affairs. That is, while much Western aid comes with requirements that outside authorities monitor how the money is used, Asian investment capital comes with few strings attached.

The new partnership between Africa and Asia has led some economists to talk of a decoupling of those regions with the West. It has been argued, for example, that increased integration with Asia has freed Africa from the effects of economic crises originating in America and Europe. But the financial crisis that began in the United States in 2007 and spread through much of the industrialized and industrializing world in 2008 has not left Africa untouched.

While it is true that the crisis that hit the world's financial system largely bypassed Africa's relatively unintegrated and backward financial sector—South Africa's being a notable exception—the freezing up of the world's credit markets has made obtaining necessary loans that much more difficult. At the same time, what limited foreign investment has come Africa's way has decreased since 2007 and the global recession has brought down prices for the mineral exports upon which so many African economies depend.

Meanwhile, the continent faces a new and far more lasting crisis from climate change, as the consensus among scientists in the field is that Africa is the region of the world that will face the most deleterious effects of rising temperatures and erratic weather patterns, including drought, spreading disease, and coastal flooding.

James Ciment

See also: Emerging Markets; Middle East and North Africa; South Africa; Transition Economies.

Further Reading

Ayittey, George B.N. *Africa Unchained: The Blueprint for Africa's Future.* New York: Palgrave Macmillan, 2005.

Meredith, Martin. *The Fate of Africa: A History of Fifty Years Since Independence.* New York: Public Affairs, 2005.

Reader, John. *Africa: A Biography of the Continent.* New York: A.A. Knopf, 1998.

Rodney, Walter. *How Europe Underdeveloped Africa.* Washington, DC: Howard University Press, 1974.

Agriculture

Human civilization's oldest economic activity, agriculture remained one of the most important components of every national and regional economy until the industrial revolution of the nineteenth century. Even today, it remains the key economic activity of many people in developing countries, though the proportion of people who make their living from agriculture has fallen to just 3 percent in the United States.

Agriculture has always been subject to the vagaries of nature. Weather, insects, and disease have traditionally produced great variations in output, as have human-caused events such as war, social unrest, and bad farming practices. In turn, the variations in output have produced great fluctuations in other sectors of the economy, though their impact in industrialized countries—where smaller numbers of people depend upon agriculture for a living and where food has become a smaller part of

consumers' budgets—has diminished significantly over the past century. Indeed, as recently as the 1930s, the average American family spent roughly one-quarter of its income on food; today, even with fluctuations in food prices, it spends less than 10 percent, a result of more productive agricultural practices and crops.

Several reasons explain why food prices have dropped even as the number of people in agriculture has declined: more efficient agricultural methods, more productive crops, and labor-saving machinery. In addition, most developed countries, including the United States, provide a variety of subsidies to farmers, both to maintain a viable agricultural industry and to keep food prices lower for consumers.

Still, in many parts of the developing world, agriculture continues to be a labor-intensive activity with little machinery, primitive farming practices, and less productive crops. Thus, while famine and even hunger have largely been eliminated from the developed world, periodic and regional food shortages continue to plague developing countries, particularly in Africa. Moreover, subsidies to domestic agriculture in industrialized countries often hurt farmers in developing countries, who find it hard to compete against subsidized food imports from the developed world or to export their crops to developed countries.

Because agriculture has been so important to regional and national economies historically, economists in the past spent much time and energy trying to explain how agricultural output affected the business cycle. The three most important schools of thought are the Malthusian theory, the sunspot theory, and the cobweb theory.

Malthusian, Sunspot, and Cobweb Theories

In 1798, the British economist and demographer Thomas Malthus developed a doomsday model of economic fluctuations. His theory was rooted in neoclassical economics, which argues that supply and demand naturally tend toward price equilibrium. That is, if demand for a product grows, then prices will rise, leading to investment, increased output, and lower prices. If supply outpaces demand, the opposite occurs.

While significant improvements in British agricultural methods had occurred by Malthus's time—notably, crop rotation and fertilizer input—they had occurred *long* before it. By the late eighteenth century, agricultural output had increased only incrementally over the previous century, primarily through increased use of land and labor. Because the amount of capital (land and equipment) remained relatively fixed, and with inputs of labor creating only arithmetic increases (adding a laborer yields a relatively small increase in production), the supply of food was limited to slow growth.

The demand side of the equation, however, was quite different. By Malthus's time, the population of Great Britain was increasing rapidly as a result of improved diet and health and increased manufacturing output. Thus, demand would inevitably outstrip supply, sending food prices soaring and sometimes leading to shortages. This, said Malthus, would lead to poverty, hunger, and starvation, thereby decreasing population. Malthus called this process the "preventive check." That is, if supply was limited to slow growth, then the neoclassical equilibrium of supply and demand required that the latter increase slowly as well. As a demographer, Malthus understood that this was not the case. In his view, therefore, the tension between food supply and demand explained the peaks and troughs of Britain's economic cycle.

There was, however, a basic flaw in the Malthusian theory—the assumption that capital inputs in the form of new technology were relatively fixed. In fact, with the industrial revolution dawning in Great Britain, new labor-saving technology arrived on the scene. That technology, along with improvements in agricultural methods and crop management, meant that a given quantity of fixed capital in the form of land, along with a fixed amount of labor, could still yield increased amounts of food, thereby increasing the supply to meet rapidly rising demand.

The "sunspot theory" was first developed by another British economist, William Stanley Jevons, in his posthumously published work, *Investigations in Currency and Finance* (1882). Jevons argued that sunspots—or increased solar activity—affected weather patterns and growing conditions on Earth. Increased solar activity caused agriculture to decline, he argued, which led to downturns in the business cycle. Jevons's main evidence was the coincidence of sunspot activity and downturns in business, which he said occurred every 10.45 and 10.43 years, respectively. But Jevons's argument had two fundamental flaws. First, he miscalculated the cycle of sunspot activity, which typically peaked every 11.11 years. Second, even if Jevons had been right that commercial activity and sunspot activity coincided, there was little evidence then—or since—that solar activity directly affects weather (even if modern science has found that solar activity does affect the ionosphere and the electromagnetic spectrum).

The Hungarian-born British economist Nicholas Kaldor (1908–1986) first formulated the "cobweb theory" in 1934. According to that view, disruptions to the stability of agricultural markets do not always correct themselves, as neoclassical theory assumes, even if prices and output are allowed to move freely without regulation or other forms of government interference. This is because farmers are literally backward-looking, taking into account last year's crop in planting decisions for this year so that prices and output form a "cobweb" of too-high prices one year, causing a rise in output the next, then too-low prices resulting in a fall in output. If prices for crops were high the year before, the farmer would plant more the next season. And with other farmers following the same course, a surplus would be produced, which in turn would drive less efficient farmers into insolvency and out of business. Such failures might well lead farmers to plant cautiously the following year, leading to shortages and higher prices—perpetuating the up-and-down cycle. Adding to the problem was the fact that, in Kaldor's time, it was difficult or expensive to store crops from one year to the next. In short, rather than moving toward a price equilibrium, crop prices tend toward volatility, which directly and significantly affects the business cycle.

The cobweb theory has less applicability in the modern world because most commodities, agricultural or otherwise, can now be stored over a long period of time, and prices are adjusted through futures markets that anticipate possible surpluses or shortages. Thus, any miscalculation about demand can be more readily smoothed over from stored inventories of the commodity in question or by sales or purchases in futures markets. If farmers can be forward-looking, a stable equilibrium is likely to be reached much faster, with less cyclical behavior. Nonetheless, cobweb-type models are used in modern explanations of bubbles and cyclical behavior or commodity prices.

The impact of price fluctuations on agricultural commodities is felt far and wide. But while they may be a burden on the pocketbooks of consumers in developed nations, price fluctuations can be a matter of life and death in the developing world, particularly in areas where people live on the edge of subsistence, such as the Sahel region of Africa. Since the 1980s, countries in the horn of Africa at the eastern end of the Sahel—notably, Ethiopia—have suffered repeated famines that have killed hundreds of thousands of people. Moreover, price fluctuations can trigger political turmoil, as was the case in Haiti and a few other countries during a run-up in agricultural commodity prices in 2008.

Financial Crisis of Late 2000s

The global financial crisis of 2008–2009 had major effects on agricultural markets and the fluctuations in price for a wide range of farm products. Indeed, the sharp and unexpected fluctuations in global agricultural prices were a direct consequence of the weakening of global financial markets. As they took their money out of the stock market, speculators placed an increasingly large portion of it in agricultural commodities markets. They did this in the hope of gaining

back losses in the financial markets by speculating on the future prices of these commodities. As a result, a bubble on agricultural products began to emerge as demand from speculators inflated the price of grains and other products far above their natural market value. Such speculative attacks on agricultural commodity markets became a serious and far-reaching problem, as they contributed directly to hunger, starvation, and related ills in many vulnerable regions of the world. In December 2008, in large part because of the speculative price bubble, the total number of hungry people in the world reached an estimated 963 million—40 million more than the previous year. As agricultural prices came down in the second half of 2008, a global recession had already started, and decreasing incomes further deepened poverty and hunger, especially in rural areas.

Mehmet Odekon and James Ciment

See also: Commodity Markets; Seasonal Cycles; Sunspot Theories.

Further Reading

Da-Rocha, J.M., and D. Restuccia. "The Role of Agriculture in Aggregate Business Cycles." *Review of Economic Dynamics* 9:3 (2006): 455–482.

Ezekiel, Mordecai. "The Cobweb Theorem." *Quarterly Journal of Economics* 52:2 (1938): 255–280.

Jevons, William Stanley. *Investigations in Currency and Finance.* London: Macmillan, 1909.

Kaldor, Nicholas. "A Classificatory Note on the Determination of Equilibrium." *Review of Economic Studies* 1:2 (February 1934): 122–136.

Magdoff, Fred, John Bellamy Foster, and Frederick H. Buttel, eds. *Hungry for Profit.* New York: Monthly Review Press, 2000.

Malthus, Thomas. *An Essay on the Principle of Population.* London: John Murray, 1826.

AIG

American International Group, or AIG, is both the world's largest insurance company and a major

Media gather outside the Manhattan headquarters of insurance giant AIG in September 2008, after the Federal Reserve authorized $85 billion to keep the firm afloat. The demise of AIG would have dealt a devastating blow to the global financial system. *(Stan Honda/AFP/Getty Images)*

financial services institution. At its peak, shortly before the global financial collapse of 2008, the New York–headquartered company employed more than 80,000 people and had operations in more than 130 countries. Once the tenth-largest corporation in the United States, AIG possessed hundreds of billions of dollars in assets. As an insurer and a financial-services institution, AIG invested heavily in exotic and risky securities—including mortgage-backed securities—which led to its near-collapse in late 2008 as the value of those securities plummeted. Deemed "too big to fail" by U.S. government officials fearful that its collapse would greatly aggravate the global financial markets—since AIG insured so many other securities with a protective instrument called a credit default swap—the company became the largest recipient of U.S. Federal Reserve (Fed) bailout funds that year, more than $150 billion in all.

AIG was founded in Shanghai, China, in 1919 by American businessman Cornelius Vander Starr, the first Westerner to sell insurance to Chinese clients.

Known as American Asiatic Underwriters, the company operated in China until the Communist takeover in 1949. Meanwhile, Starr launched other companies, including the Asia Life Insurance Company and, with British and Chinese partners, the International Assurance Company. Together they expanded operations into other parts of Asia, as well as Latin America, Europe, and elsewhere. Starr also founded such other companies as the American International Underwriters Overseas Company and American International Reinsurance (AIRCO), which, as its name implies, was involved in the business of backing the policies of other insurers by spreading the risk inherent in offering insurance among various firms. Through AIRCO, Starr also expanded his operations in the United States in the 1950s and 1960s by acquiring other insurance companies.

The American holdings did poorly, however, and in 1962 Starr hired a New York lawyer and financier named Maurice "Hank" Greenberg to turn them around. Five years later, the two partners formed American International Group, or

AIG, as Greenberg reoriented his firm's business from personal to more lucrative corporate coverage, offering industrial, commercial property, and casualty insurance. Starr died the following year, and Greenberg took over as president and chief executive officer. After going public in 1969, AIG expanded into a variety of businesses in subsequent decades, including credit services, real estate, health care, oil drilling, and the leasing of commercial jetliners. In retrospect, the most fateful of the new ventures was AIG Financial Products, launched in 1987, when several traders from Drexel Burnham Lambert, a pioneer in junk bond sales and corporate mergers and acquisitions, convinced Greenberg to utilize AIG's sterling credit rating to develop and invest in complex financial instruments known as derivatives. Akin to reinsurance, derivatives allow investors to take out a kind of insurance policy on other investments, with the price of the instrument derived from the value of another security.

Initially, derivatives were a useful and relatively low-risk tool for spreading investment exposure. That gradually changed over the course of the 1990s and 2000s, as traders at AIG and other financial institutions came to realize that derivatives could provide large returns as well as hedges against other investments. Better still, they were virtually unregulated in the United States and most other countries, allowing financial institutions to avoid including them in the assets-to-investment ratios that governments required for more traditional investments. By 2005, however, despite the favorable regulatory environment, AIG became the subject of government fraud investigations, culminating in substantial fines and the removal of Greenberg as CEO.

Nevertheless, high returns and lax oversight had helped expand the derivatives market into a multitrillion-dollar business, with AIG being one of the most aggressive of the businesses involved in it. Its AAA credit rating allowed AIG, under standard financial industry practices, to avoid having to come up with collateral to cover its positions in the derivatives market; the firm therefore

was able to invest huge sums against relatively few assets. Thus, when the crisis hit the financial markets in the summer of 2008, AIG found itself especially exposed. And when its credit rating was downgraded on September 16, it found itself unable to come up with the required tens of billions of dollars in collateral. Meanwhile, the company's stock price had plummeted to just $1.25 by mid-September, a fraction of its high of more than $70 the previous year, putting further stress on the company's finances.

AIG was on the verge of collapse, and this was a source of concern not only to the company's shareholders and management. AIG was not just a giant company. Because it insured so many securities of all kinds, it was integral to the very functioning of global financial markets. U.S. government officials, including Secretary of the Treasury Henry Paulson and Federal Reserve chairman Ben Bernanke agreed that the failure of AIG could destroy confidence in the financial markets, freeze the credit that drove the global economy, and plummet the world into a deep recession. The Fed moved quickly, providing some $85 billion in credit to AIG, secured by the company's assets, to meet its collateral obligations. In exchange, the government received a roughly 80 percent equity stake in the company.

As enormous as the credit line was, it proved insufficient to keep AIG afloat. In October, the government provided an additional $37.8 billion in credit, and in November it purchased $40 billion in newly issued preferred stock. In the process, AIG emerged as a symbol of the excesses and greed of Wall Street and as the target of popular outrage when it was learned that company executives had treated themselves to a lavish retreat at a California resort days after receiving the first bailout money and paid themselves large bonuses several months later.

With government backing, however, AIG remained solvent through the worst of the financial crisis in late 2008, though it was a now largely government-owned company. The revelation of AIG's involvement in high-risk, unregulated derivatives trading spurred calls in Congress and from the White House for tighter regulation of these markets. Nevertheless, many of the same executives who had led the company to the verge of bankruptcy were kept on, as first the George W. Bush and then Barack Obama administrations came to the conclusion that only they had the knowledge and experience to undo the damage they had caused.

James Ciment

See also: Collateralized Debt Obligations; Credit Default Swaps; Financial Markets; Mortgage-Backed Securities; Recession and Financial Crisis (2007–); "Too Big to Fail."

Further Reading

AIG Web site: www.aig.com.

Cohan, William D. *House of Cards: A Tale of Hubris and Wretched Excess on Wall Street.* New York: Doubleday, 2009.

Shelp, Ronald, with Al Ehrtar. *Fallen Giant: The Amazing Story of Hank Greenberg and the History of AIG.* 2nd ed. Hoboken, NJ: John Wiley & Sons, 2009.

Airline Industry

A relatively stable industry in its first sixty or so years of operation—barring wartime—the commercial airline industry both in the United States and around the world became much more susceptible to market forces and fluctuations in the business cycle as a result of government policies to deregulate the industry, beginning in the United States in the 1970s and soon spreading around the world. Indeed, the airline industry represents a test case for the pluses and minuses of deregulation: while airline deregulation initially promised more competition and lower prices for consumers, it eventually led to more bankruptcies, more consolidation, and deteriorating service.

Growth of Industry

Commercial aviation—that is, the carrying of passengers, mail, and freight as a for-profit business—began roughly a decade after the first heavier-than-air flight by the Wright brothers in 1903. Government contracts to carry the mail beginning in 1918 offered a kind of subsidy to help fledgling airlines start and stay in business. But technical considerations—planes were small, limited to daytime flight, and incapable of long-distance flight without refueling—limited the industry's potential until the 1930s and the introduction of Douglas DC-3, which could fly passengers across the United States in relative comfort, in fifteen to twenty hours with just three refueling stops.

The advent of pressurized cabins in the late 1930s, although not widely used in commercial aircraft until after World War II, allowed planes to fly higher, escaping the turbulence of low-altitude flight. The introduction of commercial jet aircraft further revolutionized the industry in the 1950s, with planes capable of transporting passengers across the continent and overseas in a matter of a few hours and at even higher altitudes.

As the commercial airline industry grew and became international in scope, governments came to realize that they would have to establish internationally recognized regulations and regulatory bodies. This began with the Convention on International Civil Aviation known as the Chicago Convention of 1944, and was further developed with the creation in 1947 of the International Civil Aviation Organization (ICAO), a United Nations agency. ICAO introduced the principle that air transport services should be arranged between nations through bilateral air service agreements. Meanwhile, countries set up agencies to regulate domestic air travel in order to ensure safety and control air traffic. In the United States, this began with the Air Commerce Act of 1926 and the establishment of the Civil Aeronautics Authority in 1938, the precursor of the current Federal Aviation Administration.

By the late 1950s and 1960s, air travel had become much more common in the developed world, with the United States leading the way. But it was expensive. Aside from the very wealthy—the so-called jet set—and well-heeled business travelers, it remained out of reach to most people. Part of this had to do with the introduction of costly new aircraft, the purchase of which had to be amortized through high ticket prices.

Regulation and Deregulation

But regulation played a role as well. It required airlines to price tickets dependent on length of flight rather than on volume of travel. That is, two flights of the same length—one between two small markets (with fewer passengers) and one between two big markets (with more passengers)—had to be priced the same, even though the economies of scale would have made the latter flight cheaper under free-market conditions.

More importantly, regulation limited competition. Fare changes, the introduction of new routes, and entry of new airlines into the marketplace were hampered by all kinds of rules and bureaucracy that made it very difficult for the industry to respond to market forces and changing customer demands. Adding to the airlines' woes were skyrocketing fuel prices, a result of the energy crisis of the early and middle 1970s.

As part of a general trend toward freeing markets from government control, many economists had been arguing that deregulation would both help the industry grow and provide better and lower-cost services for air travelers. Responding to such arguments, Congress passed the Airline Deregulation Act in 1978. For small start-up airlines, the timing could not have been better. A slow economy had weakened the major carriers and made it possible to purchase idle aircraft at low prices and hire out-of-work airline personnel at lower wages.

Airline deregulation fulfilled many of its supporters' hopes. All kinds of new low-cost carriers entered the market, offering fewer frills but cheaper ticket prices, particularly between high-volume markets. This forced the majors, as the larger, more established airlines were known, to lower their own prices. In addition, airlines were given more freedom to change routes and add

more flights to suit market needs, allowing them to respond to customer demands more quickly. One of the major innovations brought about by deregulation was the hub-and-spoke system, in which airlines fed travelers from smaller markets into major markets and then on to their ultimate destination, rather than directly between smaller markets, thus allowing for fuller flights, lower costs, and lower ticket prices. The result of all of this was increased capacity and lower costs; a study done by the Government Accountability Office twenty years after deregulation found that ticket prices (adjusted for inflation) overall were 30 percent lower than they had been before deregulation. These results partly influenced other countries to follow suit, as was the case in much of Europe beginning in the early 1990s.

But there was also a downside to deregulation. First, by allowing market forces to have a greater impact on ticket prices, deregulation ensured that people flying between smaller markets—where economies of scale did not come into play—would pay more proportionally than people flying between major markets, upsetting a long-standing principle of equitability in transportation that went back to the first regulations of railroads in the late nineteenth century. In addition, as airlines found their profit margins on each ticket reduced due to competition, they were forced to cut back on services, making air travel less pleasant. In addition, increased competition taxed the existing air travel infrastructure, leading to more delays for travelers.

Finally, by increasing competition and the role of market forces in the industry, deregulation led to a series of high-profile bankruptcies, particularly among the majors, as well as consolidation within the industry, as airlines attempted to further cut costs by gaining market share and exploiting economies of scale. Among the most high-profile bankruptcies were two from 1991: Eastern Airlines and Pan American World Airways (Pan Am). Major consolidation efforts include American Airlines's acquisition of Trans World Airlines (TWA) in 2001 and Delta Airlines's purchase of Northwest Airlines in 2008, the latter deal creating the world's largest commercial air carrier.

Such consolidation is meant to help airlines weather an ever more volatile era, as carriers respond to political, health, and economic disruptions that have an impact on the volume of air travelers, revenue streams, and profits. Indeed, the first decade of the twenty-first century saw a series of unprecedented shocks to the industry, including the terrorist attacks of September 11, 2001, which undermined air traffic for a time and led to increasing security delays and costs; the severe acute respiratory syndrome (SARS) outbreak, which undermined travel to the fast-growing Asia market in 2002–2003; and the financial crisis and recession of 2007–2009, which hit the lucrative business traveler market especially hard.

James Ciment and M.V. Lakshmi

See also: Oil Shocks (1973–1974, 1979–1980).

Further Reading

Belobaba, Peter, Amedeo Odoni, and Cynthia Barnhart. *The Global Airline Industry.* Chichester, UK: John Wiley & Sons, 2009.

Cento, Alessandro. *The Airline Industry: Challenges in the 21st Century.* New York: Springer Heidelberg, 2008.

Doganis, Rigas. *The Airline Business.* New York: Routledge, 2005.

Sheth, Jagdish, Fred C. Allvine, Can Uslay, and Ashutosh Dixit. *Deregulation and Competition: Lessons from the Airline Industry.* Thousand Oaks, CA: Sage, 2007.

Akerman, Johan Henryk (1896–1982)

Johan Henryk Akerman was among the economists of the early twentieth century who defined the growing discipline of econometrics. He applied a rigorous scientific approach, modeled on the study of physics, to economic research in general, and he was one of the first economists to apply it to the analysis of business cycles.

Akerman was born in 1896 in Sweden, the younger brother of economist Gustav Akerman (1888–1959). His book *Rhythmics of Economic Life* (1928), based on his dissertation, examined business cycle theory. While defending his dissertation, Akerman began a long-running debate with economist and review-board member Ragnar Frisch over the definition of business cycles. The debate not only served to sharpen the definition of business cycles but also the methods by which they were studied. Akerman taught at the University of Lund and his approach came to be known as the Lund school of economics.

Using a combination of deductive and inductive approaches, Akerman suggested that a business cycle was not an isolated event but rather a collection of smaller business cycles that combined to form larger cycles, which in turn create still larger cycles. He believed that changes within the smaller cycles created their own variations, which would eventually cause variances in the larger-scale cycles. There were, he believed, interdependencies between seasonal and cyclical changes. In spring and fall, there is typically a rise in economic activity. These seasonal variations, however, become less pronounced—and even nonexistent—during the boom phase of a cycle as well as during depressions. According to Akerman, economies had seasonal, agricultural, political, "Juglar" or fixed-investment, and building cycles, each one of a certain duration. His theories of business cycles, published in *Theory of Industrialism* (1960), were not met with universal agreement, although the idea of a political cycle (the four-year period between presidential elections) gained some support in the United States. Akerman died in 1982.

Robert N. Stacy

See also: Classical Theories and Models; Frisch, Ragnar.

Further Reading

Akerman, Johan. *Economic Progress and Economic Crises.* Philadelphia: Porcupine Press, 1979.

———. *Some Lessons of the World Depression.* Stockholm: Nordiska Bokhandeln, 1931.

———. *Theory of Industrialism: Causal Analysis and Economic Plans.* Philadelphia: Porcupine Press, 1980.

Boianovsky, Mauro, and Hans-Michael Trautwein. "Johan Akerman vs. Ragnar Frisch on Quantitative Business Cycle Analysis." *European Journal of History of Economic Thought* 14:3 (September 2007): 487–517.

Argentina

Located in the southern cone of South America, and with a population of just over 40 million, Argentina is a country with vast natural resources and a relatively literate and educated workforce. Yet, because of bad economic policy and corruption, much of its history has been marked by a series of rapid economic expansions and severe recessions. Its high inflation rates of the late twentieth century surpassed those of nearly any other country in history. The periodic economic crises have resulted in forced changes in government, most recently in 2002, when rioting forced the president from office. The rapid shifts in Argentina's economic fortunes have had a lasting effect on its population and the way in which lenders regard Argentine investment.

Argentina achieved independence from Spain in 1810. Sparsely populated at the time, it was divided into two climate zones. The coastal region was temperate with abundant rainfall, while the interior was drier and more mountainous. A majority of the inhabitants in the interior were associated with the silver mines in Bolivia. When the silver was depleted, most people migrated to the coast. The interior grasslands then depended on less-labor-intensive ranching. Until the last quarter of the nineteenth century, Argentina's economy remained largely dependent on exports of animal hides, leather, salted beef, and wool.

After 1875, the Argentine economy expanded at a rapid pace. Real income approached that of the United States. Rapid immigration, particularly by skilled laborers, helped alleviate the chronic labor shortage. Foreign investment, especially from Great Britain, allowed the development of infrastructure including an extensive railroad network that opened markets to products from the interior. Wheat, flax, and maize became major exports, thanks to advances in agriculture. The use of refrigeration permitted the export of meat products, and the more affluent European population provided the demand.

In 1890, a banking crisis nearly caused the collapse of the Argentine economy. Government bonds promising a large return had been purchased by many British investors, especially the Baring Bank. When payments on these bonds became too great, the Argentine government defaulted. Only a bailout by the Bank of England prevented major bank failures in Great Britain. As a result, foreign investment in Argentina, along with immigration, sharply declined for several years, until observers were satisfied that stability had returned.

By 1914, Argentina once again had one of the leading economies in Latin America. Although the economy was dependent mostly on exports, some industrialization had taken place. Printing plants, metalworking factories, and textile mills had been established to meet domestic demand. When World War I broke out in 1914, many imports were no longer available. Foreign investment went to supporting the war effort and was not available for investment. The decline in worldwide demand after the war caused a decline in Argentina's economy. Conditions remained poor during the 1930s because of the Great Depression. Subsidies for agriculture and an agreement with Great Britain to buy some exports helped limit the decline.

In 1930, the Argentine army staged a bloodless coup against the leftist civilian government of Hipólito Yrigoyen because of the economic conditions. A policy of import-substitution industrialization was adopted by the new government. Domestic industry was created to produce products formerly imported. These industries were given tariff protection and subsidies as necessary. When World War II broke out, exports of food products increased, resulting in a trade surplus of nearly $2 billion by 1945.

In 1946, populist Juan Perón took power in

Argentina, promising better economic conditions through greater government intervention. He nationalized financial institutions like the central bank, as well as the railroads and public utilities. Perón also created a single government purchaser for all grain products intended for export. The economy grew at first under Perón, and the quality of life improved, with many schools and hospitals being built. When the international grain market declined, however, the government limited production. Trade deficits after 1949 led to inflation. Perón adopted more business-friendly policies in 1952, but was overthrown in 1955.

Succeeding governments adopted a policy of "developmentalism." Investment, particularly from foreign countries, was encouraged in industry, energy sources, and public works, with assistance in the mortgage and business lending sectors. When combined with an austerity program for government spending, recession and inflation resulted. The subsequent foreign investment caused the economy to rebound, with real growth in wages for workers.

In 1973, Perón returned to power. The oil crisis of that year caused trade deficits resulting in budget deficits and inflation. Perón's government responded with poorly timed wage freezes and hikes that did little to improve conditions. Perón died in July 1974, and the army staged a violent coup in March 1976. The military was unable to stop the galloping inflation that reached over 100 percent annually. Public confidence declined because of human rights abuses and repression by the military government. Humiliated after an unsuccessful war with Great Britain over the Falkland Islands (Islas Malvinas) in 1982, the military was forced to turn power over to a democratically elected government in 1983. During the rest of the 1980s, Argentina was plagued by inflation, labor unrest, corruption, and the inability to achieve financial stability.

In 1990, President Carlos Menem adopted new policies. The Argentinean peso was tied to a fixed exchange rate with the U.S. dollar, and limits placed on unsecured currency. The inflation rate fell from 1,300 percent in 1990 to almost zero in 1995. Almost all state-run companies were sold to private investors, and their subsidies were abolished. Trade agreements with Brazil and other Latin American countries increased exports. Although the Argentine economy improved in the early 1990s, the rest of the decade was marred by sporadic growth because of external events.

In 1999, Argentina entered a recession largely because other countries' currency declined relative to the dollar. Imports increased because they were cheaper, while exports were more expensive for foreign customers. Fearing a devaluation of the peso, many Argentineans converted their savings to dollars. To prevent money from being sent out of the country, the government enacted a law known as the *corralito*, freezing most bank accounts and making it difficult for businesses to operate. Many Argentineans took to the streets to protest. The most common form of protest was the *cacerolazo*, consisting of banging pots and pans together. Frustrated citizens soon began to destroy property of large and foreign businesses. On December 20 and 21, 2001, violent protests ended with several protesters being killed and President Fernando de la Rúa resigning. Argentina defaulted on $93 billion in loan payments that month.

Most Argentine politicians refused to assume a leadership role. Eduardo Duhalde, vice president of Argentina from 1989 to 1991 and governor of Buenos Aires from 1991 to 1999, accepted the presidency and ordered a devaluation of the peso in January 2002. Inflation, unemployment, and most other economic indicators skyrocketed. In May 2003, Néstor Kirchner took office. The devalued peso made Argentinean exports more attractive, and a trade surplus had been created. Kirchner encouraged domestic industry and used the inflow of dollars to pay off many of Argentina's international loans. Wages increased and inflation was held largely in check. Thanks to Argentina's success in weathering this crisis, it was largely able to avoid the worst effects of the 2008–2009 recession.

Tim J. Watts

See also: Brazil; Emerging Markets; Latin America.

Further Reading

Coatsworth, John H., and Alan M. Taylor. *Latin America and the World Economy Since 1800.* Cambridge, MA: Harvard University Press, 1998.

Della Paolera, Gerardo, and Alan M. Taylor, ed. *A New Economic History of Argentina.* New York: Cambridge University Press, 2003.

Edwards, Todd L. *Argentina: A Global Studies Handbook.* Santa Barbara, CA: ABC-CLIO, 2008.

Asian Financial Crisis (1997)

The financial crisis that hit many East and Southeast Asian economies in the summer of 1997 was arguably the worst and most widespread of its kind in the modern history of the developing world. Triggered by a rapid withdrawal of foreign investment funds in Thailand—which caused a large and rapid devaluation in that nation's currency—the crisis quickly spread to other fast-growing economies in the region, such as Indonesia, Malaysia, and South Korea, among others. In the aftermath, economists pointed to a number of underlying causes—some endogenous, or internal, and some exogenous, or external—including weak national financial regulatory systems, real-estate bubbles, excessive foreign borrowing, and panic selling by foreign investors. The Asian financial crisis of 1997 set back economic growth in many of the affected countries for the rest of the decade and into the early 2000s. The crisis also had political ramifications, particularly in Indonesia, which saw the fall of the more than three-decade-old Suharto dictatorship. In addition, many countries imposed tighter regulations on their financial sectors, though calls for larger international reforms—including stricter controls on capital flows—went largely unheeded.

Causes

With economic globalization heating up in the 1980s, many developing economies in Asia ex-perienced a sudden and massive inflow of investment money from the United States, Western Europe, Japan, and other developed-world nations. At the time, however, Asian financial institutions were generally ill equipped to deal with the inflow. Banks, according to many economists, were poorly regulated, and standards for determining the credit of borrowers were largely inadequate. Meanwhile, financial liberalization across Asia promoted dramatic shifts toward speculative financing and development, as local banks became heavily involved in risky domestic lending and local firms gained access to large amounts of foreign capital.

Much of the borrowing and investment was aimed at the real-estate sector. Asian governments, looking to further attract foreign investment, offered tax breaks and other incentives to local developers to build residential and commercial properties in the hope of luring developed-world businesses to make direct foreign investments in the region. Prices for these real-estate assets, as well as the value of stock shares in local companies that owned them, rose dramatically. The increases in valuation induced further capital inflows. Much of the collateral (or guarantees) the banks accepted for foreign loans was real estate and equities, assets whose prices included a large "bubble" element (i.e., prices had risen far above the assets' intrinsic value).

Adding to this financially risky situation was the heavy borrowing local banks were engaging in, usually with U.S. banks as creditors. This left the banks exposed. Should Asian currencies weaken relative to the dollar, it would be that much harder to service the loans because they were in U.S. dollars. In some regional economies, the ratio of foreign debt to gross domestic product (GDP) skyrocketed, from roughly 100 percent in the early 1990s to nearly 200 percent by mid-1997.

The crisis began in Thailand in July 1997. Finding itself with a rising foreign debt, the Thai government had been trying desperately for some time to prop up its currency, the baht, to keep it pegged to the dollar. As these efforts became too costly, the Thai government decided to float the baht, which triggered its rapid devaluation. Foreign investors began to panic, pulling their funds out of Thailand. The contagion—foreign capital flight and monetary devaluation—spread to other emerging Asian economies, such Malaysia, the Philippines, and, especially, Indonesia. Yet even developed economies in the region—such as those in South Korea, Hong Kong, Taiwan, and Singapore—were affected. The only relatively unaffected countries were those more closed to unregulated inflows of foreign investment at the time—including Vietnam and the two Asian

giants, China and India—though asset valuations declined in those countries as well. Meanwhile, the Japanese stock market, full of companies that had invested massively in other parts of Asia, was also hard hit. Farther afield, stock markets around the world saw dramatic declines that many economists linked to the Asian financial crisis. In the so-called minicrash of October 27, 1997, the Dow Jones Industrial Average, to take the most closely watched of the world's major indexes, fell by more than 550 points, or about 7 percent. In Asia itself, the medium-term effects on the affected economies were profound. Over the next four years, GDP losses amounted to 24 percent in South Korea, 26 percent in Malaysia, 54 percent in Thailand, and 83 percent in Indonesia, one of the steepest recorded downturns in modern economic history.

IMF Response

As the crisis was unfolding, it became clear that local governments were unable to address the financial panic—some, like Thailand, were even on the verge of bankruptcy—and required outside help. The institution set up at the end of World War II to offer emergency assistance in such circumstances was the International Monetary Fund (IMF), an international lender largely financed and controlled by the governments of the major economies of developed world. Operating under the premise that the causes of the crisis were largely endogenous to the region—that the crisis arose from structural distortions in the affected nations' financial systems and economies—the IMF decided to lend the countries money to shore up and stabilize their currencies.

As is often the case with IMF assistance, the loans were offered on the condition that significant short- and long-term economic reforms would be made. First, the IMF insisted that central banks raise interest rates to cool the overheated national economies and fight inflation. Participating governments were also required to cut spending dramatically and close down

A tourist exchanges Thai currency, the baht, at an exchange booth in Bangkok in 1997. The collapse of the baht led to slumping currencies, stock market declines, and economic hardship across East Asia. (*Pornchai Kittiwongsakul/AFP/ Getty Images*)

struggling financial institutions. Regardless of whether or how effective this proved to be, it added to the immediate economic pain felt by the citizens of these countries, many of whom had already lost money in the devaluation and collapse of asset prices.

Many inside and outside the region criticized the IMF for its assessment of the crisis and the requirements it imposed on rescued governments. Some, such as Nobel Prize–winning economist Joseph Stiglitz, argued that many of the affected countries already had economies and financial sectors as well run as those in many industrialized countries and that the source of the crisis was the "herd" mentality of foreign investors who suddenly panicked and withdrew their funds. What was needed, Stiglitz and other IMF critics said, were better international controls on the flow of investment capital. Other economists charged that the IMF's belt-tightening solution was exactly the wrong one for reviving the affected economies since it strangled demand, which was critical to growth. Moreover, it was said, the minimal efforts to help the most vulnerable segments of society deal with rapidly rising prices and falling incomes led to ethnic violence and political unrest. In Indonesia, rioters attacked ethnic Chinese enclaves, and escalating instability led to the overthrow of the Suharto regime the following year.

The Asian financial crisis provided economists with stark insights into the role of irrational behavior in economic decision making and how such behavior affects exchange rates. Foreign exchange markets, some experts argued, may suffer from herd behavior that gives rise to sudden surges in capital inflow, followed by dramatic capital outflows as euphoria turns to panic. The consequences of such pronounced fluctuations include persistently unstable exchange rates, which can result in banking and financial crises with painful consequences for the real economy. As a result of such psychological forces, speculative bubbles may generate exchange rates wildly out of sync with such fundamental economic factors as inflation and interest rates, exports and imports, growth

and productivity, and domestic saving and investment rates.

If there is a lesson to be learned from the 1997 crisis, say some economists, it is that developing and transitional economies need to consider the trade-offs between higher rates of growth, financed by rapid expansion of foreign and domestic debt, and financial stability. Slower growth may be preferable if it is more sustainable in the long run.

John Lodewijks and James Ciment

See also: Business Cycles, International; China; Emerging Markets; Korea, South; Southeast Asia.

Further Reading

Arndt, H.W., and Hal Hill, eds. *Southeast Asia's Economic Crisis: Origins, Lessons and the Way Forward.* St. Leonards, Australia: Allen and Unwin, 1999.

Bhagwati, Jagdish. *The Wind of the Hundred Days: How Washington Mismanaged Globalization.* Cambridge, MA: MIT Press, 2002.

Goldstein, Morris. *The Asian Financial Crisis: Causes, Cures and Systemic Implications.* Washington, DC: Peterson Institute for International Economics, 1998.

McLeod, Ross, and Ross Garnaut, eds. *East Asia in Crisis: From Being a Miracle to Needing One?* London: Routledge, 1998.

Stiglitz, Joseph. *Globalization and Its Discontents.* London: Penguin, 2002.

Stiglitz, Joseph E., and Shahid Yusef, eds. *Rethinking the East Asian Miracle.* New York: Oxford University Press, 2001.

Asset-Price Bubble

An asset-price bubble occurs when the price of a certain asset or class of assets rapidly rises above the underlying historical value of the asset based on measured criteria other than price or by balancing price with other criteria. For example, an asset-price bubble in corporate securities would mean that the price of corporate shares had exceeded normal price-to-earnings or price-to-revenue ratios. In the case of housing, an asset bubble might be said to occur when the housing prices in a given market rise above their historic ratio relative to rents or to median income levels.

It is often difficult amid the complexity of market forces to ascertain when a bubble is occurring. That is to say, economics and other experts often have a hard time defining the intrinsic value of a given asset at a given moment in time, thereby making it hard to be sure those prices are rising too far and too rapidly above that value. Thus, many asset-price bubbles are only understood in retrospect.

Economists disagree about the causes of asset-price bubbles, though there is general consensus that excessive financial leverage plays an important role. In other words, when credit is too widely available and too easy to access, there will be asset-price bubbles. Two examples from American history back up this idea—one from the late 1920s and one from the late 2000s.

The middle and latter 1920s saw a dramatic run-up in the price of many corporate securities. Economic historians, however, differentiate between the price increases in the middle years of the decade and those of the latter years. Between the end of the recession in 1922 and the height of the economic boom in 1927, the Dow Jones Industrial Average (DJIA) rose from about 80 to about 150. This was a substantial increase, to be sure, but one merited by increases in corporate profits and revenues, many generated by the real gains in productivity created by new forms of energy (electricity) and transportation (motor vehicles). In other words, the rise in corporate securities did not represent an asset-price bubble. But then, between 1927 and 1929, the DJIA soared from about 150 to more than 380 points, even as underlying economic growth—including corporate revenues and profits—was slowing down. In other words, the growth in prices of corporate securities was far outpacing values.

Much of the explanation for this was excessive financial leverage. Low interest rates and the easy credit policies they permitted encouraged people to borrow for the purpose of investing. Brokerage houses allowed people to buy stock with just 10 percent down, financing the rest, a transaction known as margin buying. In turn, the brokerage houses were able to borrow from banks, often because they were part of the same company. Inevitably, with people able to buy far more stock than their own resources permitted, share prices rose dramatically, far in excess of their intrinsic value.

A parallel situation occurred in the early and middle 2000s in the U.S. housing market. Low interest rates orchestrated by the Federal Reserve and a flood of foreign capital coming in to pay for America's trade imbalance made it possible for financial institutions to lend on more liberal terms. Rather than buying corporate securities on margin—an act that had been severely curtailed in the wake of the 1929 stock market crash with margin requirements being increased from 10 to 50 percent—people began to take out loans to buy homes or refinance existing mortgages at lower interest rates.

Traditionally, people taking out mortgages were required to come up with 20 percent of the purchase price of the property from their own funds. But with credit standards loosening, lenders began to drop these standards, increasing the leverage of homebuyers. In addition, bankers began to lower their standards on who qualified for a mortgage to persons who previously would have been deemed too risky to lend to. Many of the latter were given adjustable-rate mortgages (ARMs), in which a low initial interest rate gave way to a fluctuating one. This increased the overall leveraging of the housing finance markets, since it increased the amount of money being borrowed to take out or refinance mortgages.

Margin buying in the 1920s and high-risk mortgages in the 2000s did not present a problem as long as the price of the asset being purchased continued to climb. In the case of the former, investors could pay back the margin call with the profits they made on the stock. In the case of the latter, mortgagors could refinance using the rising equity in their homes.

Of course, increasing the level of financial leveraging cannot go on forever. When stock and housing prices began to decline in 1929 and 2007 respectively, the dangers of financial leveraging were revealed in bankruptcies and foreclosures. In both cases, prices dropped precipitously precisely because they had been driven up by financial leveraging. That is, just as leveraging drove prices up rapidly, so deleveraging drove them down just as quickly and dramatically.

As the Great Depression of the 1930s and the so-called Great Recession of 2007–2009 reveal, the impact of asset-price bubbles can reverberate throughout the economy and can be felt around the world. The dramatic fall in corporate securities prices in the early 1930s forced banks—many of them having participated in the margin buying frenzy—to cut back on lending, leading to a drop in investment and hiring. Moreover, many of the biggest banks that had been involved in financing the purchase of corporate securities cut back on their credit to smaller banks, thus sending out shock waves from New York through the rest of the American financial system. Finally, the tightening of credit in the United States— then the world's leading creditor nation—led to a dramatic downturn in much of the world economy.

With the collapse of housing prices in the late 2000s, the scenario played out somewhat differently. Not only did many banks suddenly find themselves with bad mortgages on their books, they were also burdened with other so-called toxic assets such as securities that were based on bundled mortgages. (Indeed, the bundling of mortgages into securities—originally seen as spreading out the risk of default to investors—had encouraged some of the reckless lending that contributed to the housing asset-price bubble in the first place.) In response, banks began to tighten credit to businesses—thereby hurting investment—and each other, causing panic in the financial markets around the world.

In addition, many homeowners had used the rising equity in their homes to go on a buying spree through cash-out refinancing. Or, as they expected to pay for their retirement with the rising equity in their homes, they saved less and spent more. With the crash in housing prices, much of this spending stopped. And, as consumer spending accounts for roughly 70 percent of economic activity in the United States, this put a major damper on the U.S. economy. Moreover, since American consumers are an important market for exporters around the world, the lowered level of spending hurt economies around the world.

James Ciment

See also: Dot.com Bubble (1990s–2000); Echo Bubble; Florida Real-Estate Boom (1920s); Housing Booms and Busts; "Irrational Exuberance"; Mississippi Bubble (1717–1720); Overvaluation; Poseidon Bubble (1969–1970); Real-Estate Speculation; Souk al-Manakh (Kuwait) Stock Market Crash (1982); South Sea Bubble (1720); Stock Market Crash (1929).

Further Reading

Barth, James R. *The Rise and Fall of the U.S. Mortgage and Credit Markets: A Comprehensive Analysis of the Market Meltdown.* Hoboken, NJ: John Wiley & Sons, 2009.

Fox, Justin. *The Myth of the Rational Market: A History of Risk, Reward, and Delusion on Wall Street.* New York: Harper-Business, 2009.

Galbraith, John Kenneth. *The Great Crash, 1929.* Boston: Houghton Mifflin, 1997.

Gramlich, Edward. *Subprime Mortgage Crisis.* Washington, DC: Urban Institute, 2007.

Krugman, Paul. *The Return of Depression Economics and the Crisis of 2008.* New York: W.W. Norton, 2009.

Posner, Richard A. *A Failure of Capitalism: The Crisis of '08 and the Descent into Depression.* Cambridge, MA: Harvard University Press, 2009.

Shiller, Robert J. *Irrational Exuberance.* New York: Currency/Doubleday, 2005.

Thomas, Gordon, and Max Morgan-Witts. *The Day the Bubble Burst: A Social History of the Wall Street Crash of 1929.* New York: Penguin, 1980.

Thornton, Mark. "The Economics of Housing Bubbles." In *America's Housing Crisis: A Case of Government Failure,* ed. Benjamin Powell and Randall Holcombe. Edison, NJ: Transaction, 2009.

Australia

Occupying the entire continent of Australia, the island nation of Australia is a wealthy, industrialized country located between the Indian and Pacific oceans, south of the equator. Aside from a small minority of native Aborigine peoples, the country's 21 million people—or their ancestors—are largely immigrant, hailing from Great Britain, other European countries, and Asia.

Australia boasts a major manufacturing and service sector, as well as large-scale agriculture, and is also a major exporter of minerals, particularly to markets in Asia. At various stages in its history since British colonization in 1788, the Australian economy has been characterized by some striking features in comparison with other Western economies. In the second half of the first century of colonial development, for example, it boasted one of the highest living standards in the world. During the 2000s, when other developed economies experienced recessions following the bursting of the dot.com bubble and the onset of the global financial crisis, the Australian economy avoided recession altogether despite slowdowns in its rate of growth. However, the nation's economic development has been subject to significant periods of boom and bust.

Nineteenth Century

Some of the recurring factors in this experience are illustrated by the country's first colonial boom-and-bust episode during the 1820s. The first half of this decade was characterized by an expansion of pastoral activity as new lands became available beyond Sydney, one of the initial centers of colonization. This expansion was facilitated by the import of substantial volumes of consumer goods and significant immigration from Britain. Increased demand for loans to support the growing boom in wool production also gave rise to the establishment of new banks, supported by the import of financial capital from London. Competition between these banks led to interest rate reductions, which added further stimulus to the expansion. A series of events in the second half of the decade interrupted this boom, culminating in the economic depression of 1828–1830. The 1825 economic crisis in Britain reduced demand for Australian wool, causing a significant decline in the wool price and in pastoral incomes. The British crisis also reduced the flow of financial

capital to the colony, thereby affecting the banks' ability to lend. The credit crisis was further exacerbated by demands placed on the Bank of New South Wales, which was in the process of capitalizing newer banks. A drought in 1827–1828 further reduced pastoral output and incomes, resulting in the subsequent depression.

Both the environment and human factors have had a major impact on Australia's economy over the past two centuries. Droughts and domestic financial crises have disrupted the economy as have international downturns, which have periodically reduced both prices and demand for Australia's agricultural exports. These experiences manifested themselves in three significant and prolonged booms—in 1850–1890, 1950–1970, and 1993–2007—and two significant economic depressions—in 1891–1899 and 1929–1932—as well as a series of milder economic recessions.

The long booms all share similar features. Principal among these is the precondition of strong economic conditions in the rest of the world, leading to rising demand for Australian agricultural commodities and resources. In the extended boom of 1850–1890, the demand was for wool and gold (discovered at Bathurst and Ballarat in 1851). During the booms of 1950–1970 and 1993–2007, the demand included a broader range of agricultural produce, such as wheat, and other resources, such as coal, iron ore, bauxite, uranium, and oil. Other boom features have included strong growth in investment spending, credit expansions to support this investment, and increased imports of capital. In some cases, the booms were also associated with the inflation of asset prices, particularly those of property and stocks. This was the case, for example, in the latter stages of the boom of 1850–1890. The Melbourne land boom of the 1880s resulted not only from increased wealth accumulated during the broader boom but from improved transport infrastructure to Melbourne's outer suburbs, technological innovations that facilitated industrial development in these areas, and strong population growth. With these developments came an expectation of higher land prices that, in conjunction with the easy availability of finance, led to the realization and extension of such expectations. This represented the classic case of what economists call an "asset bubble"; it also led to a deterioration of credit standards as financial institutions competed with each other for business, further fueling the bubble.

Australia's two severe depressions reflect similar forces to those that caused the depression of 1828–1830. In 1890, London's Baring bank crisis precipitated a contraction of capital flowing to the Australian economy and an economic downturn in England that reduced the world price of wool. The first of these led in turn to a restriction of credit in the Melbourne market, stemming property demand, causing property prices to fall and the expectation of further price declines to reinforce the downward movement. The combined impact of the falls on overextended borrowers and reduced incomes from lower wool prices led to loan defaults and bank failures that compounded the economic contraction. National income fell by about 10 percent in 1892 and did not return to its 1891 peak until 1899. Unemployment also increased significantly during this period.

Twentieth and Twenty-First Centuries

While not usually included in the list of booms, the Australian economy experienced solid growth immediately following the end of World War I. This resulted primarily from increased government spending, a significant rise in population, and a faster pace of growth in the manufacturing sector than previously experienced. Economists Chay Fisher and Christopher Kent have argued that over the course of the 1920s this growth also led to increased construction activity and property speculation similar in nature to that of the 1880s property boom.

In 1929, Australia had already been in mild stagnation for a number of years due to a combination of overinvestment in industrial capacity following World War I, a contraction of demand for Australian exports due to unfavorable shifts in the ratio of the price of Australian goods to those available from other parts of the world, and *expectations* that these forces would lead to depressed economic conditions. The disruptions to financial markets in New York and London caused by the October 1929 stock market crash led to similarly sharp drops in Australian stock prices, higher domestic interest rates due to the reduced supply of funds from London, and depressed expectations that significantly curtailed spending. In conjunction with the existing situation in the Australian economy, these events caused a similar reduction in economic activity in 1930 to that experienced in 1892, albeit with an even greater increase in unemployment. The Great Depression was not, however, associated with a significant number of bank failures in Australia, as was the case in the United States and as had been the case in the depression of 1891–1899, which some economists argue accounts for the more rapid recovery of the Australian economy than was the case in the two other episodes.

Following World War II, the Australian economy showed mixed results. Its geographic isolation and limited internal market made it difficult for its manufacturing sector to grow and increase its competitiveness in international markets. In addition, the government protected the industry from outside competition, which tended to slow gains in productivity. But at the same time, its mineral sector boomed, with Australian commodities helping to fuel the economic miracle in Japan and later East Asia from the 1950s onward.

In addition to these events, a boom in stock and property prices that occurred in the late 1980s is noteworthy. While this coincided with a short period of strong economic growth between recessions in 1981–1882 and 1991–1992, this boom is frequently attributed to financial deregulation in the first half of the 1980s. Removal of restrictions on interest rates led to a rapid expansion of lending that fueled a pattern of increased asset prices, expectations of further price rises, increased asset demand financed by credit expansion, and further asset price increases. An additional factor frequently identified by economists in relation to the boom of 1993–2007 is increased labor market flexibility and reduced levels of industry protection progressively introduced during the 1980s and early 1990s.

And while banks were to come under considerable pressure when the stock and property bubble of the late 1980s burst following significant increases in interest rates engineered by the central bank, no bank was to fail in that episode, and its impact on the Australian economy was small by comparison with the Great Depression or the depression of the 1890s.

The Australian economy was also able to avoid recessions altogether following the bursting of the dot.com bubble and the global financial crisis of 2008–2009, partly due to carefully regulated banks and partly due to the prompt and aggressive use of fiscal and monetary policies to boost aggregate demand.

Thus, while the boom-and-bust experience of the Australian economy has largely reflected international economic forces, the impact of these forces has been significantly magnified or mitigated by domestic events, structures, and policies.

Peter Docherty

See also: New Zealand; Poseidon Bubble (1969–1970).

Further Reading

Boehm, E.A. *Prosperity and Depression in Australia, 1887–1897.* Oxford, UK: Clarendon Press, 1971.

Butlin, S.J. *Foundations of the Australian Monetary System, 1788–1851.* Sydney: Sydney University Press, 1953.

Edwards, John. *Australia's Economic Revolution.* Sydney: University of New South Wales Press, 2000.

Gizycki, Marianne, and Philip Lowe. "The Australian Financial System in the 1990s." In *The Australian Economy in the 1990s,* ed. David Gruen and Sona Shrestha, 180–215. Sydney: Reserve Bank of Australia, 2000.

Kindleberger, Charles P. *Manias, Panics, and Crashes: A History of Financial Crises.* Hoboken, NJ: John Wiley & Sons, 2000.

McLean, Ian W. "Australian Economic Growth in Historical Perspective." *Economic Record* 80:250 (September 2004): 330–345.

Merrett, David. "Some Lessons from the History of Australian Banking." Special Edition, *Economic Papers* (December 2006): 52–60.

Schedvin, C.B. *Australia and the Great Depression.* Sydney: Sydney University Press, 1970.

Austrian School

Founded in the mid-nineteenth century by financial journalist-turned-economics-professor Carl Menger, the Austrian school of economics—so named because its founder and many of its leading adherents hailed from that Central European country—emphasized ideas that continue to influence economic thinking. Austrian school economists maintained that the value of goods and services depend not on the labor and material that went into producing them, but on the perceived utility they provide to the seller, the purchaser, and the user. Austrian school economists also pointed to entrepreneurs as key agents of economic change. So central are these ideas that the Austrian school is referred to as the "psychological school" or "entrepreneurial school" of economics.

In addition, the emphasis on the subjectivity of value has led members of the Austrian school to maintain that market forces—that is, the decisions made by millions of individuals—always optimize economic performance. Politically, then, Austrian school economists have argued that government intervention in the economy—beyond the strict enforcement of contracts reached freely and voluntarily between individuals and maintaining a stable money supply—inevitably disrupts the workings of the market in negative ways. Fiercely antisocialist as well, Austrian school economic thinking has been adopted by libertarians and other radical free-market advocates in the years since its founding. Among its most important practitioners have been Friedrich von Wieser and Eugen Ritter von Böhm-Bawerk in the late nineteenth and early twentieth centuries, Ludwig von Mises and Joseph Schumpeter in the first half of the twentieth century, and Nobel Prize–winner

Friedrich von Hayek and Murray Rothbard in the mid-to-late twentieth century. Aside from Rothbard, an American, all of these individuals were born and educated in the Austro-Hungarian Empire or, after its demise in 1918, Austria.

Utility and Opportunity Cost

At the heart of Austrian school thinking is the concept of marginal utility, or the amount that utility increases by the addition of one unit of an economic good or service. For example, if a purchaser of potatoes is hungry, the utility of the first potato is very high; but as the person's appetite is satiated, the marginal utility—and, hence, value to the purchaser—of each additional potato decreases, since the value of the second potato sitting in his or her larder as a ward against future hunger is not as great as the value of the first potato in satisfying immediate hunger. In other words, the value of a potato is not determined by how much work went into sowing it, tending it, reaping it, and bringing it to market, but on how much individual economic agents, at a given point in time, want it.

Also critical to Austrian school economic theory is the idea of opportunity cost—the idea that the value a person places on a commodity is determined not just by how much that person desires the commodity, but by the alternative foregone in purchasing that good. An example can be found in the decision made by an hourly-wage worker who takes a day off and goes to the movies. The value of enjoying the movie, according to the theory of opportunity cost, is not determined solely by the ticket price, but also by amount of his lost wages.

In his 1871 book *The Principles of Economics*, Menger was a contributor to the "marginal revolution," a new approach that challenged the thinking of classical economists in the British tradition—as well as the Marxist tradition—who maintained that the value of goods and services can be determined objectively, based on the cost of the labor that went into them. The marginal revolution

represented a major intellectual paradigm shift in that it placed the study of individual choice and decision making at the center of economic inquiry.

Entrepreneurialism and Money Supply

The Austrian school emphasizes the role of entrepreneurs as the agents of economic change, always alert to the competitive advantages made possible by new technologies or business methods. Collectively, the decisions of profit-seeking entrepreneurs steer a free market toward the most efficient use of economic resources.

Monetary policy is another focus of Austrian school economics. According to adherents, money is not a neutral medium, as classical economists argued, but has a direct effect on market decision making. By increasing the money supply too fast, they maintain, central banks can trigger inflation. But because inflation affects the price of some goods faster or more intensely than others, increases in the money supply beyond what is required for the natural growth of the economy distort the normal exchange of goods and services and have a broad damaging effect.

The twin focuses on entrepreneurialism and monetary policy have led a number of Austrian school economists to the study of the business cycle. Entrepreneurial innovation, they argue, is a key ingredient of economic expansion. Joseph Schumpeter, a leading Austrian school economist of the early twentieth century, qualified this view by pointing out that too many entrepreneurs seeking to exploit an innovation causes profit margins to shrink, bankruptcies to multiply, credit to dry up, and a recession to result. Moreover, while entrepreneurial innovation affects economic growth and contraction over the long term, monetary policy—specifically, the setting of interest rates by central banks—has a more immediate effect. By setting interest rates too low, central banks, like America's Federal Reserve, create too much credit and an "artificial" boom. While this can be politically expedient for a government in power, it can have disastrous effects on the economy if pursued too aggressively or for too long. Cheap credit triggers more borrowing, thereby flooding the market with capital, much of which flows inefficiently after the diminishing profit margins of over-exploited new innovations or, worse, toward purely speculative purposes. This, say Austrian school economists, is precisely what happened in the mid-2000s. Inevitably, an overabundance of credit cannot be sustained and the credit markets contract, often sharply and suddenly—as in 2008 and 2009.

According to the Austrian school, then, the best role of government in helping avoid boom and bust cycles is to maintain a stable money supply. Interference in the natural workings of the market through economic stimulus plans like that introduced by President Barack Obama in early 2009 is anathema to Austrian school, as they will inevitably produce deleterious distortions in the allocation of economic resources. Because of its relatively laissez-faire approach to government economic policy—as well as its suspicion of the activities of central banks—the Austrian school has appealed more to the far right side of the political spectrum, with libertarians, such as 2008 Republican presidential candidate Ron Paul, being particularly strong advocates. More traditionally, Austrian school economics have provided arguments for those critical of socialism and communism, on two fronts. First, as noted, government involvement in the economy inevitably distorts the free market—the most efficient allocator of economic resources—in negative ways. Second, as the importance of private property diminishes, so does the capacity of individuals to make efficient economic choices.

Finally, Menger's Austrian school was not just revolutionary in the ideas it propounded, but also in its methodology. Adherents argued that general theories can explain economic behavior in all circumstances. This contrasted with the view of the contemporary German historical school, which argued that economic behavior is rooted in specific historical circumstances and

that the purpose of economics is to accumulate data on those circumstances that the government can then use to make effective economic policy. At the same time, Austrian school economists maintain that economics is not a science in the same sense as natural sciences are. For one thing, they maintained, standard experimental methodology cannot be reproduced in economics, since individual factors cannot be isolated. Second, the actions of human beings are of such complexity that strict empirical inquiry and mathematical models are useless. Instead, as Ludwig von Mises, an influential twentieth-century Austrian school adherent, argued, economists should focus on the logical processes people use to make economic decisions—a study he called "praxeology."

While some aspects of Austrian school thinking have been adopted by mainstream economists—notably, the role of entrepreneurial decision making in microeconomic theory—it is largely viewed as an iconoclastic body of thought by most practicing economists and economic policy makers today.

James Ciment

See also: Böhm-Bawerk, Eugen Ritter von; Haberler, Gottfried von; Hayek, Friedrich August von; Mises, Ludwig von; Monetary Policy; Monetary Theories and Models; Schumpeter, Joseph.

Further Reading
Hutchinson, T.W. *The Politics and Philosophy of Economics: Marxians, Keynesians, and Austrians.* New York: New York University Press, 1981.
Kirzner, Israel M. *The Meaning of Market Process: Essays in the Development of Modern Austrian Economics.* New York: Routledge, 1992.
Meijer, Gerrit. *New Perspectives on Austrian Economics.* New York: Routledge, 1995.
Reekie, W. Duncan. *Markets, Entrepreneurs, and Liberty: An Austrian View of Capitalism.* New York: St. Martin's, 1984.

Automated Trading Systems

An automated trading system is any computer program that enacts trades on a stock or securities exchange in response to user-inputted instructions. Such systems match bids and offers automatically and can "make decisions" based on market behavior, according to the instructions encoded in the software.

Automated trading systems are also known as algorithmic (or algo) trading systems, robo trading, or black-box trading, each term emphasizing a different aspect. The systems are especially popular among institutional investors and fund managers, and can accommodate a wide range of risk and yield preference. There is no one trading system, nor one trading system style; different systems can be designed with different goals, making comparisons difficult.

The use of trading systems has greatly accelerated since the computerization of financial markets in the 1970s and 1980s. The decimalization of the U.S. stock market—moving from sixteenths of a dollar to hundredths of a dollar (pennies) as the basic unit of stock value—encouraged algorithmic trading by creating smaller differences between bids and offers, as well as more price differentials to be exploited by arbitrage. As more and more traders use automated trading, trade volume increases, which in turn increases the amount of data to keep track of. This, in turn, encourages more traders to use automated trading, and so on. The use of software allows real-time analysis of, and interaction with, the global financial markets at every hour of the day. Today, more than half of the trades made on most stock exchanges, and about a quarter of trades made on foreign exchange markets, are entered through trading systems.

Trading systems are rules based and algorithmic. An algorithm is a set of instructions, often represented by flowcharts or "if . . . then" statements—used in data processing and other fields. A simple example of an algorithm is the set of instructions for what to do when a customer orders a cheeseburger: collect further information (doneness, type of cheese, toppings, special instructions) and then enact specific predetermined procedures based on that information. This is a deterministic algorithm. A probabilistic algorithm incorporates

a degree of randomness at some point in the instructions. In the rules to Monopoly, for example, each player begins his turn by rolling the dice to determine how many spaces to move.

Trading systems are particularly well suited to arbitrage, which takes large amounts of capital and uses it to generate a profit from the price differential among multiple markets, buying low on one market and selling high on another. "Low" and "high" are relative terms here, and the difference may be very small. But as long as there is a difference, a trade large enough for the profit to exceed the transaction cost is a trade worth making. Arbitrage is most common, then, where transaction costs are lowest. When arbitrage is conducted by a trading system, much less labor is involved, so the price differential can be even lower while still yielding a profit. Further, computers can identify such price differentials extremely quickly. Of course, this means that all the other arbitrageurs are scouting out the same "deals."

Alternative Trading Systems

Automated trading systems should not be confused with alternative trading systems (ATS), a regulatory term referring to trading venues that are approved by the Securities and Exchange Commission (SEC) for trading outside of exchanges. Nevertheless, there is a relationship between automated and alternative trading systems. Many ATSs operate electronically, such as broker "crossing networks" that use an automated trading system to match buy and sell orders without publicizing either before the trade is made; this is often what is meant by "black-box trading." Many crossing networks are referred to by the ominous term "dark pools of liquidity." These are designed to allow for large trades without impacting the market, keeping knowledge of the trade private or disclosing it at the last possible moment. Generally, the presence of such pools in the market can be inferred by monitoring market depth—an easy task for trading systems—and noticing that the bid and offer have decreased simultaneously by the same amount. But because this could just as easily be a coincidence, it is risky to act on the assumption that major trades are being made in the dark. Dark pools are favored by institutional investors, who usually make trades in large quantities.

Electronic communication networks (ECNs), authorized by the SEC in 1998, are publicly visible crossing networks that execute trades in stocks and foreign currencies (and, less commonly, other securities). Well-known ECNs include NASDAQ (an electronic stock exchange established in 1971) and Baxter-FX (an electronic foreign currency exchange). Automated trading generally transpires on an ECN (which is not to say that all trading transpiring on an ECN is automated).

Especially risk-averse traders, such as pension fund managers and other institutional investors, depend on the Volume-Weighted Average Price (VWAP) benchmark, which is the ratio of the combined value of all the trades of a stock over the course of the day so far, divided by the total number of shares traded. Brokers using automated trading systems can offer a "guaranteed VWAP execution," which means that the investor's trade is guaranteed to be performed at the VWAP. For a lower commission, a broker can offer a VWAP target execution, which has a margin of error but will enact the trade very near the VWAP price.

Fundamental, Quantitative, and Technical Analysis

Traditionally, investment strategy depended on fundamental analysis, which evaluates the soundness of a stock by examining the business itself—its financial statements, its industry, its position in the industry, and its plans for the future—and treating a stock purchase as an investment in the company (which of course it is). Healthy companies made for healthy investments. Quantitative analysis, while not exactly opposed to this, developed alongside it in the 1930s as economic science gained new prominence during the Great Depression. Such analysis uses the tool of calculus to examine stocks and other securities, and is fundamental to most trading systems. The Black-Scholes model developed out of quantitative analysis.

Technical analysis ignores most of the data crucial to fundamental analysis. Indeed, it barely acknowledges that there is a company behind the shares of stock. Instead, technical analysis focuses on the performance of a particular stock in the market. What the company makes and how good a job it does in making it does not really matter—all that matters is what the stock sold for yesterday, last week, and last year, and how much of it was sold. Technical analysis worries some investors for exactly that reason, and its claims to predict stock behavior are often dismissed as pseudoscience. On the foreign exchange market, however, it is quite popular.

Technical analysis, like quantitative analysis, can be built into algorithmic trading systems more easily than fundamental analysis can be. Moreover, the increased use of automated trading systems has contributed to the prevalence of technical analysis. The underlying belief of the "chartists," as technical analysts are often called, is that investor behavior and market trends can be accurately predicted. This fuels not only many legitimate and useful trading systems, but stacks and stacks of popular economics pulp, as one author after another claims to predict the size and shape of the next big crash or the next big boom.

Moreover, the increased use of trading systems leads to the same kind of security-hacker or virus-antivirus "arms race" as exists in the computing industry at large. While dark pools of liquidity conduct secret trades in the shadows, as it were, "shark" algorithms try to detect them by making small market orders to locate the pools. The pools, in turn, can be equipped with pattern-recognition algorithms and avoid or subvert identification. The more popular an algorithm or algorithm type becomes, the more likely someone will develop and market another algorithm to subvert or exploit it.

While automated trading has produced much

more responsive financial markets in general, it can also lead to, or accelerate, panics. Many analysts, including those involved in a presidential task force set up to investigate it, blame the crash that took place on Black Monday, October 19, 1987, in part on automated trading. (On this day, the Dow Jones Industrial Average experienced its largest single-day fall in terms of percentage.) Huge blocks of stock were sold off automatically, based on algorithms geared to specific market conditions, contributing to the downward slide in stock prices. In the wake of Black Monday, New York Stock Exchange officials instituted a rule which said that if the Dow fell by more than 250 points in a session, program trading would be prohibited, allowing brokers to contact their clients and infuse the process with human decision making.

Bill Kte'pi and James Ciment

See also: Stock Market Crash (1987); Stock Markets, Global.

Further Reading

Chan, Ernie. *Quantitative Trading: How to Build Your Own Algorithmic Trading Business.* Hoboken, NJ: John Wiley & Sons, 2008.

Kaufman, Perry J. *New Trading Systems and Methods.* Hoboken, NJ: John Wiley & Sons, 2005.

McDowell, Bennett A. *The Art of Trading: Combining the Science of Technical Analysis with the Art of Reality-Based Trading.* Hoboken, NJ: John Wiley & Sons, 2008.

Stridsman, Thomas. *Trading Systems That Work: Building and Evaluating Effective Trading Systems.* New York: McGraw-Hill, 2000.

Babson, Roger (1875–1967)

Known as the "Seer of Wellesley Hills," Roger Babson was an entrepreneur, statistician, and business and economic forecaster who pioneered the use of charts in the analysis and prediction of business cycles. Like many of his contemporaries in the first half of the twentieth century, including Ragnar Frisch, Babson sought to analyze business cycles using what he regarded as scientific methodology. Where he differed from his contemporaries was in adopting a loose—or, according to his critics, pseudoscientific—model, compared to their more rigorous scientific and mathematical tools and methodologies. He is also known as the founder of Babson Institute—later Babson College—a private business school established in Wellesley, Massachusetts, in 1919.

Roger Ward Babson was a member of the tenth generation of Babsons of Gloucester, Massachusetts, where he was born on July 6, 1875. He attended the Massachusetts Institute of Technology and, after graduating in 1898, worked for investment firms in New York and Boston. In 1904, he founded the Babson Statistical Organization in Wellesley to analyse stocks and business

reports for banks and investors; the firm continues operations today as Babson-United, Inc. Babson's interest in forecasting business cycles began to earn him recognition in the late 1920s, especially after September 5, 1929, when he predicted the stock market crash that occurred less than two months later. Unfortunately, he had been bullish only a few months earlier and would again become bullish by 1930.

Babson's approach to understanding and forecasting business cycles was founded on the basic concepts of Newtonian physics, in particular Newton's third law of motion ("for every action, there is an equal and opposite reaction"). Babson applied the same principle to cycles of business expansion and contraction. Although his method did not gain unanimous respect from economists who took a rigorous scientific approach, his weekly bulletin, *Babson's Report*, published under the aegis of the Babson Statistical Organization, attracted a wide readership and gained a reputation for accurate predictions.

As early as 1912, Babson wrote that a common mistake among businessmen and economists was that they were interested only in what happened in their own geographic regions, rather than in the country or the world as a whole. Additionally, he maintained, too many businessmen and economists optimistic and pessimistic maps showed areas in which business opportunities were said to exist and those in which they were lacking. In addition to books, Babson wrote hundreds of magazine and newspaper articles. He was also a popular lecturer on business financial trends.

Among his many interests and activities, Babson was one of the world's leading collectors of Newtoniana. In 1940, he ran against Franklin D. Roosevelt for president of the United States on the Prohibition Party ticket. In addition to Babson College, he founded Webber College (now Webber International University), in Babson Park, Florida, and Utopia College (now defunct) in Eureka, Kansas. Roger Babson died on March 5, 1967, in Lake Wales, Florida.

Robert N. Stacy

See also: Boom, Economic (1920s); Frisch, Ragnar; Great Depression (1929–1933).

Further Reading

Babson, Roger Ward. *Actions and Reactions: An Autobiography of Roger W. Babson.* New York: Harper & Brothers, 1935.
———. "Ascertaining and Forecasting Business Conditions by the Study of Statistics." *Publications of the American Statistical Association* 13:97 (March 1912): 36–44.
Barsky, Robert B., and J. Bradford DeLong. "Bull and Bear Markets in the Twentieth Century." *Journal of Economic History* 50:2 (June 1990): 265–281.
Friedman, Walter A. *The Seer of Wellesley Hills: Roger Babson and the Babson Statistical Organization.* Boston: Harvard Business School, 2008.
Smith, Earl Leo. *Yankee Genius: A Biography of Roger W. Babson.* New York, Harper, 1954.

Statistician Roger Babson, the founder of Babson College in Wellesley, Massachusetts, applied an array of mathematical tools and a loose scientific methodology to the study of business cycles in the early twentieth century. *(Library of Congress)*

viewed the behavior of the marketplace and the economic system from the narrow perspective of their own particular service or product. Babson urged entrepreneurs and investors to become familiar with all aspects of the business world, recommending his own publication as a source of such information. The advent of more rigorous and broad-based models for forecasting business cycles in the later half of the twentieth lent credence to Babson's approach. By the late twentieth century, Babson's holistic approach to forecasting was well established and influential in the field.

Among Babson's more than forty books on economic and social issues were the texbooks *Business Barometers Used in the Accumulation of Money* (1909) and *Business Barometers Used in the Management of Business and Investment of Money* (1923), both of which went into multiple editions. The use of statistics was only part of Babson's approach to business analyses and instruction. His so-called

Balance of Payments

The balance of payments (BOP) is a financial statement measuring the monetary transactions (or flows) between the residents of a specific country and the residents of all other countries. The BOP is determined for a specific period of time, usually a year, but sometimes monthly or quarterly. A transaction is recorded in a specific country's BOP only if one party is a resident and the other is a nonresident: transactions between two residents or two nonresidents are omitted from the calculation.

The BOP reflects the structure of a country's sources of foreign financing and its use of these sources. It also helps economists and policy makers understand how a country's foreign reserves have changed and how its gross domestic product has risen or fallen. Because most countries follow the same or almost the same rules for compiling their BOPs—published in the International Monetary Fund's *Balance of Payments and International Investment Position Manual* (sixth edition, 2008)—it is also possible to compare their balances of payments, to compare saving and investment behaviors, and, in some cases, to predict changes in their economic policies—that is, whether they will impose import restrictions, provide export subsidies, or change the value of their currencies.

The main components of a BOP are the current account (export and import of goods and services, as well as transfer payments) and the financial, or capital, account (outflow and inflow of financial securities). These, in turn, are divided into several sub-accounts. The financial account, for example, has four main sub-accounts: (foreign) direct investment(s), portfolio investment(s), financial derivatives, and other investments. Sometimes reserve assets are recorded as a fifth sub-account of the financial account, while sometimes they are treated as a separate account.

The BOP indicates flows (such as how much a country exported or invested abroad in a certain year, quarter, or month) rather than accumulations (such as the total value of the investments it has received from abroad or the goods it has imported in all years since its independence). The sum and structure of all of the country's international financial liabilities and assets can be found from its international investment position.

Although different currencies are used for foreign transactions, a country prepares its BOP in a single currency, usually its own. Transactions in other currencies are recalculated based on the exchange rate at the time they took place. Occasionally, BOP is calculated in other currencies, as this makes it easier for one country to compare its own BOP to that of another country.

In calculating the BOP, the double-entry system is used. This means that every transaction is recorded with two entries of equal amounts but with different signs: one with a plus sign (indicating a credit, including exports of goods and services, inflows on transfers and incomes from abroad, decreases in reserves and other external assets, and increase in foreign liabilities) and the other with a minus sign (indicating a debit, including imports of goods and services, outflows on transfers and incomes, increase in external assets, and decrease in foreign liabilities). As a result, the net balance of all entries should equal zero, and it is not correct to say that a country's balance of payments has either a deficit or a surplus. That is, in the aggregate, a deficit in the balance of a goods and services account must be exactly offset by a surplus in the capital account or vice versa. Hence the BOP always balances.

At the same time, of course, different accounts and sub-accounts may have different signs. For example, a country might have a current-account deficit that is covered with a positive financial account (capital account surplus), and these deficits or surpluses may be stable or may change from year to year. Because several data sources—state agencies, banks, and/or independent surveys—are used for compiling the BOP, and because it is difficult to get information about absolutely all transactions that took place during a certain period, the net balance is not always equal to zero. Thus, an additional account—net errors and omissions—is created for balancing the other accounts. The sign of this account is always opposite to the sign of the sum of all other accounts.

As is often the case, additional information becomes available after compiling and publishing the initial BOP. Thus, countries typically publish one or several corrected versions of their BOP during the course of a year. In addition to such regular adjustments, sometimes—because of significant methodology changes, for example—extraordinary adjustments are also made. In such cases, countries might revise data from earlier years, being careful to identify the causes and sizes of the alterations.

Tiia Vissak

See also: Capital Account; Current Account; Exchange Rates.

Further Reading

International Monetary Fund (IMF). *Balance of Payments and International Investment Position Manual.* 6th ed. Washington, DC: International Monetary Fund, 2010.
———. *Balance of Payments Statistics Yearbook.* Washington, DC: International Monetary Fund, 2008.

Baltic Tigers

Comprised of the former Soviet republics of Estonia, Latvia, and Lithuania, the Baltic Tigers represented, for a time, a success story in the transition from communism to capitalism in Eastern Europe. Liberalizing their economies from state control led to a flood of foreign capital, which, in turn, produced a consumer and construction boom. But the boom, which began in the wake of the Russian financial crisis of the late 1990s, was short-lived, undermined by growing deficits, inflation, and the global financial crisis of the late 2000s. (The term "Baltic Tigers" comes from the countries' location—on the Baltic Sea—and the fact that, like the East Asian "Tigers" of Hong Kong, Singapore, South Korea, and Taiwan, they were relatively small political entities that experienced rapid economic growth over a short period of time.)

Long dominated by powerful neighbors, the Baltic Tigers achieved a brief period of independence after World War I, only to find themselves occupied and annexed by the Soviet Union at the end of World War II. Between the mid-1940s and the end of the 1980s, all three states were transformed into Soviet command-style Marxist economies, where the state controlled most of the land and means of production. Among the most advanced of the Soviet republics, the Baltic Tigers experienced rapid industrialization in the years immediately following World War II, although, as with the rest of the Soviet Union, heavy bureaucracy and a lack of market forces led to increasing economic stagnation in the 1970s and 1980s.

The political liberalization of the Soviet Union under Premier Mikhail Gorbachev from the mid-1980s encouraged a growing independence movement in these highly nationalist republics. When they declared themselves independent in 1990 and 1991, Moscow opposed the decision but did not occupy the countries militarily. Finally, under pressure from European leaders, the rapidly collapsing Soviet government recognized the independence of the three countries in September of 1991. Most historians consider the declarations of independence of the three Baltic countries to have been a major contributing factor in the collapse of the Soviet Union in December 1991.

Post-Independence Slump and Boom

The decade following independence was a trying time for the three Baltic republics. Their economies remained tightly bound up with Russia and other former Soviet republics at a time when those economies were experiencing freefalls in industrial output, gross domestic product (GDP), and per capita income. All three were hit hard by the Russian financial crisis of 1998, when falling oil and commodity prices led to a rapid devaluation of the Russian currency, massive inflation and joblessness, and near-bankruptcy for the government in Moscow.

But just as the Russian economy rebounded rapidly from the crisis—largely as a result of rising commodity prices—so too did the economies of the Baltic republics. From 2000 to 2007, Latvia's GDP per capita (at current prices) increased from roughly $7,700 to $17,000, an increase of more 220 percent; Estonia's went from $9,900 to $20,200, a rise of more than 200 percent; and

Local businessmen line up for loans at the Latvian Investment and Development Agency in Riga in 2006. The newly independent Baltic states—Latvia, Lithuania, and Estonia—thrived in the transition from communism to capitalism in the early 2000s. *(Ilmars Znotins/Stringer/AFP/Getty Images)*

Lithuania's from $8,400 to $18,900, an increase of 225 percent. These growth rates were among the highest in Europe. But the countries also had to catch up with the more advanced European economies: before the boom, their GDP per capita was only about a quarter of the European Union (EU) average.

To a large extent, the growth of the Baltic Tigers was based on substantial inflows of foreign capital. Their liberal economic environments, successful economic reforms, favorable location (near Nordic and other European markets), relatively low taxes, good infrastructure, cheap but skilled labor, and accession to the EU made them attractive to foreign investors. Moreover, as large Baltic banks were taken over by Scandinavian banks, the latter increased the lending capacity of their Baltic subsidiaries, which led to a real-estate and economic boom and increased wage pressures (for instance, while in 2000 Estonia's average monthly salary was $289, in 2007 it was already $991: 3.4 times higher). However, foreign trade deficits began expanding; while both imports and exports

grew in these countries, imports increased more, as did inflation. These problems, combined with the financial crisis and global recession of the late 2000s, ended the Baltic Tigers' economic boom by late 2007, early 2008.

Financial Crisis of 2007–2008

Of the three countries, only Lithuania experienced growth—a modest 3.2 percent—in 2008. That same year, Estonia's industrial production fell by 6.5 percent compared to 2007. As the real-estate boom ended, the manufacture of building materials decreased the most: by 28.1 percent. Overall, enterprises have not met their income predictions as demand has fallen, unemployment has increased, and an increasing share of borrowers is causing solvency problems.

On the other hand, the decline has also led to some positive changes for Estonia: while in 2008 its inflation rate was 7.0 percent, in January 2009 prices decreased by 0.6 percent compared to December 2008, and its foreign trade deficit has also been decreasing. Moreover, the banks have become more conservative in issuing loans as their Nordic owners have also cut down their financing.

Despite its economic problems, however, Estonia has continued its relatively liberal economic policy to keep up investors' confidence. It has not increased taxes (except the value-added tax) and it has made cuts in the budget to meet the fiscal requirements necessary for adopting the euro in 2011 (such as a maximum deficit of no more than 3 percent of GDP).

Latvia fared just as badly. In 2008, the country's annual inflation rate was 15.4 percent, its unemployment rate increased to 7.0 percent of the economically active population, and the economy shrank, though to what degree was disputed by various economists. Meanwhile, Latvia's currency weakened and the government had to intervene to keep the exchange rate from falling further. Moreover, the government had to take over—or nationalize—one of the country's major banks, Parex Bank, to prevent its going bankrupt. Because of a large budget deficit, Latvia had to take a $2.4 billion loan not only from the International Monetary Fund (IMF), but also from the central banks and governments of Sweden, Denmark, and Finland. The country also increased taxes and cut public sector wages by 25 percent.

Like Estonia and Latvia, Lithuania also experienced weakening demand at the end of 2008, although in annual terms, private consumption still increased by 4.7 percent and government expenditure by 4.3 percent. It struggled as well with high inflation (11.1 percent in 2008), and less favorable borrowing terms. While in the fourth quarter of 2008, Lithuania's economy started falling; for the year overall, it grew by 3.3 percent. The Bank of Lithuania expects GDP declines for 2009 (by 4.9 percent) and 2010 (3.9 percent). A recovery is not predicted until 2011. It is expected that domestic demand will continue falling, and exports will also drop in 2010, but imports will decrease more.

Clearly, the economic boom times for the Baltic Tigers have been derailed by the global economic crisis of the late 2000s, at least temporarily. It is not clear when the decline will end and the new boom will start. Indeed, for these three countries, predictions have been changed frequently. Their recovery depends not only on their own actions—including adoption of the euro (although they do not meet all the requirements yet); making investments in education, infrastructure, and innovation; increasing productivity; creating high-technology clusters; and increasing firms' interest in cooperating—but also on the recovery of the economies of their main trade and investment partners from the European Union.

Tiia Vissak and James Ciment

See also: Eastern Europe; Emerging Markets; Russia and the Soviet Union; Transition Economies.

Further Reading

Andersen, Camilla. "IMF Helping Counter Crisis Fallout in Emerging Europe." *IMF Survey Magazine,* January 14, 2009. Available at www.imf.org/external/pubs/ft/survey/so/2009/int011409a.htm. Accessed February 2009.

Bank of Estonia. "Overview of Recent Economic Developments and the Future Outlook." December 15 2008. Available at www.eestipank.info/pub/en/press/Press/kommentaarid/Arhiiv/_2008/_218.pdf. Accessed February 2009.

Bank of Lithuania. "Economic Outlook for Lithuania." Available at http://www.lb.lt/news/pg.dll?lng=EN&did=2112. Accessed February 2009.

Lucas, Edward. "The Fall and Rise and Fall Again of the Baltic States." *Foreign Policy*, June 22, 2009. Available at www.foreignpolicy.com/articles/2009/06/18/the_collapse_of_the_baltic_tigers?page=0,1. Accessed September 10, 2009.

Bank Cycles

Bank cycles are periods of expanding and contracting credit. During expansions, lending standards are loosened, allowing greater borrowing for investment and consumer spending. During contractions, those standards are tightened, making it more difficult for businesses to borrow for the purposes of investment, expansion, and hiring and for households to invest in homes or spend more money on goods and services. The housing boom and bust from 2003 to 2009 was a vivid demonstration of a bank cycle.

The Role of Credit in the Business Cycle

In modern capitalist economies, there is a close relationship between money and production. To initiate production, entrepreneurs must have access to money to pay for the factors of production. Bank credit plays an important role in financing firms' investment in capital assets in order to expand their production processes. Thus, bank credit has a critical impact on the business cycle. Indeed, in the early twentieth century, Austrian school economist Joseph Schumpeter, among others, emphasized the role of credit creation in financing new techniques of production, which spur innovation.

Investment decisions require that income-producing activities will be sufficient to generate profits in order to validate current and future commitments of capital. From the bank's perspective, a loan represents a claim on a borrower. It is a promise to receive more money later. It involves time, uncertainty, and expectations that the loan will be repaid when it is due. If the bank's customer is successful, the loan will be repaid and the lender will make a profit. Customers also may pledge collateral to borrow from the bank. In this case, the investment decision is made based on the quality and the liquidity of the pledged collateral. If the collateral is expected to increase in value in the near future, this may shift the bank's preference toward collateralized loans.

However, given the nature of investment and uncertainty about future economic conditions, today's decisions may stimulate dynamic processes that lead to financial fragility and instability in the future. Thus, the way in which capital assets are financed and the structure of the credit system have important impacts on the business cycle. This view is reflected in the works of economists from varying political perspectives, including Schumpeter, John Maynard Keynes, and Hyman Minsky.

A bank cycle occurs when increases in the availability of credit and the willingness to borrow boost the demand for financial assets, thereby pushing up asset prices and encouraging further lending. Optimism about future economic growth has an impact on the expectations of both lenders, who increase the supply of credit at favorable terms, and borrowers, who are more willing to take out loans. Credit booms can lead to greater financial fragility if reliance on bank credit increases the overall level of indebtedness and compromises borrowers' ability to meet future interest payments when financial conditions change. In short, rising debt service compromises borrowers' ability to repay their loans. As businesses and households reduce their expenditures to meet increasing financial commitments, falling aggregate expenditures translate into falling sales and revenues. Firms cut back on production, investment, and employment, which depresses incomes and reduces spending even further. Rising unemployment causes substantial reductions in income, forcing borrowers to default on their loans and, in turn, leading to massive bank losses, insolvencies, and bankruptcies. As a result, banks reduce the supply of credit, tighten lending standards, and cut credit limits, causing a credit "crunch."

Monetary policy also can exacerbate the bank cycle. In this case, changes in the money supply by the Federal Reserve can lead to changes in short-run economic activity and in the level of prices. For example, tightening monetary policy leads to a contraction of bank credit and slower economic activity—a policy that usually is employed to cool an overheated economy. However, an overly strict contraction of the money supply can lead to bank failures and insolvencies that reduce the supply of credit. Many economists believe that the Great Depression was made worse by the Federal Reserve's unnecessary tightening of the money supply during a period of economic contraction.

Housing Boom and Bust of 2003–2009

The housing bubble that occurred in the first decade of the twenty-first century and the subsequent recession are an extreme example of a bank cycle. Much of the expansion in U.S. economic activity was boosted by the leveraging of households, businesses, and financial institutions. The U.S. economy experienced unsustainable housing price increases, allowing the household sector to increase spending and purchase property and speculative assets with borrowed funds.

The meltdown in the global financial markets in 2007–2008 and the severe recession that followed challenged economists worldwide to find its root causes and to formulate policies that would address its consequences. Over the past several decades, new nonbank financial institutions—such as monoline mortgage lenders, venture capital firms, and investment companies—engaged in liquidity creation as an alternative to traditional demand deposits for short-term investors. These nonbank financial institutions operated outside the regulatory structure of the Federal Reserve and the Federal Deposit Insurance Corporation, and they relied on short-term funds to finance their activities, which included buying risky mortgage-backed securities.

The crisis began in late summer 2007 as a liquidity problem, triggering the sale of assets at "fire sale" prices. The major disruption in credit markets caused instability among traditional banks, as they, too, proved unwilling to lend to—and borrow from—each other, fearing the troubled assets on one another's books. The result was massive insolvency in the global financial system. By 2010, the crisis appeared to be over, but without financial reform that could prevent another rise and fall of the bank cycle.

Felipe C. Rezende

See also: Banks, Commercial; Capital Market; Credit Cycle; Financial Markets; Financial Modeling of the Business Cycle; Leveraging and Deleveraging, Financial.

Further Reading

Black, William K. "'Control Frauds' as Financial Super-Predators: How 'Pathogens' Make Financial Markets Inefficient." *Journal of Socio-Economics* 34:6 (December 2005): 734–755.

Fisher, Irving. "The Debt-Deflation Theory of the Great Depression." *Econometrica* 1:4 (October 1993): 337–357.

Hume, Michael, and Andrew Sentance. "The Global Credit Boom: Challenges for Macroeconomics and Policy." Discussion Paper no. 27, Monetary Policy Committee, Bank of England, June 2009.

Kregel, Jan A. 1998. *The Past and Future of Banks.* Rome: Ente Einaudi, 1998.

———. "Using Minsky's Cushions of Safety to Analyze the Crisis in the U.S. Subprime Mortgage Market." *International Journal of Political Economy* 37:1 (Spring 2008): 3–23.

Minsky, Hyman P. *Stabilizing an Unstable Economy.* New Haven, CT: Yale University Press, 1986.

Schumpeter, Joseph A. *The Theory of Economic Development: An Inquiry into Profits, Capital, Credit, Interest, and the Business Cycle.* Cambridge, MA: Harvard University Press, 1934.

Wojnilower, Albert M. "The Central Role of Credit Crunches in Recent Financial History." *Brooking Papers on Economic Activity,* no. 2 (1980): 277–326.

Wolfson, Martin H. *Financial Crisis: Understanding the Postwar U.S. Experience.* Armonk, NY: M.E. Sharpe, 1986.

Wray, L. Randall. "Financial Markets Meltdown: What Can We Learn from Minsky." Public Policy Brief no. 94, Levy Economics Institute, April 2008.

Bank of America

One of the largest financial institutions in the world, Bank of America (often referred to as BofA) suffered significant losses during the financial crisis of 2008 and 2009, largely because of the financial setbacks sustained by Merrill Lynch, a troubled brokerage house it acquired in September 2008, at the height of the crisis. These losses, which dramatically reduced BofA's market capitalization, threatened the very solvency of the institution, leading the bank to accept tens of billions of dollars in funds from the Troubled Asset Relief Program (TARP), a 2008 U.S. federal program designed to shore up the finances of troubled financial institutions.

Origins and Growth

Founded as the Bank of Italy in San Francisco in 1904 by Italian immigrant Amadeo Giannini, BofA began as institution aimed at serving the financial needs of working-class immigrants in the Bay Area. Giannini's rescue of the bank's records during the San Francisco earthquake of

1906 helped cement the institution's reputation for probity, while the founder's willingness to lend money to individuals and businesses turned down by other banks gained it a wide customer base.

In 1928, Giannini merged his bank with the Bank of America of Los Angeles, adopting the latter's name for the new institution. The latter had pioneered the business of branch banking, which Giannini expanded throughout the West. Such interstate banking had only recently been allowed for nationally chartered banks under the McFadden Act of 1927. Federal banking regulations, however, required BofA to divest itself of its branches outside California in the 1950s. Around the same time, in 1958, BofA pursued a new avenue of business, introducing the BankAmericacard (renamed Visa in 1975), one of the first consumer credit cards that allowed customers to make purchases at different participating businesses. In the 1960s, BofA began licensing other banks to issue the card and then turned over control of the business to a corporation run by the issuing banks.

In the 1970s and early 1980s, BofA branched out into foreign banking, lending billions of dollars to the government of Mexico, then flush with oil export revenues. One of the two largest lenders to Mexico, along with Citibank of New York, BofA was hit hard when oil prices collapsed in the early 1980s and Mexico was unable to service its massive foreign debt and went into default. Accompanied by bad loans to other developing world countries, the Mexican default forced BofA to sell a number of its operations to raise capital. By the time of the stock market crash of October 1987, BofA stock had plummeted in value and the institution had lost its position as the nation's largest bank by asset holdings.

Under new management, however, BofA took advantage of regulatory changes in the 1980s that once again permitted interstate banking, acquiring a number of banks in other states and opening branches across the country. After suffering large losses in the Russian default of 1998, BofA was acquired by NationsBank of North Carolina, then the nation's biggest commercial bank, in what was then the largest banking acquisition in history. While its headquarters was moved to Charlotte, North Carolina, the new institution retained the name Bank of America. With the merger, BofA once again emerged as the largest bank in the United States, with assets of $570 billion and nearly 5,000 branches in more than twenty states coast to coast.

Countrywide Acquisition

Through the early 2000s, Bank of America continued to acquire other banks. In 2008, it purchased Countrywide Financial, a California-based mortgage lender with a reputation for aggressively marketing subprime mortgages and home equity loans to borrowers with less than sterling credit histories. The early and middle 2000s had seen a boom in the mortgage industry, fueled by rising home values and the Federal Reserve Bank's low interest-rate policies. Countrywide had ridden that boom to become America's largest home mortgage lender, financing roughly one in five U.S. home mortgages and creating securitized mortgage instruments that it sold to investors.

By 2007, however, Countrywide was in trouble. Many of both the conforming and subprime mortgages it financed were adjustable, meaning that an initial interest-only payment—which offered borrowers low monthly payments, allowing many to purchase homes beyond their means—was adjusted upward after a period of time, increasing the monthly payment beyond the borrower's capacity to meet it. That was not a problem as long as credit was easy to obtain and rising home equity allowed borrowers to refinance. But when home prices began drop in 2007, many of those borrowers went into default. The rising default rates, in turn, led to tighter credit by lending institutions, both to mortgage holders and other financial institutions.

By the time BofA got regulatory approval to purchase Countrywide in mid-2008, rumors began to swirl that the latter was on the verge of bankruptcy—rumors that both BofA and Country-wide's management vigorously denied. True or not, access to BofA's vast assets shored up Countrywide's finances, and the division was renamed Bank of America Home Loans as a way to disassociate it from Countrywide's now besmirched reputation.

Merrill Lynch Acquisition and the Financial Crisis

Despite the troubles at Countrywide and the collapse of the credit markets in the late summer of 2008, BofA appeared to be in relatively sound financial shape, even as other major commercial and investment banks began to fail. In September, BofA took advantage of the crisis to acquire Merrill Lynch, a financial services firm best known for having pioneered the branch stock brokerage business. Highly exposed to collapsing securitized mortgage financial instruments, and under threat of government lawsuit for misrepresenting such securities to investors, Merrill Lynch had seen its stock price plummet to the point that the firm was on the verge of bankruptcy. Paying a fraction of Merrill Lynch's once sky-high share price in an all-stock deal, BofA was seen to have purchased the world's largest financial services company at a bargain price. (Even at that reduced share price, the $50 billion price tag represented more than 80 percent of Bank of America's own falling stock valuation in September 2008.)

The acquisition proved disastrous for BofA, as it soon became clear that Merrill Lynch was in a far worse financial shape than originally understood by BofA management, posting more than $20 billion in losses in the fourth quarter of 2008 alone. Dragged down by the acquisition of Merrill Lynch and Countrywide, as well as its own plummeting stock price, BofA was in serious financial trouble by the late 2008. It therefore accepted $25 billion from TARP, with an additional bailout of $20 billion following in January 2009. Another $118 billion guarantee against potential losses on toxic assets, such as securitized mortgage instruments, was also offered by TARP.

Whether or not the bailout funds actually rescued the giant bank from insolvency, as some financial experts claimed, BofA survived. In early 2009, however, the Barack Obama administration and Congress included BofA among the many large financial institutions that it charged with using the bailout money to shore up its assets rather than to ease credit, as the TARP money was originally intended. For his part, CEO Ken Lewis maintained in sworn testimony before Congress in April 2009 that the government was at least partly responsibly for the crisis at BofA. Having learned of Merrill Lynch's true financial predicament, Lewis testified, he wanted to back out of the acquisitions deal but was coerced into completing it by former secretary of the Treasury

Bank of America, with headquarters in Charlotte, Carolina, became the largest financial services firm in the world by acquiring the ailing investment bank Merrill Lynch in 2008. But massive losses necessitated billions of dollars in federal bailouts. (Davis Turner/Stringer/Getty Images)

Henry Paulson, who feared what the failure of Merrill Lynch would do to the global financial system. In his own sworn testimony, Paulson denied the accusation.

Meanwhile, by the second quarter of 2009, BofA was back in the black, posting profits of $3.2 billion. This allowed Lewis to assert that the bank would shortly be able to begin redeeming, in installments, the preferred stock the government obtained in exchange for the TARP money it lent.

James Ciment and Andrew J. Waskey

See also: Banks, Commercial; Merrill Lynch; Troubled Asset Relief Program (2008–).

Further Reading

Bonadio, Felice A. *A.P. Giannini: Banker of America.* Berkeley: University of California Press, 1994.

Johnson, Moira. *Roller Coaster: The Bank of America and the Future of American Banking.* New York: Ticknor & Fields, 1990.

Nash, Gerald. *A.P. Giannini and the Bank of America.* Norman: University of Oklahoma Press, 1992.

Banking School/Currency School Debate

Arising in opposition to the British Banking Act of 1844, which granted the Bank of England (the nation's central bank) a monopoly on the issue of banknotes (paper money), the banking school was a group of economists who held that the Bank of England should not be required to back its notes with full gold parity, a stipulation of the 1844 law. In other words, adherents of the banking school believed that the notes issued by the bank should not be fully convertible into gold upon demand of the bearer. Opposing them were members of the currency school, who argued in favor of full gold parity.

The source of the controversy lay in the disruptive, often devastating swings of the business cycle that marked British and, indeed, transatlantic economic history in the nineteenth century. Members

of the currency school maintained that the excess issuance of banknotes (by many lending institutions before 1844) were the cause of both inflation and the speculative excesses that triggered financial bubbles and busts. Members of the banking school argued that speculative excess operated independently of banknote issues and that strict gold parity would constrain the money supply and hence economic activity. Ultimately, the currency school won the debate, as Britain maintained gold parity through World War I.

The foundation for the banking school's argument lay in the so-called real bills doctrine, first enunciated by Scottish economist John Law in the early eighteenth century and later elaborated by fellow Scotsmen James Steuart and Adam Smith. According to this doctrine, banks should be allowed to issue notes at will. Proponents maintained that the money supply was not the result of exogenous forces (those external to the economy, such as the arbitrary fiat of bank directors) but endogenous ones (according to the actual needs of business). In other words, banknotes could not produce inflation since they were issued and accepted only as people needed them, and people needed them because the economy was growing. Even if a bank were to accidentally issue excess notes, the argument went on, they would not produce speculation or inflation. Instead, the excess notes would be returned to the banks as merchants and other holders no longer needed them, a process known as the "reflux principle."

Currency school advocates—which included English economists Henry Thornton, John Wheatley, and David Ricardo—maintained that without the requirement of gold parity, banks would be tempted into issuing too many notes, since doing so would inflate their institution's profits. Members of the currency school also challenged the real bills doctrine, pointing out that merchants would have an incentive to request more and more banknotes if the rate of return on those banknotes exceeded the interest rate the bank charged on them. In other words, the self-correcting mechanism of the real bills doctrine had a loophole that could lead to a situation where banknotes flooded the economy, producing speculation and inflation.

Such arguments weighed heavily in the decisions of British policy makers, who, through the eighteenth century, maintained laws that required banks to keep enough gold in their vaults to redeem all notes. (Scotland had a partial exemption to this rule until 1765, which explains why so many of the economists who opposed full gold parity hailed from there.) In 1797, rumors of a French invasion of Britain led to a run on banks, as depositors sought to convert their notes into gold, leading the government to suspend full convertibility.

As Britain gained the upper hand militarily, the fear passed and the economic crisis ebbed. Nevertheless, the government continued to suspend full convertibility through the end of the Napoleonic Wars in 1815. By then, however, a major debate had emerged over the convertibility issue, a debate known as the "Bullionist Controversy." The Bullionists—arguing for full gold convertibility—pointed to the inflation of the early 1800s as vindication of their position; Anti-Bullionists insisted that the inflation was due to government war purchases, which caused price-hiking shortages. The end of the war offered support for the latter view, as deflation kicked in despite the fact that full convertibility remained suspended.

Nevertheless, the political forces arrayed behind the Bullionists won the day, gaining passage in 1819 of the Resumption Act, which returned British banks to full gold convertibility in 1821. For the next two decades, the debate remained largely confined to economists—until passage of the 1844 Banking Act. While the measure did not require full convertibility by the Bank of England, it did require a specific ratio of gold to banknotes issued. Supporters of the currency and free banking schools maintained, on various grounds, that such a ratio was necessary to avoid excess note issues that would result in inflation, speculation, and swings in the business cycle.

Meanwhile, members of the banking school— including economists Thomas Tooke, John Fullarton, and a young John Stuart Mill—had modified the arguments of the old Anti-Bullionists. They did not fully accept the real bills doctrine and argued that a degree of convertibility was probably a good thing. They also held to a new reflux principle, which stated that even if an excess issue of banknotes produced inflation, the inflation would not last. Note holders, they reasoned, would rush to redeem them in gold, thereby contracting the money supply and easing inflationary pressure.

Ironically, various economic crises in the mid-nineteenth century forced the government to suspend the convertibility clauses of the Banking Act, which seemed to have lent credence to the banking school's position. By this time, however, adherence to the principles of the gold standard were too strong to overcome and Britain maintained convertibility until World War I. Thereafter, huge external debts, largely to the United States, so undermined the value of the pound that convertibility to gold was no longer tenable. As for the banking school itself, the ideas it promoted helped lay the foundations for modern monetary economics and policy in Britain and much of the rest of the industrialized world.

James Ciment

See also: Banks, Central; Smith, Adam.

Further Reading

Hixson, William F. *Triumphs of the Bankers: Money and Banking in the Eighteenth and Nineteenth Centuries.* Westport, CT: Praeger, 1993.

White, Lawrence H. *Free Banking in Britain: Theory, Experience, and Debate, 1800–1845.* Cambridge, UK: Cambridge University Press, 1984.

Banks, Central

Central banks, which exist in most countries today, are institutions granted the exclusive right to create legal tender by purchasing government securities, giving them control over the nation's currency. Central banks can loan funds (reserves) to commercial banks, serving as a "lender of last resort." Like ordinary banks, central banks charge interest on the loans they make, both to the government and to commercial banks.

The earliest institution that could be likened to a central bank was Sweden's Sveriges Riksbank, established in the mid-seventeenth century. The first reference to the term "central bank" dates to Great Britain in 1873, when Walter Bagehot, editor of the *Economist*, used the term in reference to the Bank of England's monopoly on the issue of banknotes. The U.S. central bank, the Federal Reserve, or Fed—actually a system of twelve regional banks, with the New York Federal Reserve Bank serving as first among equals—was established in 1913. The Fed and most other central banks enjoy a great amount of political autonomy. Although directors are usually appointed by elected government leaders, they typically have long tenures and experience little oversight by the head of state or legislature. Such autonomy is essential to the role and purpose of the central bank, ensuring that politicians do not exert pressure to accelerate economic growth—especially prior to elections—in ways that might damage the overall long-term health of a nation's economy.

Functions and Goals

The most important function of a central bank is to set a country's—or, in the case of the European Central Bank, a region's—monetary policy. In establishing and executing monetary policy, a central bank pursues three basic goals: price stability (maintaining a low rate of inflation and avoiding deflation); financial stability (preventing financial crises and ensuring the smooth operation of the credit system); and a strong real economy (maintaining low unemployment and steady economic growth).

The most important means at a central bank's disposal for achieving these ends is referred to as "open market operations," or the buying and selling of government securities and other financial instruments to other institutions and individuals. By purchasing government securities, central banks inflate the money supply, a step usually reserved for periods of slow or negative economic growth that are accompanied by low inflation or, more rarely, deflation. By buying securities, the central bank effectively lowers the interest rates on government securities, which reduces the cost of borrowing on other loans as well.

By making it cheaper to borrow, the purchase of government securities spurs business investment, hiring, consumer purchasing, and, as a result, overall economic growth. Conversely, by selling government securities, a central bank shrinks the money supply—or, more typically, slows its growth. This tends to slow economic growth because it raises interest rates, making it more expensive for businesses to borrow for capital improvements and hiring and for consumers to borrow money to purchase a home, car, or other goods and services typically paid for with credit. Central banks typically sell government securities during periods of high inflation or when they suspect inflation is looming because of unsustainable real-economy growth rates.

Other responsibilities of central banks include setting the discount, or interest, rate they charge to commercial banks to borrow reserve assets. Most central banks also set the required reserve ratio, which will translate to the amount of reserve assets that banks must keep on hand versus the amount of funds they lend. The goal in making this determination is twofold. By increasing reserves, the central bank makes it more difficult for commercial banks to lend, thereby slowing economic activity. In addition, reserve requirements are designed to ensure stability in the financial markets, so that banks do not overlend and expose themselves to too much risk.

A central bank can also be charged with issuing a country's banknotes, managing foreign exchange rates, and regulating commercial banks. Banking regulations include measures to protect customer deposits, maintain the stability of the financial system, and prevent the involvement of banks in

Central bank governors of the G-7 nations—Canada, France, Germany, the United States, Italy, Japan, and the United Kingdom—and officials of the International Monetary Fund meet in Washington, D.C., during the global financial crisis in October 2008. *(Getty Images)*

criminal activities. Given that the failure of even a single major banking institution can trigger a larger-scale financial crisis, financial regulatory measures seek to ensure that no bank takes on too much risk. They are required to maintain a specified level of cash reserves against customers' deposits and to make provisions against prospective losses. Regulators attempt to make banking operations transparent by setting financial reporting and disclosure requirements.

Finally, central banks often act as lenders of last resort to troubled commercial banks, a role often criticized by economists and others for contributing to excessive risk taking. If distressed commercial banks are rescued by a lender of last resort, it is argued, they may be encouraged to continue lending and investing irresponsibly. Supporters of this central bank function, while they tend to acknowledge the danger, say that the importance of avoiding the collapse of a major commercial bank outweighs the risk of encouraging bad lending practices.

Financial Crisis of 2008–2009

The unprecedented scope of the global financial crisis of 2008–2009 led to an expanded role for central banks in a number of countries. In the United States, for instance, the Fed facilitated merger deals whereby failing investment banks would be purchased by solvent institutions. It provided hundreds of billions of dollars in bailout money to troubled financial institutions, with no guarantees the money would be repaid, taking on equity stakes in those institutions. Indeed, it extended its reach beyond the financial industry per se by rescuing a major insurance company, AIG, with some $150 billion in federal money and taking a majority stake in the corporation. Under the Troubled Asset Relief Program (TARP) of 2008, the Fed and the U.S. Treasury provided hundreds of billions of additional dollars to financial institutions, either in the form of loans or in exchange for equity stakes. The Fed also created numerous special lending facilities that lent to banks, primary dealers, money market mutual funds, and commercial paper dealers. The assets the Fed created by the loans more than doubled the assets on the Fed's balance sheet in an unprecedented expansion, invoking special powers for crises under the Federal Reserve Act of 1913. It remains to be seen how these positions will be unwound as the financial system stabilizes and the need for the emergency facilities lessens.

Fed chairman Ben Bernanke defended the expanded role of the Fed by pointing out the dangers of doing nothing in the face of the greatest financial crisis since the Great Depression. Failure to prop up troubled financial institutions, he maintained, could have resulted in a complete freeze in the international credit markets, which in turn could have halted the short-term lending that keeps banks afloat. The result would have been a wave of bank failures, business bankruptcies, and mass layoffs. In short, Bernanke and other defenders of the expanded Fed role argued, the financial crisis of 2008–2009 had the potential to plunge the United States and the global economies into another Great Depression.

At the same time, the expanded role of the Fed and other central banks led to concerns in the United States and elsewhere that these politically autonomous institutions, which often operate in secrecy, were gaining too much power and influence. In the United States, there was talk of expanding Congress's auditing authority over the Fed, an idea opposed by Bernanke and criticized by many economists. The Barack Obama administration, for its part, was moving in the opposite direction, arguing that the Fed should be given the right to regulate investment banks and other major financial institutions outside its traditional purview, though its powers to write and enforce consumer financial protection rules would be shifted to a new agency. The financial industry reform act introduced by Senator Christopher Dodd (D-CT) in March 2010 gave the Fed expanded powers to regulate banks and other financial institutions.

James Ciment and Lyudmila Lugovskaya

See also: European Central Bank; Federal Reserve System; Monetary Policy.

Further Reading

Davies, H. "What Future for Central Banks?" *World Economics* 7:4 (2006): 57–85.

Epstein, G. "Central Banks as Agents of Economic Development." In *Institutional Change and Economic Development*, ed. H.J. Chang. New York: United Nations University Press, 2007.

Banks, Commercial

Commercial banks are financial institutions—usually chartered by governments and highly regulated—that function as intermediaries between depositors and borrowers, taking in money from the former and lending it out to the latter. Commercial banks offer depositors a number of advantages, including safekeeping of their money, interest on their deposits, and, in the case of checking accounts, the convenience of being able to pay for purchases through checks or debit cards rather than carrying around large amounts of cash. Banks pool the money of depositors and then lend it out to businesses and individuals for interest. Commercial banks make their money in two basic ways: the difference between the rate they charge borrowers and the interest rate they pay depositors—known as the "spread"—and fees they collect for any number of financial services, such as checking accounts, overdraft protection, credit cards, automatic teller machine (ATM) fees, and the like.

Almost as old as trade itself, going back thousands of years, commercial banks play several critical roles in modern economies. As major lenders to businesses, they allocate capital to various sectors of the economy, and through the loans they offer individuals, they play a critical role in financing consumer spending, especially for purchases of homes, cars, college education, and other costly goods and services. In these various ways, banks facilitate economic activity and, hence, economic growth.

At the same time, however, commercial banks can also serve to destabilize economies. By their very nature, they are highly leveraged institutions, maintaining a small base of liquid assets to meet depositor demands for funds. At any given time, the bulk of a bank's deposits have been loaned out to businesses and individuals, making them unavailable to depositors. Backstopping banks, should there be a loss of confidence that leads to sudden mass demand by depositors for their money, are a web of short-term interbank loans and, as a last resort in the United States, the Federal Reserve (Fed), which lends funds to banks. The fact that most banks have deposit insurance offered by the Federal Deposit Insurance Corporation (FDIC), a federal agency that guarantees depositor accounts up to a given amount, makes bank runs much more unlikely than before the creation of the FDIC. Many other countries have similar agencies.

To avoid having to put these protections into action, commercial banks are heavily regulated, either by state agencies in the case of most state-chartered banks, or, in the case of national banks, by the Fed. These government agencies require banks to maintain a certain ratio of assets-on-hand to loans. The Fed, America's version of a central bank, sets a range of 3 to 10 percent reserves against loans, a figure that varies according to the institution. Reserves can be held either by the bank as vault cash or by a reserve deposit account at the Fed itself.

Commercial banks are only one of several types of financial institutions that provide similar services; others include credit unions (a kind of cooperative bank); savings and loans; and mutual savings banks.

Financial Products and Risks

Commercial banks typically offer a number of financial products for both depositors and borrowers. For the former, there are checking accounts, which typically pay little or no interest but give depositors access to their funds to make purchases; savings accounts, which offer relatively low interest rates but allow depositors to withdraw funds at any time; and certificates of deposit, which offer higher interest rates but require depositors to maintain principals for a fixed period of time. In general, the more liquid the deposit, the lower the interest rate the account provides.

Borrowers can obtain financing from commercial banks in a number of ways, with less secured and riskier lending coming with a higher interest rate. Secured loans require borrowers to use some of their own assets as collateral; unsecured loans, usually in the form of purchases or advances made on credit cards, do not require collateral but usually come with significantly higher interest rates to reflect the greater risk on the part of the bank. Mortgage loans are a subset of secured loans, with the home or commercial property itself acting as collateral.

For businesses, there are syndicated loans in which a group of commercial banks provides credit to a borrower, thereby spreading costs and risks. Project financing is a more ongoing type of partnership with the borrower, in which the bank commits itself to financing a project over the long term, providing credit as necessary.

Many commercial banks also offer trade financing, where the institution acts as an agent in international trade by making use of a letter of credit. Because the parties who are involved in trade do not know and trust each other, the seller hesitates to send the goods without some guarantee that payment will be made. In this case, commercial banks provide the guarantee and charge a fee.

Some activities of commercial banks generate income but do not require the bank to put its own capital at risk. These are called noncredit services and typically entail some fee or commission. Among such services are keeping financial documents, financial securities, and other items in safe deposit boxes; providing financial advice and cash management to bank customers; acting as clearing agents using various payments and clearing systems around the world through electronic transfers; electronic funds transfer at point of sale (EFTPOS); ATM access; and currency exchange transactions.

In taking depositor money or lending out their own assets, banks assume a variety of risks. These include credit risk, the danger that a borrower cannot repay a debt; liquidity risk, or not keeping enough cash and reserves to meet depositor demands or cover nonperforming loans; interest rate risk, caused by a mismatch in the maturity and volume of interest-sensitive assets (loans) and interest-sensitive liabilities (deposits); market or price risks, caused by price fluctuations in capital markets; foreign exchange or currency risks, caused by fluctuations in currency valuations; sovereign risk, triggered by political or economic conditions in a particular country; operating risks, involving fraud, unexpected expenses, or technological failures; and settlement payment risk, in which a borrower fails to meet the terms of a contract.

History of Banking

Although banks have existed since ancient times to facilitate trade and guard people's assets, limited trade and Christian bans on interest during the Middle Ages prevented the establishment of banks in Europe until the fourteenth century. Early European banks—first in Italy, then spreading to northern parts of the continent by the sixteenth and seventeenth centuries—offered a number of services, including bills of exchange that allowed traders from one city to obtain money in another, a form of early checking services. Many banks also issued notes, which acted as currency in a given locale, though by the nineteenth century this operation had largely been assumed by governments, usually through central banks.

In the United States, many of the earliest banks were operated by goldsmiths, who accepted precious metal from their clients and issued receipts against the deposit. The receipts were then used as currency, even as some goldsmiths began to offer credit against the gold deposits in their safes. By the mid-eighteenth century, land banks had emerged, issuing notes against land deeds deposited with them. Such institutions issued currency against the land deposits and offered loans, though most individuals and businesses turned to merchants or private lenders for credit.

By the early years of the republic, the demand for credit and capital—as well as the growing complexity of business—had created a greater need for commercial banks. They soon sprouted up across the country, issuing banknotes, holding depositor

money, and making loans. Until the 1830s, the Bank of the United States, an early central bank, tried to impose rules on how much assets a bank should hold against the notes it was issuing and the loans it was offering. But such regulations were usually ignored, and banks often participated—indeed, were often the prime actors—in the varied real-estate bubbles of the period, most of which led to crashes and financial panics.

By the late nineteenth century, the U.S. government had become the prime issuer of currency, leaving banks in the business of making money by taking in depositor assets at a given interest rate and making loans at a higher one. This was also the period in which the modern checking account system emerged. With the advent of the Federal Reserve System in 1913, U.S. commercial banks came under tighter regulation by the federal government. Despite such oversight, many lending institutions developed new corporate structures that allowed them to engage in much riskier investment banking, especially as rules against such activities were lifted during the probusiness political climate of the 1920s.

But by engaging in securities underwriting and other investment activities, commercial banks were putting their depositors' assets at greater risk. This proved disastrous to both the banks and their customers in the wake of the stock market crash of 1929. The wave of financial bankruptcies that followed prompted the federal government to pass the Glass-Steagall Act of 1933, which barred commercial banks from engaging in such businesses as investment banking and insurance, both of which carried greater risks.

From 1933 through the 1970s, U.S. commercial banking returned to its roots of offering customers basic financial services and interest on their deposits, and then lending the money, usually to businesses. Savings and loans were left to handle most consumer business, such as mortgage lending. Banks became highly regulated and stable businesses, offering solid if not spectacular returns to shareholders. By the 1970s, however, the industry entered a period of crisis. With inflation high and other financial institutions offering higher rates of return on money market accounts and certificates of deposit, banks began to lose money; regulations either prevented them from conducting such business or limited the interest rates they could charge on loans and credit cards, even as the money they borrowed from the Fed became more expensive.

Deregulation, Mergers, and New Services

The commercial banking industry responded to the crisis in three ways during the 1980s and 1990s. First, it lobbied the federal government for regulatory relief, allowing it to charge more interest, offer a variety of financial instruments, and expand across state lines. Meanwhile, the savings and loan industry was granted the freedom to make investments in more speculative real-estate ventures and other risky assets including junk bonds, a departure from its traditional role of providing financing for home purchases. Second, banks began to merge with one another, creating much larger institutions that did business regionally and even nationally. Third, the industry began to offer more services, taking advantage of new technologies to set up ATMs, Internet banking, and debit cards.

Banks also began to lower their credit qualification standards, allowing them to expand their customer base. The number of credit cards increased dramatically, as did the interest payments on those cards, providing banks with vast new revenue streams. Along with credit cards, banks provided more and more overdraft protection on checking and debit card accounts, allowing customers to withdraw more money than they had in their accounts and charging them hefty fees for the service. By offering more credit, of course, banks were also increasing their exposure to defaults and bankruptcy. But the banking industry also lobbied for stricter rules on the latter, winning passage of a new bankruptcy act in 2005 that made it more difficult for consumers to liquidate their debts.

Six years before, the commercial banking industry had won another major political victory, overturning the section of the Glass-Steagall Act that prevented it from engaging in insurance and investment banking activities. Thus, by the mid-2000s, huge new bank holding companies, such as Citigroup, had subsidiaries that provided everything from brokerage services to savings accounts to insurance. Banking thereby became a far more lucrative but far riskier business—as the financial crisis of 2008–2009 made clear.

Financial Crisis of 2008–2009

The crisis began in the housing sector. After the greatest run-up in home prices in modern U.S. history, valuations began to slide beginning in late 2006 and early 2007. With many homeowners subject to adjustable rates, foreclosure rates began to climb, hurting the balance sheets of many commercial banks. Moreover, many of the mortgages had been bundled into securities that were purchased by the investment-banking arm of many commercial banks, adding to their exposure. By September 2008, the entire global financial sector was in crisis. Interbank loans, essential to the functioning of international credit markets, began to freeze up, as confidence in the solvency of U.S. banks began to sag. Various investment banks, which were especially exposed to the mortgage-backed securities, teetered on the edge of collapse, culminating in the September 15 bankruptcy filing of Lehman Brothers. On September 25, the U.S. Office of Thrift Supervision seized Washington Mutual Bank from its holding company after a ten-day bank run by depositors, placing it in receivership. It was the largest bank failure in U.S. history.

To prevent further collapses, the George W. Bush Administration and the Fed pushed for a massive bailout package, which ultimately amounted to some $700 billion. In addition, a large chunk of the money, about $150 billion, went to insurance giant AIG, whose business included collateral debt obligations, a kind of insurance policy on other instruments, including mortgage-backed securities. Tens of billions of dollars were doled out to some of the biggest bank holding companies in the country, including Bank of America and Citigroup. The Fed also established numerous special lending facilities that increased lending to banks, primary dealers, money market mutual funds, and commercial paper lenders. Such lending injected more than a trillion dollars into the economy to prop up the financial system.

Although it was politically unpopular, the bailout was a financial success. The feared wave of bank failures was averted, and the credit markets began to unfreeze, though lending became far more restricted than it had been before the crisis. Still, some economists argued that the money would have been better spent on helping homeowners who faced foreclosure; that was, after all, the underlying source of the crisis in the first place. Nevertheless, by mid-2009, most commercial banks in the United States were no longer facing imminent collapse. Some even saw a return to profitability, a recovery reflected in the rapid rise of their share prices from the deep troughs into which they had fallen in 2008.

In the aftermath of the crisis, the new Barack Obama administration and the Democratic majority in Congress began talking about new regulations on the financial industry, including new forms of executive compensation and a new agency to regulate the consumer financial industry, so as to prohibit excessive fees and rein in the loose credit that had contributed to the crisis. Yet few people were talking about a return to the highly regulated days of the 1970s, and there was little evidence that Congress would pass laws preventing commercial banks from engaging in investment banking, insurance, and brokerage businesses.

Still, according to many economists, the commercial banking industry was not out of the woods yet. There were fears of a second crisis hitting the industry as consumers, many of whom were laid off in the deep recession that accompanied the first mortgage-related financial crisis, defaulted on record high levels of unsecured—largely credit-card—debt. This, said some of the gloomier prognosticators, could lead to a second wave of bank failures and yet another government bailout of the financial industry.

James Ciment and Asli Yuksel Mermod

See also: Bank of America; Bank Cycles; Capital One; Citigroup; Depository Institutions; Federal Deposit Insurance Corporation; IndyMac Bancorp; Northern Rock; Panics and Runs, Bank; PNC Financial Services; Regulation, Financial; Troubled Asset Relief Program (2008–); UBS; Washington Mutual.

Further Reading

Barth, James R. *The Rise and Fall of the U.S. Mortgage and Credit Markets: A Comprehensive Analysis of the Market Meltdown.* Hoboken, NJ: John Wiley & Sons, 2009.

Cecchetti, Stephen G. *Money, Banking, and Financial Markets.* Boston: McGraw-Hill/Irwin, 2006.

Hempel, George H., and Donald G. Simonson. *Bank Management Text and Cases.* 5th ed. Hoboken, NJ: John Wiley & Sons, 1999.

Hughes, Jane E., and Scott B. MacDonald. *International Banking: Text and Cases.* Boston: Addison Wesley, 2002.

Krugman, Paul. *The Return of Depression Economics and the Crisis of 2008.* New York: W.W. Norton, 2009.

Posner, Richard A. *A Failure of Capitalism: The Crisis of '08 and the Descent into Depression.* Cambridge, MA: Harvard University Press, 2009.

Rose, Peter S. and Sylvia C. Hudgins. *Bank Management and Financial Services.* 7th ed. New York: McGraw-Hill/Irwin, 2008.

Banks, Investment

Investment banks offer services that deal principally with the restructuring of business ownership, including securities underwriting through initial public offerings (IPOs) and seasoned offerings, and by arranging mergers and acquisitions, securitization and securities trading, private placements, and leveraged buyouts. Investment banks typically work for companies and governments, not individuals, and their profits come from fee income for their securities services, including underwriting, and from fees as strategic consultants. In the United States—which from the Great Depression until the late 1990s separated the functions of investment banks and commercial banks—an investment banker acting in an advisory capacity must be licensed as a broker-dealer and performs his or her job under the oversight of the Securities and Exchange Commission (SEC).

IPOs

Businesses over a certain size generally benefit from establishing themselves as corporations, while most small businesses begin as partnerships or proprietorships. The bulk of a corporation's stock is usually owned by the company's founders and loyal employees. However, revenue streams from ordinary day-to-day business activity often are not strong enough to meet demand, and offering stock to outsiders expands the company's funding and reinvestment capacity.

Private placements provide the first source of outside funding. Originally, the initial stock issues in a private placement could not be resold by their purchasers for a two-year period and were exempt from the costly SEC registration process. In 1990, the SEC adopted Rule 144A, which allowed large institutions to trade privately placed securities among themselves with no two-year waiting period. This new rule greatly increased the participation of investment bankers in the private placement market, which bypassed the registration process. There is no limit on the number of accredited private placement purchasers—institutional investors such as banks and pension funds, wealthy individuals, and the officers of the company—but there can be no more than thirty-five unaccredited purchasers. Private placements are also done by larger firms for the issuance of new securities where they want to bypass the costly registration process.

After private placements, it is common for investment banks to court a venture capital fund—a limited partnership that pools the money of its investors (usually institutional investors) and is managed by a venture capitalist who is an expert in a specific sector of business and can gauge which companies are sound investments for his or her fund.

After the venture capital stage, an IPO of stock may follow. Unlike private placements, this stock can be traded on the secondary markets and is registered with the SEC. This is generally the primary activity of investment banks: preparing companies to go public. The bank helps determine the stock's initial offering price by comparing the performance and growth prospects of the company to those of similar corporations, acts as an intermediary in selling some of the stock to its clients, and maintains investor interest in the stock after the IPO by producing reports on its prospects.

Investment banks that underwrite IPOs purchase all of the stock being offered and resell it on their own, which guarantees that the company raises the money it needs. This is the typical scenario. In some cases, a bank will refuse to make a guarantee and will only offer a best-efforts sale—selling the stock on consignment, as it were, without putting its own money up front. Underwriting is a risk for the bank. If it misjudges the market price for the IPO, it can be stuck with unsold stock.

All IPOs over $1.5 million are regulated by the SEC, and state agencies generally have regulations that must be met as well. The stock is registered with the SEC twenty days before the IPO, at which point the investment bank sends representatives on what the industry calls "the road show" to present information and sales pitches to prospective investors in order to promote the company and its stock offering. This not only gets the word out, but it also gives the bank a sense of what investors will be willing to pay and how many investors are likely to be interested. The road show cannot include any data that appear in the SEC filing, which prevents spurious claims and unlikely projections. Thus, the road show generally consists of marketing spin and selective emphasis. If there is too little interest in the IPO stock, the SEC registration can be withdrawn.

Mergers, Acquisitions, and Leveraged Buyouts

Investment banks also consult with businesses involved in mergers and acquisitions. In both kinds of transactions, one company is created where previously there were two or more. A merger is regarded as an equal arrangement—two companies merge into a new entity, preserving the rights of the original management of both. In an acquisition, one company absorbs or assumes control of the other. In practice, many arrangements that are really acquisitions are called mergers as a condition of the deal; this saves face for the management of the absorbed company.

Mergers and acquisitions are overseen by the antitrust division of the U.S. Justice Department to ensure that the new entity does not constitute a monopoly. Stockholders, for their part, may have a variety of responses to a proposed merger or acquisition. Sometimes the deal strengthens a company unequivocally, as when a large, healthy company buys out small regional competitors to increase its market share or expand into new markets. Other times, as when a shoe company attempts to buy a motion picture studio, investors fear that the company has become too diversified and no longer dominant in its field. Investors like to have a clear sense of what they are investing in—shoe stock or movie stock—and typically shy away from shares in a company without a clear identity.

Ideally, a merger or acquisition creates a new entity that is greater than the sum of its parts, thanks to an increase in efficiency and market power, tax benefits, and economies of scale. Many corporations expanded to a national scale by starting out as local or regional companies and merging with or acquiring other local companies and restructuring.

Leveraged buyouts constitute a similar form of restructuring, except that in this case, a publicly held company is wholly purchased by an investor group that wants to take it private. Typically, this occurs when the company's senior management wishes to take it private. It must therefore raise the funds necessary to buy the stock back from the public and thereby retain sole control of the business. Leveraged buyouts tend to be less common when the stock market is healthy, because a buyout is relatively more expensive. The motivation is usually to take the company in a direction that stockholders will not agree to, for one reason or another. Because of the potential for management to drive down the stock of its own company in order to afford the buyout, the transaction must be handled very carefully so that there is no hint of wrongdoing.

Securities

Investment banks deal with securities on both the buy side (managing or consulting on hedge funds, mutual funds, and pension funds) and the sell side, which includes not only the sales and promotion of stock but also the securitization of various assets. Securitization is the process of creating a publicly traded and more liquid security out of a debt instrument. The effects of the 2006–2008 subprime mortgage crisis were as widespread as they were in part because collateralized debt obligations (CDOs) that used subprime mortgages as their backing assets had become so common. Pools of such mortgages were used as the collateral to issue bonds, and sometimes these CDOs were themselves bundled into new collateral pools. The credit rating of a bond backed by such collateral was often higher than the credit rating of the constituent parts, which meant that investors who normally avoid high-risk investments—especially institutional investors like pension funds—became exposed to the toxicity of subprime-backed securities that had gone bad.

Securitization is an advanced and increasingly sophisticated process, as is the accurate valuation and rating of such instruments. Since the late 1990s, investment banks have hired more and more holders of PhDs in math, physics, and other hard sciences to work as "quants." In the language of Wall Street, a quant is a quantitative analyst. The field of quantitative finance, like modern investment banks themselves, began in the 1930s, after the stock market crash of 1929 created a desire for strong empirical methods that could be used to analyze finance and financial risk. Today, working as a quant requires advanced computer knowledge, because numerous types of specialized software have been developed for complex mathematical analysis.

History of Investment Banking in the United States

Investment banking in the United States began with brokers of government- and railroad-issued bonds, and became more sophisticated over the course of the nineteenth century thanks to the large amounts of money changing hands among the robber barons and other tycoons of the industrial revolution. During the Civil War, the Union Army was funded with the first mass-marketed war bonds. When the war ended, banks continued to mass-market similar securities to investors in search of something to do with their money. When industrialist J.P. Morgan opened his New York banking house in the 1890s, it was not to do business as a commercial bank but primarily to deal in gold, foreign currency, and securities.

Before the Great Depression, most commercial banks in the United States also offered investment-banking services. Likewise, most investment banks were also commercial banks. The onset of the Depression was only the latest in a series of banking panics that stretched back decades, and the severity of its consequences further convinced the public at large and many in public office that banking mismanagement was among the principal causes of the crash. The federal finance reforms of the early New Deal created the SEC in 1934 and required banks participating in the Federal Reserve System—commercial banks—to give up their activity in the securities trade in that same year. In addition, the reforms prohibited excessive

interaction between securities firms and commercial banks. (For example, no individual could serve on the board of both kinds of institutions.) As a result, banks spun off their investment services into separate entities, just as busted trusts of the era spun off their regional branches into separate companies.

The U.S. banking industry remained relatively stable until the 1980s, when the combination of inflation and stagnant economic growth (stagflation) contributed to a new round of bank failures at a time when political conservatives were rising to power. Although liberals and Democrats had long declared Franklin D. Roosevelt's New Deal initiatives largely responsible for pulling the country out of the Great Depression—with the heavy industrial activity of World War II undeniably responsible for restoring the country to genuine prosperity—various economists and political conservatives now challenged that notion, denied the efficacy of such regulations and reforms, and argued against the need to retain them.

From the 1980s through the 1990s, conservatives pushed for and won gradual deregulation of many sectors of the finance industry. Results included the rise of savings and loans (S&Ls, which were more appealing to consumers under deregulation); a slew of bank mergers, as lending institutions were allowed to acquire others outside the state holding their charter; and, eventually, the recoupling of investment banking with commercial banking. The 1999 Gramm-Leach-Bliley Act, or Financial Services Modernization Act (FSMA), repealed parts of the Glass-Steagall Act of 1933 that had segregated investment and commercial banking activity. Some restrictions on banking activity remained intact: banks were not allowed to own nonfinancial companies, and vice versa, preventing the possibility of an Apple Bank chain or of Capital One buying out Starbucks, for example. In the interest of financial privacy, the commercial and investment activities of a particular institution had to remain separate as well; bankers even had to use separate business cards in each context. Much of the debate over the FSMA in the years since its passage has centered on questions of privacy and the protection of personal data of banking customers.

Beginning in 1999, banking activities in the United States were allowed to intermingle under common corporate auspices, which led to the creation of companies like Citigroup (established in 1998 by the merger of Citicorp and Travelers Insurance, after the latter bought investment bank Salomon Smith Barney). As a result of both deregulation and the 2008–2009 financial crisis, there are no major Wall Street firms that do business exclusively as investment banks. Companies like JPMorgan Chase, Citigroup, Credit Suisse, and HSBC had already engaged in both commercial and investment banking; and as the financial crisis came to a head in September 2008, the last two stalwarts of pre-deregulation Wall Street—Goldman Sachs and Morgan Stanley—resumed traditional commercial banking activity. Meanwhile, other investment banks met different fates in 2008. Lehman Brothers collapsed after various acquisitions deals fell through, and Merrill Lynch became a part of Bank of America.

Bill Kte'pi

See also: Banks, Commercial; Bear Stearns; Citigroup; Glass-Steagall Act (1933); Hedge Funds; Investment, Financial; JPMorgan Chase; Lehman Brothers; Merrill Lynch; PNC Financial Services; Securities and Exchange Commission; Troubled Asset Relief Program (2008–).

Further Reading

Bookstaber, Richard. *A Demon of Our Own Design: Markets, Hedge Funds, and the Perils of Financial Innovation.* Hoboken, NJ: John Wiley & Sons, 2007.

Brigham, Eugene F., and Michael C. Ehrhardt. *Financial Management: Theory and Practice.* Mason, OH: South-Western, 2008.

Chancellor, Edward. *Devil Take the Hindmost: A History of Financial Speculation.* New York: Farrar, Straus and Giroux, 1999.

Madura, Jeff. *Financial Markets and Institutions.* Mason, OH: South-Western, 2008.

Shefrin, Hersh. *Beyond Greed and Fear: Understanding Behavioral Finance and the Psychology of Investing.* New York: Oxford University Press, 2007.

Bauer, Otto (1881–1938)

A leader of the Austrian Social Democratic Party, Otto Bauer was a major theoretician of left-wing socialists who followed Austro-Marxist ideology, which sought a "third way" to socialism—between capitalism and communism. In this role, Bauer became a leading spokesperson for the Marxist view that economic cycles lead to political instability and social revolution in the capitalist West.

Bauer advanced many of his views in the daily *Arbeiter Zeitung* (Workers' Times), of which he was coeditor beginning in 1907. His writings greatly influenced Marxist economic thinkers in the 1920s, 1930s, and the decades following World War II. In the 1960s and 1970s, Bauer's thinking served as inspiration for the New Left movement in Europe, which advocated social activism. In the 1980s, his ideas inspired the Eurocommunist movement, which moved away from totalitarian Soviet-style communism toward more democratic social reforms.

Otto Bauer was born on September 5, 1881, in Vienna, Austria. He earned a PhD in law from the University of Vienna in 1906, and published his first book, *Die Nationalitätenfrage und die Sozialdemokratie* (Question of Nationalities and Social Democracy), the following year. In it, Bauer advocated the creation of separate nation-states as a solution to the conflict among ethnic minorities in the Austro-Hungarian Empire (Czechs, Slovaks, Ruthenians, Croats, Italians, Hungarians, Roms, and others), which he viewed as class struggles. Anticipating intense ethnic conflict in the Balkans, he called for a United States of Europe organized on a confederate basis, much like today's European Union.

After earning his doctorate, Bauer became active in the Austrian Social Democratic Party and began a rapid rise through its ranks. He founded a socialist educational movement called *Die Zukunft* (The Future) and, in 1907, founded and edited a theoretical party journal called *Der Kampf*. He held the position of party secretary from 1907 until 1914.

While serving in the Austrian army on the Eastern Front during World War I, Bauer was captured and spent three years in Russian prisoner-of-war camps in Siberia. After returning to Austria in 1917, he became the head of the Austrian Social Democratic Party. With the outbreak of revolution in November 1918—which ended the Habsburg Empire and forced the abdication of Emperor Charles I—Bauer and the Austrian Social Democrats joined forces with the Christian Social Party to lead Austria as a coalition government. As minister of foreign affairs in the new regime, Bauer was a leading advocate of unification and signed a secret *Anschluss* (unification) agreement with Germany in 1919 that was later repudiated by the Allies. After resigning as foreign minister in 1919, Bauer became an opposition leader to Austria's conservative governments and concentrated on developing the foreign and domestic policies of the socialists.

Among Bauer's most important published works is *Die Österreichische Revolution* (1923; *Austrian Revolution,* 1925), in which he identifies Austrian socialists of the time as the "third force" between capitalism and communism. In 1926 he published a Social Democrat manifesto that had enduring influence on socialist movements in Europe. Other books include *The World Revolution* (1919), *The Road to Socialism* (1919), *Bolshevism or Social Democracy?* (1920), *The New Course of Soviet Russia* (1921), *Fascism* (1936), *The Crisis of Democracy* (1936), and *Between Two World Wars?* (1937).

In 1933 members of the Christian Social Party and the Heimwehr (demobilized home guards) put an authoritarian corporatist dictatorship into power that sought to suppress the Social Democrats. After taking part in the abortive Viennese Socialist revolt of February 1934, Bauer was forced into exile. In Brno, Czechoslovakia, he organized and ran the Austrian Social Democrats' resistance movement (Auslandsbüro Österreichischer Soz-

ialdemokraten-ALÖS) from 1934 to 1938, until, in the face of the Nazi threat, he fled to Paris. He died there on July 4, 1938, just months before Adolf Hitler's Third Reich united Austria with Germany.

Andrew J. Waskey

See also: Marxist Cycle Model.

Further Reading

Boyer, John W. *Culture and Political Crisis in Vienna: Christian Socialism in Power, 1897–1918.* Chicago: University of Chicago Press, 1995.

Rabinbach, Anson. *Crisis of Austrian Socialism: From Red Vienna to Civil War, 1927–1934.* Chicago: University of Chicago Press, 1983.

Bear Stearns

Bears Stearns was a venerable international investment bank, brokerage house, and securities trading firm that, at the time of its demise, specialized in risky asset-backed securities. Its collapse in March 2008 and subsequent distress sale to the JPMorgan Chase financial services company helped trigger—or at least portended—the crisis in the financial industry that paralyzed global credit markets in late 2008 and early 2009.

Bear Stearns was founded in 1923 in New York City as an equities trading firm to take advantage of another period of rapid growth in the U.S. securities markets. Founded on limited capital, the firm thrived as new small investors rushed to put their money into corporate stock and government bonds, which sent security prices—and the company's profits—soaring. With that money as a foundation, the firm was able to survive the Great Depression and prosper in the post–World War II economic boom. By the 1970s, Bear Stearns had gained a reputation as a risk taker, investing in high-yield bonds, including those issued by New York City when it was on the verge of bankruptcy, and specializing in the corporate takeovers that sent Wall Street prices soaring in the 1980s. To bring in more capital to finance such deals, company executives took Bear Stearns public in 1985, morphing from a brokerage house to a full-service securities trading firm and investment bank.

Along the way, the company had known its share of scandal. In the mid-1980s, to facilitate corporate takeovers, Bear Stearns pioneered agreements that allowed clients to buy stock in the firm's own name—a tactic deemed illegal by the U.S. Securities and Exchange Commission. In 1997, Bear Stearns was caught in another scandal when it served as a clearing broker for a smaller house, which subsequently went bankrupt and was found to have defrauded investors of tens of millions of dollars.

Its reputation and share price declining in the face of such incidents, the company retrenched to avoid a hostile takeover. The move proved successful, allowing Bear Stearns to avoid the worst of the dot.com crash of the early 2000s. Moreover, as it shifted its emphasis away from mergers and acquisitions in the 1990s, the firm also averted the effects of an industry-wide slump in that segment of the investment banking business in the early 2000s. Thus, Bear Stearns survived as one of the last independent financial services companies on Wall Street.

By this time, the firm had come to focus on three major activities: the clearinghouse business, where it worked with securities exchanges to ensure that executed trades were settled efficiently and on time; bond selling; and the packaging and bulk reselling of home mortgages as asset-backed securities—or the securitization of risky housing investments. Bear Stearns was among the most aggressive in the latter field, recognizing the enormous profits to be made in what was becoming a red-hot housing market, driven by low interest rates and increasingly lax credit standards for borrowers.

The business proved exceedingly lucrative for several years. Bear Stearns invested heavily in mortgage-backed securities, many of them involving the subprime market. In subprime mortgages, lenders offered homeownership loans to borrowers with little or even bad credit histories, at variable rates that would rise precipitously after a fixed time period. At the same time, Bear Stearns also invested heavily in various kinds of financial derivatives, or investment instruments whose price is derived from the value of another asset—a kind of insurance policy for investments.

The strategy seemed brilliant, at least for a time. By late 2007, Bear Stearns had assets of nearly $400 billion and derivative financial instruments whose notional contract value stood at a staggering $13.4 trillion. Meanwhile, the company had been voted America's most admired securities firm in the prestigious *Fortune* magazine's "America's Most Admired Companies" survey three times running, and its "Early Look at the Market—Bear Stearns Morning View" was one of the most widely read market information publications on Wall Street.

As characterized in a best-selling 2009 account of the firm's demise, Bear Stearns was a house of cards. Its nearly $400 billion in securities assets was supported by just $11.1 billion in actual equities positions, giving it a highly risky leverage ratio of more than 35 to 1. In other words, the firm had borrowed more than $35 for every dollar it held—and for very risky investments. Thus, when the U.S. housing market began to cool in 2006–2007, Bear Stearns found itself in deepening trouble. With equity drying up, highly leveraged homeowners were unable to refinance and, as rates rose on adjustable mortgages, went into default. This undermined the value of the mortgage-backed securities in which Bears Stearns was so heavily invested. Meanwhile, civil suits were being pressed against the company for misleading investors regarding the exposure of its investment funds to certain high-risk securities.

As investors learned of the financial difficulties engulfing the firm, they began withdrawing money from their investment funds. The stability of Bear Stearns became a source of industry and media speculation, which rapidly eroded its very foundation—the foundation of any investment firm—public trust. The process devolved into a full-scale "run" on the company by early 2008. In March, events cascaded rapidly as major banks

Protesters outside Bear Stearns headquarters in New York City demonstrate against the government-backed sale of the venerable but crippled investment bank and brokerage house to JPMorgan Chase in March 2008. *(Bloomberg/ Getty Images)*

refused to lend Bear Stearns the funds it needed to cover losses, resulting in even more investor withdrawals. Unable to raise funds from other banks, the company turned to the New York Federal Reserve and received a $30 billion emergency loan on Friday, March 14. It was not enough to stave off investor fears. Concerned about the impact a collapse of such a major investment bank would have on the global securities markets, the federal government hastily arranged over the weekend to have JPMorgan Chase buy Bear Stearns for $2 a share. As the firm's stock had sold for more than $150 a share less than one year earlier, this provoked a shareholder revolt, forcing JPMorgan—prodded by Secretary of the Treasury Henry Paulson and

New York Federal Reserve Bank president Timothy Geithner—to up the offer to $10 a share.

In the wake of the financial crisis that froze credit markets around the world in late 2008 and early 2009, and the hundreds billions of dollars in Washington bailout money given to U.S. banks since that weekend in March, there has been much second-guessing about the federal government's approach to the Bear Stearns collapse. Some have argued that a bailout package proportionate to the company's liquidity shortfall would have reassured the credit markets early on that the government was ready to take bold action to save major investment banks and might have helped minimize the subsequent financial crisis. Whatever the case, the Bear Stearns crisis proved to be a harbinger of dark economic times to come for the U.S. securities markets and for the global economy as a whole.

James Ciment

See also: Banks, Investment; Bernanke, Ben; Paulson, Henry; Recession and Financial Crisis (2007–).

Further Reading

Bamber, Bill, and Andrew Spencer. *Bear-Trap: The Fall of Bear Stearns and the Panic of 2008.* New York: Brick Tower, 2008.

Cohan, William D. *House of Cards: A Tale of Hubris and Wretched Excess on Wall Street.* New York: Doubleday, 2009.

Kansas, Dave. *The Wall Street Journal Guide to the End of Wall Street as We Know It: What You Need to Know About the Greatest Financial Crisis of our Time—and How to Survive It.* New York: HarperBusiness, 2009.

Waggoner, John. *Bailout: What the Rescue of Bear Stearns and the Credit Crisis Mean for Your Investments.* New York: John Wiley & Sons, 2008.

Behavioral Economics

Behavioral economics is a branch of economics that incorporates behavioral assumptions, including psychological, sociological, and institutional factors, into the analysis of economic realities. It critiques the conventional economic assumption that human beings act in a narrow, materially selfish, calculated, and deliberative manner—called "rationality" in neoclassical economics—and that their actions can and should be reduced to mathematical models that apply in all circumstances.

This branch of economics made a key contribution to the understanding of business cycles—and, more precisely, of booms and busts—by introducing realistic behavioral assumptions into business cycle models. A fundamental premise of behavioral economics is that making correct behavioral and institutional assumptions is vital in order to understand causality and to generate robust analytical predictions. One cannot arbitrarily make behavioral and institutional assumptions because they are mathematically convenient, because these assumptions traditionally have been made, or because they fit into a particular worldview of rational or intelligent behavior. Rather, behavioral and institutional assumptions must be context specific and must fit the economic reality.

According to behavioral economists, conventional economic theories fail to explain important facts about human behavior with respect to business cycles. For example, George Akerlof, a pioneer of behavioral macroeconomics, pointed to the failure of contemporary macroeconomic theory to explain the existence of involuntary unemployment (conventional economists assume that if the unemployed really wanted work, they would work for less—thus unemployment represents a strong preference for leisure); the real impact of monetary policy on output and employment (conventional economists assume that monetary policy has no impact on output and employment in the long run); the failure of deflation to accelerate when unemployment is high (conventional economists assume that prices will fall when unemployment is high); and the excessive volatility of stock prices relative to their fundamentals (conventional economists assume that actual stock prices should reflect fundamentals—part of efficient market theory). For behavioral economists, what is critical is building models of business cycles that have a robust foundation in microeconomics, inclusive of their psychological, sociological, and institutional dimensions.

Assumptions Matter

In conventional economics, which follows the prescriptions of Milton Friedman, behavioral assumptions are not at all important. Of critical importance, rather, is that individuals behave as if they know and can apply the mathematical formulas that are consistent with producing, on average, optimal outcomes. Individuals are assumed to have perfect knowledge of the alternatives relevant to a choice problem and to be able to forecast the consequences of particular choices in the present and into the future, even when that future is highly uncertain. These behavioral assertions assume that individuals have an unbounded computational capacity to determine the outcomes of alternative choices, and that they make choices independent of other individuals. What matters to conventional economists is that the model predicts well even if the behavioral assumptions are wildly inaccurate. In other words, a good model predicts well even if it explains nothing. For behavioral economists, on the other hand, analytical prediction is important, as is the ability to explain economic phenomena. They are interested in understanding how people actually behave in the real world in the process of generating both optimal and suboptimal economic outcomes.

Herbert Simon, one of the pioneers of behavioral economics, argued that in constructing economic models of human behavior, the physiological and institutional constraints that characterize human decision making must be taken into account. Real people who are intelligent and rational cannot and therefore will not behave in the calculating and all-knowing manner prescribed by conventional economics, nor will rational agents behave in the narrowly selfish, materially maximizing manner that the conventional wisdom assumes must characterize rational beings. Such thinking produces a different causal and predictive narrative than that generated by conventional economics.

Simon coined the term "bounded rational-ity" to refer to rational choice in the context of a decision maker's cognitive limitations, as well as the limitations of knowledge and computational capacity. According to Simon's theory of bounded rationality, individuals do not maximize but rather satisfy (do the best they can), based on decision rules according to which a particular choice appears satisfactory given the objectives of the decision maker. In other words, smart decision makers use context-dependent heuristics, or experience-based techniques, which Gerd Gigerenzer referred to as "fast and frugal heuristics," to make investment- and employment-related decisions.

Animal Spirits, Herding, and Confidence

To explain booms and busts in the economy, be-havioral economics emphasizes behavioral factors along with real variables such as supply shocks (e.g., a spike in oil prices or technological change). The field seeks to provide the best possible un-derstanding of business cycles, which, behavioral economists argue, cannot be achieved without ad-equately incorporating behavioral variables into macroeconomic modeling. Behavioral economics also is concerned with the relationship between policy actions and behavioral factors, such as the way in which monetary and fiscal policies influ-ence consumer and investor behavior given the importance of "animal spirits"—that is, human emotions and moods.

Behavioral models are influenced by John May-nard Keynes's *General Theory of Employment, Interest, and Money* (1936), which introduced psychological variables into the economic modeling narrative. Keynes argued that "animal spirits"—whether a person is confident or pessimistic based on imper-fect information and emotive factors—contribute directly to business cycles. Animal spirits play a role in motivating borrowing and spending behav-ior, which, in turn, has an impact on business cycle volatility and the degree to which monetary and fiscal policies can affect macroeconomic outcomes.

Keynes referred to animal spirits as behavior that is motivated by emotive as opposed to calculating or hard-core economic rationality considerations:

> Most, probably, of our decisions to do something positive, the full consequences of which will be drawn out over many days to come, can only be taken as the result of animal spirits—a spontaneous urge to ac-tion rather than inaction, and not as the outcome of a weighted average of quantitative benefits multiplied by quantitative probabilities.

Keynes's notion of the "liquidity trap" is also important to understanding macroeconomic out-comes. A liquidity trap exists when individuals have little confidence in an uncertain future in light of a dismal present, and thus refuse to bor-row money in order to invest or consume, even at very low real interest rates. This behavior plays a role in sustaining economic downturns. Reducing interest rates to drive economic recovery will not be sufficient if animal spirits—that is, consumer confidence—are at low levels. Efforts must be made to restore confidence in the economy as well; monetary policy, which emphasizes the price of borrowing, is only a piece of a much more complex policy puzzle.

Hyman Minsky introduced the concept of financial fragility, which is closely related to the ideas of animal spirits and overconfidence or over-optimism. Minsky argued that market economies are naturally subject to business cycles, largely as a function of psychological variables that might be allayed by smart government policy. As the econ-omy expands (booms), investors gain confidence and engage in speculative financing, believing that profits will cover the cost of interest payments. Growth is fueled by speculative investment, and speculative investment is fueled by growth. Lend-ers execute loans with confidence that those debts will be repaid. Eventually, however, loans become risky as more investments (including the purchase of shares) are funneled into assets whose prices have little relation to their fundamental values. When a negative shock hits the economy—exposing the overall riskiness of investment—the bubble bursts, and the economy moves into a recession (bust), driven by increasing defaults and bankruptcies.

Another concept pioneered by Keynes relates to "choice behavior," which uses predictions about the behavior of other individuals as a proxy for best practice behavior. For example, an individual is not sure how best to invest in the stock market. Therefore, he or she follows the leader. In a world of asymmetric information, such "herding behavior" may make sense, but it is not part of mainstream theory. Keynes used the analogy of a beauty contest:

> It is not a case of choosing those [faces] that, to the best of one's judgment, are really the prettiest, nor even those that average opinion genuinely thinks the prettiest. We have reached the third degree where we devote our intelligences to anticipating what average opinion expects the average opinion to be. And there are some, I believe, who practice the fourth, fifth and higher degrees.

Herding behavior, whereby individuals follow the leader at a rapid clip, generates asset-price cascades. Such behavior creates asset-price bubbles and crashes that drive assets prices far above their fundamental values in the short run. Such deviations are inconsistent with an important facet of the efficient market hypothesis—that asset prices should reflect fundamental value at all points in time.

A very important variable introduced by George Akerlof and Joseph Stiglitz to help explain business cycles is "asymmetric information," meaning that different people have access to different and incomplete information that is pertinent to a particular decision problem. For example, investment bankers know more about the riskiness of assets than buyers, borrowers know more about their creditworthiness than bankers, sellers of used cars know more about their vehicles than prospective buyers, and workers know more about their effort inputs than their employers. In these cases, individuals must make educated guesses to fill in their information gaps.

Other important variables, which behavioral economists refer to as "cognitive biases," include overconfidence, money illusion, framing, panic, and fairness. Overconfidence or overoptimism bias is also referred to as "irrational exuberance," a term coined by former Federal Reserve chairman Alan Greenspan and adopted by economist Robert Shiller, a pioneer of behavioral finance. Overconfidence occurs when individuals believe that they can do better than they actually can, objectively speaking. This drives animal spirits in a manner that yields bubbles.

Money Illusion

Akerlof argued that individuals tend to suffer from a "money illusion," causing them to act in a quasi-rational manner. That is, they do not bother to correct for small decreases in money wages that result from low rates of inflation. In the view of workers, it is not worth the transaction costs of attempting to secure compensating money wage increases. Workers also may not notice real wage cuts that are a consequence of low rates of inflation (true money illusion). Therefore, government can cut real wages by adopting a targeted low inflation policy.

To the extent that real wages must fall in order for employment to increase during a recession, this can be achieved with the help of smart monetary policy. The contemporary wisdom rejects the hypothesis that money illusion exists and that monetary policy can reduce real wages, given that individuals are assumed to be rational (not easily fooled).

Keynes rejected the hypothesis of money illusion as well. He argued instead that workers will knowingly accept small real wage cuts through inflationary policy during an economic downturn, especially a severe one that is associated with increases in employment, as this does not reduce their relative wages. However, workers will resist employers' efforts to cut their real wages directly. Therefore, Keynes argued that unions and workers "do not raise the obstacle to any increase in aggregate employment which is attributed to them by the classical school." Keynes's argument builds on the rationality assumption, but, like Akerlof, he regarded monetary policy as one weapon in a larger arsenal required to move an economy out of a downturn.

Efficiency Wages, Reciprocity and Fairness, and Business Cycles

Conventional macroeconomists tend to agree that one cause of economic downturns or busts is that workers refuse to accept wage cuts as aggregate demand falls. Thus, wages are inflexible or "sticky" downward, meaning that wages cannot always be lowered in response to an economic downturn. In this sense, many economists argue that workers are responsible for the persistence of unemployment.

Behavioral economists argue that firms will not cut wages during a downturn—as predicted by some conventional economists (new classical school)—for efficiency wage reasons. Workers will retaliate against wage cuts that are judged to be unfair by reducing their effort inputs. This is possible in the real world of asymmetric information and incomplete contracts, and increases the real cost of labor and unit production costs. This provides a rational reason why nominal wages are sticky downward. Given the money illusion or rational workers' acceptance of inflation-generated real wage cuts, monetary policy can be effective at reducing real wages without spurring workers to retaliate by cutting effort inputs, thereby facilitating rising employment on the supply side.

An alternative efficiency wage argument is that even in the absence of money illusion, employment will grow without cuts to real wages if firms respond to increasing demand by increasing firm efficiency. Firms will increase the demand for labor if rising efficiency makes increasing employment cost effective. Higher wages are sustainable when they provide incentives for sufficient increases in productivity (increasing effort inputs). Inflationary policy is not a necessary condition for increasing employment in this case (consistent with the

classical economic perspective). But increasing demand to encourage firms to increase output and productivity is necessary. This is consistent with the evidence that there is a positive relationship between employment growth and increases and levels of real wages internationally.

Policy Based on Behavioral Economics Insights

An important school of thought within behavioral economics argues that behavioral variables such as overconfidence, herding, and greed are cognitive biases or errors in judgment, and therefore are irrational. Thus, irrationality in decision making is a leading cause of booms and busts in the economy. This suggests that policy makers should attempt to modify human behavior so that agents behave rationally, therefore moderating the extent of business cycle volatility. An alternative perspective argues that these variables represent rational behaviors in a world of bounded rationality. One cannot reduce the extent of business cycle volatility by modifying these behavioral characteristics. Rather, the extent to which volatility can be reduced is contingent on changing environmental variables such as information and legal parameters that, in turn, affect decision making.

An important cause of excess market volatility, especially severe crashes, is inappropriate regulation of public and private financial institutions. Many investment decisions that generate large social and private losses are products of incentive systems that do not internalize gains and losses to individual decision makers. If it is profitable for individuals to make decisions that predictably can bankrupt their firms by selling toxic assets, for example, then it is highly rational to engage in these activities, even though it is to the detriment of the firm's shareholders. Also, what appear to be irrational decisions often are the products of a lack of knowledge or misleading information. Assets might be packaged or framed in a positive light even when the fundamentals are weak. From this perspective, public policy needs be directed toward institutional design as opposed to the reconfiguration of human behavior.

An important implication for monetary or fiscal policy is that government must consider the impact of policy on animal spirits, and hence on the propensity to consume and invest. For example, low interest rates alone, given a pessimistic public, will not generate expected increases in borrowing and expenditure. During an economic downturn, nonstimulatory fiscal policy or negative financial analysis can, through pessimistic animal spirits, push the economy further downward even in the face of easy money. To the extent that mild inflation helps grease the wheels of growth in the labor market, targeting inflation rates at very low levels keeps unemployment unnecessarily high. Finally, given efficiency wages, efforts to cut real wages will not have the predicted effect of spurring increased employment. Rather, incentives should be developed to encourage increases in economic efficiency in the context of increases in aggregate demand.

Booms and busts are part and parcel of vibrant market economies, but their magnitude can be moderated by public policy, thereby avoiding major crashes, only with a greater appreciation of the behavioral variables underlying decision making.

Morris Altman

See also: Confidence, Consumer and Business; Keynes, John Maynard; Minsky, Hyman.

Further Reading

Akerlof, George A. "Behavioral Macroeconomics and Macroeconomic Behavior." *American Economic Review* 92:3 (2002): 411–433.

Akerlof, George A., and Robert J. Shiller. *Animal Spirits: How Human Psychology Drives the Economy, and Why It Matters for Global Capitalism.* Princeton, NJ: Princeton University Press, 2009.

Altman, Morris. "Behavioral Economics, Economic Theory and Public Policy." *Australasian Journal of Economic Education* 5 (2009): 1–55.

———. "Economic Theory, Public Policy and the Challenge of Innovative Work Practices." *Economic and Industrial Democracy: An International Journal* 23 (2002): 271–290.

———. *Handbook of Contemporary Behavioral Economics: Foundations and Developments.* Armonk, NY: M.E. Sharpe, 2006.

———. "Involuntary Unemployment, Macroeconomic Policy, and a Behavioral Model of the Firm: Why High Real Wages Need Not Cause High Unemployment." *Research in Economics* 60:2 (2006): 97–111.

———. *Worker Satisfaction and Economic Performance: Microfoundations of Success and Failure.* Armonk, NY: M.E. Sharpe, 2001.

Friedman, Milton. "The Methodology of Positive Economics." In *Essays in Positive Economics,* ed. Milton Friedman. Chicago: University of Chicago Press, 1953.

Gigerenzer, Gerd. *Gut Feelings: The Intelligence of the Unconscious.* New York: Viking, 2007.

Kahneman, Daniel. "Maps of Bounded Rationality: Psychology for Behavioral Economics." *American Economic Review* 93:5 (2003): 1449–1475.

Keynes, John Maynard. *The General Theory of Employment, Interest and Money.* London: Macmillan, 1936.

Lewis, Michael. *The Big Short: Inside the Doomsday Machine.* New York: W.W. Norton, 2010.

Minsky, Hyman P. *Stabilizing an Unstable Economy.* New Haven, CT: Yale University Press, 1986.

Shiller, Robert J. *Irrational Exuberance.* Princeton, NJ: Princeton University Press, 2001.

Simon, Herbert A. "Behavioral Economics." In *The New Palgrave: A Dictionary of Economics,* ed. John Eatwell, Murray Milgate, and Peter Newman. London: Macmillan, 1987.

Stiglitz, Joseph E. "The Causes and Consequences of the Dependence of Quantity on Price." *Journal of Economic Literature* 25:1 (1987): 1–48.

Belgium

With a population of almost 11 million and a landmass the size of Maryland, Belgium is one of the smallest member states in the European Union (EU). The capital city of Brussels is a major financial center and the headquarters for the EU and the North American Treaty Organization (NATO). Due to its geographic location at the crossroads of Western Europe, a well-developed transport network, and the high productivity of its workforce, Belgium has historically enjoyed a strong economy. In 2008, it was one of the fifteen largest trading nations in the world and had a gross domestic product (GDP) of $390 billion, which ranked thirtieth in the world. Despite its comparatively strong economy, the Belgian financial sector suffered significant losses in the global economic crisis of 2008–2009, with major banks and investment firms reeling from bailouts and bankruptcies like their counterparts in the United States.

One of the Low Countries of Western Europe, Belgium is part of the Benelux group of nations (along with the Netherlands and Luxembourg). It was a founding member of the European Economic Community (a precursor to the modern European Union), created in 1957 to bring about economic integration among Belgium, France, Germany, Italy, Luxembourg, and the Netherlands; in 1992 it became a founding member of the EU.

The Senne River, which passes through Brussels, divides the country roughly in two. The northern part, Flanders, speaks Flemish (a form of Dutch) and is primarily Protestant. The southern part, Wallonia, is inhabited by the French-speaking Walloons, who are primarily Roman Catholic. Despite its ethnic, linguistic, and religious differences, Belgium has been able to survive as a constitutional monarchy since Napoleonic times. In the days of European colonialism, it was a minor power ruling over its African colony of the Belgian Congo (present-day Congo).

Since the Middle Ages, Flanders has been economically important as a center for trade and textiles. As the Italian city-states declined, Antwerp and Brugge (Bruges), today the capital city of West Flanders, became important commercial centers for shipbuilding, food processing, and chemicals. In the 1830s, Belgium followed Great Britain as it experienced its own industrial revolution and became a center for textiles and steel because of its natural deposits of coal and metal ores. This was particularly true of the French-speaking Wallonia. The Flemish-speaking north remained mostly agricultural, with some processing facilities. This economic and linguistic split has persisted through the country's history, and has led to political stalemate and even talk of separatism into the twenty-first century. Still, despite such divisions, Belgium boasted one of the most advanced industrial sectors in Europe through the early twentieth century.

Because it was so heavily industrialized and so dependent on trade, Belgium was hit by the global economic contraction of the 1930s, before being occupied by the Nazis during World War II. In the wake of that conflict, however, Belgium participated in the postwar economic miracle in Western Europe, seeing its living standards rise dramatically and a major chemical and petroleum refining industry develop around the port of Antwerp in the northwest. Indeed, the rise of Antwerp was part of a general geographic shift in the Belgium economy in the postwar era, in which the industrial heartland, saddled with older and inefficient heavy industry, began to lag behind the prospering north.

Overall, by the mid-1990s, manufacturing industries and mining had declined, while the country's service sector (consumer and financial services) expanded significantly, accounting for nearly 70 percent of the GDP and employing 70 percent of the labor force. The oil crisis of the 1970s and economic restructuring led to a series of recessions during the 1980s. In the early 1990s—in an effort to give its manufacturing regions greater control over their economic problems—the government extended each region broad economic powers to control trade, industrial development, and environmental regulation while at the same time privatizing many formerly state-owned companies.

Belgium has been one of the foremost proponents of regional economic integration, with approximately 75 percent of its trade with other EU countries, including Germany, the Netherlands, and France. After the initiation of the euro as the official currency of the EU member states in 2002, currency exchanges became more efficient and cheaper. Nevertheless, the financial crisis that began in 2008 hit the Belgians hard as shareholders in the nation's two largest financial institutions, Fortis and Dexia, saw their assets evaporate in the global monetary meltdown.

Fortis, the largest Belgian financial-services firm with branches in all three of the Benelux

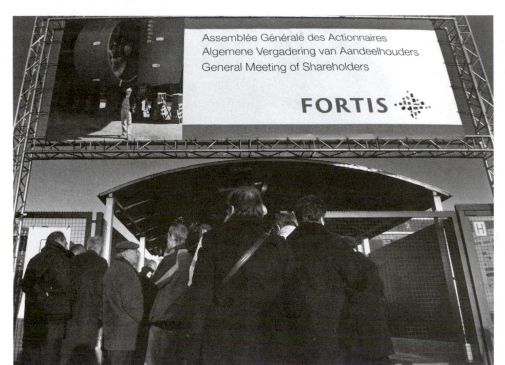

Shareholders of the Belgian financial services and insurance firm Fortis—once the country's largest—convene in Brussels in late 2008 to discuss the future of the company. The following April, BNP Paribas SA bought a 75 percent share. *(Bloomberg/ Getty Images)*

countries, had 41.7 billion euros (US$60.7 billion) of structured investments at the end of June 2008, including collateralized debt obligations and U.S. mortgage-backed securities. Its banking operation was put in jeopardy by the global financial crisis brought on by the collapse of the U.S. subprime mortgage market. In order to meet the Fortis financial crisis, in September the Benelux countries invested a total of 11.2 billion euros (US$16.3 billion) into a rescue package; however, a run on Fortis banking units in the Netherlands forced the government to nationalize the Dutch units. This meant that Fortis's branches in the Netherlands were taken away from Fortis by the Dutch government. (Finally, in early 2009, the Belgian portion of Fortis was sold to the French bank BNP Paribas.)

The 2008 Belgian financial crisis deepened after the Belgian financial institution Dexia, a major lender to governments and public agencies in Europe, received 6.4 billion euros (US$9 billion) from the Belgian, French, and Luxembourg governments in order to provide the company with additional capital after it was unable to sell more stock to increase its capitalization. However, the capital infusion was not enough to keep Dexia solvent, and in November 2008 it announced that

it had lost 1.5 billion euros and was forced to sell its insurance operations.

On December 15, 2008, Dexia announced that some of its financial problems were related to the collapse of the Wall Street firm Bernard L. Madoff Investment Securities. Madoff, a former chairman of the NASDAQ stock exchange, resigned as chairman of his firm on December 11, 2008, when it was discovered that he had defrauded investors of an estimated US$50 billion in a Ponzi investment scheme, of which Dexia was a victim.

A third major shock to the Belgian economy came in October 2008, when the Belgian unit of Ethias, a European company engaged in banking and insurance, announced that it would be receiving 1.5 billion euros from the Belgian government in order to shore up its capital reserves. As the country's financial crisis deepened, news of the assistance brought confidence in the Belgian banking sector to an all-time low.

Economic growth and foreign direct investment declined in 2008. The depth of Belgium's financial and economic crisis remained uncertain for 2010 and beyond, as EU leaders formulated an action plan to cope with Europe's economic crisis.

Andrew J. Waskey

See also: Netherlands, The.

Further Reading

Cook, Bernard A. *Belgium: A History.* New York: Peter Lang, 2002.

Meerten, Michaelangelo van. *Capital Formation in Belgium, 1900–1995.* Ithaca, NY: Cornell University Press, 2003.

Mommen, Andre. *The Belgian Economy in the Twentieth Century.* London: Routledge, 1994.

Bernanke, Ben (1953–)

Chair of the Board of Governors of the Federal Reserve System (Fed) since early 2006, Ben Shalom Bernanke was a key player in the U.S. government's response to the financial crisis of 2008–2009, arranging for the bailout of insurance giant AIG (American International Group) and working with Secretary of the Treasury Henry Paulson to design and implement the $700 billion federal bailout plan, known officially as the Troubled Asset Relief Program.

Bernanke was born in Augusta, Georgia, in 1953, and grew up in a small town in South Carolina. He received a bachelor's degree in economics from Harvard University in 1975 and a doctorate in economics from the Massachusetts Institute of Technology in 1979; his doctoral dissertation focused on the dynamics of the business cycle. Bernanke was a professor of economics and public affairs at Princeton University from 1985 to 2002. Before joining the faculty at Princeton, he was an associate professor of economics (1983–1985) and an assistant professor of economics (1979–1983) in the Graduate School of Business at Stanford University. He also taught as a visiting professor of economics at New York University (1993) and the Massachusetts Institute of Technology (1989–1990). Bernanke is a fellow of the Econometric Society and the American Academy of Arts and Sciences, and he has served as editor of the *American Economic Review.*

As an academic, Bernanke focused his scholarly efforts on examining the causes of the Great Depression. He confirmed the argument presented by Milton Friedman and Anna Jacobson Schwartz in their study *A Monetary History of the United States* (1963), that the activities of the Fed to reduce the money supply during the early 1930s contributed significantly to the duration of the Depression. Bernanke also published important works on the role of financial information and creditworthiness during the Depression. In his 1983 article "Nonmonetary Effects of the Financial Crisis in the Propagation of the Great Depression," he highlighted the impact of widespread bank failures during the Depression. These, he argued, contributed to a loss of invaluable financial information about the creditworthiness of firms, thereby leading to greater risks in investing and, in turn, causing the real cost of credit to rise. Bernanke also emphasized the importance of comparative research into prices, wages, and production across a number of countries in order to better understand the causes and transmission of the Depression.

While still teaching, Bernanke entered public service as a member of the Academic Advisory Panel at the Federal Reserve Bank of New York from 1990 to 2002. In the latter year, he took a leave of absence from Princeton to become chair of President George W. Bush's Council of Economic Advisers from 2005 to 2006. He was a member of the Board of Governors of the Federal Reserve System from 2002 to 2006 before succeeding Alan Greenspan as chair on February 1, 2006.

Upon taking the helm at the Fed, Bernanke instituted a number of reforms that attempted to make the institution more transparent by declaring specific inflation goals. At first, Bernanke made a point of issuing clearer statements about Fed policy than had Greenspan, who was famous for his oracular remarks. Some criticized the Fed's new openness, arguing that such clear declarations of intent caused fluctuations in the stock market.

But it was Bernanke's response to the financial crisis of late 2000s that garnered the greatest criticism—and praise—from economists and other experts. Some contended that he was slow to react to the economic crisis as it unfolded over the course of 2008. Indeed, many said that his decision to let the investment bank Lehman Brothers fail in September 2008 helped precipitate the crisis in the first place. However, Bernanke's research into the causes of the Great Depression clearly influenced the policy outlook of the Fed during the financial crisis. This can be seen in the interventionist, and often controversial, stance of both the Fed and Congress in preventing a contraction of the money supply, and in their actions to "bail out" many financial institutions. Bernanke maintained—along with many other supporters of the bailout—that this was critical in order to ensure the stability of, and the public's confidence in, the larger financial system, thereby limiting the damage and duration of the initial crises.

At first, Bernanke intended to buy up "toxic" mortgage-backed securities that were poisoning the global financial system. The Emergency Economic Stabilization Act, passed on October 3, 2008, authorized $700 billion to do so. Within a few days, however, the Treasury Department, in conjunction with the Fed, decided to use an initial $250 billion to purchase preferred stock in American banks. The thinking was that by shoring up the capital of the largest banks, institutions would begin lending again and the financial crisis would be resolved.

Bernanke was criticized for his role in arranging the acquisition of troubled brokerage house Merrill Lynch by Bank of America in late 2008. New York State Attorney General Andrew Cuomo, for one, alleged that Bernanke and Paulson had failed to inform Bank of America officials of the true scope of Merrill Lynch's losses when persuading it to take over the company. At congressional hearings on the subject in June 2009, Bernanke insisted that he had not forced Bank of America president Ken Lewis into taking over Merrill Lynch, and did not admit to covering up the latter company's economic woes. Bernanke also was widely criticized for his decision to provide $80 billion, prior to the passage of the $700 billion bailout legislation, to rescue insurance giant AIG. At least one senator alleged that Bernanke had made the decision against his staff's recommendation.

Despite these criticisms, President Barack Obama nominated Bernanke for a second term as Fed chairman in August 2009. But rising political anger at the bailout, a still sputtering

Federal Reserve Board chairman Ben Bernanke testifies before a Senate committee on the $700 billion Wall Street bailout request by the Bush administration in fall 2008. The Senate elected Bernanke to a second term in January 2010. *(Alex Wong/Getty Images)*

economy, and double-digit unemployment led to an unusual amount of resistance on Capitol Hill, with both conservatives and liberals questioning the president's decision. Nevertheless, Bernanke was confirmed by the Senate in a 70–30 vote in January 2010, the narrowest margin in the history of Federal Reserve chair confirmation votes.

James Ciment

See also: Federal Reserve System; Troubled Asset Relief Program (2008–).

Further Reading

Bernanke, Ben S. "Nonmonetary Effects of the Financial Crisis in the Propagation of the Great Depression." *American Economic Review* 73:3 (June 1983): 257–276.

Grunwald, Michael. "Person of the Year: Ben Bernanke." *Time*, December 16, 2009. Available at www.time.com/time/specials/packages/article/0,28804,1946375_1947251_1947520,00.html. Accessed February 2010.

Harris, Ethan S. *Ben Bernanke's Fed: The Federal Reserve After Greenspan.* Boston: Harvard Business, 2008.

Bethlehem Steel

Once the second-largest steel manufacturer in the United States, the Pennsylvania-based Bethlehem Steel corporation was laid low in the late twentieth century by internal management issues, foreign competition, and the overall decline of the U.S. steel industry that began in the 1970s. Facing huge losses by the 1980s, the company was forced to shut down most of its plants and restructure. These efforts only slowed its decline, however, and in 2001 the company declared bankruptcy.

Founded in 1857 as the Saucona Iron Company, the company moved to Bethlehem, Pennsylvania, and changed its name to the Bethlehem Iron Company four years later. The company prospered in the late nineteenth century—despite intense competition from industry leader Carnegie Steel (later U.S. Steel)—providing iron and then steel for the nation's growing rail network, the skyscraper construction boom, and the U.S. Navy,

which was replacing its wooden ships with steel ones and expanding dramatically after the 1880s. The company changed its named to the Bethlehem Steel Company in 1899, then reorganized under a corporate charter as the Bethlehem Steel Corporation in 1904. It also grew by introducing innovative steel manufacturing techniques—including the Grey rolling mill, which revolutionized the manufacture of steel girders—and acquiring other companies in the steel business as well as in railroads, coal mining, and shipbuilding.

To meet government demand, Bethlehem Steel expanded again during World War II, building more than 1,000 ships for the U.S. armed forces, leaving it with a huge capacity to meet the needs of the postwar economic boom. Bethlehem Steel became a leader in the production of steel for both old uses (such as building construction) and new ones (including production of uranium rods for nuclear power plants). The 1950s and 1960s saw some of the U.S. steel industry's most profitable years, as the economy boomed and the former steel-making capacity of Europe and Japan struggled to rebuild after the devastation of World War II. By the mid-1950s, Bethlehem Steel reached its peak production of more than 20 million tons (18.1 million metric tons) annually. In 1955, it reached number eight on *Fortune* magazine's list of America's biggest businesses.

Steel was America's bellwether industry during this period, with both economic analysts and politicians keeping a close eye on it. In 1962, for example, President John F. Kennedy intervened when the industry—led by U.S. Steel—raised its prices; Kennedy forced the company to roll back the increases out of fear they might produce destabilizing inflation throughout the economy.

But America's dominance of the global steel industry did not last. As European and Asian manufacturers revived, they soon began to compete both in the American and foreign markets. Steel producers in Europe and Asia enjoyed lower labor costs—this was particularly true for Asian producers—and more modern manufacturing facilities. In the long run, the destruction wrought by World

War II allowed European and Japanese steelmakers to introduce cutting-edge technology more quickly in subsequent decades. Thus, by the 1970s, foreign steel of the same high quality could be produced for substantially less than American steel.

Bethlehem Steel began seeing regular annual losses in the middle years of that decade, a result not just of foreign competition but of a sputtering American economy and a decline in large, steel-intensive infrastructure projects. Management contributed to the company's problems as well, failing to close unprofitable facilities, upgrade other plants, and adjust to changing market demand for more varied steel products. In 1982, the company reported more than $1.5 billion in losses, which forced it to close down many of its operations. Along with declines at other steel and heavy manufacturers, the closings helped create what came to be known as the "rust belt," a swath of the Northeast and Upper Midwest pockmarked by empty and decaying factories, declining tax bases, and persistent high unemployment. More generally, scholars of the era began to talk of an American "deindustrialization."

While Bethlehem's belt tightening returned it to profitability in the late 1980s, the comeback was short-lived. Further losses in the 1990s forced the company to divest its coal mining, railroad car manufacturing, and shipbuilding businesses. In 1995, it also closed its main plant in Bethlehem, ending an almost 140-year history of steelmaking in that city. But the restructuring was a case of too little, too late. In 2001, the corporation was forced to file for protection under U.S. bankruptcy laws. Two years later, many of its remaining assets were sold to International Steel Group, which merged with the Netherlands-based Mittal Steel in 2005.

While some of the company's old plants continue to produce steel, part of the flagship facility in Bethlehem was turned into an industrial-themed casino and resort in 2009.

James Ciment

See also: Manufacturing.

Further Reading

Loomis, Carol J. "The Sinking of Bethlehem Steel." *Fortune*, April 5, 2004.

Strohmeyer, John. *Crisis in Bethlehem: Big Steel's Struggle to Survive.* Bethesda, MD: Adler & Adler, 1986.

Warren, Kenneth. *Bethlehem Steel: Builder and Arsenal of America.* Pittsburgh, PA: University of Pittsburgh Press, 2008.

Böhm-Bawerk, Eugen Ritter von (1851–1914)

Eugen Ritter von Böhm-Bawerk was an Austrian economist, minister of finance, and founding member of the Austrian school of economics. He developed a number of the early theories that influenced such students of economic growth and business cycles as Joseph Schumpeter.

Böhm-Bawerk was born on February 12, 1851, in Brno, Czech Republic (then Brünn, Moravia). He studied law at the University of Vienna, receiving a PhD in 1875. There, his views on economics were greatly influenced by Austrian school founder Carl Menger's *Principles of Economics* (1871), and by his classmate and future brother-in-law, Friedrich von Wieser. From 1881 to 1889, while teaching at the University of Innsbruck, Böhm-Bawerk published two of the three volumes of *Capital and Interest*, his most important work. He worked with the Austrian Ministry of Finance on a proposal for tax reform, and in 1895 he became minister of finance, a post he would hold off and on until 1904. In this position, he supported the institution of a legally fixed gold standard, a balanced budget, and financial stability. He strongly opposed government subsidies and spending on large public projects. He returned to academia in 1904 as a professor at the University of Vienna. There, his students included Ludwig von Mises, Henryk Grossmann, and Schumpeter.

Böhm-Bawerk's Theory

In *Capital and Interest* (1884), Böhm-Bawerk examines interest—including use, productivity, and abstinence theories. For example, people agree to pay interest in order to have immediate access to goods. If they must give up the privilege of immediate consumption, they in turn demand positive interest. He also maintains that there is a "technical superiority of present over future goods," an argument that was both controversial and complex. He views production as a roundabout process (that is, the process by which capital, such as machinery and equipment, is produced first and then used to produce consumer goods) that requires time. Thus, investment in capital is necessary to transform future factors of production (land and labor) into higher output.

Although today Böhm-Bawerk's theories on the roundabout process are somewhat obscure, prior to World War I they were much discussed. He was among the first economists to challenge Karl Marx's view that capitalism exploits workers. Böhm-Bawerk argued that capitalism actually favors workers, since they are paid based on expected (future) revenue from the goods they produce. Workers could not receive all the benefits (profits) from production because some of the product would be necessary to finance the production process. Böhm-Bawerk criticized Marx's exploitation theories, arguing that workers, in fact, receive their wages before the owner receives revenues on goods produced. Hinting at his theory of the roundabout process, Böhm-Bawerk pointed out that Marx's theory ignored the time of production and thus the present value factor. Therefore, workers produce only part of a good's value; labor can only be paid according to the present value of a future output.

In *Karl Marx and the Close of His System* (1896), Böhm-Bawerk argues that there is a contradiction between the law of value, which Marx explained in the third volume of *Capital*, and his own theory of value. According to Böhm-Bawerk, the allocation of profits to the different factors of production does not follow political decisions but rather follows economic imperatives, such as supply and demand.

Positive Theory of Capital (1889), the second

volume of *Capital and Interest*, focuses on the time of production processes and the need of interest payments to bridge the gap between present and future output. In it, Böhm-Bawerk supports Menger's ideas of marginal utility, stating that goods only have value based on what people are willing to pay for them.

The last volume of Böhm-Bawerk's *Capital and Interest, Further Essays on Capital and Interest* (1921), published posthumously, contains clarifications of his theories and his responses to critics. At the time of his death on August 27, 1914, in Tyrol, Böhm-Bawerk was considered one of the period's leading economists.

Carmen De Michele

See also: Austrian School; Hayek, Friedrich August von; Mises, Ludwig von; Monetary Policy; Monetary Theories and Models; Schumpeter, Joseph.

Further Reading

Garrison, Roger W. "Austrian Capital Theory: The Early Controversies." In *Carl Menger and His Legacy in Economics*, ed. Bruce J. Caldwell. Durham, NC: Duke University Press, 1990.

Kirzner, Israel. *Essays on Capital and Interest: An Austrian Perspective.* Brookfield, VT: Edward Elgar, 1996.

Kuenne, Robert E. *Eugen von Böhm-Bawerk.* New York: Columbia University Press, 1971.

Boom, Economic (1920s)

The period between the end of World War I in November 1918 and the stock market crash of October 1929 saw one of the most dramatic and rapid economic expansions in U.S. history. Industrial output, corporate profits, and stock prices all experienced significant and sustained growth, aside from a short but sharp recession from late 1920 through early 1922. So dramatic was the country's economic performance during these years that the Roaring Twenties have been forever etched in the public imagination as the epitome of boom times.

In reality, the 1920s were not as universally

cheerful as people commonly believe. Large sectors of the economy, including agriculture, textiles, and coal, remained mired in recession, while the enormous wealth generated during the period was unequally distributed; most working-class and lower-middle-class Americans saw little growth in their incomes. And, of course, the boom economy of the 1920s was living on borrowed time, with a number of important flaws that contributed to the "Great Crash" and the worst catastrophe in U.S. economic history.

Rough Start

The 1920s did not begin with a roar. Indeed, economic performance in the several years immediately following World War I was shaky at best, largely as a result of a hasty and poorly thought-through demobilization effort. During the war, which, for the United States lasted from early 1917 through late 1918, federal spending grew exponentially, from several million dollars annually to more than $2 billion per month. The nation's factories could barely keep up with defense demands, and unemployment virtually disappeared (partly due to the fact that nearly 4 million people were in uniform).

With the end of the war, consumers went on a buying spree with their wartime earnings, as defense efforts had caused a relative dearth of consumer products during the war period. Since companies could not keep up with demand, prices soared—the inflation rate reached 30 percent in 1919—far outpacing wage growth. The gap led to what was perhaps the largest wave of strikes in U.S. history to that time. Approximately 4 million workers, or about 20 percent of the nation's workforce, participated in some 3,000 strikes during 1919 alone, crippling productivity and contributing to inflation and demobilization problems.

Determined to bring inflation down, the Woodrow Wilson administration and the semi-independent Federal Reserve—just six years old in 1919—made what later economists considered several major mistakes. Believing that federal borrowing dried up capital needed by private enterprise, the Wilson administration quickly moved to shrink spending, putting many companies out of business and many workers out of a job. Meanwhile, convinced that its previous low-interest, money-supply-expanding policies, while necessary to pay for the war effort, had fueled inflation, the Federal Reserve raised interest rates, thereby tightening credit and slowing growth of the money supply. The subsequent contraction was exacerbated by a drop in exports—from more than $13 billion in 1920 to less than $7 billion the following year—as the economies of many of the European belligerents were restored and began producing the necessities once imported from the United States. While the administration's efforts did have the desired effect—a deflationary cycle wiped out most the gains in prices from the early postwar years—they also led to a major contraction in industrial output and an unemployment rate of more than 10 percent.

The recession did not last long, however, and by late 1922 the economy was growing again. The trend continued through virtually the end of the decade, with unemployment never rising above 4 percent and inflation almost nonexistent. The numbers were impressive, with the economy as a whole expanding by about 40 percent, from a gross national product (GNP) of $74.1 billion in 1922 to one of $103.1 billion in 1929. What explains this dramatic expansion? Economists point to two key ingredients: innovation, both of the technological and managerial variety, and the growth in aggregate demand, as consumption trumped savings and consumers went on a spending spree for new and exciting products, such as the automobile.

Innovation

Technological innovation undoubtedly played a key role in two ways. First, new technologies or, more precisely, the application and expansion of existing technologies on a new scale, led to significant gains in productivity. Expansion of the electricity grid—from 39 million kilowatts in 1919 to 97 million kilowatts in 1929—allowed industry to switch from cumbersome steam engines to smaller, more efficient, more versatile electric motors. Expansion in the number of telephone lines—from 30 million in 1920 to 70 million in 1930—allowed for better communication within growing corporate enterprises, between businesses, and between businesses and consumers. And while the 1920s is famous for its embrace of the automobile, less heralded was the growth in internal combustion–driven trucks, a far more effective form of transportation than horse-drawn wagons and far more adaptable geographically than railroads. Finally, many companies took a more active role in technological innovation rather than waiting for independent inventors to come up with new ideas. By the late 1920s, more than a thousand U.S. corporations had created research and development programs. The most famous of these was Bell Labs, which American Telephone & Telegraph incorporated as a separate company in 1925.

Technological innovation also spurred demand, as industry introduced—or expanded production and lowered the cost of—a panoply of new and highly desirable consumer products. Among them was a variety of electrically driven household appliances, such as the radio. Between 1923 and 1930, approximately six of every ten American households had purchased a radio set. Even more important to economic growth was the automobile. With Henry Ford's Model T leading the way, car purchases increased from about 2.2 million in 1920 to 5.3 million in 1929. Such growth in aggregate demand provided a major engine of economic growth, allowing industries to take advantage of economies of scale, thereby lowering prices and spurring new demand in what economists call a "virtuous cycle."

Yet as students of economic innovation also note, technological change is usually only half the explanation for an upturn in the business cycle. New managerial practices, designated under the rubric "scientific management," also contributed to the gains in productivity that fueled the economic expansion of the 1920s. These included tighter managerial control of workers, more on-the-job training, and the implementation of scientifically determined "best practices" in the workplace, which improved output per worker on assembly lines and in the bureaucracies of corporate headquarters. At the managerial level, companies—led by the innovative General Motors—began to separate day-to-day management from long-term planning.

Meanwhile, the financial sector was innovating and expanding as well. Banks began to offer more affordable mortgages, allowing more Americans to purchase their own homes, even as they helped finance new factories and corporate headquarters. All of this helped fuel a boom in real estate and construction. The financial sector also provided the funds for an unprecedented wave of corporate mergers. Indeed, no equivalent period produced more mergers than the six years from 1924 through 1929—about 1,250 in all. Credit helped make the financial sector—and Wall Street in particular—a major player in the nation's economy, with bank assets rising from $48 billion to $72 billion between 1919 and 1929, half of this controlled by the largest 1 percent of banks.

Government policy under successive pro-business Republican administrations and Congresses also contributed to corporate growth. The government relaxed its efforts to break up large corporations, allowing for the rapid growth in business consolidation, even as it cut taxes on the wealthy to free up funds for investment. The Commerce Department under Secretary Herbert Hoover offered a number of more innovative ideas, particularly through its efforts to allow companies to share information and collectively market their products at home and overseas—practices once considered violations of antitrust laws. Washington also supported manufacturers with high tariffs on imported goods.

Uneven Growth

For all the wealth and exuberance it generated, the boom of the 1920s was neither a universal

Flourishing consumerism, the rebellious exuberance of flappers, and the freedom afforded by automobiles characterized the Roaring Twenties. An ailing farm sector and a widening gap between rich and poor were among the underlying economic weaknesses. *(Stringer/Hulton Archive/ Getty Images)*

phenomenon nor one built on the most solid foundation, as the stock market crash of 1929 and the Great Depression of the 1930s proved. First, a number of key industries remained ailing throughout the decade. This included textile production in the Northeast, as factories moved south to take advantage of cheaper labor; coal, which faced new competition from oil and gas; and railroads, facing increasing competition from trucks and buses. But no sector suffered more than agriculture, which still employed about one in four working Americans at the beginning of the decade. Having greatly expanded output to meet wartime demand—often by going into debt— farmers faced a dramatic collapse in commodity prices after the war. The prices never really recovered, and the farming sector was left in a state of recession through the entire decade. Thus, while nonfarm yearly incomes averaged around $750 during the decade, farm incomes hovered at one-third that level.

Discrepancies in income were not confined to the farm sector. Indeed, many Keynesian economists point to stagnant wages and the rapidly growing inequality between rich and poor as a major reason why the Wall Street crash, which directly affected only a small proportion of the population, caused a depression that affected every corner of the American economy. Despite the enormous productivity gains of the 1920s, the vast majority of workers saw their wages rise modestly if at all. According to a study released by the National Bureau of Economic Research (NBER) in 1921, a typical American family of five (the average household was larger than in the twenty-first century) required at least $2,000 a year in income for basic necessities. In 1919, approximately 70 percent of American income earners fell below that mark. By 1929, that figure had only fallen to 60 percent, and the drop occurred mostly among skilled workers, themselves a relatively small portion of the overall working-class population. Among the unskilled, fully 42 percent had household incomes of less than $1,500. At the other end of the income scale, meanwhile, the gains were dramatic. Between 1919 and 1929, the average income for the top 1 percent of American households rose some 75 percent. Their share of total national income rose from 12 to 34 percent, the largest ten-year increase in U.S. history. Likewise, household wealth was being distributed more and more unequally. By 1929, the top 1 percent of Americans held more than 44 percent of the nation's wealth, while the bottom 87 percent held just 8 percent.

Several factors contributed to the growing inequality, including a drop in union membership, which undermined wages; falling income tax rates on the rich; and the spectacular growth in the values of securities, most of which were owned by upper-middle-class and wealthy households. In fact, the growth in stock values did not just contribute to greater wealth among the rich; it also resulted from it. In other words, while much of the new wealth accruing to the top households went into conspicuous consumption, a good deal of it also went into speculative financing. Such investments drove stock prices spectacularly upward in the late 1920s, especially as the other avenue for speculation—real estate—went into a slump after 1927. Between that year and the crash of 1929, the average price of stocks rose 50 percent; high flyers such as RCA rose many times faster. Soon, not only the rich were investing in corporate securities, so was the middle class. By the time of the crash, some 10 percent of American households had invested on Wall Street. Encouraging this growth was a particularly dangerous form of financing,

whereby brokerage houses and investment banks offered loans to stock purchasers for up to 90 percent of the value of the securities they were buying, collateralized by the ever higher valuations themselves.

It was a classic bubble, and it finally burst. The fall in asset values produced a liquidity crisis that reverberated throughout the economy when confidence in the ability of individuals and institutions to pay back loans and credits evaporated. The crisis in the financial markets might have remained largely confined there, much as during earlier panics, had it not been for the underlying weaknesses of the "boom" of the 1920s.

James Ciment

See also: Florida Real-Estate Boom (1920s); Great Depression (1929–1933); Stock Market Crash (1929).

Further Reading

Bernstein, Irving. *The Lean Years: A History of the American Worker, 1920–1933.* Boston: Houghton Mifflin, 1960.

Best, Gary Dean. *The Dollar Decade: Mammon and the Machine in the 1920s.* Westport, CT: Praeger, 2003.

Ciment, James, ed. *Encyclopedia of the Jazz Age.* Armonk, NY: M.E. Sharpe, 2008.

Goldberg, David J. *Discontented America: The United States in the 1920s.* Baltimore, MD: Johns Hopkins University Press, 1999.

Leuchtenberg, William E. *The Perils of Prosperity, 1914–1932.* Chicago: University of Chicago Press, 1958.

Boom, Economic (1960s)

In the popular imagination, the 1960s are remembered as a time of social upheaval—urban rioting, anti–Vietnam War demonstrations, feminist protest. For those who study the intersection of politics and economics, however, all of the protest seems incongruous for the times. Social upheaval, it is understood, tends to occur during times of great economic upheaval—the industrial union movement and sit-down strikes of the Great Depression being a classic example. But the 1960s were, arguably, the most prosperous decade in modern American history, with virtually every economic index—from the Dow Jones Industrial Average (DJIA) to the number of people living above the poverty line—showing remarkable gains.

Extent of the Boom

Before examining why the 1960s were so prosperous, a few words on the time frame and scale of the expansion are helpful. According to most economists, the recovery from the mild recession of 1957–1958 marks the onset of the great expansion, and the oil shocks and far deeper recession of 1973–1975 mark the end. Whatever the specific time frame, the actual decade of the 1960s saw remarkable gains across the U.S. economy. Between 1960 and 1970, the gross national product nearly doubled from $503.7 billion to $976.4 billion in non-inflation-adjusted dollars. Inflation remained largely in check until deficit spending to fund the Vietnam War sent it higher in the late 1960s. The unemployment rate was cut in half, from just under 7 percent at the end of the recession to 3.5 percent in 1970, a trend made even more noteworthy by the fact that millions of women were entering the workforce in these years. In 1960, about one-third of all adult American women worked; a decade later, the figure was well over 40 percent.

The financial markets boomed as well, with daily shares traded on the New York Stock Exchange nearly quadrupling from 3 million to almost 12 million. As late as the recession of 1957–1958, the DJIA had stood at just under 420, up just 10 percent from its pre-Depression high of 381; by 1969, it had more than doubled to nearly 1,000. At the other end of the spectrum, the gains were equally remarkable, as the economic expansion, along with a host of government anti-poverty programs launched by President Lyndon Johnson, collectively dubbed the "Great Society," lowered the percentage of households living in poverty from 22.4 percent in 1959 to 12.6 percent

in 1970, the fastest and most dramatic recorded drop in American history.

In fact, the 1960s economic expansion represented the culmination of a much a longer growth period. Referred to by economists as the post–World War II economic boom, the surge encompassed virtually the entire noncommunist industrialized world, including Western Europe, Canada, Japan, and elsewhere. Indeed, the growth rates of such high-flying countries as Italy and Japan outpaced that of the United States in these years. Between 1960 and 1970, Japan posted gross domestic product (GDP) gains of between 7 and 10 percent annually, raising per capita income from about $6,000 to more than $14,500 in 1970 (or from 40 percent of the U.S. figure to 60 percent). In Italy, per capita income rose from about $9,600 in 1960 to just over $17,000 in 1973, a rise of about 75 percent. During the same period, U.S. per capita income rose from about $17,600 to about $26,000, an increase of nearly 50 percent. (All figures, except where noted, are represented in 2008 U.S. dollars.) While Europe and Japan experienced the same forces that propelled the U.S. economy—principally, pent-up aggregate demand—they also prospered as they rebuilt and modernized economic infrastructure that had been devastated by the war. U.S. government policy also helped, going beyond the massive foreign aid to Europe and Japan after the war. As the dominant player in the global economy and international institutions, the United States promoted international trade and a stable global financial system based on a strong U.S. dollar.

Causes

What explains these remarkable numbers? Much of it had to do with international circumstances, innovation, and government policy. The story begins with World War II. While Europe and Japan saw their infrastructures devastated by the conflict, the United States remained largely untouched. Indeed, its industrial capacity expanded dramatically as a result of the war effort. At the same time, deprived of consumer goods, Americans accumulated some $140 billion in savings between 1942 and 1945. When the war ended, pent-up aggregate demand fueled a consumer-led economic surge as Americans spent lavishly on new automobiles and household durables such as washing machines, refrigerators, and television sets. Millions of Americans decamped from the cities to the suburbs, and from the Northeast and Midwest to the South and West, fueling an unprecedented construction boom.

The federal government contributed to the boom in two major ways. The GI Bill, 1944 legislation designed to help more than 15 million men and women in uniform readjust to civilian life, provided government-backed mortgages, making buying a home much more affordable for working- and middle-class Americans. Whereas about four in ten families owned their own homes in 1940, more than six in ten did so in 1960. Meanwhile,

the GI Bill paid other dividends. By providing scholarships and low-interest loans for veterans to attend college, it greatly increased the overall productivity of American workers. The second policy was the Interstate Highway Program, launched by President Dwight Eisenhower in 1956, which not only connected suburbs to cities (and cities to other cities) with high-speed, limited-access highways, but also fueled a major construction boom.

The government also played a more indirect role in the postwar boom period. Many of the scientific and technological innovations of World War II—largely financed with government research money—were commercialized in the 1950s and 1960s. Among the industries that took advantage of wartime innovation were plastics, synthetic fibers, and aerospace. The latter, in particular, was aided by a massive expansion in defense spending, as the United States ended its long tradition of maintaining a tiny peacetime

Low-interest, government-backed mortgages for World War II veterans, standardized building techniques, new highways, and growing families gave rise to single-family housing developments across America during the boom of the 1960s. *(American Stock/Hulton Archive/Getty Images)*

military establishment. Whereas defense spending represented 25 percent of much smaller federal government outlays in 1930—about $50 billion in all—it commanded more than 40 percent in 1970, or about $700 billion, which went to the Vietnam War effort.

The dramatic rise in per capita income during the 1960s allowed tens of millions of Americans, including many blue-collar workers, to join the ranks of the middle class. But not only were members of the vast middle sector of the U.S. economy seeing their incomes rise, their share of national income remained significantly higher in these years than in any other period of the twentieth and twenty-first centuries. Whereas the top 1 percent of income earners garnered 15 to 20 percent of all income in the 1920s (and the 2000s), the figure stood at about 10 percent throughout the postwar boom.

The more equitable distribution of income was the result of several factors, including a lack of competition from other countries. Even as late as 1970, to take one important example, imported passenger cars (other than those built by Canadian subsidiaries of U.S. corporations) represented just 13 percent of all new sales. Commanding the largest market for cars in the world allowed U.S. auto manufacturers to pay high wages and offer plentiful benefits, for the most part negotiated by a powerful union movement. Indeed, during the 1960s, union membership in the United States was at or near record levels, with roughly one in three workers organized. High union membership not only meant a higher percentage of national income going into the pockets of unionized workers, but nonunionized workers also did well, since union pay scales set the standard in most industries. Thus, as productivity rose dramatically, so did the income of the working and middle classes, fueling ever more consumer demand.

Supercharged Late 1960s and the Fall of the 1970s

While the postwar boom began in the late 1940s, it became supercharged in the period between the end of the 1957–1958 recession and the oil crisis and persistent recession beginning in late 1973. Much of this was the result of government policy. To help boost a somewhat sluggish economy in the early 1960s, President John F. Kennedy proposed the largest tax cut as a percentage of national income in U.S. history, though it did not go into effect until signed into law by his successor, Lyndon Johnson, in February 1964. The measure significantly lowered tax rates on all income groups and corporations while liberalizing the rules on the depreciation of capital. All of the extra posttax income, corporate profits, and spending produced a sustained period of extraordinary growth, as the nation's GDP climbed from less than $3.6 trillion in early 1964 to $5.42 trillion in late 1973—a rise of nearly 44 percent in one decade, more than economic growth during the 1980s and 1990s.

But it could not last. For even as the huge tax cut was going into effect, Johnson was expanding government expenditures, both for the War on Poverty and, even more significantly, for the war in Vietnam. Fearing that opposition to the war and his social programs would be fueled by raising taxes, Johnson instead allowed the federal debt to grow and put pressure on the Federal Reserve to increase the money supply. This resulted in rising levels of inflation through the late 1960s and early 1970s, which hit 5.7 percent in 1970. To deal with the inflation, Johnson's successor, Richard Nixon, instituted two major policy decisions in August 1971. The first was a ninety-day wage and price freeze followed by a three-year period of regulated increases. The second was a devaluation of the U.S. dollar. With inflation running high and the federal debt growing, foreigners were attempting to convert their dollars into gold, creating unsustainable pressure on the value of the dollar. In 1973, the global financial system that had been in place since the end of World War II, whereby currency values were pegged to the U.S. dollar, was replaced by freely floating currencies for most nations.

The final nail in the coffin of the 1960s economic expansion was the oil shock of 1973–1974, whereby major Arab oil producers raised their prices and cut supplies to the West as punishment for the latter's support of Israel in the 1973 Arab-Israeli War. As a result, oil prices nearly quadrupled and, since oil was central to just about every facet of the U.S. economy, the effect was widespread. The inflation rate climbed to more than 11 percent in 1974. Meanwhile, economic growth slowed, stalled, and then slipped into negative territory through the mid-1970s, not recovering significantly until after the deep recession of 1981–1982, when inflation was brought to heel. The economic crises of the 1970s confounded governments around the world, as they combined inflation with slow economic growth in a pattern that baffled the Keynesian economists who had driven government economic policy making since the end of World War II.

James Ciment

See also: Recession, Stagflation (1970s).

Further Reading

Andrew, John A. *Lyndon Johnson and the Great Society.* Chicago: I.R. Dee, 1998.

Karier, Thomas. *Great Experiments in American Economic Policy: From Kennedy to Reagan.* Westport, CT: Praeger, 1997.

Matusow, Allen J. *Nixon's Economy: Booms, Busts, Dollars, and Votes.* Lawrence: University Press of Kansas, 1998.

Mayer, Thomas. *Monetary Policy and the Great Inflation in the United States: The Federal Reserve and the Failure of Macroeconomic Policy, 1965–1979.* Northampton, MA: Edward Elgar, 1999.

Brazil

Located in South America, Brazil, with a population of roughly 190 million, is one of the large emerging countries (along with Russia, India, and China) expected to play a prominent role in the global economy in the twenty-first century. Despite its growing economy and substantial industrial and agricultural exports, Brazil still suffers from widespread poverty, high illiteracy, and a poor education system. Brazil also has one of the highest Gini coefficients, the most common measure of income inequality, of any country in the world. This inequality is a remnant of Brazil's uneven economic development over the past 500 years.

This is not the first time that Brazil has been characterized as an emerging economic power. Since the explorer Pedro Cabral first claimed Brazil as Portuguese territory in 1500, Brazil has experienced four major economic development cycles. The first three cycles were driven by booms in different exports in the seventeenth, eighteenth, and nineteenth centuries, respectively. In contrast, the last of the four cycles, in the twentieth century, was stimulated by intentional government policies designed to spur domestic industrial development by restricting international trade. Each of the development cycles ended with Brazil's standard of living still far below those of leading contemporary economies.

Sugar Cycle

When Pedro Cabral accidentally bumped into the Brazilian coast on his way to India around the Horn of Africa, Portugal was a small country more interested in establishing trading posts in Africa and the East Indies than in colonizing vast foreign territories in the Americas, as its Iberian neighbor Spain did after 1500. However, in Brazil there was little to trade; the most valuable early resource export was brazilwood, the source of a red dye that proved to be of little value beyond giving the new territory its name. The Portuguese thus switched to the colonization strategy of awarding large tracts of land (*capitanias*) to wealthy Portuguese citizens (*donatários*) willing to go to Brazil to invest in their properties and attract colonists. In exchange for land titles, *donatários* agreed to pay the crown 20 percent of the revenues generated on the land. According to economic historian William Glade, this system made early Brazilian colonization "a business venture, combined with aspects of private subgovernment." A small elite came to dominate Brazil's society and economy.

With no easy riches to exploit except for fertile tropical lands, the Portuguese *donatário* introduced crops from elsewhere in the Portuguese empire, most notably sugarcane from the Portuguese Azores and Cabo Verde islands in the Atlantic. Sugarcane grew very well in the Northeast region of Brazil where the Portuguese first settled. But sugar production was labor intensive, and labor was in short supply in the *capitanias*. There were few Portuguese settlers, and the native population mostly fled into the interior of the country to escape disease and hard labor. Brazilian landowners thus began importing slave labor from Portuguese outposts in Africa, initiating the Atlantic slave trade. By 1600, Brazil was the world's leading sugar producer, and slaves outnumbered Portuguese settlers in Brazil.

The Brazilian sugar boom ended in the late seventeenth century when other European colonial powers introduced sugar to their own colonies. Most colonial empires limited foreign trade to their own colonies, and Brazil's "mother country," Portugal, offered a very small market for sugar. Other products such as tobacco and cotton faced the same limitations. The Brazilian plantations stagnated, leaving a society characterized by huge income inequalities and little lasting economic development, although plantation owners had accumulated substantial riches. The Northeast region of Brazil remains the poorest region of the country today.

Mining Cycle

During the 1690s, gold and diamonds were discovered in parts of what is today the state of Minas Gerais (General Mines) in the interior of the country. Nearly half of the world's output of gold during the eighteenth century would come from Minas Gerais. Some planters from the Northeast moved their slaves to the region to work in the gold mines, but mostly the mining boom attracted new settlers from Portugal and

elsewhere. The gold cycle generated more diverse economic development than did the sugar cycle because gold mining was based on small operations. Miners' demand for food and transportation stimulated farming and the raising of mules to carry supplies and gold between Minas Gerais and the coastal city of Rio de Janeiro.

The gold cycle also led to a greater government presence in Brazil as Portuguese bureaucrats were deployed to collect a 20 percent government tax on gold. To minimize tax evasion, Portugal limited transport to a single mule trail between Rio and Minas Gerais. Also, ships leaving Brazil had to sail in annual convoys accompanied by government escorts back to Portugal. Of course, some smuggling occurred, but the economically oppressive measures mostly fueled resentment of the crown. The first open uprising against the Portuguese colonial government occurred in Minas Gerais in 1788. Another effect of the gold cycle was the emergence of Rio de Janeiro as the colony's largest city, through which all commerce with Minas Gerais passed.

Rio de Janeiro gained a huge increase in stature when, in 1807, the Portuguese royal court fled Napoleon's Iberian invasion and made Rio the capital of the Portuguese Empire. The wealthy Brazilian families schemed to declare independence in 1822 when the Portuguese crown returned to Lisbon and reduced Brazil's status once again to a distant colony. Interestingly, the Brazilian elite opted for a monarchy rather than the republican form of government most former Spanish colonies in Latin America chose after independence. They urged the son of the Portuguese king to remain in Brazil as Emperor Dom Pedro I, which he did; he was succeeded by his son in 1831. Brazil remained a monarchy until 1889, effectively ruled by a somewhat shaky coalition of elite business and agricultural classes. A republican form of government was finally adopted in 1889 after years of debate within the elite about slavery (abolished in 1888) and monarchy. The republic, like the monarchy, was increasingly dominated by wealthy coffee barons, the new elite that emerged from the third development cycle.

Coffee Cycle

Coffee trees were introduced to Brazil from the Middle East early in the eighteenth century. The trees require a combination of cool but never cold weather, and they die from frost, which is often found in the higher altitudes of tropical countries. The vast coastal highlands of Brazil fit the requirements for coffee cultivation perfectly. Worldwide demand for coffee grew rapidly during that nineteenth century as the incomes of middle-class consumers in Europe and the United States grew and as Brazil's efficient production lowered costs. The coffee trade was also helped by Europe's abandonment of protectionist colonial trade preferences, and by the decline in shipping costs by over 70 percent between 1840 and the early twentieth century due to the development of metal steamships. Coffee cultivation spread from the Paraíba valley near Rio de Janeiro southward toward the state of São Paulo and westward into the former mining region of Minas Gerais. The port of Santos, just below the São Paulo plateau, became the world's largest coffee port.

Coffee farming required large amounts of labor, and because the importation of slaves was no longer permitted, the coffee boom attracted large numbers of immigrants from Portugal, Italy, Spain, Germany, and many other parts of Europe. The Southern region of Brazil, from São Paulo down to the Uruguayan border, became a melting pot of European immigrants, augmented later by immigrations from Japan and the Middle East, and by internal migration of Brazilians from the poor Northeast region. British investment in infrastructure followed, and railroads soon fanned out from the port of Santos and the nearby city of São Paulo into the interior of the state. By 1900, Brazil produced half the world's coffee, and the export accounted for 80 percent of the country's export earnings.

The wealth accumulated by São Paulo coffee barons laid the basis for Brazilian industrialization. At the start of the twentieth century, the growing immigrant population was creating a viable market for locally produced textiles, clothing, footwear, woodworking, and processed foods. Most of the new industries were established in the city of São Paulo. However, coffee's role as the "engine of growth," as one historian called it, was weakened by the volatility of coffee prices and by overproduction, as other countries, such as Colombia and Mexico, planted more coffee trees. The politically powerful Brazilian coffee interests pushed the government to guarantee prices and purchase excess stocks. After the sharp rise of prices in the 1920s following the world economy's recovery from the war, there came a price decline of over two-thirds at the start of the Great Depression; the Brazilian government's political response to this latest coffee bust would effectively create the next development cycle: the import substitution industrialization cycle.

Import Substitution Industrialization

The collapse of coffee prices in 1930 greatly reduced foreign exchange earnings and government tax revenues. In response, the Brazilian government imposed foreign exchange controls and sharply devalued the national currency but guaranteed Brazilian coffee farmers the same local currency prices they received before devaluation. By making imports much more expensive, foreign trade was balanced by causing imports to fall from $417 million in 1929 to just $108 million in 1932. The price support of coffee was a huge subsidy to the largest sector of the Brazilian economy; it effectively constituted a huge fiscal stimulus. The government's payments were largely financed by printing money, not raising taxes, so the fiscal expansion was effectively augmented by an expansionary monetary policy, just as John Maynard Keynes (1936) would some years later prescribe as the solution to the Great Depression. Economic historian Celso Furtado writes: "Unconsciously Brazil undertook an anticyclical policy of larger relative proportions than had been practiced in industrial countries until that time." The "accidental" Keynesian program worked, and while much of the world was in the Depression, Brazilian industrial production grew rapidly throughout the 1930s as augmented internal demand was channeled toward domestic producers when the price of imports rose sharply after the devaluation of the currency.

The 1930s experience influenced Brazilian policy makers in the 1940s and 1950s, when World War II and the postwar economic worldwide economy recovery increased demand for Brazil's raw materials. The value of the Brazilian currency rose as a result of export expansion, and the prices of domestic goods relative to foreign goods moved in the opposite direction from what occurred in the 1930s. In response to the pleas from the new Brazilian industrialists, and justified by various popular economic and political arguments popularized by the United Nations Economic Commission for Latin America and its head Raúl Prebisch, the Brazilian government imposed strict import restrictions to protect Brazilian industries. Such intentional trade restrictions to promote domestic industrial production came to be known as "import substitution industrialization" (ISI).

Brazil passed the "law of similars" in 1948, which explicitly banned all imports of "similar" products as soon as any domestic firm showed it could supply the domestic market. Under this legislation, any product would be protected, whether it cost twice as much or five times as much to produce in Brazil as it did in the rest of the world. The law of similars thus severed the link between underlying comparative advantage and domestic production. It effectively awarded domestic producers indefinite subsidies paid for by Brazilian consumers, who faced the high prices charged by producers protected from foreign competition. Despite the apparent cost of ISI, it seemed to work. Domestic industrialization grew rapidly, and by the late 1950s Brazilian factories, often owned and operated by foreign multinational firms, were producing automobiles, electrical equipment, nearly all consumer goods, construction equipment, tools, and, by the late 1960s, aircraft. Brazil's status

today as one of the emerging world industrial powers has its roots in the ISI period after World War II. Brazil also achieved some of the fastest growth rates of any developing country during the 1960s and 1970s.

The ISI policies made São Paulo and its surroundings the industrial capital of Brazil. They also made the southern part of the country much wealthier than the rest of Brazil. The near middle-class living standards in many parts of southern Brazil combine with the historically based extreme poverty of the Northeast and the poverty-fed slums of the major cities housing migrants from the country's poor regions to give Brazil its very unequal income distribution.

In addition to worsening the income distribution, ISI caused other unsustainable economic changes, as evidenced by the financial crisis of 1982. That year, the Brazilian government and its agencies defaulted on nearly $100 billion in foreign debt, and the sudden reversal of capital inflows brought Brazilian growth to a complete halt. After several decades of rapid per capita income growth, between 3 and 6 percent per year in real terms over the three decades between 1950 and 1980, per capita income actually fell between 1980 and 1990. It grew at just 1 percent during the 1990s. Economist Victor Elias's data also show a sharp slowdown in total factor productivity—the rate at which output increases in excess of the growth of all inputs—from 3.7 percent per year in the 1950s to just 1 percent per year in the 1970s, and to −1 percent by the early 1980s. The rapid economic growth of the 1970s under ISI thus seems to have led to investment that did little to increase productivity, while foreign borrowing greatly increased Brazil's foreign debt burden.

Brazil borrowed overseas because, under ISI, export earnings as a percentage of gross domestic product (GDP) fell from over 7 percent prior to the ISI period to just 4 percent in the 1950s, and then to just above 2 percent by the late 1970s. As should have been expected, ISI reduced Brazil's capacity to produce exports because the protected

Traders at the Brazilian Mercantile and Futures Exchange in São Paolo celebrate a rebound in stock prices in early 2008 after the U.S. Federal Reserve cut interest rates to stave off recession. The United States is Brazil's main export market. *(Bloomberg/Getty Images)*

Brazilian industry had little incentive to compete in export markets. Yet Brazil had to import increasing amounts of oil, industrial equipment, parts, components, other raw materials, and technology to sustain the growing domestic industrial sector. The external imbalance from the ISI period represented a challenge to Brazilian policy makers after the 1982 debt crisis stopped Brazilian growth and effectively brought the fourth development cycle to an end.

A Fifth Economic Development Cycle?

In his analysis of ISI policies, economist Henry Bruton suggests that while "some form of protection is in order to enable a country to establish its place in the world economy," the period of protection must also be used to "establish an economy that is flexible and resilient." Under pressure to repay loans from the International Monetary Fund and the World Bank, Brazilian leaders introduced so-called Washington consensus policies designed to improve its ability to repay foreign

debt, namely trade liberalization, free investment flows, balanced government budgets, and a reduced government role in the economy. During the 1980s and 1990s, Brazilian leaders struggled to balance the domestic economic interests that had developed under ISI with policies linking the Brazilian economy more closely to the global economy.

Under the recent presidencies of Fernando Henrique Cardoso and Luiz Inácio (Lula) da Silva, both left-leaning politicians, Brazilian economic policy has moved toward an eclectic mixture of open trade policies and continued active government involvement in the economy. Since barely escaping another foreign debt crisis 1998, Brazil has accumulated foreign reserves of over $200 billion, which has stabilized its currency. Foreign investment increased after 2000, and transnational firms increased their industrial and agricultural exports from Brazil. Brazil's own mixed state-private companies Petrobras (oil) and Vale do Rio Doce (mining) have transformed themselves into global corporations. A number of private Brazilian firms that grew up under ISI protectionism have also become "outward oriented," some even investing overseas, a sign that Brazil has abandoned ISI policies in favor of integration with the global corporate economy.

Per capita real growth of GDP rose to about 2.5 percent between 2000 and 2009, an improvement on the 1980s and 1990s. Meanwhile, international economists had praised Brazil for getting its macroeconomic fundamentals together, keeping inflation low and even boasting growth through the financial crisis and global recession of the late 2000s. And this fiscal probity did not come at the expense of the poor, as is often the case in developing economies seeking to balance budgets, as Brazil saw a gradual reduction in income inequality and poverty, previously two of the main weaknesses of the country's economic and social order. Finally, with the discovery of potentially large oil fields off its southern coast, Brazil looked to become a major petroleum producer as well.

Now the question for the country, agree economists, is whether the gradual moves toward more income inequality and lower levels of poverty will turn the modest growth recovery of the past decade into a new development cycle that finally puts Brazil on a consistent path toward economic development.

Hendrik Van den Berg

See also: Argentina; BRIC (Brazil, Russia, India, China); Emerging Markets; Latin America.

Further Reading

Baer, Werner. *The Brazilian Economy: Growth and Development.* 4th ed. Westport, CT: Praeger, 1995.

Elias, Victor J. *Sources of Growth: A Study of Seven Latin American Economies.* San Francisco: ICS Press, 1989.

Furtado, Celso. *The Economic Growth of Brazil: A Survey from Colonial Times to Modern Times.* Berkeley: University of California Press, 1963.

Glade, William P. *The Latin American Economies: A Study of Their Institutional Evolution.* New York: American Book, 1969.

Maddison, Angus. *Monitoring the World Economy, 1820–1992.* Paris: OECD, 1995.

Prebisch, Raúl. *The Economic Development of Latin America and Its Principal Problems.* Lake Success, NY: United Nations Department of Social Affairs, 1950.

Skidmore, Thomas E., and Peter H. Smith. *Modern Latin America.* 3rd ed. New York: Oxford University Press, 1992.

Stein, Stanley J. *Vassouras: A Brazilian Coffee County, 1850–1890.* New York: Atheneum, 1974.

Summerhill, William R. "Railroads in Imperial Brazil, 1854–1889." In *Latin America and the World Economy Since 1800*, ed. John H. Coatsworth and Alan M. Taylor, 383–405. Cambridge, MA: Harvard University Press, 1998.

Thorp, Rosemary. *Progress, Poverty, and Exclusion: An Economic History of Latin America in the 20th Century.* Washington, DC: Inter-American Development Bank, 1998.

BRIC (Brazil, Russia, India, China)

BRIC is an acronym coined by the investment company Goldman Sachs in 2003 to represent the group of four rapidly expanding economies that consists of Brazil, Russia, India, and China—sometimes referred to as "the BRIC" or "BRICs." By the year 2050, each of these developing countries is expected to be wealthier than most of today's major economic powers. According to Goldman Sachs and adherents of its view, China and India will become the world's largest suppliers of manufactured goods and services, respectively, while Brazil and Russia will dominate as suppliers of raw materials. Because of their lower labor and production costs, these nations are also expected to represent a growing opportunity for foreign expansion on the part of firms in the developed world.

The BRIC countries, taken together, have contributed almost 40 percent of global economic growth since 2000. As of 2008, their combined economies (adjusted for cost of living) exceeded that of the United States and accounted for 22 percent of the global economy. China has been the single-largest driver of growth, with its share of world output rising from 6 percent to 11 percent in just one decade.

Although the BRICs are unlikely to organize as a trading bloc like the European Union, or even a formal trading association like ASEAN (the Association of Southeast Asian Nations), there are strong indicators that the four countries recognize their growing economic power and look forward to transforming it into greater geopolitical clout. The BRIC countries encompass more than a quarter of the world's landmass, account for 40 percent of the world's population, and held a combined gross domestic product (GDP) of some $15.5 trillion in 2009. With or without a formal trading bloc, they constitute the largest economic entity in the global market by virtually any measure.

According to several forecasts, the BRIC economies together will account for more than half the market size of the G-8 nations (Canada, France, Germany, Italy, Japan, Russia, United Kingdom, and United States) by 2025 and exceed them by 2050. (As of 2009, they accounted for less than 15 percent of the aggregate G-8 GDP.) Of the G-8 nations, only the United States and Japan are expected to be among the world's six largest economies in 2050. The shift in GDP is expected to be most dramatic through 2030, with a significant deceleration in the following two decades. Only India is likely to see growth rates above 3 percent in the 2030–2050 period. With the exception of Russia, individuals in the BRIC countries are likely to remain poorer than their counterparts in the G-8 economies. China's per capita income is forecast to grow to about $30,000 by 2050, according to some economic analyses.

In order to help these nations reach their economic potential, policy makers in the four countries have continued to focus on education, foreign investment, domestic consumption, and domestic entrepreneurship. India has the potential to grow the fastest among the BRICs, primarily because the decline in average age will occur later for India than in Russia, China, and Brazil. According to Goldman Sachs, India's per capita GDP will quadruple between 2007 and 2020, the Indian economy will exceed that of the United States by 2043, and the four BRIC nations as a group will overtake the G-8 by 2032.

World Rankings, BRICs, 2009

	Brazil	Russia	India	China
Population	5	9	2	1
Total area	5	1	7	3
GDP (nominal)	10	11	12	4
GDP (PPP*)	9	7	4	2
Exports	21	11	23	2
Imports	27	17	16	3
Received FDI	16	12	29	5
Foreign exchange reserves	7	3	4	1
Number of mobile phones	5	4	2	1
Number of Internet users	5	11	4	1

*Purchasing power parity.

Impact of Global Recession

All four countries in BRIC have suffered economic downturns as a result of the 2008–2009 global recession, albeit to different extents. Brazil was the hardest hit, but the effects of the recession were softened by the boom period that preceded it and by a relatively strong economic foundation. The Brazilian stock market (Bovespa) had skyrocketed from 9,000 in 2002 to more than 60,000 in 2008, and government policies, such as lowered interest rates, favored investment. In addition, much of the nation's foreign debt was retired and the economy was bolstered by strong capital inflows and booming exports in 2008, primarily due to the global commodity boom of the previous year.

Russia, which averaged growth of more than 7 percent over a period of ten years, has shown signs of economic contraction on par with other hard-hit countries. Exports plummeted, and industrial production fell by almost 9 percent in 2008. Especially damaging to the Russian economy was the collapse of oil prices in mid-2008. Foreign exchange reserves dropped significantly despite currency depreciation, and refinancing of external loans became extremely difficult.

India, too, was hurt by the global recession of 2008–2009, suffering a sharp economic deceleration following the international credit crunch. Merchandise exports fell by 12 percent in 2008, with sales data from a wide array of industries and services suggesting further slowdowns in the future. India's currency, the rupee, depreciated by 20 percent in just one year, and stock prices remained low despite a mild recovery in late 2008.

China has been the major economic force among the four BRICs, primarily because of the global growth spurt of 2003–2005, which propelled a massive commodity boom from 2006 to 2008. Yet even China's export growth turned negative in 2008, resulting in the closure of thousands of factories that had produced toys, textiles, electronics, and other labor-intensive exports.

Future Economic Growth

Among the four countries, China has registered the strongest economic growth in recent years— 11.9 percent in 2007 and 9.4 percent in 2008. Forecasts for 2009 by the World Bank, Goldman Sachs, and Citibank ranged from 1.5 to 3.0 percent. India has recorded the second-highest growth among the BRICs—9.0 percent in 2007 and 6.3 percent in 2008, with forecasts of 5.5 to 6.0 percent for 2009. The Russian economy expanded by 8.1 percent in 2007 and 6.0 percent in 2008, with projections of 1 to 4 percent for 2009. The Brazilian economy grew by 5.4 percent in 2007 and 5.2 percent in 2008, and was expected to grow by 2 to 3 percent in 2009.

According to an Ernst & Young research report published in December 2008, titled "For Richer, For Poorer: Global Patterns of Wealth," the BRIC countries will contribute 40 percent of global economic growth between 2009 and 2020, with China alone accounting for one-quarter. China is also expected to be the largest economy in the world in terms of purchase parity by 2019 (taking cost of living into consideration). The BRIC countries are also expected to account for 65 percent of global basic metal consumption as well as 38 percent of chemical products, 30 percent of motor vehicles, and 28 percent of electronics by 2020. In all sectors, China will contribute the lion's share of growth.

Assumptions and Criticisms

The major assumptions underlying BRIC projections are that the four countries will continue to pursue established economic policies and to develop institutions supportive of growth. Bad public policy, natural disasters, and any number of external factors could derail the projections. Proactive growth policies will have to continue at both the national and the global levels, and the pace of reform must be steady or accelerate, given the political and social tensions in these countries. Demographic factors such as declining fertility rates represent another area of potential risk.

Another assumption underlying the BRIC thesis is that the four countries have abundant untapped energy sources, such as oil, coal, fossil fuels, and natural gas. However, should any of the countries reach peak production before renewable energy sources can be developed and commercialized, economic growth will be slower than anticipated. Furthermore, given the current technology, there is a limit to how much the BRICs can develop their natural resources before exceeding the ability of the global economy to absorb them. These countries also have enormous populations of impoverished people, which could hinder economic progress, increase social unrest, and limit market demand. Finally, factors that are impossible to predict or plan for—such as international conflict, civic unrest, acts of terrorism, or outbreaks of disease—can have an impact on the destiny of any country.

Abhijit Roy

See also: Brazil; China; Emerging Markets; India; Russia and the Soviet Union; Transition Economies.

Further Reading

Bird, Robert C. "Defending Intellectual Property Rights in the BRIC Economies." *American Business Law Journal* 43:2 (2006): 317–363.

Tamazian, Artur, Juan Piñeiro Chousa, and Krishna Chaitanya Vadlamannati. "Does Higher Economic and Financial Development Lead to Environmental Degradation? Evidence from BRIC Countries." *Energy Policy* 37:1 (2009): 246–253.

Wilson, Dominic, and Roopa Purushthaman. "Dreaming with BRICs: The Path to 2050." *Goldman Sachs Global Economics Paper No. 99,* 2003. Available at www2.goldmansachs.com/ideas/brics/brics-dream.html. Accessed May 2010.

Brunner, Karl (1916–1989)

A Swiss-American economist who was a leading early member of the monetarist school, Karl Brunner was influential in the founding of two economic watchdog groups that monitor global economic policy: the Shadow Open Market Committee and the Shadow European Economic Policy Committee, both established in the early 1970s. As a monetarist, Brunner believed that prices and inflation are closely tied to the growth of a nation's money supply. He was known as a critic of the U.S. Federal Reserve, citing its failure to maintain steady growth in the money supply as a destabilizing factor in the nation's economy.

Born on February 16, 1916, in Zurich, Switzerland, Brunner attended the University of Zurich from 1934 to 1937, studied at the London School of Economics for the next two years, and then earned his PhD back at the University of Zurich in 1943. After working for the Swiss National Bank, Brunner arrived in the United States in 1948 on a Rockefeller Foundation fellowship. After spending a semester at Harvard, he moved to the University of Chicago, where he was greatly influenced by Milton Friedman, Frank Knight, and others, who advocated a brand of free-market libertarianism, took a neoclassical approach to price theory, and attempted to bring economic reasoning to other realms of social science. Outside the discipline of economics, Brunner also wrote and taught in such fields as logic and the philosophy of science.

Eventually becoming a U.S. citizen, Brunner went on to teach at the University of California–Los Angeles (UCLA), Ohio State University, and the University of Rochester, where he served until his death as the Fred H. Gowen professor of economics at the William E. Simon Graduate School of Business Administration and as director of the Simon School's Bradley Policy Research Center.

In addition to his academic work, Brunner advised international governments on economic and financial policy, and established a number of influential economic research and policy bodies. An active organizer, academic, and policy advocate, he founded the Carnegie-Rochester Conference Series on Public Policy, the Konstanz Seminar on Monetary Analysis and Policy, and the Interlaken Seminar on Analysis and Ideology, later renamed the Karl Brunner Symposium. He also served as an adviser to the Swiss National Bank and other European central banks, in which capacity he advocated a policy of low inflation as critically important to economic growth.

Much of Brunner's work was in collaboration with the economist Allan H. Meltzer and in agreement with Milton Friedman and the Chicago school of economics. Brunner and Meltzer argued that the modern system of monetary circulation is profoundly affected by the lending practices of banks and the control of the money supply. In developing his theories on monetary supply and its relationship to business cycles, Brunner examined the activities of central banks, commercial banks, and other lending institutions in order to gauge the supply of money and credit at a given time and to understand its effect on business cycles and economic stability within different countries.

In addition to founding the *Journal of Money, Credit and Banking* and the *Journal of Monetary Economics,* Brunner wrote or co-wrote more than a dozen books, including *Monetary Economics* (1989), and *Money and the Economy: Issues in Monetary Analysis* (1989), both with Meltzer, and well over a hundred published papers. He also edited *The First World and the Third World* (1978) and *The Great Depression Revisited* (1981). He died on May 9, 1989, in Rochester, New York.

Andrew J. Waskey

See also: Friedman, Milton; Monetary Theories and Models.

Further Reading

Brunner, Karl. *Money and the Economy: Issues in Monetary Analysis.* New York: Cambridge University Press, 1993.

Brunner, Karl, and Allan H. Meltzer. "The Uses of Money in the Theory of an Exchange Economy." *American Economic Review* 61 (December 1971):784–805.

Lys, Thomas, ed. *Economic Analysis and Political Ideology: Selected Essays of Karl Brunner.* Cheltenham, UK: Edward Elgar, 1996.

Bullock, Charles (1869–1941)

Charles Jesse Bullock was a Harvard economist and monetary expert whose career flourished during the early years of the 1900s. His work touched on a number of the important economic issues of the day as well as significant aspects of the history of economics. His most important achievements centered on the measurement and forecasting of business cycles.

Bullock was born on May 21, 1869, in Boston. After beginning his higher education through a correspondence course, he graduated from Boston University in 1892 while working as a high school principal. After obtaining his PhD from the University of Wisconsin in 1895, Bullock became an instructor in economics at Cornell University, taught at Williams College from 1899 to 1903, and then took a position at Harvard University, where he remained for the next thirty-one years.

Bullock's area of expertise was public finance, though he also notable made contributions to the study of international economics before 1914 and to the history of economics. He served as a tax adviser to Massachusetts, among other states, and was a member of Phi Beta Kappa, the American Academy of Arts and Sciences, the American Economic Association, the Statistical Association, the Harvard Economics Society (president, 1927), and the National Academy of Arts and Sciences. From 1917 to 1919, Bullock served as president of the National Tax Association.

As director of Harvard's Committee on Economic Research from 1917 to 1929, Bullock worked with colleagues to develop the "barometric" approach to business cycles. Their "three-curve" barometer, also known as the Harvard barometer, was used to measure expansions and contractions in business cycles. The A curve was based on stock prices and the loans of New York City banks; the B curve was based on wholesale prices and loan totals of banks outside New York; and the C curve used short-term interest rates as a reflection of financial conditions. Together, the A, B, and C curves were grouped into a statistical description that could be used to examine economic fluctuations as deviations from major trends. For example, seasonal fluctuations in economic areas such as jobs, harvests, and travel might be grouped into composite indices. The Harvard barometer was widely used in the 1920s as an economic forecasting tool and became the basis of a variety of other quantitative measures. Bullock's committee published its findings in the *Review of Economic Statistics* (later titled the *Review of Economics and Statistics*), which provided a forum for discussions about business cycles, their size, and timing.

In addition to his work on business cycles, Bullock made significant contributions to the study of economic history, especially financial practices in colonial America. His study of colonial monetary policy examined its impact on the American Revolution and consequences for the new republic. Bullock concluded that British colonial authorities had mismanaged the financial resources of their day. His major published works include the *Finances of the United States from 1775–1789, with Special Reference to the Budget* (1895); *Introduction to the Study of Economics* (1897); *Essays on the Monetary History of the United States* (1900); and *Finances of Massachusetts, 1780–1905* (1907).

In his last years, Bullock focused his studies on the effects of economic and financial practice in politics and society, resulting in his influential *Economic Essays* (1936) and *Politics, Finance and Consequences* (1939). Bullock died on March 17, 1941, in Hingham, Massachusetts.

Andrew J. Waskey

See also: Fiscal Policy; Tax Policy.

Further Reading

Bullock, Charles Jesse. *Economic Essays.* Reprint ed. Freeport, NY: Books for Libraries Press, 1968.
———. *Elements of Economics.* Boston: Silver Burdett, 1905.
———. *Essays on the Monetary History of the United States.* Reprint ed. New York: Greenwood, 1969.

Burchardt, Fritz (1902–1958)

German economist Fritz Adolph "Frank" Burchardt is best known for his extensive theoretical work on economic growth and business cycles. His research encompassed the related areas of employment, monetary policy, production theory, and international trade. A founder of the so-called Kiel school, whose members included some of the most important German academic economists, Burchardt became known as a prominent critic of monetary trade-cycle theories in Weimar Germany.

Born in Barenburg, Germany, in 1902, Burchardt received a doctorate in economics from the University of Kiel (Germany) in 1925. He remained at Kiel from 1926 to 1933, working closely with sociologist and economist Adolph Lowe. The Kiel school was affiliated with the Kiel Institute of World Economics, a center for the study of business cycles founded in 1914 by Bernhard Harms. Under Lowe's leadership, the school's reformist mission attracted a group of brilliant young economists, including Gerhard Colm, Hans Neisser, Wassily Leontief, and Jacob Marschak. During the same period, Burchardt also pursued postdoctoral training in economics at Frankfurt's Goethe University, where his thesis was accepted in the winter of 1932–1933. His studies were cut short with the rise to power of the Nazi Party and his subsequent dismissal from his academic post.

Fleeing the Nazis, Burchardt moved to England in 1935 and joined the Oxford Institute of Statistics. Four years later, however, after the outbreak of World War II, he was among 65,000 young Germans interned by the British as enemy aliens on the Isle of Man. Thanks to the protests of influential colleagues, including British economist John Maynard Keynes, Burchardt was released from the internment camp in November 1940.

Back at Oxford, Burchardt revamped the *Bulletin* of the Institute of Statistics and coordinated the research of various colleagues. At the same time, he was also developing his theories of business cycles and economic growth, which expanded on his work with Lowe at the Kiel Institute. In 1944, Burchardt edited a famous cooperative study titled *The Economics of Full Employment*, with contributors from such notable Central European émigrés as Thomas Balogh, Kurt Mandelbaum, Ernst F. Schumacher, and Burchardt himself. Their flight from Central Europe before and during World War II would impoverish the economics departments at German and Austrian universities for the next generation and beyond.

Burchardt's work focused on monetary explanations of business cycles, including a comprehensive survey of the topic from a historical perspective, written in 1928 when he was still in Germany. In 1932, Burchardt made a significant contribution to the development of economic growth theory with a comparative analysis of Austrian and Marxist approaches to that subject. He was particularly interested in showing how the study of both vertically integrated production systems and interindustry linkages informs economists about patterns of economic growth and the ups and downs of the business cycle.

Burchardt sought to apply the same theories to government. His criticisms of the Weimar Republic's trade-cycle theories were in keeping with the reforms sought by the Kiel school, which aimed to develop innovative theories of growth in light of monetary policy, production structures, and the business cycle. Burchardt was also interested in applying his research to the issue of international trade. In a May 1943 article in *Economica* titled "Multilateral Clearing," he addressed the problems of international trade and capital movements within the context of Keynesian economic theory. In 1948, he became the first economist (and nonmathematician) to be named director of the Oxford Institute of Statistics. Burchardt died on December 21, 1958.

Andrew J. Waskey

See also: Austrian School; Growth, Economic; Kalecki, Michal; Marxist Cycle Model.

Further Reading

Burchardt, F.A., et al. *The Economics of Full Employment: Six Studies in Applied Economics.* Oxford, UK: Basil Blackwell, 1944.

Lowe, A. "F.A. Burchardt, Part I: Recollections of His Work in Germany." *Bulletin of Oxford University Institute of Statistics* 21 (1959): 59–65.

Worswick, G.D.N. "F.A. Burchardt, Part II: Burchardt's Work in Oxford." *Bulletin of the Oxford University Institute of Statistics* 21 (1959): 66–72.

Burns, Arthur (1904–1987)

Arthur Frank Burns was an American economist whose career spanned academia and government. He was considered an expert on the measurement of business cycles and served as chairman of the Federal Reserve System (Fed) during the Nixon administration, from 1970 to 1978.

Burns was born on April 27, 1904, in Stanislau, Galicia, in the Austro-Hungarian Empire (now part of Ukraine). His parents immigrated to Bayonne, New Jersey, when he was a child. Burns attended Columbia University in New York City, where he received bachelor's and master's degrees in 1925, pursued graduate studies under Wesley Clair Mitchell, and was awarded a PhD in 1934. Burns taught economics at Rutgers University from 1927 until 1944, at which time he joined the faculty at Columbia. There, in 1959, he was appointed John Bates Clark professor of economics.

Burns's research at Columbia focused on business cycles. He became a member of the National Bureau of Economic Research (NBER) in 1933,

serving as director of research from 1945 to 1953 and as president from 1957 to 1967. NBER, founded in 1920 as a private, nonprofit research center, sought to promote understanding of the U.S. economy through rigorous research projects and to share the results of its research as nonpartisan economic information. A major interest of the NBER was the business cycle and its relationship to long-term economic growth, which it investigated in detail.

Burns's work on business cycles, much of it in collaboration with his former mentor at Columbia, Mitchell, explored the factors that determine booms and busts as an economy expands and contracts. Together, Burns and Mitchell set the standards for the NBER committee on business cycles as it sought to assign dates to them. Through this work, Burns became known as an expert on the timing and movement of business cycles.

From 1953 until 1956, Burns served as chairman of the Council of Economic Advisers under President Dwight D. Eisenhower. He returned to government service three years later as an economic adviser to President Richard M. Nixon. He was elevated to chairman of the Federal Reserve System in February 1970 and served in that capacity until late January 1978. As Fed chairman, Burns came under attack for his economic beliefs, often by those who were in power. Burns believed in fiscal and monetary restraint (reduced money supply and government spending) as a way to achieve low unemployment and economic growth, but many thought he was too susceptible to political pressures and influences. President Nixon, who had attributed his defeat in the 1960 presidential election to the Fed's tight money policy, now encouraged Burns to follow an easy-credit policy—the very opposite of Burns's belief in fiscal and monetary control. The issue was at the center of U.S. policy debate during the oil crisis of 1973, when the national economy underwent an unusual and debilitating condition called stagflation—a decline in business activity and increased unemployment (stagnation) at the same time that consumer prices were rising (inflation). Contributing to the problem of inflation were government spending on the Vietnam War, congressional deficit spending, and the ongoing cost of Great Society programs. When Burns's term as Fed chair expired in 1978, Democratic president Jimmy Carter chose not to reappoint him to the position. One short-term consequence of this decision was a plunge in value of the dollar.

After leaving government, Burns joined the conservative think tank American Enterprise Institute, where he was free to lecture and write, publishing *Reflections of an Economic Policy Maker* in 1978. He was appointed ambassador to West Germany by President Ronald Reagan, and served in that capacity from 1981 to 1985. He died on June 6, 1987, in Baltimore, Maryland.

Andrew J. Waskey

See also: Federal Reserve System; Monetary Policy; National Bureau of Economic Research; Recession, Stagflation (1970s).

Further Reading

Tuch, Hans N. *Arthur Burns and the Successor Generation: Selected Writings of and About Arthur Burns.* Lanham, MD: University Press of America, 1999.

Wells, Wyatt. *Economist in an Uncertain World: Arthur F. Burns and the Federal Reserve, 1970–1978.* New York: Columbia University Press, 1994.

Business Cycles, International

The study of international business cycles, a relatively new field of inquiry in economics, attempts to explain how swings in national economies or economic groupings affect other national economies and economic groupings. The central question in the study of international business cycle studies is whether and how the business cycles in developed-world economies affect economies in the developing world.

Prior to the rise of international business cycle studies, economists focused their efforts on understanding national economies or, more typi-cally, trying to develop foundational theories and assumptions for economic conditions and performance generally. By the 1970s, however, many economists had come to recognize that the global economy was becoming increasingly integrated. Key to the integration were new communication and transportation technologies (the Internet and container shipping, for example) that made doing business across continents and oceans far simpler and easier. At the same time, increasing computer capacity was making it possible to digest, analyze, and utilize the enormous quantity of economic data being generated around the world—data that made better investment decision making possible. A second key factor in the integration of the world economy was the emergence of new economies in the developing world, most notably those of East and South Asia. Finally, there was a growing awareness among economists that economic "shocks," which began in developed-world economies, could spread to developing world economies, leading economic decision makers in the latter to design and adopt response strategies.

While developing nations were insignificant players on the world scene as late as the 1960s, their economies have come to play an increasingly influential role in the global economy. By the late 2000s, China and India alone accounted for approximately one-quarter of world economic output. Meanwhile, businesses in the developed world began to take advantage of opportunities in the developing world in the form of direct investment or by establishing trade links with suppliers. A number of factors play into these decisions, including government policies in the developed and developing world, geographic location, natural resources, and, importantly, labor markets. With their huge populations of manual workers—and, in some cases, a growing cohort of educated workers—developing world countries offer enormous advantages to firms in the developed world trying to lower costs. Even more rapid has been the financial integration of the world economy, as individuals and institutions take advantage of new communications to invest in

The small town of Wilmington, Ohio, suffered thousands of job losses after the German shipping company DHL closed its hub there in early 2009. In the age of globalization, international business cycles can have a major effect on local economies. *(John Moore/Getty Images)*

national financial markets, in the process creating an integrated global financial system.

Students of international business cycles study this process of integration, as well as its wide-ranging ramifications. The essential question is the extent to which upswings and downswings in one part of the international economy affect other parts—in particular, how much do trends in developed-world economies affect their counterparts in the developing world. This question divides the field into two intellectually competing camps. On the one hand, some theories under the idea of "co-movement" maintain that the more open a country is to international trade the more vulnerable it becomes to external economic shocks. Specifically, proponents argue, the economies of developing world countries that depend on investment from and trade with the developed world are more likely to go into recession when their investment and trading partners do. According to advocates of this view, the United States is crucial in this regard, as it is not only a major source of investment in the developing world but also the world's largest importer, with an increasing portion of that import trade coming from China and other developing world economies. Thus, they argue, while the recession of 2007–2009 may have

begun in the United States, its effects soon spread to the developing world—evidenced by slower growth rates in China and other economies dependent on trade with and investment from the United States. As American consumers closed their wallets and international credit froze up (much of it having come from U.S. financial institutions), so new investment in China slowed, factories shut down, workers were laid off, and the economy slowed.

An opposing theory points to a phenomenon referred to as "decoupling." Adherents of this view maintain that, despite growing economic integration, developing world economies, particularly large ones such as Brazil, China, and India, have effectively become disconnected from swings in the business cycle of the United States and other countries of the developed world. Proponents of decoupling note that, despite the deep recession in the United States, Japan, and Europe, large developing countries either continued to grow or experienced only minor recessions. Decouplers maintain that government policies, trade among developing countries, and, most importantly, dramatic growth in internal markets—as evidenced by enormous increases in the number of middle-class consumers in China and elsewhere—make these countries relatively immune from business downturns in the developed world, even as severe as the 2007–2009 recession.

Current empirical research paints a mixed picture, with data to support both the co-movement and decoupling views of international economic influence. In any event, the rigorous study of international business cycles provides an evolving context for understanding the relationship between the economies of the developed and developing worlds and other aspects of the emerging global economy in the twenty-first century.

Michael Rawdan and James Ciment

See also: Asian Financial Crisis (1997); Emerging Markets; Shock-Based Theories; Transition Economies.

Further Reading

Backus, David, Patrick J. Kehoe, and Finn E. Kydland. "International Business Cycles: Theory and Evidence." Available at www.nber.org/papers/w4493. Accessed April 2009.

Crucini, Mario J., Ayhan Kose, and Christopher Otrok. "What Are the Driving Forces of International Business Cycles?" NBER Working Paper Series No. 14380, October 2008. Available at www.nber.org/papers/w14380.pdf. Accessed March 2010.

Engelhardt, Lucas M. "Business Cycles in an International Context." Available at www.mises.org/journals/scholar/Engelhardt.pdf. Accessed April 2009.

Kose, M., C. Otrok, and E. Prasad. *Global Business Cycles: Convergence or Decoupling?* Washington, DC: International Monetary Fund, 2008.

Lewis, A. *Nobel Lectures, Economics 1969–1980.* Singapore: World Scientific Publishing, 1992.

Canada

Canada is a land of contrasts. It is both a large nation and a small one. The second biggest in the world by landmass, it has the least number of inhabitants of the G-8 group of major economies. While its vast expanses reach to the extreme latitudes of the north, politically, economically, and socially, it is situated somewhere in the middle of the Atlantic. That is to say, Canada stands halfway between the more statist and socialist polities of Western Europe and the freewheeling capitalism of its huge neighbor to the south, the United States.

Sharing a 3,000-mile (4,825-kilometer) border with the largest economy on Earth, Canada has often experienced the same economic ups and downs as the United States, even if its more extensive social safety net has sometimes better cushioned its citizens from the privations of the latter. Canada was one of the nations hardest hit by the Great Depression, for example, though it has been less deeply affected by the financial crisis and recession of the late 2000s.

Economic History

Canadian history has often paralleled that of the United States. Home to hundreds of thousands of indigenous people in the pre-Columbian era, it was settled by Europeans beginning in the seventeenth century and became an important British colony in the eighteenth. Unlike the United States, Canada did not win its freedom as a result of revolution but was granted increasing autonomy during the nineteenth century, culminating in its independence in 1867. The late nineteenth and early twentieth centuries saw Canadians settle the vast expanses of the West and build a substantial industrial and transportation infrastructure. Like the United States, Canada is a land of immigrants, with similar waves of Eastern and Southern Europeans coming to the country around the turn of the twentieth century and another wave of peoples arriving from the developing world in the latter half of the century. The parallels are not perfect. One significant difference between the two countries has to do with ethnicity; Canada had almost no slavery, little history of racism, and, until recently, few persons of African descent. Instead, it has a sizable French-speaking population—largely situated in the eastern province of Quebec—which has often seen itself as an oppressed minority.

The modern Canadian economy owes much to the work of John A. Macdonald, the country's first prime minister. In the 1870s and 1880s, he pushed

Trade ministers of the United States, Canada, and Mexico (left to right) convene in Vancouver in 2007 for their annual meeting to oversee the North American Free Trade Agreement. Free trade has been a boon to the Canadian economy, one of the world's most stable. *(Bloomberg/Getty Images)*

through a transcontinental railroad that helped unite the far-flung reaches of the continent-wide country economically. Macdonald also pushed for protective tariffs to allow the country's infant industrial base to grow. But for all Macdonald's efforts, Canada remained mired in an economic slump throughout much of his administration. Most immigrants preferred the warmer climes of the United States, and the long global recession from the 1870s through the early 1890s meant that there was slack demand for the country's vast natural resources—from timber to minerals to fish.

Only with the revival of the world economy in the 1890s did Canada itself truly begin to grow into an economic power and draw in large numbers of immigrants. Huge new mineral deposits were discovered in northern Ontario, along with the last great gold discovery of the nineteenth century in the Yukon. A burgeoning population on the country's vast great plains led to soaring wheat production while new transportation infrastructure allowed for the more effective exploitation of the country's vast timber resources.

In the twentieth century, the Canadian economy became closely linked to that of the United States. As with its neighbor to the south, Canada

enjoyed flush economic times in the 1920s—buoyed by increasing consumer spending—but was hard hit by America's Great Depression, experiencing similarly high levels of unemployment and shrinking gross domestic product (GDP). Although under conservative leadership for the first half of the 1930s, Canada developed its own set of New Deal–like programs to regulate business and provide jobs, though it was only with the country's 1939 entry into World War II that unemployment dropped to pre-Depression levels.

Emerging out of World War II as one of the largest economies in the world (like the United States, its infrastructure was spared wartime destruction), Canada basked in the global prosperity of the 1950s and 1960s, its natural resources in great demand from industries in the United States, Europe, and Japan, and its industrial capacity expanding to meet rising consumer demand at home. During these years, Canada expanded its social welfare system to provide Social Security–like public old-age pension and welfare programs to aid the poor. Unlike the United States, however, Canada also created a universal health care program from the late 1940s onward that eventually evolved into a single-payer system, whereby provincial governments—aided by the federal government—use tax revenues to pay for the health services provided by private doctors and hospitals.

With its economy heavily dependent on natural resources, which experienced steep price hikes in the 1970s, parts of Canada, particularly the oil-rich province of Alberta, prospered even as industrial Ontario and Quebec experienced a recession due to a flagging U.S. economy. When commodity prices, including oil, fell in the 1980s, Canada went into a prolonged period of slow or negative growth, with high unemployment and growing government deficits.

The slump produced political disaffection, as voters turned from the Progressive Conservatives, the center-right party, to the Liberals, the center-left party, in the early 1990s. The new government, under Prime Minister Jean Chrétien, soon began to put Canada's fiscal house in order, with the federal government posting surpluses in every fiscal year since 1996. It was aided in this by a rapidly growing North American economy, now more integrated than ever since the passage of the Canada–United States Free Trade Agreement of 1988, renamed the North American Free Trade Agreement (NAFTA) with the inclusion of Mexico in the early 1990s.

The dot.com bust of the early 2000s left Canada largely unaffected, though market valuations on the Toronto Stock Exchange, the country's main securities exchange, fell. Thus, while the United States fell into recession in 2002, the Canadian economy continued to grow, one of the few times in history that has occurred.

Financial Crisis of the 2000s

Canada has not been as fortunate in the wake of the financial crisis originating in the U.S. housing market in 2007, though the Canadian banking system has weathered the crisis better than that of many other countries. There are a number of reasons for this. First, Canada has much stricter lending rules for mortgages. By law, homebuyers must put down 20 percent of the cost of the home and there are strict rules against adjustable rate mortgages. Unlike Americans, Canadians do not receive tax breaks for mortgage interest, thereby discouraging people from taking on mortgages they could not normally afford. At the same time, there are tighter rules against homeowners walking away from mortgages when they cannot make the payments. Such regulations have meant that Canada avoided the subprime mortgage crisis experienced in the United States.

Canadian banks operate in similarly more cautious ways, both out of custom and because of tighter regulations. They tend to operate in a more traditional manner, being more liquid and less highly leveraged, though some had invested in the mortgage-backed securities that brought down a number of major U.S. banks.

Still, Canada is not expected to escape the reverberations of the financial crisis entirely. With more than 80 percent of its exports going to the United States, Canada cannot help but be affected by the deep recession south of its border. In particular, timber exports have plummeted with the crash in housing starts in the United States. More generally, falling commodity prices across the board—a result of lessening demand in a global downturn—have undermined Canada's economic growth, sending unemployment up from 6.4 percent in 2006 to nearly 9 percent by late 2008.

Still, compared to the United States and other developed-world countries, Canada was in relatively good financial shape through the first couple of years of the recession. Its government had the smallest debt load per capita of any G-8 country and its fall in home sales—at 20 percent—was not nearly as dramatic as that in the United States. And unlike most industrialized world economies, Canada experienced positive growth—2.7 percent—in its GDP in 2008, but saw that figure fall by 2.9 percent in 2009.

James Ciment

See also: United States.

Further Reading

"Canada's Economic Growth Offers Hope." *The Globe and Mail*, August 31, 2009. Available at www.theglobeandmail.com/report-on-business/canadas-gdp-back-in-black/article1270430/. Accessed September 11, 2009.

"IMF Slashes Canada's GDP Growth for 2009 and 2010." CBCNews, January 28, 2009. Available at www.cbc.ca/money/story/2009/01/28/imf-canada-growth.html. Accessed September 11, 2009.

Johnson, Harry G. *The Canadian Quandary: Economic Problems and Policies.* Montreal: McGill-Queen's University Press, 2005.

Naylor, R.T. *Canada in the European Age, 1453–1919.* 2nd ed. Montreal: McGill-Queen's University Press, 2006.

Statistics Canada Web site: www.statcan.gc.gov.

"Worldwide Financial Crisis Largely Bypasses Canada." *Washington Post*, October 16, 2008. Available at www.washingtonpost.com/wp-dyn/content/article/2008/10/15/AR2008101503321.html. Accessed September 11, 2009.

Capital Account

The capital account constitutes one part of the balance of payments of a given country, the other two components being the current account and the financial account. The balance of payments is the cumulative measure of net income coming into a country via international trade, overseas investments, and other foreign sources. The capital account records transfers of assets, such as patents, trademarks, stocks, and bonds, while the current account includes payments for exported and imported goods and services, interest, and foreign aid.

The financial-derivatives account records financial instruments that allow or obligate their owners to buy, sell, or exchange financial assets at an agreed time (or period) in the future, at an agreed price, or in an agreed amount. Such instruments are known in the financial community as forwards, futures, options, and swaps. Employee stock options are also a part of this account.

Other investment accounts record all assets and liabilities that are not reflected in the capital, financial, or reserve assets accounts. Hard currency and deposits, trade credits and advances, loans, and other assets and liabilities are reflected there.

The reserve-assets account records the assets of a nation's central bank—such as the U.S. Federal Reserve (Fed), including the assets that can be used to meet the country's balance-of-payments needs. The reserve assets must actually exist and be readily available; potential assets, or those that may be realized in the future, may not be included. Reserve assets can take a number of forms, including foreign currency, monetary gold, International Monetary Fund (IMF) reserves, and other liquid assets. A positive sign associated with a reserve-asset account means that, during the specified period, the country's reserves have decreased; a negative sign means they have increased.

A country with a positive capital account balance (and negative current account balance) is called a "net borrower"; a country with a negative capital account balance (and positive current account balance) is called a "net lender." However, because not all capital takes the form of loans, a country with a large current account deficit may not actually have large foreign loans. Instead, it may have attracted a lot of foreign direct investment, which can have important economic benefits.

Most economists argue that countries should maintain relatively liberal capital account policies, which allows for the free flow of capital across borders, stimulating trade and, theoretically, increasing the prosperity of all countries. But if countries remove virtually all barriers to capital flows, they risk being swept along by market fluctuations. For example, many East Asian countries removed most of the barriers to capital flows from the late 1980s onward, allowing foreigners to invest heavily in East Asian securities. Soon, these economies became heavily dependent on having a positive capital account balance. But when fears about the values of those securities caused foreign investors to pull out their capital, Asian economies found themselves with their foreign reserves depleted, causing depreciation of local currencies and a regional crisis known as the Asian financial crisis of 1997–1998. The event has led some financial analysts to call for more capital account controls.

Economists also cite the role of America's capital account deficit as a factor in the 2008–2009 financial crisis and the 2007–2009 recession. With the country running a major current account, or balance-of-trade, deficit, it needed a capital account surplus to finance the gap between the imports and exports. This need drew in large financial investment from abroad, especially from the exporting economies of East Asia and the oil exporting nations. All of this new capital flowing into the United States contributed to the run-up in asset prices, including mortgage-backed securities and, indirectly, housing. But to keep the flow of foreign capital coming, the Fed had to raise interest rates on government bonds. When it did so, it caused rises in adjustable rate mortgages, which were tied to the Fed rate. This contributed to the rapid decline in housing prices that most economists say was at the heart of the financial crisis and recession of 2007–2009.

Tiia Vissak

See also: Balance of Payments; Current Account; Exchange Rates.

Further Reading

International Monetary Fund (IMF). *Balance of Payments and International Investment Position Manual.* 6th ed. Washington, DC: International Monetary Fund, 2010.
———. *Balance of Payments Statistics Yearbook.* Washington, DC: International Monetary Fund, 2008.

Capital Market

The capital market is the market for both debt and equity securities. It is where businesses and governments turn when they need to raise long-term capital, usually defined as capital that they can use for more than a year.

Capital markets are divided between primary and secondary markets. In the primary market, businesses, governments, and public sector institutions sell debt (bonds) or equity (stocks) via securities dealers, such as brokerages and investment houses. These dealers then sell the stocks and bonds to investors in a process known as underwriting. Secondary markets are where investors buy and sell the stocks and bonds among themselves. For stocks this is usually done through exchanges, such as the New York Stock Exchange, while bonds and structured products, such as derivatives, are sold directly from investor to investor in the over-the-counter market.

In some countries, such as the United States and the United Kingdom, business firms typically use primary capital markets, whereas in others, such as Germany and Japan, businesses rely on the banking system more. The main difference between the two ways of raising money is that the access to funds in the former case depends on the combined judgment of the market participants, whereas in the latter it depends on the judgment of the particular bank to which the project is presented. The many agents that participate in primary capital markets can provide a more reliable profit outlook for a project than a particular bank, though the latter may have more accurate knowledge of a particular local business than capital investors do.

In the primary capital markets, the borrowers get money and the lenders get documents that specify the conditions under which the money is lent. These documents, or titles, fall into to two basic categories: equity and bonds. The lender who purchases equity acquires a share in the ownership of the company and, accordingly, acquires the right to share in its profits. The portion of the profits that the company's management decides to pay out to shareholders is called "dividend"; accordingly, an investor who purchases equity acquires the right to be paid dividends. By contrast, the purchaser of bonds issued by a company (or government entity) does not acquire an ownership share and, accordingly, acquires no right to dividends. The obligation of the bond issuer to the bond purchaser is to repay the total amount, plus interest as stipulated. When a company or government borrows money by issuing bonds, it is said that it finances not with *equity*, but with *debt*.

Not every business project or enterprise has access to the primary capital markets. A firm can "float an issue" (borrow funds) only if the authority that runs the market allows it to do so. A company admitted to a capital market—often with an initial public offering (IPO)—becomes a "publicly listed firm"; in colloquial terms, it is also said that the firm "goes public." This does not mean that the company becomes nationalized, only that it has been admitted to the capital market, where the public can purchase its issues. Nor is access to the primary capital markets restricted to private business enterprises. Public institutions and, in particular, the government can float issues—that is, borrow money—in the primary capital markets.

Shares and bonds, private or public, can be either negotiable or nonnegotiable. Titles are negotiable if the owner can transfer them to a third party; titles are nonnegotiable if the owner is barred from doing so. Negotiable titles are sold and purchased in a *secondary capital market.* More attention is often paid to secondary markets such as the stock market, perhaps because more than ten times as much wealth exchanges hands in the secondary market than in primary markets. However, the primary market is equally important because it is the original source of investment funding. Obviously, there are no secondary capital markets for nonnegotiable titles. Secondary capital markets arise when the titles issued in the primary market are negotiable and their owners are willing to exchange them either for other titles or for money. The reason why lenders may want to sell or purchase their titles is to maximize the yield on their investment. This may require, first, to exchange one's titles for other titles that promise larger dividends. Second, the desire to maximize the return on investments in capital markets could lead investors to exchange titles they currently possess for other titles whose price they expect to rise in the future; if that expectation if fulfilled, the investor makes a *capital gain.* Investors who expect changes in the dividend policy of publicly traded companies or who expect increases in the prices of titles are said to be *speculating.* Thus, both primary and secondary capital markets are speculative; in both cases, the investor acts in accordance with an expectation of future dividends on asset prices.

In addition to equity and debt, participants in the capital markets can issue titles, which confer the right or the obligation to buy or sell a given title at some future time and/or at some definite price. These titles are called "derivatives." If the contract stipulates an *obligation* to buy or sell the underlying title at some future date, then the derivative title is called an "option." If, by contrast, the property of the derivative title confers a *right* to buy or sell the underlying title, it is called a "future." Futures and options are issued in primary capital markets and traded in secondary capital markets. (With regard to futures, it is also necessary to differentiate *commodity* markets—in which the participating agents buy and sell titles that stipulate prices for future deliveries of ordinary commodities, such as pork bellies or corn—from *capital* markets—in which the item being traded is money.)

Kepa Ormazabal

See also: Financial Markets; Stock and Bond Capitalization; Stock Markets, Global.

Further Reading

Chisholm, Andrew. *An Introduction to Capital Markets: Products, Strategies, Participants.* The Wiley Finance Series. Hoboken, NJ: John Wiley & Sons, 2002.
Fabozzi, Frank J., and Franco Modigliani. *Capital Markets: Institutions and Instruments.* 4th ed. Upper Saddle River, NJ: Prentice Hall, 2008.

Capital One

Based in McLean, Virginia—located in Fairfax County, the second-richest county in the country and home to seven Fortune 500 companies and Freddie Mac—the Capital One Financial Corporation is one of America's most successful financial companies, built primarily on the mass-marketed credit cards it pioneered in the 1990s. Thanks to the quantity of direct mail the company sends to offer its services to consumers, Capital One is the fourth-largest customer of the United States

Postal Service and the second largest of the Canadian post office.

Capital One was founded in 1988 by Richard Fairbank (chairman and CEO to the present) and his British partner, Nigel Morris (chief operating officer until retiring in 2004), to provide more customized financial services to customers. Shortly after retiring, Morris was involved in the Cash for Honors scandal in the United Kingdom; his donation of 1 million pounds to the Labour Party was part of an investigation into political contributions given in exchange for peerages and other special favors.

Originally a monoline business specializing in consumer loans, Capital One weathered the circumstances that drove other single-service financial companies like the Money Store out of business and saw others like First USA scooped up in acquisitions. Underlying Capital One's success, and part of Fairbank's initial business plan, was a new sophistication in data collection and information processing. Capital One radically expanded the breadth and quantity of customer data it collected; ten years after its founding, the company had one of the largest consumer information databases in the world. This approach, among other things, allowed Capital One to offer loans and other financial services to prospective customers who represented too great a risk to lenders who relied on conventional metrics. Capital One's willingness to extend credit to college students and others with little or no income, and to offer secured credit cards to those rebuilding bad credit or emerging from bankruptcy, prefigured the craze for subprime mortgage loans in the early twenty-first century.

As in the case of many subprime mortgage lenders, Capital One's ethics and practices have been called into question. In order to offset the risk of issuing credit cards to consumers with little means of paying them off, for instance, the company charges high penalty fees and interest rates sometimes so high that the cards cannot be issued in states with strict anti-usury laws. In addition, Capital One has a reputation for of-fering some customers multiple cards, each with its own limit and fees, rather than raising the limit on an existing card; this can quickly lead to hundreds of dollars per month in fees without paying off the principal. Some Capital One cards are issued with a debt already approaching the credit limit, because of annual and one-time processing fees.

Capital One Financial Corporation is the holding company for Capital One (the original credit card issuer), Capital One Bank (a retail bank chain), and Capital One Auto Finance (COAF). Like the credit card company, COAF built its fortune on specifically tailored marketing, offering its services through direct mail targeted at specific consumer types. Later acquisitions and diversification have made it the largest online lender of car loans, with approvals communicated online in a matter of minutes. Although Capital One's international operations are not as significant as those of other financial companies, Canadian and British operations are extensive.

The second half of the 2000s brought several significant changes at Capital One. The company began retail banking operations under the Capital One Bank brand after acquiring New Orleans–based Hibernia National Bank (negotiating a lower price than originally offered, in the wake of Hurricane Katrina) in 2005. Then, with financial crisis looming later in the decade, the company abandoned subprime mortgage lending in response to investor demands. In 2009, however, after the collapse of that market and the devastation to the entire credit industry, the company cut its quarterly dividend by 87 percent in order to preserve capital in a volatile economic environment. At the same time, Capital One raised interest rates on many existing credit card accounts, offering holders the option of closing the account and paying off the balance under the previous terms. In November 2008, Capital One received just over $3.5 billion in bailout funds from the Troubled Asset Relief Program (TARP), established by the federal government to assist financial institutions facing liquidity problems.

In June 2009, Capital One repaid the federal government, freeing itself from restrictions placed on TARP recipients.

Bill Kte'pi

See also: Banks, Commercial.

Further Reading

Chin, Amita Goyal, and Hiren Kotak. "Improving Debt Collection Processes Using Rule-Based Decision Engines: A Case Study of Capital One." *International Journal of Information Management* 26:1 (February 2006): 81–88.

Clemons, Eric K., and Matt E. Thatcher. "Capital One Financial and a Decade of Experience with Newly Vulnerable Markets: Some Propositions Concerning the Competitive Advantage of New Entrants." *Journal of Strategic Information Systems* 17:3 (September 2008): 179–189.

Catastrophe Theory

Catastrophe theory is a branch of mathematics that describes dynamic phenomena in which sudden, dramatic jumps, or "catastrophes," may occur in apparently stable, calm situations or during regular, continuous processes. The theory originates from the works of the French mathematician René Thom in the 1960s, though some elements had been articulated by earlier thinkers, including the French mathematician Jules-Henri Poincaré in the late nineteenth century and even, to some extent, Leonardo da Vinci during the Renaissance. In addition to mathematics and finance, catastrophe theory has been applied to other areas of study, including biology, geology, chemistry, archaeology, physics, medicine, demographics, psychology, education, politics, road traffic, and aviation.

Catastrophe theory became popular among academic economists in the 1970s, after the Japanese-born British mathematician Sir Erik Christopher Zeeman—who is credited with coining the term—used it to study financial market dynamics, in particular booms and busts in the stock market. For that analysis, Zeeman divided investors into "fundamentalists"—who can gauge the true value of assets, buying them when the market value is below that level and selling them when it is above; and "chartists"—who do not know the true value and therefore "chase trends" (i.e., buy assets after prices rise and sell them after prices fall). In Zeeman's view, the behavior of the stock market reflects the interactions of these two types of agents, causing underlying instability and unexpected crashes in capital markets.

At the macroeconomic level, catastrophe theory has been used to study the relationships among national income, capital stock, gross investment, savings, and wealth. In addition, it has been used in studying the links between actual inflation, unemployment, and expected inflation, as well as studies of urban and regional economics, bank failures, real-estate prices, consumer purchasing behavior, business management, the decision making of monopolists, the dynamics of balance of payments (especially trade balance), and foreign currency speculation. An example is the Asian financial crisis of the late 1990s, in which inflows of vast amounts of capital from outside the region suddenly evaporated and then reversed themselves as a result of a single government's—specifically, Thailand's—inability to prop up its currency, the baht.

Since the late 1970s, catastrophe theory has also been used as well to explain several cyclic economic phenomena at the microeconomic level that cannot be adequately described with traditional analytical techniques—such as why some firms continue producing goods even when market prices do not cover their production costs (i.e., they are suffering losses), while others do not restart production when prices are considerably higher than they had been before the shutting down. Thus, during an economic recession, some firms continue producing goods longer than they should, while during periods of economic recovery, some firms do not resume production soon enough.

Catastrophe theory has also been used to explain other illogical economic behavior—such as why firms decide to open new plants too late to maximize their profits (after demand has peaked) or do not close less efficient plants soon enough (amid declining demand). Likewise, it can show why some companies raise prices as demand diminishes or lower prices as demand increases. Such decisions are explained by the lack of complete information regarding costs and revenues, resulting in overproduction during economic recessions and delays or underproduction during economic recoveries.

The popularity of catastrophe theory has generally declined since the 1980s, the theory having been the object of questioning, criticism, and even ridicule among some scholars. Critics have variously contended that the theory or its applications—including those in economics—have relied excessively on qualitative methods, have been incorrectly calculated (using arbitrary variables or improper statistical methods), or have relied on overly narrow or restrictive mathematical assumptions. According to another line of criticism, catastrophe theory is suitable only for the study of very specific—and unrealistic—economic systems and scenarios. Despite the waxing and waning of academic interest, and despite the various criticisms, catastrophe theory remains actively and widely applied in economics, business, and related disciplines.

Tiia Vissak

See also: Shock-Based Theories.

Further Reading

Balasko, Yves. "Economic Equilibrium and Catastrophe Theory: An Introduction." *Econometrica* 46:3 (1978): 557–569.

Dodgson, J.S. "Kinks and Catastrophes: A Note on the Relevance of Catastrophe Theory for Economics." *Australian Economic Papers* 21:39 (1982): 407–415.

Pol, Eduardo. "Theoretical Economics and Catastrophe Theory: An Appraisal." *Australian Economic Papers* 32:61 (1993): 258–271.

Rosser, J. Barkley, Jr. "The Rise and Fall of Catastrophe Theory Applications in Economics: Was the Baby Thrown Out with the Bathwater?" *Journal of Economic Dynamics & Control* 31:10 (2007): 3255–3280.

Scott, Robert C., and Edward L. Sattler. "Catastrophe Theory in Economics." *Journal of Economic Education* 14:3 (1983): 48–59.

Varian, Hal R. "Catastrophe Theory and the Business Cycle." *Economic Inquiry* 17:1 (1979): 14–28.

Zhang, Wei-Bin. "Theory of Complex Systems and Economic Dynamics." *Nonlinear Dynamics, Psychology, and Life Sciences* 6:2 (2002): 83–101.

Central America

Consisting of seven small nations—Belize, Guatemala, Honduras, El Salvador, Nicaragua, Costa Rica, and Panama—Central America, sometimes referred to as Mesoamerica (though the latter appellation also includes southern Mexico) is an isthmus that connects North America to South America. Approximately 202,000 square miles (523,000 square kilometers) in area and with a population of about 42 million, Central America is a largely Spanish-speaking and Roman Catholic region, though there are sizable English-speaking and Protestant minorities. Most of the people in the region are of mixed Spanish and Indian heritage, or mestizos, with significant populations of persons of other European and African backgrounds.

Economic development in the region varies. Nicaragua and Honduras are among the poorest nations in the hemisphere, while Panama and Costa Rica rank as middle-income countries. The economy of the region rests on commercial agriculture, light manufacturing, tourism, and, in the case of Panama—with its ocean-linking canal—trade and finance.

Central America was home to millions of indigenous people prior to the arrival of Europeans at the end of the fifteenth century, and, along with southern Mexico, was home to the Mayan civilization. Aside from Panama, which offered the quickest overland route between the mines of Peru and the Atlantic Ocean, the region was largely bypassed by the Spanish in the early years of their conquest of the Americas due to its thick jungles, stifling equatorial climate, and lack of precious metals. Land was parceled out to conquistadores, who developed large plantations and ranches worked by indigenous and mestizo workers. In

1540, the Spanish organized much of the territory into the Captaincy General of Guatemala.

With the independence of Mexico in 1821, the region was absorbed into the Mexican Empire for two years, before gaining independence as the United Provinces of Central America, with its capital in Guatemala. Ideological and regional disputes led to great instability and dissolution into five separate countries—Costa Rica, El Salvador, Guatemala, Honduras, and Nicaragua—between 1838 and 1840. Meanwhile, Panama had become a province of Colombia with that country's independence from Spain in 1810. Remote Belize was settled by the British from the seventeenth century—who began bringing in black Jamaican slaves as timber workers—and became a British colony (known eventually as British Honduras) in the late eighteenth century, remaining part of the empire until independence in 1981.

With the breakup of the United Provinces, the various countries of Central America followed parallel but different economic and political trajectories. With large indigenous and mixed-race populations ruled over by a European-descended elite, the countries remained economically underdeveloped and politically unstable. They were often ruled by military dictators who had come to power in various violent and nonviolent *golpes*, or coups, through much of the nineteenth century, and they remained underdeveloped, exporting small amounts of agricultural products, such as coffee, to North America and Europe. With power in the hands of a tiny landed elite, manufacturing was slow to develop and the middle class remained a tiny minority, largely located in the various capitals of the region.

Around the turn of the twentieth century, the various countries of the region came increasingly under the political and economic hegemony of the United States. Guatemala and Honduras, in particular, became major exporters of bananas to North America with the economies of these two countries, as well as their politics, dominated by the U.S.-owned United Fruit Company. Nicaragua saw a U.S. occupation from 1912 to 1933,

resisted by an insurgency under Augusto César Sandino, while Panama came into existence as a country separate from Colombia in 1903 with the assistance of the United States, which soon began construction of a transoceanic canal that was completed in 1914.

By the middle of the twentieth century, however, two of the region's countries had embarked on efforts at economic and political reform. In Guatemala, voters put into power leftist president Jacobo Árbenz, who began to challenge the United Fruit Company's power, including its control of roughly 40 percent of the country's arable land. Following a brief civil war in 1948, Costa Rica abolished its army and implemented political reforms that established a working democracy in the nation. While Costa Rica's efforts were successful, Guatemala saw its reformist president overthrown in a U.S.-sponsored coup. Meanwhile, Nicaragua remained under the control of dictator Anastasio Somoza García, who had been put into power with the help of U.S. occupation forces, while El Salvador continued to be effectively ruled by the so-called fourteen families of wealthy landowners.

Continuing inequalities in wealth and a lack of land reform led to insurgencies in much of the region from the 1960s through the 1990s, fought vigorously by the military or conservative civilian governments in power, often with military aid from the United States. Guatemala saw a bitter civil war begin in the 1960s that would eventually result in the deaths of 200,000 persons, most of them civilians. Meanwhile, in 1968, a populist general named Omar Torrijos came to power in a coup in Panama, vowing to win back control of the canal from the United States, which he achieved by treaty in 1977, with a takeover date of 1999. In El Salvador, some 75,000 persons—again, largely civilians—were killed in an insurgency that began in 1980. And in Nicaragua, the Sandinista National Liberation Front (FSLN, its Spanish acronym) rose up against the Somoza dictatorship in the 1970s.

The Sandinistas were successful in coming to power, overthrowing the dictatorship in 1979.

The new government then tried to implement land reform and other measures to equalize the great discrepancies of wealth in the country. But once in power, the FSLN was confronted by an insurgency of its own, consisting largely of disaffected remnants of the Somoza dictatorship backed by the United States and largely based in Honduras.

U.S. support for right-wing governments in Central America had always been premised on keeping the countries of the region from falling under the influence of communists, backed by Cuba and the Soviet Union. But with the end of the cold war that urgency evaporated, and eventually the various conflicts in the region wound down, either through negotiated settlements, as in El Salvador in 1992 and Guatemala in 1996, or through a change in government, as was the case of Nicaragua in 1990. A U.S.-led invasion in late 1989 ended the rule of dictator Manuel Noriega in Panama.

Since the return to peace and civilian government in the 1990s, the various countries in the region have embarked upon free-market reforms, opening their countries up to foreign investment, which has led to the development of more light manufacturing. Costa Rica has emphasized ecotourism to draw in foreign capital while Panama has emerged as a major center of trade and finance, especially since its takeover of the canal. Many of the countries of the region also depend heavily on remittances from the hundreds of thousands of Central American immigrants—both legal and illegal—working in the United States.

In 2004, the countries of Central America—along with the Dominican Republic, but minus Belize and Panama—signed the Central America Free Trade Agreement with the United States. CAFTA, as the agreement is known, lowered tariffs for Central American imports into the United States while easing restrictions on U.S. investment in the region. CAFTA has accelerated the economic integration between the United States and Central America and was seen by many experts as a boon to the latter's economy. Opponents in the latter region, however, argue that it will lead to further U.S. domination of the Central American economy. Moreover, they point out, increased integration will expose Central American economies to the U.S. business cycle. And, indeed, exports to the United States have declined somewhat as a result of the 2007–2009 recession, and growth rates have slowed significantly or fallen in all of the Central American countries, barring Panama.

James Ciment

See also: Latin America; Mexico.

Further Reading

Desruelle, Dominique, and Alfred Schipke, eds. *Economic Growth and Integration in Central America.* Washington, DC: International Monetary Fund, 2007.

Jaramillo, Carlos Felipe, et al. *Challenges of CAFTA: Maximizing the Benefits for Central America.* Washington, DC: World Bank, 2006.

Pearcy, Thomas. *The History of Central America.* Westport, CT: Greenwood, 2006.

Robinson, William. *Transnational Conflicts: Central America, Social Change, and Globalization.* New York: Verso, 2003.

Chile

A long sliver of a nation, tucked between the Andes Mountains and the Pacific Ocean in the southern cone of South America, Chile, a nation of roughly 17 million, has an economic history that shares many experiences with other Latin American economies. Its economic development has been inconsistent and, at times, volatile: export booms and busts occurred, import substitution industrialization policies were adopted in the twentieth century, and those policies were recently abandoned in favor of trade liberalization. Chile's economic history differs from the rest of Latin America, however, in that its economic ups and downs did not exactly parallel those of other countries in the region. Chile's distinctive domestic economic policies interacted in unique ways with its export booms and busts.

It experienced subpar economic growth for most of the post–World War II period, when most of Latin America grew rapidly, and its very recent economic growth performance has been substantially better than that of its neighbors.

Early Development

Before gaining independence from Spain in 1818, the region that is today Chile was sparsely populated by both descendants of Spanish settlers and native groups. Probably fewer than 1 million Chileans lived and farmed in the central valley at the start of the nineteenth century. Central valley farmers exported tallow, beef, and grain to other Spanish colonies in present-day Peru and Colombia, and there were mines in the Andes Mountains that defined the long eastern border of the country. Most of the northern deserts remained largely unpopulated, and native societies continued to occupy most of the southern part of the country until the nineteenth century.

The export of food continued after Chile and Spain's other South American colonies gained their independence. Agricultural exports received a boost from the California gold rush in 1849, as the direct ocean supply route from Chile was more convenient than overland routes to California from the eastern United States.

Chile's first major export was nitrate. In the 1870s, Chilean entrepreneurs opened nitrate mines on land claimed by Bolivia and Peru. Chile won the War of the Pacific (1879–1884), fought over the disputed territory, and extended its national territory to its present northern borders. Bolivia was permanently denied access to the Pacific Ocean, an issue that troubles Bolivian-Chilean relations to the present day.

Chilean mines soon faced competition from British mining firms that opened large-scale nitrate mines to supply the growing world market. Nitrate was a critical raw material for manufacturing explosives, and it was a basic ingredient in agricultural fertilizers that were increasingly applied by farmers in Europe and the United

States in the latter half of the nineteenth century. Nitrate accounted for half of Chile's exports and up to one-quarter of its gross domestic product (GDP) by 1890.

The nitrate mines in the remote northern region of Chile are an example of *enclave development.* British mines employed few Chileans, and much of the revenue from exporting nitrate accrued to the foreign firms. However, the Chilean government learned to capture a greater share of the nitrate earnings by raising taxes on nitrate exports to over 30 percent. In the early twentieth century, nitrate taxes accounted for three-quarters of government revenues.

The Second Export Boom: Copper

Chile's second major export product was copper, mined in the remote Andes. By the early twentieth century, the U.S. copper companies Anaconda and Kennecott controlled Chile's major copper deposits. The global market for copper grew rapidly as electric power and telephone communications expanded throughout the world. The Chilean government again sought to capture an increasing share of the value of copper exports, but copper tax revenues never exceeded 20 percent of all government revenues. For one thing, the foreign firms fought back with threats to leave the country. For another, they actively lobbied domestic politicians to resist calls for higher taxes.

A Larger Economic Role for Government

Chile's democracy was dominated by the country's economic elites and, occasionally, the military. The political system did transmit enough pressure from all segments of the population to induce the government to undertake popular programs in education and social services in addition to the infrastructure and transportation projects favored by businesses and large farmers. Chile was well ahead of most of the rest of Latin America in terms of literacy, living standards, and health. The military sometimes sided with labor during the frequent labor disputes early in the twentieth century.

Politicians were able to satisfy most Chilean factions because nitrate and copper export taxes provided the revenues. The Chilean government spent over 15 percent of national income early in the twentieth century, a very high share at that time in history, but Chileans did not pay many of the taxes. By the end of the 1920s, Chile's per capita real income was equal to that of Germany and the Scandinavian nations.

The government's role was expanded at the start of the Great Depression of the 1930s. And, even though Chile owed its relatively high (for Latin America) levels of government-provided education, health care, transportation, and social services to export tax revenues, when exports fell by 80 percent and GDP per capita fell by 42 percent between 1929 and 1932, the political response was to reduce Chile's dependence on exports. Chile introduced high tariffs and import quotas to protect domestic producers who "substituted" foreign imports. Chile thus anticipated the import substitution industrialization (ISI) policies popularized by the United Nations Economic Commission for Latin America and its director, Raúl Prebisch, and embraced by most Latin American countries after World War II.

Chile soon went beyond restricting imports. In the late 1930s, the government established the Corporación de Fomento de la Producción (CORFO) to fund government-owned industries in steel, energy, and food processing when private investors appeared reluctant to expand domestic output. The results of these policies were disappointing. Chile's per capita real income grew annually at rates of 1.3 and 1.9 percent during the 1950s and 1960s, respectively, when Latin America's overall per capita real income grew at 2.2 and 2.6 percent. As a result, Chile did not sustain its per capita GDP relative to the European countries with which it had enjoyed near parity at the start of the century. Instead, Chile's per capita real GDP regressed to the Latin American average.

Increased domestic taxes to pay for growing government activities split political sentiments more clearly between those who wanted the government to reduce its share of the economy and those who supported more socialistic policies and the expansion of government social and economic programs. After World War II, left-of-center parties demanded that the government take over the copper industry so that Chile could capture the full surplus from its exports. Many politicians and commentators accused the U.S. copper firms of intentionally reducing production and, therefore, tax revenues in order to pressure the government.

More fundamentally, Chile's ISI policies were costly because the country's domestic market of less than 7 million low-income people was not large enough to sustain large-scale manufacturing industries. An example of the failure of import substitution was Chile's attempt to establish a domestic automobile industry in the 1960s. Some twenty local factories used the ban on imports of complete automobiles to begin assembling autos from imported parts. A total of 8,180 automobiles were assembled in 1963 and 7,558 in 1964. The near-artisan production methods resulted in cars costing five times their overseas price, with inferior quality. Once launched, however, ISI policies were not easily dismantled because protectionism created a constituency of domestic industries and workers who feared their demise if protectionist import tariffs and quotas were abandoned.

Three political factions fought for power during the post–World War II period: the conservative Right, the socialist Left, and a "centrist" party that favored some modifications in the ISI regime but also promised to nationalize the copper industry. The centrists often won by attracting votes from conservatives who feared that the Left would win if they split the center-right vote. In the presidential election of 1970, however, the conservatives backed their own candidate, and the left candidate, Salvador Allende, won with only 36.3 percent of the vote, barely above the Right's 34.9 percent and the center's 27.8 percent.

Against strong resistance from established private business and landholders, the Allende administration not only completed the nationalization of the copper industry started by earlier governments, but began nationalizing many other foreign and Chilean industries. Allende also honored his campaign promise for a major redistribution of land, something many earlier governments had promised but never actually carried out. There were reports that some of Allende's government officials were urging workers to occupy factories and invade farms in order to spur owners to agree to government takeovers. In any case, occupations and invasions soon became a common occurrence. After a 7 percent rise in per capita income in 1971, a direct result of expanded government programs and a hike in the minimum wage, per capita GDP declined in 1972 when private investment collapsed. The Allende government accused the business sector of intentionally sabotaging the economy, and it pressed ahead with its nationalization of private industry. The Right argued that investment fell because of the threats of government nationalizations and worker occupations. Inflation rose as goods became scarce with the disruptions of production, and the government began printing money to fund the difference between falling tax revenues and the rising cost of nationalizations, unemployment benefits, and new government benefits. Under cover of the economic difficulties, the U.S. Central Intelligence Agency (CIA) helped a Chilean military junta launch a coup in 1973 in which Allende was killed. General Augusto Pinochet headed the new military government.

The Pinochet regime reversed Allende's socialist economic policies, but economic growth did not recover. The privatization of government assets was a major component of Pinochet's new economic program, designed by mostly U.S.-educated Chilean economists who came to be known as the "Chicago boys" because several held degrees from the University of Chicago. Chicago is famous for its advocacy of free-market and free-trade policies, or what most Latin Americans describe as "neoliberal ideology." Privatization was difficult because of the lack of private Chilean capital to buy the government-owned firms, banks, and utilities.

At the urging of the government, purchases were highly leveraged through bank borrowing. A large portion of the bank funds were acquired through foreign borrowing, enabled by foreign banks anxious to lend to a country led by what they saw as a pro-business regime. When the worldwide debt crisis caused foreign lending to stop in 1982, Chilean private banks and their highly leveraged clients defaulted en masse. Domestic lending immediately stopped, real investment declined, unemployment surged to 20 percent, and GDP per capita fell by 15 percent in 1983 and another 5 percent in 1984. The economic collapse reduced real per capita GDP below its level at the time of the 1973 military coup. Domestic opposition to the Pinochet regime became quite visible despite the continued political oppression.

The Pinochet government responded with a more gradual approach, and policies to further liberalize foreign trade and privatize the economy were balanced by more social expenditures to deal with Chile's poverty, uneven education, and unemployment. After 1985, Chilean per capita GDP rose again, albeit from low levels. Growth was spurred in part by rising copper prices and taxes, and there was also rapid growth of agricultural exports, such as fruits, farmed fish, wood products, and wines, from food-processing industries created decades earlier under ISI policies. After a century during which Chile sought to reduce the role of exports in its economy, policy had clearly come full circle. Like 200 years earlier, exports by miners and the central valley's farmers drove economic development. Would the nation's per capita income once again approach that of the world's most developed countries as it had 100 years earlier?

After the restoration of democracy with the election of 1990, the new left-of-center government kept many neoliberal "Chicago" policies in place while increasing the share of government revenue to social programs. Chilean real per capita GDP grew 4.8 percent during the 1990s, a period when the rate for all of Latin America grew 1.5 percent. Growth of per capita income was more than 3 percent per year between 2000 and 2008, and poverty was significantly reduced. The global recession sharply cut Chilean exports in 2009, however, and growth turned negative in the first quarter of that year despite fiscal stimuli in the form of direct payments to households and direct support of bank lending. Chile's return to the ranks of the wealthy countries was further set back by a massive earthquake and tsunami in February 2010.

Hendrik Van den Berg

See also: Argentina; Latin America.

Further Reading

Bruton, Henry J. "A Reconsideration of Import Substitution." *Journal of Economic Literature* 31 (1989): 903–936.

Collier, Simon, and William F. Sater. *A History of Chile: 1808–1994.* New York: Cambridge University Press, 1996.

Economic Commission for Latin America and the Caribbean (ECLAC). *Economic Survey of Latin America and the Caribbean: 2008–2009.* Santiago, Chile: ECLAC, 2009.

Frank, Andre Gunder. *Dependent Accumulation and Underdevelopment.* London: Macmillan, 1967.

Glade, William P. *The Latin American Economies: A Study of Their Institutional Evolution.* New York: American Book, 1969.

Maddison, Angus. *The World Economy: A Millennial Perspective.* Paris: OECD, 2001.

Skidmore, Thomas E., and Peter H. Smith. *Modern Latin America.* 3rd ed. New York: Oxford University Press, 1992.

Thorp, Rosemary. *Progress, Poverty, and Exclusion: An Economic History of Latin America in the 20th Century.* Washington, DC: Inter-American Development Bank, 1998.

China

Encompassing one of the oldest continuous civilizations in human history, the People's Republic of China is a hybrid state, blending a dynamic and rapidly growing capitalist economy with a one-party, communist-inspired political system.

Until about the eighteenth century, China was arguably the richest and most advanced economy on Earth, before entering a long period of stagnation and foreign occupation, which came to an end with the Communist takeover of 1949. Over the next thirty years, a dictatorial political system and command style economy ensured that land and virtually all of the means of production were controlled by the state, eliminating the gross inequalities in wealth that existed prior to the revolution, but at the cost of famine, economic stagnation, and political repression.

An ideological reorientation following Communist Party chairman Mao Zedong's death in the mid-1970s encouraged the growth of markets in China and produced astounding growth rates beginning in the 1980s, although the state retained control of large swaths of the economy. Despite the Asian financial collapse of the late 1990s—as well as various recessions in the West, including the very deep one of 2007–2009—China continued to grow at near or above double-digit rates into the late 2000s, by which time the country had become a leading exporter, as well one of the largest economies in the world.

Pre-Communist Economy

China emerged as one of the first large, organized states around the end of the third millennium BCE and, within the next thousand or so years, developed an infrastructure of cities, roads, and canals that allowed for extensive internal trade in textiles, metals, handicrafts, and food, all administered by a centralized government. China was also the birthplace of many key innovations in human history, including coinage, paper, and gunpowder over the millennia.

But its history was also punctuated by great upheavals, in which central government control withered, long-distance trade diminished, and conflict among local authorities hampered agriculture and manufacturing, until a new strong and centralized authority, known as a dynasty, emerged and the country was once again united and prosperous. There were roughly a dozen of these dynasties between the formation of the centralized state under the Xia dynasty around 2,000 BCE and the Qing, or Manchu, dynasty, which began ruling from the late seventeenth century CE.

While China under the early Qing dynasty saw great advances in internal trade and economic development, it also turned inward, rejecting many of the new technologies and economic ideas of the burgeoning West. Still, China in these years enjoyed a favorable trade balance that saw the West exporting large quantities of precious metals to the country in exchange for China's many coveted goods, including tea, silk, and various finely crafted artisan products.

But by the nineteenth century, the Qing dynasty's resistance to outside ideas left China vulnerable to an aggressive and militarily advanced West. In the first half of the century, the country experienced a series of humiliating military defeats—known as the Opium Wars—in which Great Britain forced China to allow Europeans to export more freely to the country as a way to address the continuing trade imbalance with the West. Among the products Britain imposed on China was opium from its colonies in South Asia.

Other European imperialists—as well as rapidly modernizing Japan—soon joined Britain and, by the end of the century, many of the country's coastal provinces, the most economically dynamic region of China, had been carved into spheres of influence. Various outside powers were granted exclusive trading rights, known as concessions, and their nationals were immune from Chinese law.

Traditionally, the Chinese viewed their country as the center of the world—indeed, the Chinese name for the country was the "middle kingdom"; they believed China to be culturally superior to countries of the foreign "barbarians," as they referred to most non-Chinese peoples. The occupation of much of their country, then, was seen as a humiliation, and led to the failed antiforeign Boxer Rebellion of 1900–1901 and the successful revolution of 1911, in which the Qing dynasty was overthrown and replaced by a republic.

While the new Republic of China under Sun Yat-sen was less resistant to Western ideas and achieved a modicum of centralized control over the vast Chinese empire, it was unable to dislodge the foreign concessions and was ineffective in moving China from a peasant-based agricultural economy to a modernizing industrial one. The country continued to stagnate economically, remaining a largely feudal state in which the peasants of the countryside—who made up the vast majority of the population—lived under the iron rule of wealthy landlords and warlords. Dire poverty for the masses, periodic local famines, and gross inequalities of wealth continued to be the hallmarks of Chinese life.

Communist Economy

Such conditions led many Chinese to turn to communism as a way to address continued political subjugation to foreign powers, ongoing economic privation, and the unaddressed injustices of feudalism. By the 1920s, a Marxist-inspired movement under Mao had emerged to challenge, both politically and militarily, the nationalist government and foreign occupiers that were ruling China, in particular the Japanese. By the early 1930s, large parts of the country were engulfed in a civil war that would continue until the Communist victory of 1949, albeit with a long hiatus in which Nationalists and Communists united in opposition to Japanese invaders. (At the time of the Communist victory, hundreds of thousands of Nationalists fled to the island of Taiwan where, under military leader Chiang Kai-shek, they established an authoritarian capitalist system independent of Beijing. By the early 1990s, under the protective wing of the U.S. military, Taiwan had emerged as both a democracy and a flourishing, export-oriented free-market economy, though Beijing has always maintained that it has sovereignty over the "renegade province.")

Meanwhile on the mainland, the ruling Communist Party utterly transformed the political, social, cultural, and economic order of China. All political parties, other than the Communist

Party of China, were banned, along with a free press. Dissent of both the ideological and cultural varieties—China is home to a number of restless ethnic minorities on its fringes—was ruthlessly crushed. At the same time, however, the Communists dismantled the feudal order, executing or taking away the powers and property of economic elites, freeing peasants from the arbitrary and brutal rule of local landlords.

Land was nationalized and peasants organized into farming collectives. As per the model of its early mentor, the Soviet Union, the new People's Republic of China government instituted tight, centralized control of the economy, directing it toward rapid industrialization under a series of plans, including the Five Year Plan of the mid-1950s; the Second Five Year Plan, or "Great Leap Forward," of the late 1950s and early 1960s; and the Third Five Year Plan, or "Agriculture First" program, of the mid-1960s.

Much was achieved under these programs, particularly in the early years, as China created a heavy industry infrastructure and improved agricultural output. But there were also systemic failures and catastrophic missteps. Despite much emphasis on the farming sector, economic inequality between the relatively prosperous cities and impoverished countryside remained large. Efforts under the Great Leap Forward to expand industrial production through decentralization—including such ill-thought-through ideas as "backyard" steel smelters—set back economic development while a program to foster communal living and farming in the countryside led to massive famine that cost the lives of millions of peasants.

A further setback occurred with the "Cultural Revolution" of the late 1960s. A largely political event inspired by Mao's efforts to renew the country's revolutionary spirit, the Cultural Revolution saw disruptions in nonagricultural production due to intensified political agitation and an anti-intellectual crusade that saw older and experienced technicians replaced by inexperienced youths whose only qualification for running things was a fervent revolutionary spirit.

"Market Socialist" Economy

With the deaths of Mao and Premier Zhou Enlai in 1976, the radical forces within both the government and the party found themselves outflanked by a more pragmatic leadership led by formerly disgraced Communist Party official Deng Xiaoping, who, beginning at the party's national conference in 1978, pushed for the introduction of market forces within a socialist political and economic system. Technocrats rather than ideologues were put in charge of national economic planning; peasants were allowed to cultivate private plots and sell their surplus on the open market for profit; and local governments were given more leeway in deciding which industries to invest in. Within a few years of these reforms, agricultural output, light industry, and the production of consumer goods expanded dramatically.

The money for all of this investment came from two sources: bank deposits of newly prospering peasants and workers, and foreign capital. Under Deng, the Chinese government set up a series of Special Economic Zones, largely in the old trading regions of coastal southern China and centered on the capitalist, British-administered enclave of Hong Kong, which funneled much of that foreign capital to entrepreneurs and entrepreneurially inclined local governments. These enclaves also allowed foreign capitalists freedom from many government regulations and offered them the ability to repatriate profits.

Much of the economic activity in these zones and in other light manufacturing centers was geared for the foreign market. Between the late 1970s, when the economic reforms were first implemented, and the mid-1980s, the value of exports and imports rose from roughly 10 percent of gross domestic product (GDP) to 35 percent. Meanwhile production for domestic consumption was also expanding dramatically, as restrictions on entrepreneurial activity, as well as price controls and subsidies, were lifted. By the mid-1980s, China had developed its own unique brand of "market socialist" economics, with the central government still running much of the country's heavy industry and engaged in overall planning, but with microeconomic decisions left in the hands of local authorities and businesspeople.

The results of these reforms were nothing short of astonishing, as China achieved an annual average growth rate of nearly 10 percent, measured in real, inflation-adjusted terms, between the early 1980s and the mid-2000s. Over the same period, GDP by purchasing power parity (PPP)—a measure that equalizes differences in currency values between countries—rose from just over $250 billion to about $8 trillion in 2008 while per capita income soared from roughly $250 annually to more than $6,550 in 2008. By 2008, China had emerged as the second-largest economy in the world, after the United States.

But while the prosperity lifted hundreds of millions out of poverty, new problems emerged, as the economic disparities between classes and between the city and countryside grew exponentially. Many Chinese also complained of widespread corruption, in which well-connected officials—oftentimes with links to the Communist Party—used their power to override local complaints about headlong development that displaced families from their homes with little compensation. Human rights issues also emerged, as stories about exploited workers, the use of coerced prison labor, and appallingly dangerous working conditions were exposed. Many of these issues were raised during the large Tiananmen Square (Beijing) protests of 1989, which were brutally put down in June by authorities at the cost of hundreds of lives.

There were also domestic and international concerns about the environmental costs of China's rapid industrialization—by the late 2000s, China rivaled the United States as the leading producer of greenhouse gases, for instance—and the poor and sometimes dangerous quality of Chinese manufactured goods and agricultural products, with stories of tainted food, toys, and cosmetics capturing headlines around the world. Western countries, most notably the United States, also complained

The southern city of Shenzhen, China's first Special Economic Zone and a center of the nation's economic transformation, was said to grow by "one high-rise a day, one boulevard every three days" during the 1990s. *(Thomas Cheng/AFP/Getty Images)*

of China's growing trade surplus, which, vis-à-vis the United States, grew from $6 billion in 1985 to $268 billion in 2008. Some economists and politicians blamed this on Beijing's policy of maintaining an artificially undervalued currency, which made its exports that much more competitive.

Financial Crises of the 1990s and 2000s

Yet for all this, China continued to sustain remarkable growth and development, even while its neighbors and much of the rest of the world stumbled. The financial crisis that hit other Asian economies hard in the late 1990s, and which was triggered by massive foreign capital flight from local securities, left China largely untouched, since most of the foreign money coming into the country had not been invested in securities but in brick-and-mortar factories and other infrastructure. Thus, while many Asian economies went into recession following the 1997 crisis, China continued to post annual growth rates in the 7 to 8 percent range, before climbing above 10 percent by the mid-2000s.

Even more astounding was China's and much of the rest of Asia's response to the global financial crisis and recession that began in 2007. With Western economies sinking into negative growth and consumers reducing spending, many experts predicted a dramatic slowdown in the growth of both Chinese exports and the Chinese economy overall. Indeed, the growth rate in Chinese exports to the world fell, but still increased at 17.2 percent in 2008. Yet, while growth rates declined somewhat, from 11.4 percent in 2007 to a still dynamic 9 percent in 2008, they soon rebounded, reaching a blistering annualized rate of more than 15 percent in the second quarter of 2009.

Economists offered a number of possible explanations of why their predictions of a slow and tepid Chinese recovery from the global slump proved so wrong. First, they said, the government actively loosened credit, allowing for more investment. Sec-

ond, energy- and resource-hungry China benefited from the falling oil and commodity prices triggered by recession in Europe and North America. China has aided itself on this front by engineering long-term deals with resource-rich countries—particularly in Africa and Latin America—to ensure itself not only access to key commodities but also more stability in their pricing. In addition, China's huge late-2008 economic stimulus package of $586 billion—some 15 percent of GDP, as compared to America's stimulus package of $787 billion in early 2009, representing roughly 5.6 percent of GDP—appeared to be having a more profound effect in a country where consumers are less burdened with debt. That is, more of every yuan of stimulus money that landed in Chinese consumers' pockets went into purchasing rather than paying off debt.

Inevitably, the United States and other Western economies will emerge from the 2007–2009 recession and begin growing again. But just as inevitably, say economists, they will not experience the same growth rates as a surging China. With its huge population, its growing technological expertise, and the entrepreneurial energy of its people, China is destined, say economic prognosticators, to emerge as the world's largest economy, outpacing the United States sometime in the late 2020s or early 2030s.

Not that there are no problems ahead. Some experts argue that unless rapid economic growth is maintained, the increasing inequalities in Chinese life could lead to social unrest. In addition, there remains the growing contradiction of a freewheeling economy coexisting with a rigid political autocracy. In many other formerly authoritarian Asian countries that contradiction was resolved relatively peacefully in favor of democracy by the 1990s. But China has a long history, going back thousands of years, in which diminished centralized authority leads to economic chaos and decline, a scenario that no doubt concerns both Chinese authorities and the Chinese people.

James Ciment

See also: Asian Financial Crisis (1997); BRIC (Brazil, Russia, India, China); Emerging Markets; Southeast Asia; Transition Economies.

Further Reading

DeBary, William Theodore, and Irene Bloom, eds. *Sources of Chinese Tradition.* New York: Columbia University Press, 1999–2000.

Eastman, Lloyd. *Family, Fields, and Ancestors: Constancy and Change in China's Social and Economic History.* New York: Oxford University Press, 1988.

Mengkui, Wang, ed. *China in the Wake of Asia's Financial Crisis.* New York: Routledge, 2009.

Naughton, Barry. *The Chinese Economy: Transitions and Growth.* Cambridge, MA: MIT Press, 2007.

Overton, Rachel H. *China's Trade with the United States and the World.* Hauppage, NY: Nova Science, 2009.

Philion, Stephen E. *Workers' Democracy in China's Transition from State Socialism.* New York: Routledge, 2009.

Schiere, Richard. *China's Development Challenges: Public Sector Reform and Vulnerability to Poverty.* New York: Routledge, 2010.

Spence, Jonathan. *Gate of Heavenly Peace: The Chinese and Their Revolution, 1895–1980.* New York: Viking, 1981.

———. *The Search for Modern China.* New York: W.W. Norton, 1999.

Wilson, Scott. *Remade in China: Foreign Investors and Institutional Change in China.* New York: Oxford University Press, 2009.

Chrysler

The smallest of the "Big Three" major American automobile manufacturers in the early twenty-first century, Chrysler was also the first to go into—and emerge from—bankruptcy when the financial crisis and recession of the late 2000s dried up credit financing and caused a plunge in automobile sales. In its efforts to survive, Chrysler lobbied for and received billions of dollars in federal bailout money. This was the second time in the company's history that it had turned to Washington for help—the first was in the late 1970s. This time, however, the money came with a catch. The Detroit-based company had to come up with a viable plan to return to solvency. After failing to do so, it was forced to declare bankruptcy in 2009.

Origins and Growth

Walter Chrysler, founder of the eponymous company, was a kind of white knight of the automotive industry of the early twentieth century. A former railroad mechanic who had helped streamline production at the Buick division of General Motors in the 1910s, Chrysler successfully restructured Willys-Overland, an independent manufacturer hit hard by the recession of 1921–1922. In 1924, he bought a controlling interest in the failing Maxwell Motor Company, which he closed down and reorganized as Chrysler a year later.

At a time when Americans idolized dynamic business leaders, Walter Chrysler was hailed in the Roaring Twenties as an industrial hero. By the late 1920s, his company had emerged as one of the leading automobile manufacturers in America, having introduced two new divisions—Plymouth and DeSoto—and acquiring Dodge. Chrysler was inspired by similar efforts at industry leader General Motors, which, under his former boss, William Durant, had introduced the concept of different divisions whose cars appealed to buyers with different budgets. In 1928, the company broke ground on its iconic art deco headquarters, the Chrysler Building in New York City, which, when it was completed in 1931, was briefly the tallest structure in the world. In 1929, *Time* magazine named Walter Chrysler "Man of the Year."

Like other automobile manufacturers, Chrysler was hit hard by slumping demand during the Great Depression. But it was not hit as hard as rival Ford, which, by 1936, Chrysler had replaced as the number two American automobile manufacturer by sales, a ranking it would hold on and off through the end of the 1940s. From the post–World War II boom of the late 1940s through the early 1970s, Chrysler thrived, emerging as one of the Big Three while most other major U.S. automakers closed their doors. Chrysler also moved aggressively into the European market, acquiring controlling interests in British, French, and Spanish firms during the 1960s and reorganizing them as Chrysler Europe.

Oil Crisis and the First Government Bailout

The company was less successful seeing its way through the troubled manufacturing climate of the 1970s. Like other American automobile companies, Chrysler generally produced large, less fuel-efficient models. When oil prices spiked after the Arab oil embargo of 1973–1974, Chrysler found itself stuck with a substantial inventory of big cars, which American consumers were spurning in favor of higher-mileage Japanese and European imports. Meanwhile, in response to growing environmental and consumer concerns, Washington had imposed new emissions and safety standards on domestically manufactured vehicles. Reengineering cars to meet those standards—and then introducing new, higher-mileage models—was expensive, especially for Chrysler. Being the smallest of the Big Three, research and design costs ate up a relatively larger portion of its revenues. Trying to save money, it introduced poorly designed small cars such as the Dodge Aspen and Plymouth Volaré, which saddled the company with high warranty costs.

By the time of the second spike in oil prices during the late 1970s, Chrysler was reeling in the United States and its European operations had collapsed. Some $4 billion in debt and on the verge of bankruptcy by the middle of 1979—its total losses for that year would hit $1.2 billion, the largest in U.S. corporate history to that time—the company requested $1.5 billion in loan guarantees from the federal government. At the same time, Chrysler's board hired Lee Iacocca—a highly regarded marketing executive at Ford, known for having designed and marketed the hugely successful Mustang in the 1960s—to head the company.

Renaissance

An effective lobbyist as well, Iacocca won over a reluctant Congress, which passed the Chrysler Corporation Loan Guarantee Act at the end of 1979. The government also helped by making large purchases of Chrysler vehicles for its own fleet. Through aggressive marketing with a patriotic message—Iacocca appealed to Americans to buy domestic rather than foreign cars—and by selling off its lucrative defense subsidiary, Iacocca turned the company around, aided by a reviving economy and surging car sales. The federal loans were paid off early, allowing taxpayers to turn a $350 million profit on Washington's loan guarantees. By 1983, Chrysler had returned to the black and Iacocca was hailed as a business genius.

With oil prices declining steadily, the nation's automobile industry thrived from the mid-1980s through the mid-2000s, though its share of domestic sales continued to be eroded by imports. Chrysler shared in the prosperity, buying American Motors and its popular Jeep brand of off-road vehicles in 1987, returning to Europe by building a manufacturing plant in Austria, and introducing one of the most popular new styles of light vehicle—the minivan—in 1983.

So successful was Chrysler that in 1998 the German automobile manufacturer Daimler-Benz purchased it and renamed the combined new corporation DaimlerChrysler. The $48 billion deal was intended as a merger of equals: Chrysler would bring its high-end German counterpart a line of more moderately priced cars and broad access to the U.S. market; Daimler would provide Chrysler with some of its own top-flight technology and engineering. But the merger did not work out as intended. A clash of corporate cultures and the weakening of the U.S. automobile market doomed the enterprise in less than ten years. In 2007, Daimler sold an 80 percent stake in the company to a private equity group called Cerberus Capital Management for $7.4 billion—a huge loss.

Even at that price, Cerberus's purchase of Chrysler proved problematic. Along with soaring fuel prices, a weakening economy beginning in 2007 and the financial crisis of 2008—which dried up the credit most buyers used to finance their vehicle purchases—produced a 25 percent drop in sales, from just over 2 million in 2007 to fewer than 1.5 million in 2008. Financial losses

Chrysler workers leave the Warren (Michigan) Truck Assembly Plant as the company faced bankruptcy in April 2009. All manufacturing was suspended during the restructuring process, 789 dealerships were terminated, and eight factories were slated for closure in 2010. *(Bill Pugliano/Stringer/Getty Images)*

mounted into the billions, forcing the company to lay off thousands of workers.

Bailout Efforts and Bankruptcy

The new owners tried a number of strategies to stave off bankruptcy, including failed merger talks with General Motors. With General Motors also in serious financial trouble by late 2008, the George W. Bush administration announced plans for a bailout of the two automobile giants. Although the $13.4 billion package was a fraction of the contemporary bailout of failing U.S. financial institutions, the plan met with a political firestorm. As with General Motors, Chrysler had not helped its case by flying its executives in private jets to testify before Congress—not the best public relations move for a company begging for taxpayer dollars. The Senate promptly voted against the package, whereupon Chrysler announced that it was running out of cash and,

absent a bailout, would be forced to declare bankruptcy within weeks.

Chastened, company executives returned to Washington—this time by car caravan—to again plead with Congress. Fearing the political fallout from seeing a pillar of the American economy collapse at a time of deepening recession, taking with it hundreds of thousands of jobs, Congress responded with an even bigger bailout than that proposed by Bush—some $25 billion in all—in September. But the money came with strings attached. Chrysler would have to present a viable plan for returning to solvency within a matter of months.

The company responded by closing plants—some temporarily and some permanently—and furloughing or laying off more workers. Its real hope lay in a merger with Fiat, Italy's largest automobile manufacturer. Sergio Marchionne, Fiat's president and the man credited with having returned that company to profitability—demurred, believing that he would get a better deal once Chrysler had been reorganized under Chapter 11 of U.S. bankruptcy laws.

Without access to Fiat's assets, Chrysler did just that on April 30, 2009. Both Chrysler and the new Barack Obama administration expressed a desire for what they called a "surgical bankruptcy," a process that would allow Chrysler to make arrangements with its many creditors, dealers, and workers in a much shorter time than was usually the case for a bankruptcy of this size and complexity. Such a process, it was hoped, would also serve as a template for the potential bankruptcy of the much larger General Motors. After a few last-minute hitches, including protests from some creditors, Chrysler emerged from bankruptcy on June 10 as a new corporate entity, also named Chrysler. More than half the stock was owned by the pension plan of the United Auto Workers, 20 percent by Fiat, and another 10 percent by the U.S. and Canadian governments.

James Ciment

See also: General Motors; Manufacturing; Troubled Asset Relief Program (2008–).

Further Reading

Curcio, Vincent. *Chrysler: The Life and Times of an Automotive Genius.* New York: Oxford University Press, 2001.

Langworth, Richard M., and Jan P. Norbye. *The Complete History of Chrysler Corporation, 1924–1985.* New York: Beekman, 1985.

Moritz, Michael, and Barrett Seaman. *Going for Broke: Lee Iacocca's Battle to Save Chrysler.* Garden City, NY: Anchor Press/Doubleday, 1984.

Circuit City Stores

Circuit City provides an important example of how even large, popular retailers can fail when cost-conscious management shift from their traditional areas of expertise and jettison core competencies during times of economic contraction. Circuit City was a U.S.-based electronics retailer that sold personal computers, entertainment software, and other electronic products. The company opened its first stores in 1949 and liquidated its final U.S.-based stores in March 2009 following a bankruptcy filing and a failed effort to find a buyer.

History

Circuit City was first founded by Samuel S. Wurtzel as a part of the first Wards Company retail store in Richmond, Virginia, in 1949. By 1959, it operated four television and home appliance stores in the city. The company continued to grow over the next two decades, experimenting with several retail formats and names, finally changing its name to Circuit City and being listed on the New York Stock Exchange in 1984. The early slogans, for example, "Circuit City—Where Streets Are Paved With Bargains," touted the company's everyday low pricing strategy. By the late 1980s, the company had begun an aggressive national growth policy, highlighting its "plug" design stores, in which the entrance was in the shape of a plug, drawing consumers in. It also accentuated its core competency of exceptional service best exemplified by its slogan, "Welcome to Circuit City, Where Service Is State of the Art."

In 2000, the company exited the large-appliance market. This had been a profitable business to date, earning it $1.6 billion in revenues in 1999, but the company decided to focus on its original "plug design" electronic and computer-based products as well as music and movie sales. The updating of the stores cost $1.5 billion. The move was met with skepticism from investors, and within a few weeks the value of the company's stock plummeted to nearly a third of its one-year high. In 2003, the company moved from having a commissioned sales force to hourly "product specialists," resulting in the laying off of 3,900 employees, but the company realized $130 million a year in savings. In 2004, Circuit City co-branded with Verizon Wireless, allowing the latter to operate full-service sales and service centers in each of its superstores. Firedog, the company's upgraded in-store and in-home theater technical support and installation services, was introduced in 2006.

Decline, Bankruptcy, and Liquidation

Philip J. Schoonover, an executive vice president from rival Best Buy Stores, Inc., took over as chairman of the board of Circuit City in June 2006 and implemented cost-cutting strategies, which began the gradual decline of the company. His initiative of slashing salaries of management and sales associates appeared to hurt employee morale. Starting wages for sales associates in 2007 were dropped from $8.75 an hour to $7.40 an hour. That same year, the company also closed seven U.S.-based superstores, one Kentucky distribution center, and sixty-two stores in Canada to cut costs and improve its financial performance.

In Schoonover's first six months in office, three handpicked senior executives, including its chief financial officer, left the company, causing concerns among analysts. In the "wage management" program, 3,400 of the better-paid associates were laid off and were offered to be rehired ten weeks later at prevailing lower wages. The policy backfired and resulted in even lower sales. Schoonover resigned in September 2008.

On November 3, 2008, hit by falling consumer demand during the worst recession in decades, Circuit City announced that it would close 155 stores and lay off 17 percent of the workforce by the end of the year. A week later, it filed for bankruptcy protection under Chapter 11 of the U.S. Bankruptcy Code. The company had assets of $3.4 billion and a debt of $2.32 billion, including $119 million to Hewlett-Packard and $116 million to Samsung. Unable to find a buyer, Circuit City decided to close all of its remaining 567 stores on January 16, 2009. Approximately 30,000 employees lost their jobs in the liquidation.

Future of Electronics Retailing

Despite the demise of its major competitor, Best Buy cannot afford to rest easy. Analysts expect Wal-Mart to pick up at least half of Circuit City's customers and compete fiercely by deeper discounting. Best Buy's new chief executive officer as of June 2009, Brian Dunn, is hoping to distinguish his company by turning his stores into a series of interactive experiences, where customers can step into the world of a new videogame or see their faces on a high-definition video camera, instead of just walking past aisles stacked with merchandise. His main philosophy is to rely on the innovations proposed by the frontline workers in his company.

Abhijit Roy

See also: Recession and Financial Crisis (2007–).

Further Reading

Berfield, Susan. "Selling Out to the Bare Walls." *BusinessWeek*, March 12, 2009.

Bustillo, Miguel. "Best Buy Confronts Newer Nemesis—With Circuit City Gone, Electronics Retailer Arms Its 'Blue Shirt' Sales Force to Take On Wal-Mart." *Wall Street Journal*, March 16, 2009.

"Circuit City Arbitration Clause Struck Down." *Dispute Resolution Journal* 58:3 (2003).

Llovio, Louis. "Circuit City's Demise Vacates Lots of Retail Space." *McClatchy-Tribune Business News*, March 10, 2009.

Citigroup

A global financial services conglomerate serving 200 million customers in more than 100 countries, New York–based Citigroup Inc. provides an array of financial services, including retail, corporate, and investment banking, insurance, and asset management. Created in a 1998 merger of Citicorp, a banking powerhouse, and the Travelers Group, an insurance and financial services provider, Citigroup prospered mightily during the financial industry boom of the early

2000s before being hit hard by the financial crisis of 2008–2009. To shore up its assets in the face of heavy losses from securitized mortgage financial instruments, Citigroup accepted $45 billion under the federal government's Troubled Asset Relief Program (TARP) in late 2008.

The Citicorp side of Citigroup began as the City Bank of New York in 1812. Over the years, the bank acquired a number of other banks in the United States and overseas, even as its corporate named changed at various times. It emerged as America's largest commercial bank in terms of assets toward the end of the nineteenth century and the largest in the world by 1929. (In subsequent years, both distinctions would be lost to other banks from time to time, but Citicorp always remained among the largest in the United States and the world.) Citicorp did suffer its share of setbacks, however. Heavily involved in loans to the developing world in the 1970s and early 1980s, it posted a record $1.2 billion loss in 1987 and was forced to set aside a $3 billion reserve fund after falling commodity prices forced several countries to default.

As its name implies, the Travelers Insurance Company, founded in 1864, began by offering insurance against death and personal injury for those traveling on steamboats and railroads. It eventually grew into one of the largest American insurance companies, though it too had its stumbles. Facing heavy losses during the real-estate bust of the early 1990s and required to pay vast sums to policyholders in the wake of Hurricane Andrew, which devastated South Florida in 1992, Travelers formed an alliance, and then merged, with rival Primerica in 1993. The new company retained the Travelers name, though changed it to the Travelers Group in 1995. Meanwhile, the company had branched out into the financial services industry, acquiring the brokerage house Smith Barney in 1987 and the investment bank Salomon Brothers in 1998.

Citicorp and the Travelers Group came together as Citigroup in one of the largest mergers in corporate history, with the new firm having a market value of $140 billion and assets of nearly $700 billion. While the Glass-Steagall Act of 1933 ostensibly prevented banks from owning insurance companies, Citigroup won government approval of the merger by promising to sell off its insurance businesses. At the same time, however, it lobbied hard to get the relevant provision of Glass-Steagall overturned. In 1999, President Bill Clinton signed the Financial Services Modernization Act, which did exactly that.

While the legal hurdle to the banking-insurance merger had been overcome, other problems emerged. Turf battles arose among the various divisions of the company, and the hoped-for economies of scale proved elusive. In 2002, Citigroup spun off the property and casualty part of Travelers into a separate subsidiary, followed three years later by the sale of the life insurance division to MetLife. With these divestments, Citigroup sought to focus exclusively on banking and financial services.

Several divisions of Citigroup were implicated in the Enron investor fraud scandal of the early 2000s, which caused a 25 percent drop in the price of company stock price and forced Citigroup to set aside $1.5 billion for litigation costs. Nevertheless, the company prospered in the financial industry boom of the early to mid-2000s, posting profits of more than $15 billion in 2002, at the height of the scandal. From 2000 to 2004, the company enjoyed a compound annual growth rate of 8 percent in net revenues and 9 percent in operating income.

Through its financial services divisions, however, Citigroup also became deeply involved in collateralized debt obligations (CDOs), many of which included mortgages bundled into tradable financial instruments. Having underestimated the possibility of a collapse in real-estate prices and widespread mortgage foreclosure, Citigroup was heavily exposed when the housing bubble burst, beginning with defaults on subprime mortgages. As the crisis began to unfold in 2007, Citigroup moved to cut costs, laying off thousands of workers, and assured investors that the bank was not heavily exposed.

As the crisis deepened through 2008, Citigroup found itself in trouble on a number of fronts. Loans in virtually every form—from home mortgages it financed directly to CDOs to small-business loans and corporate financing—went into default. By November, the company was floundering, with losses close to $20 billion for the year; $10.1 billion in losses came in the fourth quarter alone, a company record. To cut costs, the company announced further layoffs, which put the total for the year at some 75,000.

The cost-cutting measures were not enough, however, and in November the company was forced to take $25 billion in TARP money to shore up its assets and avoid insolvency. When that proved insufficient, another $20 billion was added. Meanwhile, the value of company stock was plunging; total market valuation plummeted from $300 billion in 2006 to just $6 billion by the end of 2008. In the face of such a decline, the company negotiated a deal in which the federal government would provide a more than $300 billion guarantee for Citigroup loans and securities. And in early 2009, the company announced a major restructuring, reorganizing itself into two separate banking and brokerage units.

In February 2009, the newly installed Barack Obama administration agreed to take a 36 percent equity stake in the company by converting $25 billion of the aid money into common shares. So reduced were Citigroup's fortunes by mid-2009 that the Dow Jones announced it was removing the company from its much-watched Dow Jones Industrial Average, replacing it with the Travelers Insurance Group it spun off as a subsidiary in 2002.

Yet amid these setbacks, Citigroup made a solid recovery during the first half of 2009, posting significant profits in the first two quarters of the year. In April, it announced first-quarter profits of nearly $1.6 billion and insisted it would pay back the entire $45 billion in government loans. Some market analysts remained skeptical, saying the company still faced potentially painful write-downs in its automobile and credit card financing businesses. Such skepticism was borne out when Citi released its earnings report for the third quar-

ter, showing $3.2 billion in losses, most it from its Citi Holdings divisions, which held most of the troubled assets on the corporation's books.

James Ciment

See also: Banks, Commercial; Banks, Investment; Troubled Asset Relief Program (2008–).

Further Reading

Citigroup Web site: www.citigroup.com.

Langley, Monica. *Tearing Down the Walls: How Sandy Weill Fought His Way to the Top of the Financial World . . . and Then Nearly Lost It All.* New York: Free Press, 2004.

Stone, Amey, and Mike Brewster. *King of Capital: Sandy Weill and the Making of Citigroup.* New York: John Wiley & Sons, 2002.

Classical Theories and Models

The dominant school of economic thought from the time it arose with the work of Scottish economist Adam Smith and French economist Jean-Baptiste Say in the late eighteenth and early nineteenth centuries through the economic catastrophe of the Great Depression of the 1930s, classical economic theory argued that markets, operating under the principles of supply and demand, naturally tend toward equilibriums of full production and full employment. More to the point, this is the intellectual legacy of this school even though a careful reading of Smith, David Ricardo, Thomas Malthus, and Karl Marx—classical economists all—shows that they were quite aware of the prospects for unemployment and fluctuations in the business cycle.

Nevertheless, classical economics holds that recessions generally tend to be short-lived and self-correcting, requiring no government interference at the macroeconomic level. Indeed, any such interference is only likely to distort the proper functioning of the market, thereby prolonging the economic downturn. Although classical economists recognized the phenomenon of the business cycle, they did not attach great importance to it.

According to Say, the most well known proponent of the self-correcting market economy, supply creates its own demand. In other words, the income paid by producers to those who own the resources—such as the rent paid by tenant farmers to a landlord—will be repaid in equal amount by the resource owners who desire the goods or commodities. Of course, this would apply only in situations where land is the sole resource and farmers are the only producers. But, according to Say, such a scenario also plays out in the complexity of real-life economies. Say argued that the production of an economy generates precisely the level of income needed to purchase the economy's output of goods and services. Or, put another way, supply generates the demand to keep resources fully employed.

AN

INQUIRY

INTO THE

Nature and Caufes

OF THE

WEALTH OF NATIONS.

By ADAM SMITH, LL. D. and F. R. S.
Formerly Profeffor of Moral Philofophy in the Univerfity of GLASGOW.

IN TWO VOLUMES.

VOL. I.

LONDON:

PRINTED FOR W. STRAHAN; AND T. CADELL, IN THE STRAND.
MDCCLXXVI.

Classical theories of economic behavior begin with Adam Smith's two-volume *Wealth of Nations* (1776), which argues that competition should dictate wages and prices and that government should avoid interfering with market forces. *(The Granger Collection, New York)*

Thus, supply is the driver of the economy; it is a product of the push and pull of free-market forces. According to classical economists, an oversupply of goods causes prices to fall. Similarly, when there is excessive demand for goods—that is, when the demand outstrips the economy's capacity to produce—prices rise. Consumers react by buying less, thereby bringing supply and demand back into equilibrium. Conversely, when the economy produces more than people want, prices fall. This, in turn, triggers a rise in demand, again returning the economy to equilibrium.

The same rules are said to apply to employment and interest rates, since these constitute the price of labor and the price of money, respectively. If there are too many workers chasing too few jobs, wages fall, which spurs employers to increase hiring. When there are too few workers, wages rise until employers can no longer afford to pay them. Before that happens, however, the higher wages trigger greater demand, causing a rise in prices that negates the wage increase. Likewise with money, when there is too little in circulation, interest rates rise, which makes borrowing for investment more difficult. When investment shrinks, production slows, thereby adjusting the supply of goods to the amount of money in the economy.

While some pre-twentieth-century economists, most notably Karl Marx, argued that the equilibrium can be set at a level that produces great suffering (indeed, building on the work of Adam Smith and classical British economist David Ricardo, Marx asserted that capitalist economies naturally tend in that direction) they nevertheless held to the idea of supply-and-demand equilibrium of high output and low unemployment.

Government involvement in the economy, according to classical economists, should be restricted to creating a climate in which the markets can operate freely. Traditionally, this meant ensuring that contracts are honored through the establishment of a court system and ensuring domestic tranquility so that economic agents are not subject to violence or coercion. More expansively, classical economists embraced government measures at the microeconomic level. If, for example, a single firm dominates an economic sector—allowing it to set prices at will and thus distort the proper functioning of the market—then it might be within the government's purview to take measures, such as antitrust action, to ensure free competition.

The tendency toward market equilibrium—the heart of the classical economist's approach to the business cycle—was sorely tested by the Great Depression of the 1930s. Here was a situation in which the economy operated far below its productive and consumption capacity, with factories going idle and farm produce left to rot in the fields—nowhere near equilibrium. The rate of unemployment, meanwhile, hovered at 25 percent in the United States, more than six times what economists consider economically robust (the percentage of workers normally between jobs or opting to stay out of the workforce).

This situation led a number of economists at the time to question the classical paradigm of market equilibrium, the most important being British economist John Maynard Keynes. According to Keynes, the classical theory of equilibrium was wrong on several critical counts. First, said Keynes, demand is the critical component in the equation, not supply. Second, he said, aggregate demand—established by the spending decisions of individuals, businesses, and governments—is the product of a host of independent factors. In addition, Keynes argued, the classical assumption of wage and price flexibility is off the mark as well, since a number of factors make them quite inflexible. In short, he said, an equilibrium can be set at which an economy operates well below its capacity and full-employment level.

Just as classical economics had implications for government policy makers—essentially, leave macroeconomics alone and let the free market work out the problems for itself—so, too, did Keynesian economics. If the key to lifting an economy out of a low-employment, low-output equilibrium was to raise aggregate demand—and if individuals and businesses are incapable of doing so—then the only agent left is government. Thus, Keynes

argued that governments should abandon their classical economics bias and inject large sums into the economy during downturns as a way to smooth out the economic cycle—a process that classical economists argued could be achieved only by the market itself.

James Ciment

See also: Law, John; Malthus, Thomas Robert; Marshall, Alfred; Mill, John Stuart; Neoclassical Theories and Models; Smith, Adam.

Further Reading

Keynes, John Maynard. *The General Theory of Employment, Interest and Money.* London: Macmillan, 1936.

Knoop, Todd. *Recessions and Depressions: Understanding Business Cycles.* Westport, CT: Praeger, 2004.

Sowell, Thomas. *On Classical Economics.* New Haven, CT: Yale University Press, 2006.

Collateral

In finance, collateral is property that the borrower of a secured loan uses to back his or her promise to pay back a debt to a creditor—an asset the creditor can acquire in the event that the borrower defaults on the loan agreement, thus reducing the creditor's risk. In most real property mortgages, for instance, the house (or land or other building) that is being purchased also serves as the collateral for the loan; if the mortgage cannot be repaid, the bank extending the mortgage takes possession of the house through foreclosure, typically auctioning it off to recoup its investment. (The process of foreclosure is generally overseen by a court, which presents the borrower with the opportunity to protest if he or she feels that the foreclosure is unjust or unwarranted; it also helps ensure that a fair price is obtained for the property.)

On a smaller scale, the vehicle purchased with a car loan acts as the collateral for that loan; reclaiming the collateral in this case is called repossession, not foreclosure. Most smaller debts are likely to be unsecured, though items bought on store credit lines, such as furniture and major appliances, can be repossessed in case of default. While most credit card debt is unsecured, some financial institutions offer secured credit cards (intended for those repairing their credit), which require an initial deposit equal to a portion of the credit limit. The security deposit required to open an account with a utility company in the case of bad or no credit serves a similar function, as does the security deposit that landlords typically require of renters.

Cross-collateralization is the process of using the same property as collateral for more than one loan issued by the same institution. While this sounds like it works to the consumer's benefit, it often means that the title of a smaller purchase—typically a car or truck—remains with the lending institution until the much larger purchase—such as a house—has been paid off. And because the life of a mortgage usually exceeds the life of a car, this puts the borrower in the position of never completely owning the vehicle, despite having paid it off. Cross-collateralization does not apply to real estate; once a house or piece of land is paid off, it remains paid off even if other outstanding loans are owed to the institution.

Title Loans

A title loan is a sum of money extended to a borrower who uses the title to his or her car as the collateral. Typically short-term and high-interest, title loans are offered by companies that fill a niche in the lending landscape by providing smaller and higher-risk loans than banks typically offer. Such loans are often available online and granted without a credit check; the interest rate can be staggeringly high compared to that for more mainstream consumer loans, with annual percentage rates (APRs) well over 100 percent and often three or four times that. Minimum payments must cover the interest and, if the principal cannot be paid off at the end of term, the loan may be rolled over into another term, with

interest continuing to accumulate. Like payday loans—which offer fast cash at high interest to people in need of money and anticipating a paycheck—title loans are manageable for the borrower only if they are paid off quickly. And like check-cashing outlets, the lender profits from individuals with few financial services options and little financial acumen. State legislation increasingly limits title loans, both by the amount of the loan that can be extended and by the number of times it can be rolled over.

Collateralization

Collateralization, or securitization, is the process of creating asset-backed securities—that is, securities backed by a pool of assets from which the income and overall value of the securities is derived. In recent years, the most famous example of this is the collateralized mortgage obligation (CMO), a type of security first created by First Boston and Salomon Brothers on behalf of Freddie Mac, the government-sponsored enterprise, in 1983. CMOs are legal entities created to serve as the owner of a pool of mortgages, which are used to back bonds issued by the CMO. Like other asset-backed securities backed by collateralized debt, CMO bonds are structured in complex ways to allow more adjustments to the risk and return than could be made if investors were to simply pool their money together and buy a mortgage debt. The process developed for Freddie Mac allowed multiple types of bonds to be issued by a CMO, at different prices, with different interest rates, and with other different characteristics. The CMO may issue a hierarchy of bonds, for example, with those in the highest tier paid first; this runs the risk that there will be no money left to pay off the bonds on lower tiers, which thus sell at a lower price. (This could occur if a mortgage is paid off early, before the full twenty- or thirty- or forty-year term expires, which yields less income in the form of interest payments.) CMOs may also be issued that pay investors from the interest payments on the underlying mortgages—hence the name interest-only CDOs. On the other hand, principal-only CDOs pay investors from the principal payments on the underlying mortgages only.

Before long, specialists developed pooling techniques to shorter-term structured notes that were similar to CMO bonds. Then the technique was extended to other debt pools, including credit card debt, insurance contracts, small business loans, and so on. CDOs were even created that were backed by other CDOs, and those CDOs backed still other CDOs, to create several layers of investment. The complexity of the instruments resulted in a significant abstraction of the structured notes from the underlying assets used as collateral. In many cases, investors did not actually know what they owned—especially given the prevalence of CDOs in hedge funds, pension funds, and mutual funds. When the subprime mortgage crisis struck, many of the CMO bonds backed by subprime mortgages became part of the plague of toxic assets that contributed to the global financial crisis in 2008, when exposure to these assets ruined so many banks and other businesses.

Bill Kte'pi

See also: Collateralized Debt Obligations; Collateralized Mortgage Obligations; Debt; Debt Instruments.

Further Reading

Ahamed, Liaquat. *Lords of Finance: The Bankers Who Broke the World.* New York: Penguin, 2009.

Davenport, Penny, ed. *A Practical Guide to Collateral Management in the OTC Derivatives Market.* New York: Palgrave Macmillan, 2003.

Garrett, Joan. *Banks and Their Customers.* New York: Oceana Publications, 1995.

Sena, Vania. *Credit and Collateral.* New York: Routledge, 2007.

Collateralized Debt Obligations

Collateralized debt obligations (CDOs) are complex financial instruments created from pools of debt securities (obligations). CDOs are backed by the principal and interest payments made on the underlying securities, which are passed through to the owners of the CDO. The payments made on the CDOs are divided into different tranches (classes), or slices, with different risks. Since principal and interest payments are not passed through in a straightforward, proportional way, various risks can be transferred among investors in different tranches within the CDO. The CDO specifies the number of tranches, which have ranged from a few to around 100.

The three categories of tranches are the senior tranche, the mezzanine tranche, and the subordinate/equity tranche. Usually at least one of the tranches pays a floating rate where the interest rate is periodically reset based on an index. Those in the highest (most secure) tranche would be repaid principal and interest payments first, while those in the lowest (least secure) tranche would be repaid last and not until the securities in all the other tranches had been fully repaid. The investor in the most secure tranche would earn a lower return than the investor in a more risky tranche because of the lower risk. Given the different risks involved in the various CDO tranches, rating agencies such as Moody's, Standard & Poor's, and Fitch Ratings rate each tranche of the security separately. Investors in high-rated tranches can use the rating system to feel more secure about their investment, and all investors can more accurately evaluate the risk/return relationship.

History of CDOs

The first CDOs were created in 1983 in the mortgage market, where a type of CDO called a "collateralized mortgage obligation" (CMO) was developed by the government-sponsored enterprise Freddie Mac. The CDO market was dominated by CMOs through the 1990s, and the CMO market remains the largest part of CDO market. However, in the 1990s, the pool of assets from which a CDO was created began to spread to other debt securities, and in the early 2000s,

CDOs in nonmortgage-related securities began to grow exponentially. Today, CDOs have been created from one or more of the following categories of debt instruments:

- Investment-grade and noninvestment-grade corporate bonds
- Credit card balances, accounts receivable, auto loans, and student loans
- Emerging market bonds
- Domestic and foreign bank loans

Example of a CDO

A CDO consisting of bank loans, called a collateralized loan obligation (CLO), is constructed as follows: Every CDO has a sponsor. Suppose that the sponsor is a bank that wants to securitize some of its loan portfolio to reduce its capital. Loans are assets to the bank, and regulatory capital requirements specify a capital-to-assets ratio that must be maintained. By sponsoring a CDO, the bank can reduce the loans on its balance sheet, thus increasing its capital-to-assets ratio. At the same time, the bank can get new funds to lend from the sale of the CDO. A second reason why a sponsor may create a CDO is if the sponsor believes a profit can be made on the CDO and this profit becomes the motivating force. The CDO will have a collateral manager that purchases the loans from the bank and issues debt obligations (CDOs) to pay for them. Again, the CDO could be based on a pool of bonds, mortgages, or pools of other debt instruments.

Consider the above case where the sponsor buys $100 million of loans from Bank A. The loans earn 10 percent interest per year for the next ten years. Thus, the loans in the pool will earn $10 million per year in interest ($100 million × 10 percent = $10 million). For simplicity, assume that the loans are bullet or balloon loans where the principal ($100 million in this case) is due at maturity. Assume there are only three tranches and that payments are made according to the table that follows.

Tranche Type	Par Value	Fixed or Floating Rate	Coupon Rate (annual percent interest paid as a percentage of face value of the CDO)
Senior	$70 million	Floating	T-bill rate + 150 basis points
Mezzanine	$20 million	Fixed	8 percent
Subordinate	$10 million	—	—

The senior tranche pays investors a floating rate equal to the one-year T-bill rate plus 150 basis points. (One basis point is 0.01 percent, so 150 basis points is 1.5 percent.) Thus, if the one-year T-bill rate is 5 percent, then senior tranches would pay 6.5 percent. CDOs in the mezzanine class pay investors a fixed interest rate of 8 percent. The subordinate/ equity class (that put up $10 million) would get the remainder if any funds are left over.

Hedging Interest Rate Risk on CDOs

In the example above, to hedge the risk that the floating rate payable to investors in the senior tranche might increase to a rate greater than the 10 percent of the underlying loans in the pool earn, the CDO sponsor can enter into an interest rate swap agreement. An interest rate swap agreement allows for a fixed interest rate stream, such as the 10 percent earned on the pool of loans, to be traded for a floating interest rate stream that resets periodically based on an index. Only the interest streams and not the principal balances that generate the income streams are traded.

In the previous example, assume that the sponsor enters into an interest rate swap agreement where the fixed stream of 10 percent earned on the loans in the senior tranche is traded for a floating stream to be paid to investors in the senior tranche based on the one-year T-bill rate plus 150 basis points. Thus, by entering into the interest rate swap, the sponsor is able to hedge (or in this case, eliminate) the risk that changes in the interest payments to the senior tranche will reduce or eliminate potential profits to the subordinate/equity class.

The flows of funds per year resulting from the CDOs are as follows.

Tranche Type	Par Value	Coupon Rate	Interest Received from CDO	Interest Paid to Investor	Return
Senior	$70 million	T-bill + 150 basis points	$7 million	–$7 million because of interest rate swap*	$0
Mezzanine	$20 million	8 percent fixed	$2 million	–$1.6 million	$0.4 million
Subordinate	$10 million	—	$1 million	—	$1 million
Residual funds left over for subordinate/equity class	—	—	$10 million	–$8.6 million	$1.4 million

*Note that the sponsor entered into an interest rate swap agreement to pay the fixed interest rate of 10 percent earned on the senior tranche in exchange for receiving the T-bill rate plus 150 basis points, which is then passed on to the investors in the senior tranches.

For example, ($70 million × 10% = $7 million) – ($70 million × 10% = $7 million) = $0 million. Therefore, the sponsor had a net receipt of $0 million.

Thus, in this case, the investors in the subordinate tranche that invested $10 million will get the original $10 million back plus an additional $1.4 million (14 percent) per year for 10 years. This, of course, assumes all the interest and principal payments on the underlying loans are paid in full. If the principal and interest on the underlying loans in the CDO are not fully repaid, or if the interest rate swap adversely affects the sponsor, the return to the subordinate tranche may be reduced or eliminated.

CDOs and the Recession and Financial Crisis of 2007–2009

CDOs played a significant role in the global financial crisis and accompanying recession (2007–2009), when investors found out that things do not always turn out as hoped for or anticipated. Defaults in the CDO market significantly contributed to and exacerbated the crisis.

The financial crisis began in the subprime mortgage market. Many of the loans involved in subprime mortgages were made to borrowers with bad credit and involved little or no down payment. They were often made at low teaser interest rates that would reset to higher rates within a few years. These and other mortgages were then repackaged and sold as mortgage-backed securities or as CMOs (a type of CDO) in the global marketplace. Many of these securities had been rated AAA by the rating agencies and hence were attractive investments for global investors.

At the same time, the issuances of other types of CDOs (which had been relatively small prior to 2000) were also increasing. In 2000, the global issuance of all CDOs was about $67 billion. CDO issuances increased to over $250 billion in 2005 and to over $520 billion in 2006. As more and more homeowners had trouble making their house payments on the reset subprime loans, borrowers started defaulting at alarming rates on loans that had been securitized into mortgage-backed securities or CMOs. This caused a crisis in these markets, and as housing prices started to fall, more and more homeowners defaulted. The crisis in the CMO market quickly spread to all CDOs, as investors became dubious about the creditworthiness of these exotic securities. Prices plummeted as the securities were dumped in the market. As the crisis spread from the mortgage market to other financial markets and then to the broader economy, the situation further deteriorated. As the securitized payment on income streams of all types of debt instruments became more uncertain, defaults on all types of securities spread. The CDO market exacerbated the crisis by the sheer volume of securities that had been sold into global markets to investors who really had little knowledge about the risks of the assets in which they were investing. By 2007, issuances of new CDOs fell to about $481 billion, and then dropped precipitously to $61 billion in 2008 and to just over $4.2 billion in 2009.

The largest banks in the country were also heavily involved in CDOs. Losses in CDOs became one of the factors limiting credit extension by the largest banks throughout the crisis and into early 2010, despite the enormous injections of cash into the banks by the Federal Reserve. Because of the large losses in these markets, questions have been raised about the appropriateness of the behavior of some of the largest banks. In January 2010, the Securities and Exchange Commission (SEC) sent subpoenas to Goldman Sachs, Credit Suisse, Citigroup, Bank of America/Merrill Lynch, Deutsche Bank, UBS, Morgan Stanley, and Barclays Capital to investigate their involvement with a particular type of CDO called a synthetic CDO, that is, a CDO based on one or more previously existing CDOs. It is feared that the largest banks could take enormous losses in the future on synthetic CDOs, similar to the losses they have already taken on CDOs backed by subprime mortgages.

It is clear that the risks involved in these securities were not understood by either the rating agencies or the investors, and that U.S. government failed to sufficiently regulate these markets.

Maureen Burton and Jamie Shuk Ki Yuen

See also: Collateral; Collateralized Mortgage Obligations; Debt; Financial Markets; Recession and Financial Crisis (2007–); Securitization.

Further Reading

Burton, Maureen, and Bruce Brown. *The Financial System and the Economy.* 5th ed. Armonk, NY: M.E. Sharpe, 2009.

Burton, Maureen, Reynold Nesiba, and Bruce Brown. *An Introduction to Financial Markets and Institutions.* 2nd ed. Armonk, NY: M.E. Sharpe, 2010.

Fabozzi, Frank J., Franco Modigliani, and Frank J. Jones. *Foundations of Financial Markets and Institutions.* 4th ed. Upper Saddle River, NJ: Prentice Hall, 2009.

Lucas, Douglas J., Laurie S. Goodman, and Frank J. Fabozzi. *Collateralized Debt Obligations: Structures and Analysis.* 2nd ed. Hoboken, NJ: John Wiley & Sons, 2006.

"Risk Management of Investment in Structured Credit Products." *Financial Institution Letter,* FIL-20–2009. Washington, DC: Federal Deposit Insurance Corporation, April 30, 2009.

Rosner, Joshua, and Jospeh R. Mason. *Collateral Debt Obligations.* Available at www.hudson.org/files/documents/Mason_Rosner percent20for percent20posting.pdf. Accessed February 2007.

Securities Industry and Financial Markets Association Web site: www.sifma.org.

Collateralized Mortgage Obligations

A collateralized mortgage obligation (CMO) is a financial instrument (security) created from a pool of mortgages or mortgage-backed securities (MBSs) that redirects the cash flows (principal and interest) from the underlying mortgages to different classes of investors. The originator of the CMO takes a pool of mortgages or a mortgage-backed security and sells new securities based upon the redistribution of the cash flows into different tranches or slices with differing risks. CMOs meet the demands of investors (usually institutions) for securities with varying risks and returns. (CMOs should not be confused with collateralized debt obligations, or CDOs, which involve various types of nonmortgage debt, though the two are similar in structure.)

History of CMOs

A mortgage-backed security is a security backed by a pool of mortgages that provides cash flows to investors. CMOs are securities like mortgage-backed securities in that they are backed by the cash flows from a pool of mortgages. However, the cash flows of the CMOs are divided into different tranches (slices) or classes to create new securities with different risks and returns that would appeal to different investors.

For example, if an investor was looking for a short-term investment, he or she could invest in the tranche where all of the flows of principal went to that tranche first. Investors in other tranches would initially receive cash flows of interest payments only until after the principal of the previous tranche was paid in full. Those investors that preferred long-term instruments could purchase securities created from the tranche that was last to receive principal payments. There are two broad types of CMOs: agency-backed CMOs and non-agency-backed CMOs.

Agency-Backed CMOs

Agency-backed CMOs are created from pools of mortgages or mortgage-backed securities issued and insured by the government-sponsored entities Fannie Mae and Freddie Mac, or the government-owned corporation Ginnie Mae (National Mortgage Association). The mortgages in these CMOs are all insured by these institutions and have no default risk. That is, their principal and interest payments are fully insured by the government or a government-sponsored enterprise and will be paid even if the original borrower defaults. However, investors in mortgage-backed securities with no default risk still face the risk that the mortgages in the pool will be prepaid sooner than expected because the property is sold or because the mortgage is refinanced due to a decrease in interest rates. This risk is called "prepayment risk." If more mortgages than expected are prepaid, then the return falls short of expectations because the investor receives his or her funds back before the full return is realized. Moreover, if there have been greater-than-expected prepayments due to decreases in interest rates, then the funds received back early will have to be reinvested at a lower rate. Likewise, if interest rates go up, fewer mortgages than anticipated will be repaid and the maturity of the securities will be longer than anticipated.

This dilemma could lead to a problem if the investor had planned to receive the funds back sooner rather than later. An agency-backed CMO deals with these problems by dividing the cash flows from the pool of mortgages into different tranches. Those who wanted shorter-term instruments could invest in a tranche that received principal payments first. Those who wanted longer-term instruments could invest in a tranche that postponed receiving any principal payments until all other investors in the various tranches had been repaid. For example, CMO tranches could be designed to amortize sequentially. One class might have the right to all of the initial principal payments, while other classes have to wait until the first class is paid off before receiving any principal payments. Once the first class is paid off, the second class begins to receive scheduled and unscheduled principal payments. By designing the classes to be paid down sequentially, it is possible to create short-term, medium-term, and long-term securities.

Thus, the CMO took a typical mortgage-backed security or pool of mortgages and divided it into a series of tranches with different prepayment risks. The newly directed CMO redirects the cash flows (principal and interest) of mortgage-backed securities to various classes of bondholders, thus creating financial instruments with varying prepayment risks and varying returns. Those who are most risk averse to a prepayment risk or who want a short-term investment can choose an instrument wherein the principal will be repaid soonest. Those who are willing to bear more risk can choose an instrument wherein the principal will not be repaid until later, and hence, is subject to a greater prepayment risk. In exchange for more prepayment risk, the investor may receive a higher return. Needless to say, such provisions make attractive choices available to a wider range of investors. Finally, since CMOs are fixed-rate debt instruments, there is an interest rate risk in that, if the interest rate goes up, the value of the fixed-rate CMOs will go down. If an investor had to sell the CMO in the secondary market before maturity, he or she would experience a capital loss.

Nonagency-Backed CMOs

Nonagency-backed CMOs are similar to agency-backed CMOs with the exception that they are backed by pools of mortgages that are not insured by Fannie Mae, Freddie Mac, or Ginnie Mae. Thus, in addition to prepayment risk, there is some credit risk that the mortgages will not be repaid and the cash flows will fall short of anticipated. Some nonagency-backed CMOs were formed from pools of relatively safe mortgages or mortgage-backed securities with little default risk. However, others were formed by pools of subprime mortgages where there was a great deal of default risk. With nonagency CMOs, the cash flows from the underlying mortgages are divided into tranches that direct principal payments to different classes of investors. Those in senior tranches receive principal and interest payments first and thus are more likely to be repaid in full. Those in lower tranches receive a higher return for accepting more default risk. Because of the default risk, each of the tranches in a CMO (except the lowest tranche) is rated by one or more of the rating agencies—Moody's, Standard & Poor's, and Fitch—to give investors some idea of the risks of investing in the various tranches. The lowest tranche is a subordinate/equity tranche that is not rated by a rating agency and is often held by the originators of the CMO. This tranche has the highest risk, but the originators believe it offers the highest possible return.

This shifting of risk creates relatively secure classes called "senior securities" and a relatively risky class called the "subordinate/equity class." Between the two lie the so-called mezzanine CMO tranches. Losses resulting from mortgage loan defaults are first absorbed by the most subordinated CMO class, followed by the next most subordinated class, and so on. If the loss of mortgage principal is large enough, even the senior class may experience losses. The ability to reallocate the cash flow in a pool of mortgages or a portfolio of MBSs makes the market for CMOs much deeper and broader than for simple MBSs. Note that even the senior tranches of the CMOs formed by pools of subprime mortgages were rated high (low risk) by the rating agencies because it was believed that the lower tranches would absorb any defaults. The number of tranches in CMOs has increased dramatically from the original three-class CMO issued by Freddie Mac in 1983. In 2007, CMOs were being issued with close to 100 classes.

CMO classes can also be structured so that a tranche receives only interest or only principal payments. These are known as interest-only securities (IOs) and principal-only securities (POs). IOs and POs appeal to investors with different needs and expectations about the prepayment behavior of borrowers. Investors in POs want the mortgages to be paid off as soon as possible because that would give them the highest return. If they have to wait a long time to receive their principal payment, the return is reduced. For example, if an investor invests $10,000 in a PO to receive $20,000 on some future date, then the return will depend on how soon the principal is paid. If the principal is prepaid in one year, the investor earns a 100 percent return because his or her investment has doubled in one year. However, if the principal payment is not received for twenty years, the return is reduced to about 3.5 percent per year since $10,000 invested at 3.5 percent for twenty years is approximately equal to $20,000. For IOs, the investor receives interest payments only until the mortgages are paid off. Thus, investors in IOs do not want mortgages to be paid off early whereas for investors in POs the sooner the mortgages are paid off, the higher the return.

Finally, since CMOs are predominantly fixed-rate debt instruments, there is an interest rate risk in investing in either agency-backed or nonagency-backed CMOs. That is, if the interest rate goes up, the value of the fixed-rate CMOs will go down. If an investor had to sell the CMO in the secondary market before maturity, she would experience a capital loss.

CMOs and the Financial Crisis of 2008–2009

CMOs played an integral role in the financial crisis of 2008–2009. Defaults in the subprime mortgage market led to losses in CMOs that were backed by subprime mortgages, a type of nonagency CMO. The crisis in the subprime market quickly spread to other mortgage markets and caused defaults on mortgages that were packaged into agency CMOs and thus guaranteed by Fannie Mae and Freddie Mac. Losses in these markets spread to other markets and led to the collapse of numerous financial institutions that eventually spilled over to the real estate sector, causing the severest recession since the Great Depression of the 1930s. Because of the losses to Fannie Mae and Freddie Mac, the two government-sponsored enterprises were put into conservatorship by the U.S. government in September 2008.

A look at the spectacular growth of these markets from the mid-1990s until 2009 is also revealing and supports the notion that the creation of these instruments allowed for huge flows of funds into the mortgage markets and contributed to the housing price bubble that eventually burst with such disastrous results. For example, the table below shows the amount outstanding of agency and nonagency MBSs and CMOs for various years from 1995 to 2009. Data for MBSs and CMOs are reported together.

In addition to the tremendous growth of these securities, note that after the financial crisis began in 2007, the amount outstanding of nonagency-backed securities actually fell by over $600 billion. The amount of agency securities—those insured by Fannie Mae, Freddie Mac, or Ginnie Mae—actually increased by over $800 billion in this period. This was despite the fact that Fannie Mae and Freddie Mac were put into conservatorship by the U.S. government and were virtually insolvent, with over $100 billion of taxpayer funds having been injected into them. Thus, firms that experienced the most severe strains still managed to increase the pool of assets that they insure by over $800 billion. Although still buying MBSs and CMOs, Fannie Mae and Freddie Mac were far from out of the woods when government officials announced in December 2009 that the U.S. Treasury would give them virtually unlimited support over the next three years. Finally, the Federal Reserve (in addition to the increased purchases by Fannie Mae and Freddie Mac) has purchased over $1 trillion in mortgage-backed securities and agency-backed securities as of February 2010. They are authorized and plan to purchase $1.25 trillion of mortgage-backed securities and agency-backed securities. This reflects the extent to which policy makers have tried to mitigate the severe downturn caused by the collapse of mortgage market and mortgage derivative markets, including MBSs and CMOs.

Maureen Burton and Jamie Shuk Ki Yuen

See also: Collateral; Collateralized Debt Obligations; Financial Markets; Housing Booms and Busts; Mortgage-Backed Securities; Mortgage Lending Standards; Mortgage Markets and Mortgage Rates; Mortgage, Subprime; Recession and Financial Crisis (2007–); Securitization.

Further Reading

Burton, Maureen, and Bruce Brown. *The Financial System and the Economy.* 5th ed. Armonk, NY: M.E. Sharpe, 2009.

Burton, Maureen, Reynold Nesiba, and Bruce Brown. *An Introduction to Financial Markets and Institutions.* 2nd ed. Armonk, NY: M.E. Sharpe, 2010.

Fabozzi, Frank J., Franco Modigliani, and Frank J. Jones. *Foundations of Financial Markets and Institutions.* 4th ed. Upper Saddle River, NJ: Prentice Hall, 2009.

Investing in Bonds.com. "The Various Type of CMOs." Available at http://www.investinginbonds.com/learnmore.asp?catid=5&subcatid=17&id=35. Accessed May 2010.

Mortgage-Backed Securities and Collateralized Mortgage Obligations, 1955–2009 (billions of dollars, amounts outstanding end of period)

Year	Agency MBSs and CMOs	Nonagency MBSs and CMOs	Total*
1995	$1,570.7	$241.5	$1,812.2
2000	$2,493.2	$604.5	$3,097.7
2003	$3,326.7	$1,009.3	$4,336.0
2005	$3,541.9	$2,131.3	$5,673.2
2007	$4,463.5	$2,946.8	$7,410.3
2009**	$5,299.7	$2,305.3	$7,605.0

*Board of Governors of the Federal Reserve, *Flow of Funds*, Z.1. December 10, 2009.
**Through September 30, 2009.

Colombia

Unlike most Latin American countries, Colombia—a nation of roughly 45 million located in northwestern South America—has enjoyed a relatively stable political and economic history, with no military coups. Still, the country is deeply divided by wealth, with most Colombians living in great poverty. Political and class violence is not unknown, and the last decades of the twentieth century were marred by widespread violence from criminal and revolutionary groups. Despite the disorder, however, Colombia's export-driven economy avoided the extremes of other economies in the region. But because of this reliance on exports, Colombia has been hard hit by the U.S. and global recessions of the late 2000s.

Before independence from Spain in the early nineteenth century, Colombia was a relatively sparsely populated country. The first decades as an independent country did not change that fact. Most people lived in the northwestern part of the country, separated into disconnected regions by branches of the Andes. Internal transportation depended largely upon pack mules, and few goods had enough value to be shipped very far. Colombia's most important export was gold. During the 1840s, however, British investment encouraged the development of tobacco exports. The Magdalena River provided a more economical route to bring tobacco from the interior to waiting ships, and profits from the trade bought steamboats to speed up the process. Tobacco was joined by other exports, including cotton, indigo, and cinchona bark, but Colombia remained an insignificant exporter until the twentieth century.

After 1865, the burgeoning international market for coffee encouraged Colombian landowners to grow it. Mountain slopes, which could be used for little else, were very suitable for the crop. By 1890, coffee had become Colombia's primary export. The first growers were large landowners, but small and medium landowners soon became the primary growers. Income from the relatively dependable coffee crop provided funds for new industries and for consumer spending. After 1910, coffee production increased rapidly, until Colombia exported 10 percent of the world's supply in 1929.

Agricultural products dominated the Colombian economy for most of the twentieth century. Cotton, sugarcane, and other tropical products supplemented the coffee exports. Colombian industry remained small and produced goods primarily for domestic consumption. Tariffs helped protect the small industrial sector from foreign competition. The economy continued to grow at a steady, moderate pace.

Politically, Colombia was divided between supporters of the Liberal and Conservative parties. Conservatives held power from 1884 to 1930, but uprisings by Liberals resulted in thousands of deaths in the 1890s. As a result, some Liberal ministers were included in all cabinets. Liberals regained power between 1930 and 1946. When a prominent Liberal leader was assassinated in 1948, rioting in the capital of Bogotá and uprisings throughout the country resulted in thousands of deaths. In 1958, Liberals and Conservatives agreed to a power-sharing arrangement, in which each party would alternate holding the presidency for four years. Other political groups were shut out of power. In the late 1960s, a number of rebel groups began a guerrilla war against the established order.

The great poverty in which most Colombians lived, as well as the widespread violence, led some to move to the sparsely inhabited lowlands in the southeastern part of the country. They found that coca, marijuana, and other crops that could become illegal drugs grew well in the climate. Beginning in the late 1960s, the worldwide demand for recreational drugs increased, and cartels formed to grow, refine, and supply them. By the 1970s, Colombian drug cartels had accumulated massive amounts of dollars, which they laundered through such legitimate operations as land purchase. The inflow of dollars helped fuel inflation, while violence associated with cartels that were protecting their markets helped destabilize the country. Government efforts to stifle this illegal economy were largely unsuccessful, but did bring increased American aid. When unemployment among the poor in legal businesses increased, drug cartels were able to provide work and income.

In 1990, President César Gaviria Trujillo

The world's third-largest coffee producer, Colombia relies heavily on exports for economic stability. The global recession of the late 2000s thus had a major impact, compounded by a small coffee harvest at decade's end. *(Rodrigo Arangua/ AFP/Getty Images)*

implemented a policy of economic liberalism. Tariffs were reduced and many industries were deregulated. State-owned businesses were privatized and a more liberal foreign-exchange rate was adopted. Free-trade arrangements were made with other Latin American countries, especially Chile, Mexico, and Venezuela. To ensure affordable food for the poor, Gaviria also adopted a policy of encouraging the growth of agricultural products that could readily be exported. Coffee, cacao, and cut flowers found ready markets in the United States, while wheat, soybeans, and corn were imported. The policy kept food prices low and the economy grew at an annual rate of 4.5 percent, but made Colombia heavily dependent on imports for survival.

The 1990s also saw the increased export of energy and mineral products. Hydroelectric plants produced electricity, which was made available to neighboring states. Petroleum deposits were developed and oil became the leading export in 1991. Oil was sent via pipeline from the interior

to the Pacific port of Tumaco for export. Coal also became a significant export, along with nickel, gold, silver, and emeralds.

Social unrest remained a stumbling block for the Colombian economy in the 1990s, however. Paramilitary groups organized by the Right assassinated many labor and indigenous leaders who spoke out for greater equality. Rebels and drug cartels attacked government installations and pipelines carrying oil, prompting U.S. military aid. Thanks to an overvalued peso and increased government spending, a deficit budget helped bring on a recession in 1999. Unemployment rose to 20 percent. Foreign investments declined, worsening the situation. In 2002, Álvaro Uribe was elected president on promises to restore peace and security. Loans from the World Bank, the Inter-American Development Bank, and the Andean Development Corporation helped Uribe to increase spending on social programs. Military forces were increased as well, and rebel threats were reduced. The power of the drug cartels was also curtailed, but not eliminated. The supply of cocaine has been limited, but international demand means that trafficking will continue.

The worldwide recession beginning in 2007 reduced the demand for Colombian exports and led to economic hardships. Growth rates slowed dramatically, from more than 7 percent in 2007 to just 2.5 percent in 2008 to −1 percent in 2009, a performance that put Colombia among the hardest hit of Latin American economies during the recession of the late 2000s.

Tim J. Watts

See also: Latin America.

Further Reading

Hylton, Forrest. *Evil Hour in Colombia.* New York: Verso, 2006.

Safford, Frank, and Marco Palacios. *Colombia: Fragmented Land, Divided Society.* New York: Oxford University Press, 2002.

Schneider, Ben Ross. *Business Politics and the State in Twentieth-Century Latin America.* New York: Cambridge University Press, 2004.

Commodity Markets

The role of a commodity market is to provide a locus for buyers and sellers to trade physical commodities at spot prices or to trade derivative instruments of the physical commodities (futures and options). Traditional commodities include agricultural products, livestock and meat, forest products, metals and minerals (precious and industrial), and energy. Commodity markets serve as mechanisms to provide market price discovery and to transfer risk. In recent decades, certain nonconventional derivative instruments have been traded on commodity markets. Nonconventional "exotic" derivatives include derivatives of financial instruments (financial futures and options) and derivative products related to environmental emissions, telecommunications bandwidth, and weather conditions.

Commodities (or derivatives of commodities) are typically traded in standardized contracts that specify the product, its deliverable grade (quality), the contract size, the pricing unit, the incremental minimum fluctuation (tick size), daily price limit trade, and, in the case of futures and options, delivery dates, settlement procedure, and any special conditions. Commodities and derivatives have individual trading symbols.

There are approximately fifty major commodity markets and exchanges around the world, known by the cities in which they are located. London and New York are the principal international commodity markets, and Chicago is the leading domestic commodity market in the United States. Some of these trade in a wide variety of offerings, while others are highly specialized. Metals are largely traded in London, New York, Chicago, and Shanghai. New York, London, and Tokyo are centers of energy-based trading. Most of the markets offer electronic trading, auction trading on a trading floor (public outcry, ring trading, or pit trading), and centrally cleared over-the-counter, off-exchange trading.

Speculation as a Positive Force

Commodity markets function on speculation. Although this term has a negative popular connotation, the activity can also serve to enhance overall utility—that is, to maximize the benefits of commodities for society in general. This does not seem to be the case at first glance, as most speculators who purchase commodity contracts have no interest in the delivery of the actual goods. Instead, they are hoping to make a profit on price fluctuations, unloading the contract before the delivery date to someone who actually wants the commodities.

Major World Commodity Exchanges

Exchange	Headquarters Nation	Products Traded
CME (Chicago Mercantile Exchange and Chicago Board of Trade)	United States	Agriculture, timber
New York Mercantile Exchange (NYMEX)	United States	Energy, agriculture, metals, freight, environment, energy
IntercontinentalExchange	United States	Agriculture, energy, environment
London Metal Exchange	United Kingdom	Metals, plastics
Minor Metals Trade Association	United Kingdom	Metals, metal by-products
Zhengzhou Commodity Exchange	China	Agriculture, plastics
Dalian Commodity Exchange	China	Agriculture, plastics
Multi Commodity Exchange	India	Agriculture, metals, energy, environment
National Commodity and Derivatives Exchange	India	Agriculture, metals, energy, plastics, financial instruments
Abuja Securities and Commodity Exchange	Nigeria	Agriculture
BM&FBovespa	Brazil	Agriculture, energy, financial instruments
Dubai Mercantile Exchange	United Arab Emirates	Energy

Source: Frank L. Winfrey.

Even barring unforeseen events—like a frost that damages a Florida orange crop or a hurricane that threatens oil production on the Gulf Coast—commodity prices vary from place to place and over time. Buying and selling commodities between markets, an activity known as arbitrage, ensures that the cost of a crop in one market will be about the same, aside from shipping costs, as in another. Similarly, most crops are harvested at a given time of year; if an entire crop were sold at harvest, the price would drop precipitously. Speculators, then, buy up the commodity, put it in storage, and sell it later—thereby smoothing out the price over the course of the year. Such activities can be a boon to consumers.

For producers and processors, the speculation inherent in commodity markets offers a form of insurance. Commodity prices, particularly those of weather-affected crops, are notoriously volatile. Producers, usually farmer cooperatives, and processors, such as those who run storage facilities and canning, freezing, or bottling plants, can lock in a price by buying a commodity futures contract. A futures contract is one in which a buyer and a seller agree today on the price and quantity of a commodity that will be delivered later. Futures agreements are standardized with regard to quantities and delivery dates. They are traded on organized commodity exchanges. Many producers will purchase futures contracts on the type of commodity they produce. Note that prices of futures contracts are highly correlated with spot prices (the price for immediate delivery). If their crop is damaged—again, using a frost in Florida as an example—it is likely that other producers will be hurt as well, pushing both spot and futures prices up. Producers then make a profit on the futures contract because they can sell the contract at a higher price than they paid, making a profit to offset the losses the frost caused in their own crop. This activity is known as "hedging."

The Chicago Mercantile Exchange, founded in 1898 as the Chicago Butter and Egg Board, merged with the Chicago Board of Trade in 2007 to form CME Group, the largest commodity futures and options exchange in the United States. *(Scott Olson/ Stringer/Getty Images)*

Hedging has benefits for processors as well. If the owner of a corn warehouse buys a crop in the fall, hoping to sell it in the spring, and the price drops significantly in the intervening months, he or she could lose a large amount of money. To offset that risk, the warehouse owner purchases futures contracts, thereby hedging against the exposure of all the corn in his or her warehouse to price fluctuations.

Speculation as a Negative Force

While most commodity speculation serves the larger societal good, it can have deleterious effects as well. Efforts to corner markets, or buy up virtually all of a given commodity, can lead to a buying and selling frenzy that often drives up prices temporarily, only to crash when the corner fails. Efforts by speculators to corner the gold market, for example, contributed to the financial panic of 1873, which led to a prolonged economic recession in the United States. More recently, many economists blame market speculators for the spectacular run-up in oil prices in 2008, worsening a recession that had begun in late 2007.

Positive or negative, this kind of commodity trading is as old as agriculture and trade itself, though the market in futures was not fully realized until the development of railroads in the mid-nineteenth century, which allowed for more timely delivery of goods over greater distances. Over time, markets have been developed for any number of commodities as they became marketable, such as petroleum in the nineteenth century and uranium in the twentieth. But these represent mere additions to an existing paradigm. In the 1990s, for example, the Texas-based energy firm Enron pioneered a host of new products for futures trading, involving energy and telecommunications bandwidth. The company collapsed in 2001, though not because of the intrinsic risk involved in futures speculation but because of excessive debt and fraudulent accounting practices.

On a vastly greater scale, financial institutions began to develop futures contracts on the products they specialize in. Beginning in the 1980s but accelerating in the 1990s and 2000s, investment banks and brokerage houses created futures contracts on mortgages and interest rates. Known as derivatives because their value is derived from other assets, these forms of futures contracts were at the heart of the crisis that struck the global financial markets in 2008. Part of the problem was that these products were so unusual that they fell outside the purview of government watchdog agencies and were too complicated for many of the institutions investing in them to understand the risk they entailed.

While financial derivatives have received a black eye because of the crisis, the expansion of futures markets to other noncommodity products continues in other areas. The cap-and-trade system on carbon emissions being promoted in various countries, including the United States, would allow companies to buy and sell their emissions. The underlying principle is that the marketplace provides a more efficient mechanism for allocating the costs of carbon emission reduction—essential in preventing catastrophic climate change—than taxes, fines, and specific government-mandated limits.

James Ciment and Frank L. Winfrey

See also: Agriculture.

Further Reading

Gallacher, William R. *Winner Take All: A Brutally Honest and Irreverent Look at the Motivations and Methods of Top Traders.* New York: McGraw-Hill, 1994.

Geman, Hélyette, ed. *Risk Management in Commodity Markets: From Shipping to Agriculturals and Energy.* Hoboken, NJ: John Wiley & Sons, 2008.

Morrison, Kevin. *Living in a Material World: The Commodity Connection.* Hoboken, NJ: John Wiley & Sons, 2008.

National Futures Association. *Opportunity and Risk: An Educational Guide to Trading Futures and Options on Futures.* Chicago: National Futures Association, 2006.

Schofield, Neil C. *Commodity Derivatives: Markets and Applications.* Hoboken, NJ: John Wiley & Sons, 2007.

Community Reinvestment Act (1977)

The Community Reinvestment Act of 1977 (CRA) was passed in the Ninety-Fifth U.S. Congress and signed into law by President Jimmy Carter. This federal law was designed to encourage commercial banks and savings institutions to reduce discriminatory lending practices in low- and moderate-income neighborhoods. The act ensures that lenders "help meet credit needs of the entire community, including low- and moderate-income neighborhoods in a manner consistent with safe and sound operation of the institution." Recently, critics of the act point to the CRA as an important factor in the financial a crisis of 2008, citing the fact that it lowered standards for mortgage lending, thereby contributing to the spread of subprime mortgages, the financial instrument at the heart of the crisis.

The goal of the act was to reduce discriminatory credit practices against low-income and minority neighborhoods, a practice known as redlining. To enforce the statute, federal regulatory agencies were required to assess each bank's and savings institution's record in terms of its compliance with the law before approving the opening of new bank branches or approving mergers and acquisitions. The law, however, does not entitle institutions to make high-risk loans that might bring about losses. Recent amendments to the CRA have allowed community groups to better access CRA information and enabled the lending organizations to increase their activities.

Does CRA Help or Hurt Lending Practices?

There is no clear consensus as to the effectiveness of the CRA. Some economists maintain that there is no solid evidence that the CRA was effective in increasing lending and homeownership more in low-income neighborhoods than in high-income ones. Even Federal Reserve chairman Ben Bernanke recently stated that more lending does not necessarily produce better outcomes for local communities. However, in some instances, Bernanke notes, "the CRA has served as a catalyst, inducing banks to underserved markets that they might otherwise have ignored."

In a hearing on the CRA before the U.S. House Committee on Financial Services in February 2008, the director of the Division of Supervision and Consumer Protection at the FDIC, Sandra L. Thompson, praised the positive impact of the CRA by pointing to increases in lending to low- and moderate-income households and minorities in the decades since the law's passage. She pointed to data from studies done at Harvard University that showed that between 1993 through 2000, home purchase lending to low- and moderate-income groups had increased by 94 percent—more than in any of the other income categories.

At the same hearing, New York University professor Larry White stated, "Fundamentally, the CRA is a regulatory effort to 'lean on' banks and savings institutions, in vague and subjective ways, to make loans and investments that [the CRA's proponents believe] those depository institutions would otherwise not make." White felt that such laws were more likely to drive institutions out of neighborhoods, and that better ways to achieve these goals would be through vigorous enforcement of antidiscrimination laws and antitrust laws, the latter to promote competition, and federal funding of worthy projects directly through community development funding.

CRA and the Subprime Crisis

The CRA was under particular scrutiny after the foreclosure and mortgage crisis of 2008–2009. Some charged that the CRA was primarily responsible for the financial crisis, as it encouraged the loosening of lending standards throughout the banking industry and encouraged banks to make bad loans. Others commented that this act, along with government-backed Fannie Mae, was primarily responsible for pushing banks and mortgage brokers into granting easy credit and subprime loans to those who could least afford them.

Many housing advocacy groups, like the Association of Community Organizations for Reform Now (ACORN), also felt that lowered credit standards resulted in unsupportable increases in real-estate values in low- to moderate-income communities. Ballooning mortgages on rental properties resulted in higher rents for lower-income tenants who could least afford them.

However, other commentators have noted that CRA-regulated loans tended to be safe and profitable, and that the subprime excesses came primarily from institutions not regulated by the CRA. A Federal Reserve survey has shown that 50 percent of the "toxic" subprime loans were made by independent mortgage companies that were not regulated by the CRA. An additional 25 to 30 percent came from only partially CRA-regulated bank subsidiaries and affiliates. Finally, others note that it is unfair to place blame on CRA for what other federal agencies did on their own. In particular, defenders of CRA point out that the Department of Housing and Urban Development (HUD) and the Office of Federal Housing Enterprise Oversight (OFHEO) allowed Fannie Mae and Freddie Mac to fulfill their affordable but ill-advised housing goals by buying mortgage-backed securities that were never part of the CRA. (Note that Congress abolished OFHEO in July 2008, putting its functions under the newly created Federal Housing Finance Agency, or FHFA, and that Fannie Mae and Freddie Mac were put into conservatorship by the U.S. government on September 7, 2008. Both actions occurred because of de facto bankruptcy of the two housing giants and the ongoing financial crisis.)

By late 2009, the House Financial Services committee was discussing an act to update the CRA. The Community Reinvestment Modernization Act of 2009 would extend the CRA's lending standard to nonbank institutions, such as credit unions, insurance companies, and mortgage lend-

ers. It would also make the act more race based, applying its standards to minorities regardless of income or whether they lived in low- and moderate-income areas.

Abhijit Roy

See also: Housing Booms and Busts; Mortgage Lending Standards; Mortgage, Subprime.

Further Reading

Ardalan, Kavous, "Community Reinvestment Act: Review of Empirical Evidence." *Journal of Commercial Banking and Finance* 5:1/2 (2006): 115–139.

Ardalan, Kavous, and Ann Davis. "Community Reinvestment Act and Efficient Markets Debate: Overview." *Journal of Economics and Economic Education Research* 7:3 (2006): 53–70.

Black, Harold A., Raphael W. Bostic, Breck L. Robinson, and Robert L. Schweitzer. "Do CRA-Related Events Affect Shareholder Wealth? The Case of Bank Mergers." *The Financial Review* 40:4 (2005): 575–586.

Brevoort, Kenneth P., and Timothy H. Hannan. "Commercial Lending and Distance: Evidence from Community Reinvestment Act Data." *Journal of Money, Credit, and Banking* 38:8 (2006): 1991–2012.

Singer, Daniel D. "Online Banking and the Community Reinvestment Act." *Business and Society Review* 111:2 (2006): 165–174.

Title VII of the Housing and Community Development Act of 1977. Pub. L 95–128; 91 Stat. 1147, 12 USC 2901–05.

Vitaliano, Donald F., and Gregory P. Stella. "The Cost of Corporate Social Responsibility: The Case of the Community Reinvestment Act." *Journal of Productivity Analysis* 26:3 (2006): 235.

———. "How Increased Enforcement Can Offset Statutory Deregulation: The Case of the Community Reinvestment Act." *Journal of Financial Regulation and Compliance* 15:3 (2007): 262–274.

Confidence, Consumer and Business

Consumer confidence, a post–World War II concept that has developed into an important economic indicator in the United States and throughout the world, measures and describes the degree of optimism or pessimism about both the national economy and individuals' personal economic circumstances. This subjective measurement, conducted monthly by several major organizations and factored into U.S. government economic projections, infers a causal link between consumers' economic optimism and greater consumer purchasing and, thus, economic growth. Demographer Fabian Linden postulated in 1967 that consumers offer clues about the nation's economic outlook faster than such "hard" data as gross domestic product growth or retails sales.

Key Measures and What They Mean

Government, investors, manufacturers, retailers, and financial institutions in the United States closely watch the principal consumer confidence indices—the University of Michigan's Consumer Sentiment Index and the Conference Board's Consumer Confidence Index—to forecast and plan. If consumers are confident, businesses take this as a signal to increase production. Conversely, if pessimism prevails or is growing, manufacturers are likely to cut inventories and delay new investment. Government can project either higher or lower tax revenues based on consumer confidence. Banks can plan for either increasing or decreasing lending. And the media widely covers these indices as bellwethers of the state of the economy.

In many ways a combination of economics and psychology that long predates behavioral economic analysis, consumer confidence reflects the partly rational, partly irrational feelings of the public. Economist John Maynard Keynes referred to consumer and business confidence as the "animal spirits" that play a significant role in macroeconomic performance. These indices are predicated on the belief that consumer mood powerfully influences spending and the economy at large.

"Consumer confidence figures are really a measure of how we feel about ourselves," said David Wyss, chief economist at Standard & Poor's, in 2003. "If consumers are worried, Main Street retailers better get worried too."

But is this true? As Nobel Prize–winning economist James Tobin asked in 1959: "Are households which express optimistic attitudes and posi-

tive intentions more likely to spend and less likely to save than other households? Do the answers to attitudinal and intentions questions provide information of value in predicting the buying behavior of households? If so, does this information supplement or merely repeat the predictive information contained in financial, economic, and demographic data concerning households?"

CCI, MCSI, and George Katona

In the United States, the Conference Board releases its Consumer Confidence Index (CCI) on the last Tuesday of each month. The University of Michigan's Consumer Sentiment Index (MCSI) is released three days later. Each index, as well as such lesser-known indices as the Washington Post–ABC News Consumer Comfort Index, is based on large-scale national surveys addressing a variety of economic topics and disaggregated into several subsidiary indicators.

The Consumer Sentiment Index is the oldest confidence index, developed in the late 1940s at the University of Michigan by economist George Katona to probe consumer feelings and behavior, what influences them, and how this data can be used to forecast and support business and government growth goals. During World War II, working for the Federal Reserve Board, Katona wrote that rising aspirations will fuel economic growth and that experts can chart, if not guide, expectations of consumer sentiment and behavior. Trained as a psychologist as well as an economist, Katona obtained funding for his research from the Fed, enabling him to establish the Survey Research Center as part of the Michigan's Institute of Social Research in 1946.

For twenty-six years, beginning in 1952, Katona directed the quarterly Survey of Consumer Attitudes. He published numerous books and articles, managed a staff of sixty-five plus several thousand part-time interviewers and a thousand-person consumer focus group, and was celebrated by business and the media as a defender of America's abundant capitalist economy. Katona—who claimed to have invented the new field of psychological or behavioral economics based on the ideas of psychologists Kurt Lewin and Abraham Maslow as much as those of Keynes—staunchly believed that consumer attitudes are at least as critical as macroeconomic data in understanding the economy. He was one of the first to detect U.S. consumer optimism immediately after the war, predicting—against conventional wisdom—that the U.S. economy was headed for a boom rather than a new depression. He was also one of most perceptive observers of the new mass-consumption economy of the postwar era.

In such books as *The Powerful Consumer* (1960), *The Mass Consumption Society* (1964), and *Aspirations and Influence* (1971); in his in-depth analyses of consumer attitudes and demand; and in the Surveys of Consumer Attitudes, Katona hailed consumers as the dynamo behind the booming U.S. economy. His basic, oft-repeated formula was that abundance depends on sustained high demand, high demand depends on consumer optimism, and optimism does not necessarily depend on income.

Contrary to neoclassical ideas of scarcity, Katona said: "Instead of being driven to avoid hardship and being satisfied with restoring an equilibrium, in an era of prosperity people are spurred by rising levels of aspiration." They continually strive for more and more income and consumption, which "may become cumulative and self-reinforcing." To Katona, capitalism, consumption, and democracy are all of a piece, complementary ingredients of an abundant society.

The MCSI is benchmarked at a value of 100 as of December 1964. The index not only fluctuates in tandem with existing economic conditions, but it has been a remarkably reliable predictor of the nation's medium-term economic outlook. Five core questions and a host of industry-specific questions are asked in thirty-minute telephone interviews of a random sample of more than 500 Americans. The major questions concern individuals' beliefs about the current business climate, personal finances, and spending. The survey asks people to assess their current financial situation and to predict what it will be one and five years in the future. It also asks about expectations of the strength or weakness of the national economy in one and five years, and present intentions to buy major household items. The MCSI is based on relative scores of the percentage giving favorable replies minus the percentage giving unfavorable replies, with adjustments derived from the sample composition and prior surveys. The index also is subdivided into three indices—the Index of Consumer Sentiment, the Index of Current Economic Conditions, and the Index of Consumer Expectations. The latter is included in the U.S. government's Index of Leading Economic Indicators.

The Conference Board, a business-sponsored economic research organization, launched its Consumer Confidence Index in 1967 as "a monthly report detailing consumer attitudes and buying intentions, with data available by age, income and region." The Conference Board mails a questionnaire to 5,000 households each month. About 3,500 reply, making the sample less representative of the general population. Expectations about future economic conditions make up 60 percent of the index, and views about current conditions comprise 40 percent. Again, relative values of "positive," "negative," or "neutral" responses are calculated against a 1985 benchmark of 100. Two subindices are released—the Present Situation Index and the Expectations Index.

Other Indices and Underlying Factors

Other opinion research about economic conditions and expectations are conducted in the United States. The Washington Post–ABC News Consumer Comfort Index asks 1,000 randomly selected adults each month to rate national and personal economic conditions and whether it is a good time to make major purchases. Many other countries have developed and issued consumer confidence indices. For example, KBC Bank Ireland and an Irish think tank have calculated such an index since 1996. An American consulting firm surveys 10,000 people in fifteen Indian cities to create an index for that country. Most developed nations of the Organisation for Economic Co-operation and Development (OECD) follow America's lead in conducting such surveys, and the Nielsen Company conducts a Global Online Consumer Survey with respondents in more than fifty countries.

Research suggests that the top factor driving consumer confidence is employment. "As the labor market goes, so goes the confidence index," says Lynn Franco of the Conference Board. "The three keys to consumer confidence are jobs, jobs, and jobs." Stock market swings and geopolitical events also have an effect; for example, after the September 11, 2001, terrorist attacks on the United States, the CCI fell precipitously, by 17 points. Younger Americans tend to be most optimistic, with optimism declining with age. Men tend to be more upbeat than women, and optimism increases with educational attainment. Not surprisingly, lower-income Americans are more pessimistic.

Similar surveys of business confidence and expectations are conducted by a number of entities, ranging from the private Moody's Investors Service to the U.S. Department of Commerce's Bureau of Economic Analysis (BEA). The Moody's Survey, which has been released every Monday since 2006, not only asks business leaders for sales and investment data, but also about their outlook for business conditions in the coming months. The BEA/Conference Board survey tracks the relative assessment of business conditions over time among chief executive officers. Several states, particular industries, and countries outside the United States also conduct surveys of business leaders' economic expectations. Data similarly are used to help assess current economic conditions and forecast future business investment, hiring, production, and other activities. But confidence indices have their critics.

Questions and Criticisms

In the mid-1950s, a Federal Reserve–appointed committee questioned the power of such surveys in predicting business trends and economic con-

ditions. C. Britt Beemer, president of America's Research Group, has said that because the questions are not open ended, they do not allow people to explain why they hold their beliefs. Sampling problems arise with the Conference Board's CCI, as it relies on a self-selected pool of respondents. Other critics say that the MCSI misses people in the highest and lowest income brackets. A frequent criticism is that most people are not well informed about macroeconomic conditions and, therefore, should not be asked about "business conditions." Instead, questions about buying intentions and perceived employment prospects are said to be more predictive. Others suggest that new questions should be asked, particularly ones that gauge people's sense of the probability of different economic developments.

Nonetheless, even the moderately skeptical James Tobin concludes that "the [economics] profession owes George Katona and his colleagues at the Survey Research Center for their imaginative and pioneering work in the collection and interpretation of buying intentions and attitudinal data."

Andrew L. Yarrow

See also: Behavioral Economics; Consumption; Savings and Investment.

Further Reading

Conference Board Web site: www.conference-board.org.

Dominitz, Jeff, and Charles F. Manski. "How Should We Measure Consumer Confidence?" *Journal of Economic Perspectives* 18:2 (Spring 2004): 51–66.

Horowitz, Daniel. *The Anxieties of Affluence: Critiques of American Consumer Culture, 1939–1979.* Amherst: University of Massachusetts Press, 2004.

Katona, George. *The Mass Consumption Society.* New York: McGraw-Hill, 1964.

———. *The Powerful Consumer: Psychological Studies of the American Economy.* New York: McGraw-Hill, 1960.

Linden, Fabian. "The Consumer as Forecaster." *Public Opinion Quarterly* 46:3 (1982): 353–360.

Moody's. "Economy.com." Available at www.economy.com/survey-of-business-confidence.asp. Accessed May 2010.

Tobin, James. "On the Predictive Value of Consumer Intentions and Attitudes." *Review of Economics and Statistics* 41:1 (February 1959): 1–11.

Weiss, Michael J. "Inside Consumer Confidence Surveys." *American Demographics* 25:1 (February 2003): 23–29.

Congressional Budget Office

The Congressional Budget Office (CBO) is a nonpartisan agency in the U.S. federal government charged with providing economic data to Congress, especially for the purpose of helping it formulate the national budget. In that capacity, it conducts research studies and prepares analytical reports that, among many other things, assess the timing and duration of past, current, and future business cycles.

The CBO was founded on July 12, 1974, under the Congressional Budget and Impoundment Control Act and began operations on February 24, 1975. The CBO is located in Washington, D.C., and has about 230 employees, mainly economists and public policy analysts. The CBO's director is appointed for a two-year term by the Speaker of the House and the president pro tempore of the Senate, in consultation with each chamber's budget committee. The CBO has six divisions that work both independently and cooperatively: the Macroeconomic Analysis Division, Budget Analysis Division, Tax Analysis Division, Health and Human Resources Division, Microeconomic Studies Division, and National Security Division. The agency also includes a Panel of Economic Advisers and a Panel of Health Advisers, consisting of experts in each area. The panels advise the CBO directorship on ways to improve transparency, reliability, and professional standards in the agency.

By February 15 of each year, the CBO is responsible for providing Congress—specifically, the House and Senate budget committees—objective and timely information, estimates, and analyses that help it make fiscally sound policy decisions and allocations on programs covered by the federal budget. Every year, it testifies before Congress on a wide variety of issues and policies, including alternative spending and revenue scenarios. It completes hundreds of formal cost estimates and impact assessments. It estimates the impact of unfunded mandates (regulations imposing costs on state or local governments for which they do not receive reimbursement from the federal government) on state, local, and tribal governments and the private sector. It estimates the president's budget proposals and generates cost estimates for all bills reported by congressional committees and, on request, possible amendments to those bills and bills at other stages of the legislative process (including alternative proposals) with a likely impact on state or local governments or the private sector. When necessary for clarification, CBO analysts contact the sponsoring legislator or the staff of the appropriate legislative committee; in all cases, however, the CBO draws its own conclusions and makes its own estimates based on independent analysis.

Specific legislation over the years has assigned additional tasks to the agency, such as assessing the financial risks posed by government-sponsored enterprises or the treatment of administrative costs under credit reform. In addition, the CBO may also conduct analytical studies if requested by individual members, committees, or subcommittees of the House or Senate. As in economic analysis and reporting, the CBO remains objective and impartial on all policy matters, offering no recommendations or proposals.

Under the Congressional Budget Act of 1974 and the Unfunded Mandates Reform Act of 1995, the CBO must fully explain its methodologies and assumptions. The agency obtains data from a variety of sources, including government statistical agencies, industry groups, and private surveys. Likewise, while it develops some of its own analytical models, it also relies on those formulated by others. Beyond the expertise of its own analysts, the CBO also seeks the help of outside experts, especially in the course of examining specific business sectors, such as agriculture or telecommunications.

The CBO issues a steady flow of studies, reports, briefs, monthly budget reviews, letters, presentations, background papers, analytic studies, and other publications, all available online. It regularly publishes a short-term economic and

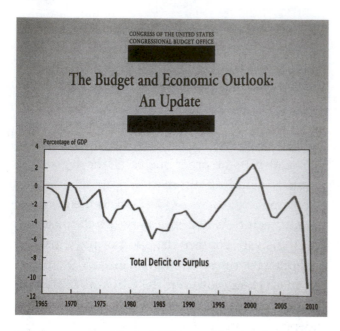

CONGRESS OF THE UNITED STATES
CONGRESSIONAL BUDGET OFFICE

**The Budget and Economic Outlook:
An Update**

The Congressional Budget Office provides detailed, nonpartisan estimates and analyses of federally financed programs. Its revised budget and economic outlook for 2010 projected a deficit of $1.4 trillion. *(Bloomberg/Getty Images)*

budget outlook report at the end of January, which includes estimates of federal spending and revenue for the next ten years. It also publishes a long-term budget outlook, with revenue and spending scenarios—and their economic implications—through the year 2050. Since 2004, the agency has also produced long-term outlooks for the Social Security program. A variety of supplemental information and revised data is available on the CBO Web site, including the most up-to-date budget estimates, economic projections, and the status of discretionary appropriations (those not mandated by existing law). Most of the agency's work is made readily available to the public; only cost estimates for legislative proposals may remain confidential until they become law. CBO assessments of its own economic forecasts for accuracy, balance, and consistency are reviewed both internally and by outside experts.

While the CBO is widely praised across the political spectrum for its nonpartisanship and the quality of its research, its assumptions and predictions are, by necessity, politically controversial, as for example ten-year estimates of the federal deficit. In addition, some in Washington and the media have criticized the CBO for an overly narrow focus on direct costs and benefits of new programs, ignoring broader savings the programs might generate. During the health care debate of 2009, for example, the CBO estimated that part of the proposal circulating in Congress could cost the federal government up to $1 trillion over ten years. Conservative opponents of the proposal seized on the report as evidence that the health care reform was too costly in an age of ballooning deficits. Supporters of the reform effort—both in Congress and the Barack Obama administration—countered that the CBO was ignoring indirect savings, such as those associated with broader preventive care.

Tiia Vissak and James Ciment

See also: Council of Economic Advisers, U.S.; Fiscal Balance; Fiscal Policy; Government Accountability Office; National Economic Council; Tax Policy.

Further Reading

Congressional Budget Office Web site: www.cbo.gov.
Congressional Budget Office. *CBO's Policies for Preparing and Distributing Its Estimates and Analyses.* Washington, DC: Congressional Budget Office, 2005.

Construction, Housing and Commercial

Among the oldest of human activities, the construction of buildings—for commercial, industrial, residential, and other uses—displays many continuities as well as many changes over the millennia. An important activity in all periods of human history, construction is one of the largest industries in the United States in the twenty-first century. Ironically, for an industry whose aim is to provide one of the most permanent of products, the construction business has proven to be one of the most volatile, rising and falling dramatically with upturns and downturns in the overall economy.

Market Characteristics

Contract construction represented more than $500 billion in value added (current dollars) and 4.6 percent of U.S. gross domestic product (GDP) from 2001 to 2004. In the United States, nearly 8 million people were employed in construction and alteration work annually from 2005 to 2006. Added to this are the ancillary industries that supply construction workers with tools and materials, expanding the construction network dramatically. For example, in 2007, 122 million tons (110.7 million metric tons) of concrete were produced in the United States alone.

But the business is also fraught with instability. There are several reasons for this. For the most part, construction is a process of building custom-designed products, on location, often with a specific user in mind. Construction sites vary from the building of a multimillion-dollar urban skyscraper to the putting in place of a sewer on a local street corner. Installation methods generally are labor intensive, and projects serve as textbook examples of the law of diminishing returns (marginal productivity theory), whereby a rising labor-to-capital ratio tends to produce decreasing returns after a maximized point of output is reached. Thereafter, efficient production becomes a balancing act between capital and labor, requiring careful supervision of workers and materials. This makes construction projects sensitive to changes in wage rates and capital costs—so sensitive that job sites have been known to shut down following periods of intense inflation, as the cost of construction rapidly exceeds the original estimate over time.

A recent snapshot of the sector would show a multitude of firms, some sole proprietorships and others with thousands of employees spanning markets worldwide. The U.S. Census Bureau reported in 2002 that there were 2,657,360 construction companies in the American market, of which more than 2.4 million were individual proprietorships. Typically, a small number of firms produce the largest share of revenue. Such an industrial structure makes the construction industry susceptible

to the upheaval of market gyrations. Low capitalization at one extreme and overexpansion at the other creates a risk profile that makes firm survival tenuous. Limited barriers to entry, such as licensing requirements and low start-up costs, allow for rapid expansion as demand rises. Conversely, these financially unsecured firms are vulnerable to downturns, causing equally rapid market exit as thin profit margins evaporate. The rapidity of turnover and the market structure combine to reinforce the cyclical nature of the construction contractor's existence.

While production and market organization are important, the real engine of market movement comes from the demand side. Construction demand is derived overwhelmingly from the needs of other economic sectors (speculative commercial construction is one exception). As a derived demand, the "wants" for construction are subject to forces ranging from a corporation's expansion plans to tax breaks for specific types of construction (e.g., health care facilities). Thus, the construction industry feeds on the success of the overall domestic economy.

Labor Markets

Modern construction is characterized by the use of skilled labor, which is divided among approximately sixteen trade categories. Trade abilities and knowledge are uniquely defined, and often gained through formal apprenticeships or informal mechanic-helper arrangements. Such skill compartmentalization requires a fair degree of coordination by job managers to keep construction projects on schedule and within budget. Total construction employment hit an all-time high of 7.8 million in 2007, propelled by a housing boom.

Traditionally, the hands-on nature of the production process led to low capital-to-labor ratios as builders and contractors struggled to impose capital substitutions for labor. The intricacies of on-site installations gave workers a fair degree of individual control over the pace of the workplace.

U.S. Employment in Construction, 1939–2009

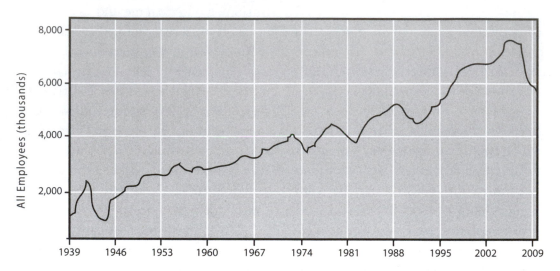

This fact lent strength to building trades unions in the twentieth century, which negotiated wage premiums for construction workers. The importance of skilled labor cannot be overestimated in understanding market-based construction. The time needed to train workers in the building trades makes labor supply problematic given the wide swings in the building sectors.

Employers are hesitant to invest heavily in training entry-level employees for two reasons. First, they may be concerned that workers will leave their firm after gaining enough knowledge to find employment with another company. Second, the employer essentially has trained its competitor, given the ease of market entry. Building trades unions solved this problem by developing multi-employer apprenticeship programs, in which costs are shared and skilled labor is made available through a hiring hall. Both the union and non-union sectors still depend on itinerant workers to make up shortfalls in labor demand when work is plentiful. Yet when work is scarce, labor market attachment among union workers remains high because of long-term benefit plans and more equitable distribution of limited job offerings. Thus, in the long run, the rise and fall of construction activity leads to a steady flow of workers into and out of the industry as employees react to the boom-and-bust economy, leaving contractors wanting for skilled labor during upswings and oversupplied

when work dries up. The graph of U.S. construction employment since 1939 shows a rising trend over time, but with clear evidence of periodic ups and downs in the market demand for labor.

Cycles

Cyclical behavior has always been apparent in construction, in the same way that the weather creates optimal seasons for agricultural production. Weather-oriented cycle durations vary by location, but developers in cold climates still rush to undertake excavation prior to the onset of the freezing cold. While these cycles are not economic swings by definition, they serve as parameters for peaks and troughs in employment and output on an annual basis.

A more practical concern is how cycles in the construction sector are affected by factors in the overall economy. Downswings produced by a slowing of economic activity cause the building sector to follow suit, while the opposite is true during rebounds. For example, an overlay of Bureau of Labor Statistics employment data for the construction industry with the National Bureau of Economic Research (NBER) listing of business cycles shows clear patterns, such as the examples listed in the following table. There are relative similarities in the first two examples. In the third, the contraction of 1990 ended in March 1991 for the

Contractions of the U.S. Economy and Construction Employment

U.S. Economy		U.S. Construction	
Peak	Trough	Peak	Trough
July 1953	May 1954	April 1953	September 1954
November 1973	March 1975	March 1974	September 1975
July 1990	March 1991	March 1990	July 1992

Sources: National Bureau of Economic Research; U.S. Bureau of Labor Statistics.

overall economy, while the decline in construction lasted considerably longer, from March 1990 until summer 1992.

Timing is of more interest. In part, this is related to the speculative aspect of the construction investment decision, and in part, it is connected to the timing of the construction process. Once the decision is made to go forward with a speculative project, the owners are affected by the overall economy. Shifts in demand, changes in use, and the cost of construction are all variable influences. In response, developers may alter the form of the building through design or scale switch (e.g., from condominiums to rentals), or shut the job down if the expected revenue negatively affects the minimum return on investment regardless of the structure's function.

Construction projects tend to be relatively long-term endeavors compared to most manufacturing processes. Thus, a time span of eighteen to twenty-four months exposes builders and contractors to a wide variety of economic factors—consider that the NBER found that post–World War II contractions averaged ten months and expansions fifty-seven months. Typically, input price change risk, which producers of consumer products (e.g., automobiles or paper towels) can limit by altering their short-run output or selling prices, negatively affects contractors who have already submitted bids based on existing costs.

Added to this is the fact that work is awarded to architects and contractors through a bidding process that tends to create short-term relationships,

so that new work is often carried out by different combinations of employers and workers. Although such continuing competition can benefit the buyers of constructions services, the inefficiencies caused by the realignment of shops calls into question the accuracy of the price estimates offered by successful bidders. Clearly, most projects are run successfully, but a by-product of the contracting process is instability when poor estimates lead to firm failures.

Although the construction industry always has seemed ripe for technological and structural advancement, it is in the last quarter of the twentieth century and the initial decade of the twenty-first that substantial progress has been made in the capital/labor trade-off. The key to cutting on-site labor hours is prefabrication. Early on, major shifts came in building techniques that were associated with breakthroughs in new materials or engineering, such as steel fabrication in the late nineteenth century and the commercialization of portland cement in the early twentieth. Though these techniques added new dimensions to the building process, they did not necessarily shorten the time needed for construction. The development of drywall in the mid-twentieth century and advances in excavating equipment, such as steam shovels and modern payloaders, cut the time for wall production, land clearing, and foundation work.

The elusive ability to significantly improve construction productivity came full circle with the advent of off-site manufacturing of building elements that incorporated many of these early innovations. Prefabricated curtain walls of brick, stone, or metal, precast concrete slabs, and prefabricated residential units have shortened the time span for erection. Technology also has been augmented by improved project management methods such as "design build" and "fast track" construction, again hastening the completion of projects. The result of this increased speed is faster turnover for skilled labor and greater urgency for employers to have another project lined up for their capital investment. This, in itself, challenges long periods of expansion and intensifies the cyclical nature of the construction process.

Yet the greatest threat to the industry in some ways is the most obvious. It is found in the funding pipeline for all parts of the construction sector. Construction is extremely sensitive to interest rates given its role in capital formation. Although some projects are self-funded, the vast majority require equity investors and construction capital. Although each form of investment undergoes its own due diligence, both are constrained by the vagaries of the broader economy.

Corporate construction (e.g., a new headquarters) or owner-financed residential undertakings often are started because of specific needs and because sufficient funding already exists. In more speculative sectors of the industry, builders and developers seek to raise capital through the sale of equity in the project. There are numerous means of raising capital at this level, but all are tied to some expected return on investment, either through the sale of finished structures or through leasing

A welder works on a new entertainment complex in downtown Los Angeles in 2006. The commercial and residential construction industry is a vital component of U.S. economic growth, with a major effect on employment rates and materials manufacturing. *(David McNew/Getty Images)*

income streams. The investment decision is tied to many traditional economic measures and interest rates, and alternative investment opportunities help determine the end result. Why is it, then, that construction booms seemingly charge ahead in the face of an impending downturn and the industry seems slower to react than other economic sectors as expansions begin? The housing market offers some clues.

Housing Market

Although private homes have a certain element of use value comparable to consumption goods, the role of the housing market is accounted for in a manner similar to that of other additions to the capital stock of a nation. Large amounts of public and private money are invested in home building, and it has long been institutionalized in public policy around the world. The demand for housing has several components, all of which may fuel and then retard construction, leading to market oscillations. Waves of immigration, domestic population growth, and rising disposable income are three well-known influences on demand. The first two demonstrate a need for additional housing, while the last creates demand as people seek larger living spaces. In addition, all of these factors are easily affected by government through legislation and executive direction.

The decision to add housing units to the existing supply is guided by interest rates, which affect the cost of financing for both the builder (loans) and the buyer (mortgages). Given a level of demand, attractive interest rates are necessary to stimulate home production, although they are not, by themselves, sufficient to do so. The prices of land, labor, and materials are other aspects of the cost of production that shape a developer's appetite for residential construction. Elements from the supply and the demand sides create a roller-coaster ride for builders, contractors, and workers. The accelerator principle, which holds that growth in real GDP leads to increases in planned investment spending, is important here.

Expected future growth in the demand for housing leads builders to shift investment capital to residential projects. The timing allows them to break ground for new units that will be completed during the current expansion or finish as an uptick is getting under way.

It is the unplanned portion of housing investment that can produce instability. If output is steady and population growth is zero, there will be only replacement additions to capital stock. However, rising standards of living and/or increases in population create conditions that spur unplanned investment in a nation's housing stock. The growing demand depletes existing inventories of homes and, given the time needed for housing production, causes planned (replacement) investments in the residential market to fall short of demand. This, in turn, sets off a cyclical upswing in home building.

The housing market then starts to attract additional investment from existing home builders, while the low barriers to entry allow new entrants in the market, further fueling investment. If, at the same time, low interest rates and government policies entice more homebuyers, the industry will experience a boom. Hiring increases, the number of housing starts explodes, and supply rises rapidly. The spigot of economic activity opens wide, and, short of government controls or a disastrous economic occurrence, such as the credit market debacle of 2008–2009, the industry will continue to add housing units—but to what point?

Consumption goods produced in factories are regulated easily through information on supply and demand. Housing, on the other hand, is a durable investment-grade good that often is custom designed, time consuming to build, and produced by both small-scale firms and large corporate builders. The boom psychology and the consistent inability to gauge real market demand historically fuel the boom-and-bust nature of housing construction. In addition, housing is an extremely durable good, making replacement investment far less predictable, which, in turn, leads to fluctuations rather than steady demand.

It is not much of a stretch to believe that commercial construction operates in a similar way. Research in the early 1960s by economist Moses Abramowitz indicated that all aspects of construction historically have suffered from a series of long swings. Commercial projects, however, tend to be larger, but more susceptible to replacement through technologically superior structures or renovations over time. Consider the fact that both the Chrysler Building and the Empire State Building were started at the end of the 1920s economic boom in New York City and completed at the onset of the Great Depression, while the Burj Khalifa in Dubai was started during the boom years of the mid-2000s but finished after the global financial crisis of 2008, which nearly rendered the emirate bankrupt. The firms in this segment of the industry tend to be bigger, better capitalized, and better able to withstand swings in demand. However, both residential and commercial construction markets often give the appearance of a game of "musical chairs," in which no builder wants to be the last one constructing during the boom or holding an undesirable structure as the market cycles downward.

Crisis

Economists long have recognized that crises play a role in the macroeconomy, initiating a catharsis in which markets are restructured, inefficiencies are exposed, and the groundwork for revival is prepared. Such economic chaos, even in construction, is far more devastating and socially destructive than the typical troughs of a business cycle. The construction industry has been caught in the tidal waves of the major downturns and certainly has faired no better than other sectors.

For example, the stagflation crisis of the 1970s started at a GDP peak in November 1973 and bottomed out sixteen months later in March 1975. Construction employment shadowed this decline, cresting in February 1974 and reaching a low point in July 1975. The more severe financial crisis that began in December 2007 and traumatized global market systems was preceded by a precipitous drop in construction employment that commenced in January of the same year. The early twenty-first-century downturn underscores the dependence of the building industry on the credit markets and confirms that demand is derived from the needs of the rest of the economy.

The initial retrenchment in housing demand that stalled the building boom at the beginning of the millennium resulted from a falloff in the demand for private residences. Rising delinquencies in the subprime mortgage markets sounded a warning to home builders in an era of easy credit, while a lack of due diligence by financial institutions created a seemingly unending pool of potential commercial and residential property failures. Builders applied the brakes to some projects and abandoned others, leading to a drop in residential construction permits and employment in 2007. Census Bureau data show that annual new, privately owned housing starts fell from a high of 2.07 million in 2005 to a low of only 554,000 in 2009, a 73 percent decrease in just forty-eight months.

Compounding the situation was the fact that banks and brokerage houses had bundled many of these mortgages into collateralized debt obligations, which were sold on the open financial markets. As arrears mounted in the paying of home mortgages, holders of these debt instruments began to suffer significant losses, making lenders at all levels reluctant to issue more debt. (By mid-2009, the same situation had developed in the commercial sector.) Builders and developers that were scaling back from a perceived falloff in demand also felt the credit crunch as liquidity dried up for existing and near-term projects. The collapse of the stock markets further reduced demand, as widespread layoffs and a dearth of economic activity arrived in the fourth quarter of 2008. Builders of all sizes were unable to secure equity loans or construction financing, leading to further cutbacks and massive labor reductions.

Additional evidence of the cyclical nature of market-based construction can be found in the securitization process. Economic historians have shown that the overly optimistic view of investors during the 1920s fueled a building boom that was unsustainable in terms of return on investment. In much the same way, the opacity of collateralized debt obligations in the early twenty-first century helped ensure that a housing bubble would emerge. As financial institutions raced to sell debt secured at the subprime level, investors failed to understand the extent of the risk to the underlying mortgages (billions of dollars in mortgages had been issued to individuals who were not creditworthy). The unrealistic expectation of future returns mimicked the real-estate failure of the Great Depression. However, the rise in delinquent mortgage holders increased the volume of foreclosed properties on the market, creating an alternative competitive market for any would-be homebuyers to choose from. This, in turn, limited the need for new housing and led to a precipitous drop in home building.

Solutions

Given the labor requirements, market barriers (or the lack thereof) to entry, and site specificity of construction projects, there is little expectation that the construction industry could be regulated into stability through supply-side intervention. The length of time for completion and contractors' inability to divine demand explains the bumpy road that the industry often takes.

A more appropriate focus, say economists, is the demand for construction services. In this case, there is room for public and private decision making as well as input from trade associations and labor organizations. The use of interest rates as a policy tool has long been the purview of the Federal Reserve, and yet the financial meltdown of 2007–2008 has been attributed, in part, to easy credit terms. In retrospect, moderate home building growth would have served the economy far better than the binge construction seen at the turn of the twenty-first century. Greater government oversight in both the credit and securities markets with respect to housing and home mortgages might have forestalled any economic disasters.

Of course, once the downturn snowballed into a deep recession, it was necessary to develop means to stimulate economic growth. Construction was curtailed by a lack of funding and, later, by a lack of effective demand as other sectors were crippled by inactivity. Building permits declined and housing starts fell off dramatically. In the 1930s, the federal government adopted a Keynesian philosophy, bolstering the construction industry through large doses of infrastructure spending (e.g., the Works Progress Administration built bridges, schools, stadiums, etc.). Many projects initiated by the Barack Obama administration have received funding from the federal stimulus program, although not nearly on the same scale as President Franklin D. Roosevelt's New Deal. In fact, Nobel Prize–winning economist Joseph Stiglitz has called on the federal government to dramatically expand government expenditures well beyond the $700 billion stimulus plan of 2009 to revive the American market system.

In contrast, the *New York Times* reported on January 23, 2009, that the centralized Chinese government undertook construction projects valued at hundreds of billions of dollars. These were focused largely on improving the nation's transportation network, but included environmental projects such as water treatment plants. State-controlled banks provided funding, whereas free-market banks in the United States have been cautious and slow to fund projects as a result of market conditions and a backlog of nonperforming loans. Stiglitz noted that the national Chinese stimulus package was valued at 14 percent of that country's GDP. An equivalent American response would have been in the trillions of dollars.

From a market perspective, construction booms are fraught with the inherent dangers of land, labor, and material price inflation. Limited urban land sites classically raise the price of existing lots for building during any expansion. The uptick translates into higher demand for skilled workers and building products until the costs of these inputs invariably put pressure on profit margins. Typically, these market-based price limits set the stage for a barrier to expansion as high-cost producers begin to fail and market demand for buildings and structures wanes. A lack of construction investment can be overcome by an influx of government projects (as occurred in China and in the United States during the Great Depression), although in noncrisis times, such projects can fuel sharply rising prices of production.

Construction is an important sector of the economy that suffers from a historical pattern of instability while generating billions of dollars in improvement to the nation's capital stock. Yet it often gets short shrift from an economic policy perspective. In part, this is because the cyclical movement stems from the derived demand for construction services and its own production process. The wide range of market influences, which spur demand for structures, homes, and facilities, say some economists, need to be considered in light of public policy. The relationship to government fiscal policy (e.g., tax incentives), public works expenditure (infrastructure), and legislative actions (e.g., immigration laws) already has been established but needs to be further explored, they argue. Additional study is also warranted to understand the effects of technology and the de-skilling process as the industry continues to reduce on-site labor hours through prefabrication and capital for labor substitutions. Finally, the U.S. economy in general, many students of the industry agree, would be better served by a more stable construction sector, given that it employs millions of workers and develops opportunities for so many companies and contractors.

Gerald Finkel

See also: Housing; Housing Booms and Busts; Mortgage, Commercial/Industrial; Mortgage Markets and Mortgage Rates.

Further Reading

Abramowitz, Moses. *Evidence of Long Swings in Aggregate Construction Since the Civil War.* New York: National Bureau of Economic Research, 1964.

Allen, Steven G. "Why Construction Industry Productivity Is

Declining." *Review of Economics and Statistics* 67:4 (January 1986): 661–669.

Barth, James R. *The Rise and Fall of the U.S. Mortgage and Credit Markets: A Comprehensive Analysis of the Market Meltdown.* Hoboken, NJ: John Wiley & Sons, 2009.

Bradsher, Keith. "China's Route Forward." *New York Times.* January 23, 2009.

Burns, Arthur F., and Wesley C. Mitchell. *Measuring Business Cycles.* New York: National Bureau of Economic Research, 1946.

Finkel, Gerald. *The Economics of the Construction Industry.* Armonk, NY: M.E. Sharpe, 1997.

Goetzmann, William N., and Frank Newman. *Securitization in the 1920's.* Working Paper no. 15650, National Bureau for Economic Research, 2010. Available at www.nber.org/papers/w15650. Accessed March 2010.

Krugman, Paul, and Robin Wells. *Macroeconomics.* 2nd ed. New York: Worth, 2009.

Mills, Daniel Q. *Industrial Relations and Manpower in Construction.* Cambridge, MA: MIT Press, 1972.

Stiglitz, Joseph E. *Freefall: America, Free Markets, and the Sinking of the World Economy.* New York: W.W. Norton, 2010.

Thornton, Mark. "The Economics of Housing Bubbles." In *America's Housing Crisis: A Case of Government Failure*, ed. Benjamin Powell and Randall Holcombe. Edison, NJ: Transaction, 2009.

Consumer and Investor Protection

One issue that often arises during or following an economic bust is whether consumers and investors were properly protected from making bad economic decisions. The degree to which consumers and investors are protected from the financial losses resulting from a crisis draws scrutiny in post-bust analysis.

Consumer protection refers to the system of safeguards that protect consumers from possible fraudulent and unfair practices of businesses. It entails enabling the consumers to attain compensation for defective or harmful products and deficiencies in the delivery of promised goods and services.

Consumer

A consumer is one who buys products or services for personal consumption. In the present context, the term "consumer" is used for anyone who makes a purchase. Globally, consumers number in the billions and collectively have the power to influence the seller. However, at an individual level, there is seldom any interaction and cooperation among consumers, which limits the scope for collective action. This greatly reduces the market power of the single buyer and puts him or her at a disadvantage whenever seeking compensation or satisfaction in any unfair deal or financial loss during or after purchase. Accordingly, sellers may indulge in any number of unfair practices, including incomplete disclosure of information, use of harmful ingredients or components in products, selling defective products, and so on.

Caveat Emptor versus Caveat Venditor

For centuries, the Latin phrase *caveat emptor*, meaning "buyer beware," was an accepted business norm, which meant that the buyer was solely responsible if the merchandise sold were found to be defective or deviated from the claims made by the seller. Hence, the buyer had to be careful in product selection and purchase. Since the mid-1960s, however, there has been a growing recognition of consumer rights in the United States, initiated in part by Ralph Nader, an attorney and pioneering consumer rights activist. Within a few years came the emergence of a movement of citizen activists, public interest litigants, and consumer advocacy groups throughout the United States. This crusade for consumer protection gained momentum and intensified into a full-fledged movement known as consumerism, which spread across the rest of the world. Governments were persuaded and compelled to pass supporting legislation that gave teeth to the movement. The main outcome of this was a shift in responsibility for product liability from the buyer to the seller, the philosophy of *caveat venditor*, or "seller beware," has gained ground. *Caveat venditor* holds the seller responsible for any liability arising out of the purchase transaction, unless the seller explicitly disclaims any responsibility and the buyer agrees to this prior to the purchase.

Rights of Consumers

Articulating the rights of the consumers is an important aspect of protection. In all the stages of purchase—from the prepurchase decision-making stage to the postusage stage—the consumer is entitled to information and the opportunity to act in case the promised value is not delivered. The rights of consumers in a number of countries are as follows:

- *Right to Satisfaction of Basic Needs.* The buyer has access to goods and services that are essential for the satisfaction of basic needs like adequate food, clothing, shelter, health care, education, public utilities, water and sanitation.
- *Right to Safety.* The merchandise bought must be safe and healthy for the consumer. Products made with ingredients or components that are hazardous or potentially harmful must be regulated. For example, children's toys painted with colors that have a high lead content and refrigerators that emit high levels of chlorofluorocarbons are harmful to health and the environment respectively. Hence, right to safety involves the development of standards by government and compliance with these standards by manufacturers and sellers to ensure a minimum level of assurance to the consumers.
- *Right to Information.* The buyer has to be informed about the quality, source of supply, dates of production and product expiration, price, quantity, and so on, in order to protect himself or herself from being misled by salespersons, distributors, advertisements, and labels.
- *Right to Choose.* Besides the availability of product-related information that will help consumers make an informed decision, the right to choose also precludes forced choice through tie-ups, that is, the purchase of a product or service being linked to the compulsory purchase of another product or service.
- *Right to Seek Redress.* If the consumer has a complaint about the product or service following purchase, representing his or her grievance to an independent body should be possible. This right involves the creation of regulatory or judicial bodies that have (1) the mandate to hear out the consumer complaints; and (2) the power to ensure corrective action or compensation from the supplier.
- *Right to Consumer Education.* Consumers can demand information or seek compensation only when they are aware of their rights. Hence, educating the consumers is an important cornerstone of consumer protection.
- *Right to a Healthy Environment and Sustainable Consumption.* Consumers have a right to expect products and services that do not endanger the environment or cause erosion of natural resources. Sellers have to ensure that the products do not cause harm to the environment or rapid resource depletion that can cause ecological imbalances.
- *Right to Associate.* Consumers must have freedom to associate and form consumer groups and to represent their views in decision-making processes at the local or federal levels affecting them.

Consumer Protection Laws and Organizations

Laws for consumer protection are essential for safeguarding consumer rights. In the absence of appropriate laws, delivering justice to consumers would be left to the discretion of the sellers since corrective action cannot be enforced. Hence, the first step toward ensuring consumer rights is to develop the necessary legal provisions. Legislation is usually in the areas of consumer complaint redress, fixing liability of sellers, assuring truth in advertisements and labels, establishing information disclosure requirements, setting resale price controls, deterring the creation of monopoly power in an industry, prohibiting unfair and restrictive trade practices, and so forth. To enforce these laws, appropriate regulatory venues are created in which consumer interests can be fairly represented.

A variety of organizations are involved in promoting consumer protection. They are in the form of citizen groups or consumer groups that are nonprofit organizations and often the first places consumers can turn for help following a purchase of a good or service. These groups gather information and guide consumers in representing their cases to judicial organizations. They also undertake campaigns for educating consumers about harmful products and consumption habits. In order to mobilize support for the consumer movement, they seek representation in decision-making bodies at national and international levels. For instance, Consumers International (CI), founded in 1960, is a nonprofit federation of 220 consumer groups from 115 countries. The organization's expressed mandate is "to secure a fair, safe and sustainable future for consumers in a global marketplace increasingly dominated by international corporations."

Once a customer case is represented, the actual process of hearing the case, assessment, passing judgment, and enforcing corrective action are undertaken by judicial organizations. These institutions differ from country to country. In the United States, the Federal Trade Commission (FTC) is the government agency responsible for consumer protection through the establishment and enforcement of commercial trade regulations. The FTC ensures effective law enforcement by sharing its expertise with federal and state legislatures and national and international government agencies. It also develops policy and research tools and runs educational campaigns. The Bureau of Consumer Protection, an arm of the FTC, fields complaints about consumer fraud and identity theft and makes them available to law enforcement agencies across the country. It also conducts investigations and sues those sellers who violate the law. The seven areas of its work include advertising practices, consumer and business education plans, enforcement, financial practices, marketing practices, planning and information, and privacy and identity protection.

The consumerism movement has assumed worldwide proportions, especially with the rise of communications technology and the Internet. Web-based campaigns and the forwarding of e-mails across continents and blogs are now a part of global coordination and concerted consumer protection strategies. For instance, World Consumer Rights Day (WCRD) 2009 was observed on March 15 with the members of Consumers International organizing supermarket sweeps, lunchbox challenges, marches, press conferences, and guest blogs. The Junk Food Generation Campaign, a worldwide campaign which calls for an end to the marketing of unhealthy food to children, was also intensified to mark WCRD. However, consumerism is also associated with the idea that global economic benefits arise though greater and well-informed consumption. As a consumer rights movement, consumerism has become a global phenomenon for consumer protection.

Investor Protection

An investor is one who commits resources to business venues that generate returns in the future. These commitments can be bank deposits, fixed assets, or financial assets like stocks and bonds or bullion, real estate, and precious items. From a professional finance standpoint, capital investment refers to the buying of a financial product or any item of value with an anticipation of earning positive future returns. Unlike a speculator who accepts a high level of risk in the hope of gaining higher-than-average returns, an investor tries to minimize risk and maximize returns. Hence the investor tries to balance the twin concerns of risk and return.

Safeguarding the interest of investors and their legal rights is known as investor protection. It includes guiding and educating investors regarding their rights and legal enforcements in the case of violation of these rights. Investors' backgrounds usually range from the technically sophisticated to those who are less so and who have resources but little knowledge in these matters. The need for protection arises due to the information and knowledge gap between the investors and the group that manages the investors' funds. If the investment is made in financial products like bonds or mutual funds, investors deal with providers of financial services; if shares are purchased, the investors' entrusted resources are used by the managers of the company. Thus the investors deal with professionals who possess greater knowledge and experience since individual investors often possess neither the information nor the capability to evaluate the information. Not all parties they deal with are honest and straightforward. At times, the self-interest of the vendors or managers may be served better by not communicating all the information to the investors, or else they may find it difficult to communicate technical information in an understandable manner to the less knowledgeable investors.

The alternative for investors is either to seek the services of professional investment advisers or to entrust funds to professional fund managers to make appropriate investment decisions on their behalf. However, even these solutions are not foolproof. The investment advisers possess better technical and market knowledge but still cannot match the product knowledge of vendors, while the fund managers may be motivated by their self-interest rather than maximization of the clients' interest. Thus the need for investor protection arises due to information gaps, potential conflicts of interest, and disparate investor capabilities.

Investor Rights

The explicit rights of the investor include the following:

Right to Complete Information (about):
- The firm and the work history and background of the person handling the investor account
- Commissions, sales charges, maintenance or service charges, transaction or redemption fees, and penalties

- The terms and conditions of transactions the investor undertakes
- Any major changes to investments

Right to Receive Advice:
- Advice consistent with the investor's financial needs and investment objectives
- Presale advice about the risks, obligations, and costs of any investment

Right to Documents and Statements:
- A copy of all completed account forms and agreements
- Account statements that are accurate and understandable, with regular updates
- Statement for the period during which transactions are made

Right of Access to Funds:
- Timely access to funds
- Information about any restrictions or limitations on funds access

Right to Be Heard:
- Right to patient hearing and clarification of investor queries
- Prompt attention to and fair consideration of investor concerns and account problems

In addition, as partial owners of the company, shareholders have all or some of the following rights depending on the nature of shares held:

- Voting rights on issues that affect the organization
- Right to the assets of the corporation
- Right to transfer the stock
- Right to receive dividends as declared by the board of directors of the company
- Right to inspect the books and records of the company
- Right to sue the company in case of wrongful deeds committed by the directors and officers of the company
- Right to share the proceeds recovered in case of liquidation of the company's assets

Free-market advocates who are averse to government regulation advocate competition as a means of ensuring investor rights. Their belief is that the government's role is to foster a competitive environment in which companies vie with each other to maximize the investors' wealth. In other words, free-market forces are expected to ensure protection of investor concerns. In their view, companies that do not divulge all of the relevant information in a clear and understandable way will be driven out of business because investors will not invest in them. However, there have been instances of market failures like the financial crisis in the 1930s and the global financial crisis of 2008–2009 that have demonstrated that markets do not always offer protection and hence there is need for regulation. The extent of the regulation needed is still a highly debated issue and is decided by the governments of respective countries based on their past experience, public demands, and political requirements.

Laws and Institutions

Effective investor protection requires a strong legal system and an effective enforcement regime. Clear ownership rights, contract laws, commercial and bankruptcy codes, and strict enforcement lend strong credibility to a country's securities market. Most countries have investor protection regimes comprised of the necessary legislation as well as the institutions that monitor relevant business practices and enforce the legislation. Countries like the United States adopt rules pertaining to registration and authorization of financial products and schemes, which is known as a top-down approach. They specify custodial, redemption, liquidity, disclosure, and reporting requirements. They also impose restrictions on leveraging, short-selling, management fee arrangements, and portfolio diversification. The purpose of this kind of regulation is to ensure information availability to investors as well as limiting their exposure to financial loss.

On the other hand, countries that adopt a bottom-up approach ensure investor protection through disclosures and self-certification by the companies themselves. In these countries, investors are expected to make their own risk assessment and judgment about the suitability of the products to their concerns. Under such regimes, like in Australia, the onus placed on the investors is clearly greater than in countries such as the United States.

The following are some examples of the regulatory provisions that nations adopt in order to protect investors:

- Entry norms like capital requirements, promoter's contribution, and lock-in period
- Liquidity norms, for instance, the percentage of the net tangible assets to be held in monetary assets
- Eligibility of the companies for public issue or rights issue, denomination of shares for public/rights issue, stipulations about the manner of specifying the information in the offer document
- Disclosure norms, including guidelines for the issue of advertisements and the prospectus, the form or forms in which the required information should be furnished, the items or details to be shown in the balance sheet and the earnings statement, etc.
- Strict separation of clients' money, maintenance of accounts, audit, and insurance requirements

The development of such rules and their enforcement is done through institutions specifically created for this purpose. The Bankruptcy Act of 1938 and Securities Investor Protection Act of 1970 are the major laws aimed at protecting the investors in the United States. More recently, the Sarbanes-Oxley Act of 2002, also known as the Public Company Accounting Reform and Investor Protection Act of 2002, was passed in the United States in the wake of a number of major scandals that eroded billions of dollars of investors' wealth and public confidence in the securities markets due to a collapse in share prices of companies like Enron and WorldCom. The Securities Investor Protection Corporation (SIPC) protects securities investors from financial harm.

SIPC organizes the distribution of the available customer cash and securities to investors. If such cash is not available, SIPC provides insurance coverage up to $500,000 of the customer's net equity balance, including up to $100,000 in cash. Note that the SIPC does not insure against losses in an investment account. It insures against losses involving crimes that a brokerage firm commits with its clients' funds, such as embezzlement.

The U.S. subprime mortgage crisis of 2007–2008 and the victory of the more regulatory-minded Democrats in the congressional and presidential races of 2008 has led to calls for a new government agency—the proposed Consumer Financial Protection Agency (CFPA), which would oversee a variety of financial products, including home mortgages, credit cards, and other consumer lending. The subprime mortgage crisis revealed a variety of problems in the way mortgages were originated and marketed, including overcomplicated contracts and misleading sales practices, as well as a general lack of financial understanding among large portions of the public, particularly those at the lower end of the income spectrum who took on the subprime mortgages.

In addition, consumer groups have long complained that banks were too aggressive in marketing credit cards, offering low teaser rates to get people in debt and then arbitrarily raising interest rates to exorbitant levels. While some of these business activities are regulated by various federal and state agencies, advocates of the CFPA argue that there needs to be a single agency, so that financial instruments are not only marketed fairly but remain uniform throughout the country. In addition, they argue that many of the existing agencies were created to help the markets run more smoothly, not to protect consumers, and they remain too closely tied to the interests of the financial industry. Detractors of the CFPA idea concede that some new consumer financial regulation is necessary but say that creating another government bureaucracy is not the answer and that more regulation would prevent the development of new and useful financial instruments that benefit consumers.

Benefits and Costs

Regulation enhances investor security and contributes to the development of financial markets that are considered imperative for strong economic growth. Inadequate investment protection leads to financing constraints and hence, increases the cost of capital. Research has shown weak investor protection to be the cause of suboptimal investment decisions like overinvestment in low-growth industries and underinvestment in high-growth industries. Low dividend payout, excessive cash holding, and more aggressive earnings management were also found in countries with weak investor protection regimes. The mandatory information disclosure required by strong investor protection regimes was found to improve information transfer and financial market liquidity. In the arena of international business, firms from countries with strong legal systems and shareholder rights were found to make more profitable overseas investment decisions while firms from weak investor protection regimes often ended up as targets for acquisition.

A number of administrative and bureaucratic costs are associated with regulation and compliance. Regulation also leads to market rigidities (inability of the market to react quickly to shifts in supply and demand), weakening of economic incentives, and increased costs of lobbying by business to influence the regulatory agenda. Obtaining an optimum balance between protection and cost of regulation is difficult. Despite these dilemmas, most countries opt for regulation because the social costs associated with real-world market imperfections are greater than the costs of regulatory intervention. The big issue is the extent of regulation. Historical evidence reveals a retreat of regulation during financial booms and a surge in regulation in the eras of financial busts. Finally, in an era of globalized financial markets, more attempts for greater global coordination of regulations are imperative. Without global coordination, market participants wishing to engage in more risky behavior than domestic regulators allow can merely take the activity offshore.

A.D. Madhavi and James Ciment

See also: Corporate Corruption; Securities and Exchange Commission.

Further Reading

Brian, Harvey W., and Deborah L. Parry. *The Law of Consumer Protection and Fair Trading.* London: Butterworths, 2000.

Consumers International Web site: www.consumersinternational .org.

Franks, Julian, and Colin Mayer. *Risk, Regulation and Investor Protection: The Case of Investment Management.* Oxford, UK: Clarendon Press, 1990.

Meier, Kenneth J., E. Thomas Garman, and Lael R. Keiser. *Regulation and Consumer Protection: Politics, Bureaucracy and Economics.* 3rd ed. Houston, TX: Dame Publications, 1998.

Page, Alan C., and R.B. Ferguson. *Investor Protection.* London: Orion, 1992.

Reinis, August, ed. *Standards of Investment Protection.* New York: Oxford University Press, 2008.

United Nations. *Guidelines for Consumer Protection.* New York: United Nations, 2003.

Consumption

"Consumption" is a macroeconomic term for the total amount of spending on consumer goods by individuals or households—or a defined group of individuals and households, such as a nation—over a given period of time. Although consumption literally refers to the goods and services consumed during the period in question, economists also include goods that are bought during the period but used or enjoyed over a longer amount of time, such as cars, appliances, home linens, or shoes. Consumption falls into three basic categories: durable goods, such as cars and appliances; nondurable goods, such as food, medicine, clothing (though this last item may be used over a long period of time, economists classify it as a nondurable); and services, such as medical care, home cleaning, and school tuition. Consumption equals individual or household in-

come, minus savings. The use of savings is either to purchase financial assets or to purchase newly constructed housing, a component of investment spending. (Only households engage in consumption spending on consumer goods and services; business firms and governments do not.)

Patterns and Trends

As in most developed economies, consumption accounts for the lion's share of total spending in the United States—roughly 70 percent in 2009. Consumption, of course, varies widely among individuals and groups, especially when it comes to income. For example, wealthier individuals and households with higher incomes tend to spend a higher percentage on health care, while poorer individuals and households with lower incomes spend a higher percentage on food. There are several explanations for the difference in consumption patterns—older people, who require more health care, tend to be wealthier and to have higher incomes; for those with tighter budgets, nonessential medical services may not be a high priority. And while wealthier people buy higher-quality food and eat out more often, there is a limit to how much food someone can eat. More importantly, wealthier individuals with higher incomes tend to put more of their income into savings. Across all demographic and social categories, aggregate consumption in the United States in recent years breaks down approximately as follows: 12 percent for durables, 29 percent for nondurables, and 59 percent for services.

Not only do consumption patterns differ among classes, but they also vary over time—in the lives of individuals, over the course of business cycles, and through historical eras. Thus, younger Americans tend to spend more of their income on entertainment, shifting the emphasis to health care when they get older. Paradoxically, people tend to save more and consume less (even as a percentage of income) during downturns in the economic cycle. While that is not the case among people who have been laid off, who cannot afford to save as much and who spend all of their unemployment benefits to buy the things they need for themselves and their families, there are still far more employed people than unemployed people in the worst of recessions. And those who are still employed tend to save more for a variety of reasons. They may fear losing their jobs or seeing their incomes go down and decide to put money away for a "rainy day." Economic downturns also tend to bring declining equity value in securities and homes; while the losses may only be on paper, they tend to make people feel less secure about their current and future (retirement) economic situation, compelling them to save more.

The housing bubble and crash of the mid-to-late 2000s illustrates how an economic cycle can play a crucial role in consumption. During the run-up in housing prices in the early and middle part of the decade, Americans found themselves with greater amounts of equity in their homes. That led to three developments. First, with more equity in their homes, many individuals worried less about saving for retirement and increased consumption. Second, with credit standards loosening, many people were able to take out home equity loans and use the money to buy all sorts of consumer goods and services. And third, with rising equity, people were able to refinance their homes at lower interest rates, which lowered their monthly mortgage payments and freed up more money for consumption. Between 2002 and 2006—at the peak of the housing boom—the aggregate personal savings rate in the United States fell from more than 2 percent of after-tax income to nearly zero. By 2009, it had climbed back up to more than 5 percent, a level not seen since the mid-1990s.

Even at 5 percent, however, the aggregate savings rate was relatively low compared to that of much of the post–World War II era. There were two basic reasons for this. First, median household income has stagnated in real, inflation-adjusted terms; according to some estimates, it has even fallen since the early 1970s, when the aggregate savings rate was above 10 percent. Moreover, to sustain even the stagnant or slightly falling income level, households have had to add an additional breadwinner—usually the wife. With both parents working, households have to spend more on day care, food (going out or buying prepared food), cleaning expenses, and other goods and services that had been provided by the stay-at-home spouse in the traditional, one-breadwinner family. Of course, in some two-breadwinner households, the savings rate may be higher since there are now two incomes.

Such consumption may be seen as a sheer necessity. But there has also been a major attitudinal change toward discretionary consumption since World War II, a change fostered by the advertising, consumer goods, and financial industries. Advertising and marketing have increased the appetite for consumption, while the consumer goods industry has both met demand and produced new and improved products. Meanwhile, the financial industry has developed and aggressively marketed a host of new products—credit cards, debit cards, home-equity loans, and other innovations—that make it easier to borrow and, at least temporarily, hide the costs of consumption by delaying payment or spreading it over longer periods of time. Between 1980 and 2008, so-called revolving debt (primarily credit-card debt) increased from $139 billion to $972 billion (in 2008 dollars), a jump of 700 percent.

Consumption in the United States has also been driven by secular trends—that is, long-term historical patterns unaffected by the business cycle. For example, improved agricultural methods and crops have brought down the cost of food, reducing that important component of consumer spending. Where Americans spent more than 40 percent of their income on food and drink in the early part of the twentieth century, a hundred years later they were spending less than 20 percent on such items. In addition, according to some economists, the advent of Social Security in the 1930s and Medicare in the 1960 lowered savings rates and increased consumption as people worried less about how they would pay for medical care in their senior years. At the same time, relentlessly rising medical costs have driven up that component of national consumption. And, of course, demographic trends also play a vital role. Living on fixed income and savings, seniors tend to consume relatively more than people at the peak of their earning lives. Thus, as the median age rises in a country, savings rates decline.

Differences Among Nations

As a function of both cyclical economic trends and secular factors, savings rates may also differ dramatically from country to country. With their high consumption rates, Americans are among the least active savers of any industrialized country, a somewhat paradoxical trend given the relative lack of a social safety net. In other words, it would seem sensible for American consumers—who receive less in unemployment, retirement, health care, and educational benefits from the government than their counterparts in Europe, say—to save more against such contingencies than people who live in countries where the social welfare system is far more generous. Indeed, in China, where the social safety net is even weaker than in the United States, the national savings rate hovers above 30 percent—the highest in the world for a major country. Even in the eurozone, the savings rate is about 10 percent, double that of the United States.

Economists offer a number of theories for the differences. On the savings side, they say that Americans are less likely to put money away because, aside from the occasional recession, Americans have only known prosperity since World War II. On the consumption side, factors include the effectiveness of advertising, the wealth of new products constantly being offered, and the innovative new financial products that have made it easier to consume thoughtlessly. In broad terms, the theorists tend to break down into two camps: liberal voices, which insist the high consumption-to-saving ratio is caused by stagnating incomes, compounded by soaring medical costs and, until the late 2000s, rising housing costs; and conservative voices, which contend American consumers have lost their sense of discipline, refusing to defer immediate gratification for long-term security. The easy availability of credit also gives some households the ability to increase their consumption beyond what they otherwise would be able to spend without credit.

Whatever the reasons, consumption patterns have an enormous impact on the national economy, given that they account for about two-thirds of all spending. High rates of consumption, combined with a decline in manufacturing capacity, can lead to rising trade deficits in the durable and nondurable goods categories (services are harder to provide from overseas), while low savings rates can stifle investment as banks and other financial institutions lack the resources to lend money to businesses for capital improvements.

James Ciment

See also: Confidence, Consumer and Business; Effective Demand; Hoarding; Inflation; Retail and Wholesale Trade; Savings and Investment.

Further Reading

Attanasio, Orazio P., Laura Blow, Robert Hamilton, and Andrew Leicester. "Booms and Busts: Consumption, House Prices and Expectations." *Economica* 76:301 (2009): 20–50.

Calder, Lendol. *Financing the American Dream: A Cultural History of Consumer Debt.* Princeton, NJ: Princeton University Press, 1999.

Censolo, Roberto, and Caterina Colombo. "Public Consumption Composition in a Growing Economy." *Journal of Macroeconomics,* 30:4 (2008): 1479–1495.

Strasser, Susan, Charles McGovern, and Matthias Judt. *Getting and Spending: European and American Consumer Societies in the Twentieth Century.* New York: Cambridge University Press, 1998.

Corporate Corruption

The fraud perpetrated by financier Bernard Madoff, whose $50 billion to $60 billion Ponzi scheme was uncovered amid the subprime mortgage crisis of 2008, was but the latest in a long history of scandals associated with corporate corruption in America. Such scandals have occurred frequently, often resulting in devastation to individual investors and to the overall economy. Ironically, corporate corruption has helped shape the financial system in many ways, making it a dominant force in world finance, as institutional and regulatory reforms initiated in response to corruption have created a more efficient and transparent marketplace that encourages investment. For example, the stock market manipulations of Assistant Treasury Secretary William Duer in 1792 led to reforms that laid the groundwork for the establishment of the New York Stock Exchange. That institution would play a key role in the capital-raising efforts that built the nation's railroads, funded insurance companies and banks, and connected isolated local markets to the national economy.

Another example of reform following fraud occurred after the Panic of 1907, a financial crisis touched off by corruption at the Knickerbocker Trust Company in New York. That panic shook the nation, but also led to the creation of the Federal Reserve System, which did much to save the economy during the subprime mortgage crisis that peaked in 2008. Similarly, congressional investigations following the stock market crash of 1929 uncovered widespread fraud and corruption. These revelations led to the passage of federal securities laws and, in 1934, to the creation of the Securities and Exchange Commission, which reshaped Wall Street and corporate governance through mandatory full-disclosure requirements.

Robber Barons

Corporate corruption became a national concern during the era of the "robber barons" following the American Civil War, when businessmen such as Jay Gould and Daniel Drew plundered the stock markets and looted the corporations they controlled. In 1872, a scandal at Crédit Mobilier of America, a service company for the Union Pacific Railroad, set the bar for corporate scandals in future centuries. Crédit Mobilier made profits of some $44 million from Union Pacific construction projects, which were funded in part by the federal government. The company's officers gave a number of its shares to Congressman Oakes Ames of Massachusetts in order to buy influence. Cash was given to other government officials to persuade them to falsely certify completion of construction and to allow the company to receive payments from Congress. Representative Ames was expelled from Congress when the scandal became public, as was Representative James Brooks of New York, who also had accepted bribes. Several other members of Congress were censured, and a motion was entered to impeach Vice President Schuyler Colfax. Numerous other politicians were found to have been involved in this affair, including James A. Garfield, the twentieth president of the United States. The secretaries of navy and war were among those who received bribes.

Another model of corruption before the turn of the twentieth century was the American Ice Company (AIC), which had a monopoly on all ice business along the Atlantic coast. Ice was then a vital consumer product, and AIC was the fifth-largest company in the United States. AIC officials bribed New York City dock commissioners to turn back competing supplies of ice. The ice fields of competitors were smashed by steamships hired by AIC, and the company lowered its prices until its remaining competitors were destroyed. Once its monopoly was in place, AIC raised its prices by well over 100 percent, causing much hardship to consumers and stirring controversy in the press. The scandal blossomed when it was discovered in 1900 that the mayor of New York City, Robert Van Wyck, and his brother, a onetime Democratic Party gubernatorial nominee, had received AIC stock valued at almost $900,000. Several other prominent New York politicians also were found to have received large amounts of AIC stock for their support of the company.

Twentieth-Century Scandals

The Teapot Dome Scandal during the administration of President Warren G. Harding was another epic case of corporate corruption. In 1921, it was discovered that Albert Fall, then secretary of the interior and a former senator, had secretly leased the U.S. Navy's oil reserves at Teapot Dome in

Wyoming to oil tycoons Harry F. Sinclair of Mammoth Oil and Edward Doheny of Pan American Petroleum. Fall, who was paid $500,000 for access to the government oil leases, was indicted and convicted for his misconduct. However, he was sentenced to only a year in prison and fined $100,000. Sinclair and Doheny were acquitted of bribery charges, though Sinclair was found guilty of jury tampering. The scandal tainted the administration of President Harding, leaving it with a reputation for corruption.

Another massive scandal involved the failure of the Kreuger & Toll Company in the 1930s. Kreuger & Toll controlled more than 90 percent of the world's production of matches. Its head, Ivar Kreuger, known as the "Match King," used counterfeit bonds to support the company's loans—but when its finances collapsed, the company failed. Although the company was based in Sweden, Kreuger & Toll securities were held widely in the United States. Claims against the bankrupt firm exceeded a then-astonishing $1 billion. Another corporate scandal in the 1930s involved the Insull Utility Holding Company in Illinois. This company generated some 10 percent of the country's electric power through a pyramid of 100 holding companies that controlled more than 250 operating companies. Investors lost hundreds of millions of dollars when this empire collapsed. The head of the company, Samuel Insull, was indicted for misleading investors and manipulating the company's stock price. Insull fled the country, but soon was captured and returned for trial in the United States, where he eventually was acquitted of all charges.

An underworld group of individuals—including Lowell Birrell, Ben Jack Cage, Earl Belle, Alexander Guterma, Serge Rubinstein, and Virgil D. Dardi—weaved a web of corporate corruption in the 1950s. These men were said to have looted and destroyed seventy-five public companies and caused investor losses of $100 million. Many of them fled to Brazil, but that exodus slowed when an extradition treaty was signed with that country in 1961. Eddie Gilbert was at the center of another

highly publicized corporate scandal in the 1950s. Gilbert acquired control of the E.L. Bruce Company, a large manufacturer of hardwood flooring. He amassed a fortune estimated at $25 million, which allowed him to live an opulent lifestyle. Gilbert used $2 million of E.L. Bruce funds to meet margin calls on stock that he owned. When the loss was discovered, Gilbert fled to Brazil, making front-page news across the nation. He eventually tired of Brazil, however, and returned to the United States, where he was prosecuted and jailed for two years. Gilbert later became a successful businessman in New Mexico.

The "go-go" years of the 1960s and the following decade saw corporate fraud ranging from the IOS (Investors Overseas Services, Ltd.) mutual fund collapse and its looting by Robert Vesco, who fled the country when the fraud was discovered, to the highly publicized collapses of the National Student Marketing Corporation, the Four Seasons Nursing Centers, and the pyramid sales schemes of Glenn W. Turner of Koscot. In the 1970s, "questionable" payments made by the Lockheed Corporation and other large companies to foreign government officials in order to obtain business resulted in the collapse of several governments. That scandal resulted in the passage of the Foreign Corrupt Practices Act of 1977, which prohibited such payments.

The 1980s revealed a mass of corporate corruption that threatened the financial system. The events of this decade included the collapse of Penn Square Bank, a strip mall bank that contributed to the failure of the giant Continental Illinois National Bank. The Bank of Credit and Commerce International S.A. proved to be a global criminal enterprise that was involved in money laundering and drug trafficking. The savings and loan (S&L) debacle in the 1980s cost taxpayers more than $125 billion. The abuses committed by the managers of S&Ls were legendary—they included hiring prostitutes to entertain customers, leasing or buying Learjets for personal use, and purchasing extravagant homes and expensive art, all paid for with S&L money. By 1992, more than 1,000 individuals had been charged with crimes in connection with S&L activities—most of whom were convicted. Two of the individuals charged with crimes were Don Dixon and "Fast Eddie" McBirney. Also implicated was Charles Keating, Jr., who controlled the Lincoln Savings and Loan Association in Irvine, California. He had paid himself and his family members $34 million for their services before the failure of that institution cost taxpayers more than $3 billion. Keating spent five years in jail before a federal court overturned his conviction.

The insider trading scandals of the 1980s involving Ivan Boesky and others, and the prosecution of Michael Milken, the "Junk Bond King," were all headline news and the subject of several books. Milken, for a time, became the high priest of corporate finance through his innovative use of high-yield "junk" bonds to fund corporate mergers. His annual "Predators' Ball," a conference on junk bonds held in Beverly Hills, was attended by hundreds of institutional investors and individuals involved in mergers and acquisitions. Milken was well compensated for his efforts to expand the use of junk bonds, receiving more than $120 million in salary and bonus in 1984 and $550 million in 1987. Milken was indicted in March 1989 on ninety-eight felony counts of securities violations, mail and wire fraud, and racketeering. The charges brought against Milken involved parking stock (holding shares controlled by another party to conceal ownership of shares) and other forms of manipulation. Milken pleaded guilty to six felony counts, agreed to pay a fine of $600 million, and was sentenced to ten years in prison, which later was reduced to three years.

Modern corporate corruption is marked by the failure of the Enron Corporation, the nation's seventh-largest company at the time it declared bankruptcy in 2001. Enron failed amid a sea of corporate corruption that involved accounting manipulations designed to boost its stock price so that company executives could reap millions of dollars in compensation from stock options. More corporate corruption was uncovered following the failure of WorldCom, a telecommunications company whose executives had engineered massive manipulations of its accounts to boost the company's share price. At the time, it was the largest bankruptcy in history. WorldCom's chief executive officer (CEO), Bernard Ebbers, was sentenced to twenty-five years in prison.

The accounting scandal at WorldCom was accompanied by others, including Tyco International Ltd., whose CEO, Dennis Kozlowski, was sentenced to more than eight years in prison, and Adelphia Communications Corporation, whose eighty-year old CEO was sentenced to fifteen years in prison. Other massive accounting scandals arose during this era at Nortel Network Corporation, Lucent Technologies Inc., Qwest Communications International Inc., Global Crossing Ltd., AOL-Time Warner, Cendant Corporation, Hollinger International Inc., and HealthSouth Corporation. The Sarbanes-Oxley Act of 2002 was passed in response to those scandals. It sought to strengthen accounting controls at public companies.

New York State Attorney General Eliot Spitzer began a crusade against corporate corruption during this period. He exposed, among other things, conflicts of interest on Wall Street by financial analysts, who privately were disparaging the same stocks they were touting to public investors. Spitzer arranged a $1.4 billion settlement between state and federal regulators and several investment banking firms involved in the scandal. Spitzer also attacked the fee arrangements of Marsh & McLennan and AIG (American International Group), two large insurance firms, ousting their chief executive officers and imposing large fines in the process.

Spitzer exposed "late trading" and "market timing" activities by hedge funds in the shares of mutual funds. Those arrangements allowed hedge funds to profit at the expense of individual mutual fund investors. The mutual fund investigations led to large settlements with several hedge funds. Spitzer's aggressive prosecutorial tactics made him a controversial figure, but he leveraged the publicity associated with his prosecutions of corporate corruption to catapult himself into the New York governor's office in 2007. However, he was forced to resign from office the following year when he was caught up in a scandal of his own involving money laundering activities that were used to cover up his involvement as a client of a prostitution ring.

The subprime mortgage crisis exposed more corporate corruption, including the largest fraud in history committed by Bernard Madoff, who was arrested on December 11, 2008, after confessing that he had been running a giant Ponzi scheme. Madoff was a well-known figure in the securities business. He was a former chair of NASDAQ and had served on the Board of Governors of the National Association of Securities Dealers, the industry's self-regulatory body. Actual out-of-pocket losses to investors were estimated at $19.4 billion. Madoff was sentenced to 150 years in prison. Among Madoff's victims were a number of Jewish charities, including one sponsored by Nobel laureate Elie Wiesel. Tufts University lost $20 million, Yeshiva University lost more than $100 million, and Bard College lost $3 million.

Marc Schrenker, an investment adviser in Indiana accused of defrauding his customers, fled in his airplane, jumping out of the plane over Alabama. The crashed, but empty, plane was discovered in Florida, 200 miles (320 kilometers) away. Schrenker was found hiding in a campground near Quincy, Florida, where he slit his wrist just before being captured. Schrenker survived and was jailed. Another massive fraud was revealed on February 17, 2009, after the Securities and Exchange Commission charged Sir R. Allen Stanford with defrauding investors of some $8 billion. He had promised high returns from certificates of deposit, but actually had invested customer funds in illiquid assets. Stanford was a high-profile financier who was an international cricket sponsor. He operated out of the Caribbean island of Antigua through his Stanford International Bank.

The subprime mortgage crisis also gave rise to concerns that executives at large financial service firms had been corrupted by compensation schemes that induced them to take excessive risks, which crippled or destroyed their firms when the subprime crisis began. Several financial services firms failed, or had to be bailed out by the federal government, during the subprime crisis. They included Merrill Lynch, Bear Stearns, Morgan Stanley, Lehman Brothers, Citigroup, Bank of America, Wachovia, Washington Mutual, Countrywide Financial, IndyMac Bancorp, and AIG, as well as the government-sponsored enterprises Fannie Mae and Freddie Mac. Those failures prompted the federal government to place restraints on executive pay at firms bailed out by the government and to allow shareholder votes on compensation arrangements.

Conclusion

Corporate corruption has had a significant impact on the American economy, often precipitating market panics. The Panic of 1884, for example, was touched off by the discovery of massive fraud at Grant & Ward, a brokerage firm in which former Union general and U.S. president Ulysses S. Grant was a partner. The Panic of 1907 was set off by the failure of the Knickerbocker Trust Company. The stock market crash of 1929 and the unveiling of much corruption on Wall Street preceded the Great Depression. The subprime mortgage crisis of 2007–2009 was a continuing scandal over corrupt lending practices and excessive executive compensation. The unraveling of Bernard Madoff's massive fraud followed those scandals.

Corporate corruption frequently leads to new regulations. Corruption on Wall Street resulted in the enactment of the Securities Act of 1933 and the Securities Exchange Act of 1934, which created the Securities and Exchange Commission. The Insull scandal led to the enactment of the Public Utility Holding Company Act of 1935, which subsequently was repealed. The savings and loan crisis of the 1980s resulted in much corrective legislation. The corruption at Enron and WorldCom led to the enactment of the Sarbanes-Oxley Act in

2002. In the aftermath of the subprime mortgage crisis, Congress considered a number of measures to prevent corruption and reckless risk taking by financial services firms.

This cycle of corruption imposes heavy costs on society in the form of onerous regulatory requirements that the innocent must bear. The Sarbanes-Oxley Act, for example, imposed significant accounting costs on public companies. This pattern of corruption, market panics, and corrective legislation also has resulted in a multilayered regulatory system in which numerous state and federal agencies seek to prevent and deter corporate corruption.

At the federal level, regulators include the Federal Reserve Board, the Office of the Comptroller of the Currency in the Treasury Department, the Federal Deposit Insurance Corporation, the Office of Thrift Supervision, and FinCEN, an anti–money laundering group located in the Treasury Department. In addition to those bodies are the Securities and Exchange Commission, the Commodity Futures Trading Commission, the Federal Trade Commission, the Occupational Safety and Health Administration (for Sarbanes-Oxley whistle-blower claims), and self-regulatory bodies such as the Financial Industry Regulatory Authority, in the securities industry, and the National Futures Association in the futures industry. The Justice Department is criminalizing every form of corporate behavior.

Corporations are policed at the state level by fifty state insurance commissioners, acting collectively through the National Association of Insurance Commissioners; fifty state securities commissioners (plus the District of Columbia), acting collectively through the North American Securities Administrators Association; and fifty state attorneys general. There also are fifty state bank regulators.

Before the subprime mortgage crisis, there was widespread concern that these layers of regulation were affecting the ability of American corporations to compete in a global economy. Efforts to reduce those burdens were dropped during the subprime crisis. Congress is now considering even more regulation in this continuing cycle of scandal and corrective legislation.

Jerry W. Markham

See also: Enron; Insull, Samuel; Securities and Exchange Commission; WorldCom.

Further Reading

Fox, Loren. *Enron: The Rise and Fall.* Hoboken, NJ: John Wiley & Sons, 2003.

Gup, Benton E., ed. *Too Big to Fail: Policies and Practices in Government Bailouts.* Westport, CT: Praeger, 2004.

Henriques, Diana B. *The White Sharks of Wall Street: Thomas Mellon and the Original Corporate Raiders.* New York: Scribner, 2000.

Markham, Jerry W. *A Financial History of Modern U.S. Corporate Scandals: From Enron to Reform.* Armonk, NY: M.E. Sharpe, 2005.

Mayer, Martin. *The Greatest-Ever Bank Robbery: The Collapse of the Savings and Loan Industry.* New York: Scribner, 1990.

Partnoy, Frank. *The Match King: Ivar Krueger, the Financial Genius Behind a Century of Wall Street Scandals.* New York: PublicAffairs, 2009.

Vise, David A., and Steve Coll. *Eagle on the Street.* New York: Scribner, 1991.

Corporate Finance

Corporate finance is the process by which corporations acquire the funds needed to start and grow their businesses, and to fund their everyday commercial activities. Corporate finance can be complex, but its essential nature begins with the corporate balance sheet. The right side of that financial statement identifies the corporation's sources of funding of its assets, which are liabilities and shareholder equity. Each of these funding sources has unique characteristics.

During boom periods, when credit comes on easier terms, corporations tend to become more leveraged, or indebted, using the additional borrowed funds to increase output and even speculate in things like other corporate securities and real estate. But during recessions, such as the one that began in the United States in late 2007 and gripped the global economy in 2008–2009, corporations find it increasingly difficult to borrow money to finance investment, expansion, and hiring. Indeed, the credit markets became so tight in late 2008 that many economists feared corporations would not be able to access even the normally routine short-term credit they often used to finance day-to-day operations, including payroll. This freezing up of the global economy was one of the critical factors leading the United States and other governments to offer bailouts of major financial institutions in late 2008.

Liabilities

Liabilities shown on the balance sheet are simply borrowings, which may include bank loans (secured or unsecured), notes, bonds, commercial paper, and a number of other lending arrangements. Interest must be paid on borrowings, which may be either a floating or fixed rate. Arrangements must also be made for the repayment of the principal of the loan on its maturity date, or at some earlier time. Earlier repayment of the loan may be required upon the occurrence of a trigger event specified in the loan documents, such as a credit downgrade.

Short-term working capital needs may be met with a number of loan arrangements, such as a revolving line of credit from a bank. A line of credit allows the corporation to borrow and repay funds as needed, up to a specified maximum principal amount set by the lending bank. Another popular short-term lending arrangement is commercial paper. This is simply a promissory note issued by a corporation to a lender, which may be another corporation with excess funds on hand. The initial type of commercial paper can range from overnight to 270 days, but averages about 30 days.

Corporations obtain loans on a medium- or long-term basis through a number of financing techniques, such as note and bond sales. Bonds sold to the public, sometimes referred to as "debentures," are sold under a trust indenture agreement that specifies the terms of the bond. The basic

"coupon" note, or bond, pays periodic interest at a set rate over the life of the note.

The interest rate on bonds is usually set by market conditions and by the creditworthiness of the borrower. That creditworthiness may be assessed by the rating agencies, such as Moody's, Standard & Poor's, and Fitch. The borrower is assigned a rating by one or more of those rating agencies, reflecting one of several levels of perceived creditworthiness, ranging from investment grade to "junk." The lower the credit rating, the higher the interest rate on the loan. The higher rate is required to compensate for the increased risk of a default on a lower-rated bond.

Bonds paying fixed rates of interest will fluctuate in value with changes in interest rates or the creditworthiness of the borrower. All other things being equal, the value of a bond will increase if interest rates decrease. This is because the higher-paying bond is more valuable than comparable bonds paying a lower rate of interest. Conversely, the value of the bond will decrease if interest rates increase.

Some bonds are "callable." This means that the corporation may redeem the loan before maturity, allowing a refunding of its debt at a lower cost if interest rates decrease. To protect the lender, there is often some "call protection" for these bonds in the form of a premium to be paid on redemption or some minimum period of time before the bonds can be called. Some debt instruments are convertible into stock. This allows the holder to receive a fixed rate of return before conversion and to participate in the success of a corporation through the increased value of its stock upon conversion. Conversion rights, call provisions, and other bells and whistles added to the plain vanilla bond, are designed to attract capital and to allow flexible funding for the corporation at the lowest or most acceptable cost.

Shareholder Equity

Shareholder equity includes capital raised by the sale of stock to shareholders, who are the owners of the corporation. Typically, stock is issued in the form of "common stock" that is given one vote per share on corporate matters at shareholder meetings and a pro rata share of dividends. "Preferred stock" is also popular. It is given priority over common stock for dividends in a specified amount. "Preferred stock" generally has a liquidation preference over common stock in the event the business of the corporation is terminated, but preferred stock usually has limited voting rights. Preferred stock dividends may be cumulative, which means that, if a dividend on the preferred stock is missed, the common stockholders may not receive a dividend until those arrears are paid to the preferred. Such rights give preferred stock many characteristics associated with debt.

Most corporations start out as private businesses. If they later seek to sell stock or bonds to the public, that offering must be registered with the Securities and Exchange Commission (SEC). The company will, thereafter, be required to submit financial reports to the SEC, which are made public on a quarterly and annual basis, and upon the occurrence of certain special events. Once registered with the SEC, the corporation's stock may be listed on a national securities exchange, like the New York Stock Exchange, or traded in the over-the-counter market on NASDAQ or some other venue, such as an electronic trading platform.

Another component of shareholder equity is retained earnings. These are the profits (or losses) of a company accumulated over the years, minus dividends paid out to shareholders. The declaration of a dividend is a discretionary matter for the board of directors of the corporation. Instead of paying out the profits to shareholders, the board may decide to use corporate profits for capital expenditures that will increase the size or profitability of the business.

A matter of some concern in corporate finance is the concept of "leverage," which is determined by the debt-to-equity ratio of the corporation. A high degree of leverage will increase shareholder profits because the profits of the corporation will be generated more by borrowed funds than

by shareholder equity. The lenders receive only interest payments. In contrast, if the funds were raised by additional stock sales, the amount of dividends the existing shareholders would otherwise receive will be diluted. This is because the new shareholders will be entitled to share in future dividends with the existing shareholders. Leverage is a wonderful thing when there are profits, but it works both ways. If the corporation is suffering losses, leverage will magnify shareholder losses and present a danger to creditors.

Corporate finance is also driven by the time value of money. This concept recognizes that a dollar earned today is worth more than a dollar earned in the future. Corporate finance requires constant attention to the present and future value of money in assessing the costs of particular financing programs and the viability and effectiveness of alternative financing programs, mergers and acquisitions, and other aspects of corporate finance.

Corporate Finance—History

Today a vast, complex, and interconnected global structure exists to meet the financing needs of corporations. It was not always so. The greatest commercial adventure in all history, Christopher Columbus's voyages to America, had to be funded by the Spanish sovereign because there was little private capital available for such an enterprise. That situation changed with the development of the "joint stock" companies, the predecessor to our modern corporations, which were used by the Dutch and the English for exploration of the world in the sixteenth and seventeenth centuries. Joint stock companies, including the Virginia Company, which established the Jamestown colony, were able to raise private capital to fund their global operations and to colonize America.

The British crown eventually suppressed commercial corporations in the American colonies, but the number of corporations grew rapidly after the Revolutionary War. These fledgling enterprises demanded increasing amounts of capital as the need arose for the building of bridges, turnpikes, canals, and other internal improvements. Much capital was raised in Europe, especially England, to fund the early American enterprises. The arrival of the railroad increased the demand for capital, with over 1,000 miles (1,600 kilometers) of track per year being laid in the period leading up to the Civil War.

Bonds, rather than common stock, largely capitalized the railroads. This was because European investors preferred a fixed return on their money. Railroads were soon issuing many levels of bonds in England, including sterling bonds, which were payable in British pounds; first, second, and third mortgage bonds; convertible bonds; and real-estate bonds. The preference for bonds over equity would have an unfortunate result. The individuals controlling the railroads through stock ownership often contributed little in the way of capital, at least in comparison to bondholders. The equity owners were all too frequently speculators who had little concern for the long-term success of the company. These robber barons used their leverage at every opportunity to loot the railroads or to otherwise abuse their positions.

Private investment banking firms expanded after the Civil War in order to meet the increased demands for capital that followed the conflict. Jay Cooke, the principal Union military financier, was a leader in one of the first joint syndicate operations for underwriting securities sold to the public, an event that occurred in 1869. Cooke's firm failed in 1873, but other investment bankers led the effort to consolidate enterprises into giant amalgamations. From 1897 to 1904, more than 4,000 firms merged into 257 surviving entities. During the same period, 319 railroads combined. The hundred largest companies quadrupled in value as a result of these combinations, controlling 40 percent of the industrial capital of the United States.

J.P. Morgan became the most famous investment banking firm and a leader in corporate finance through its reorganizations of faltering railroads at the end of the nineteenth century. The firm's most famous combination was the creation of United States Steel Corporation as the twentieth century began, with a then staggering total capitalization of $1.4 billion.

The United States was the largest industrialized country in the world at the beginning of the twentieth century. At the time, it was producing 24 percent of manufactured goods in the world; by 1913, the figure would increase to one-third. Corporate finance provided the foundation for that growth. The United States became a net creditor with the outbreak of World War I. Before that conflict, securities issues over $1 million were considered to be large. By the 1920s, $25 million issues were not unusual. Stock trading grew during the 1920s, until the stock market crash of 1929, and the ensuing Great Depression, crippled the economy.

Congress responded to concerns over corporate finance raised by the market crash with the adoption of the federal securities laws in the 1930s. That legislation included the Securities Act of 1933, which regulated initial public offerings of stocks and bonds, and the Securities Exchange Act of 1934, which regulated trading of securities on stock exchanges, and later the over-the-counter market. The latter measure also created the Securities and Exchange Commission, which has become the nation's principal regulator of corporate finance for public companies.

Until the 1970s, corporate finance was a largely unexciting business of raising capital from stock offerings and borrowing funds through bond offerings, bank loans, or commercial paper. That changed dramatically as a result of the rampant inflation that arose in the 1970s, reaching 13 percent in 1979, with short-term interest rates climbing to nearly 20 percent in 1981. This resulted in an increased focus on corporate finance, leading to the rise of the chief financial officer as one of the leading executives at most public companies. These individuals employed many imaginative techniques for borrowing, investing, and managing short-term funding needs through such means as "repos" (repurchase agreements), asset-backed commercial paper, sweep accounts, and other arrangements designed to minimize borrowing costs and maximize profits from surplus funds.

Corporate finance was also exposing a dark underside of its character. The insider trading scandals involving Ivan Boesky and other well-known financiers on Wall Street resulted in several high-profile criminal prosecutions in the 1980s. The "junk bonds" promoted by Michael Milken, a broker at the investment banking firm of Drexel Burnham Lambert, were used to fund highly leveraged corporate mergers. These bonds became highly controversial because the mergers they financed sometimes resulted in business failures and massive layoffs. The buyouts relied on heavy borrowing to buy public companies.

A revolution in corporate financing techniques involving derivative instruments was also under way. These included stock option contracts traded on the Chicago Board Options Exchange, beginning in 1973. The futures markets also developed a number of innovative contracts, including futures on Government National Mortgage Association (GNMA, or Ginnie Mae) pass-through securities. More innovation followed with futures on stock indexes, resulting in a convergence of the stock and commodity markets. That convergence raised concerns with the effects of new trading techniques in these derivatives, such as "dynamic hedging" and "portfolio" trading through computerized trading programs on the stock market. Those concerns seemed justified when the stock market crashed in 1987. However, the stock market soon recovered and financial innovation proceeded apace.

Swap contracts that allowed corporations to hedge their interest rate, currency, and other risks became popular in the 1980s. For example, a firm with an unwanted floating interest rate exposure could swap that rate for the fixed rate payments of a firm seeking floating rate exposure. More complex swaps led to problems on the part of some firms that did not understand their complexities. The variations of derivative instruments multiplied into the hundreds and included such things as "worthless warrants," "death-backed bonds," and even "exploding options."

An important development in finance was the so-called pass-through security, or collateralized mortgage obligation, which involved mortgage pools in which investors were sold participations. This process facilitated the raising of a significant amount of capital for the mortgage market. This "securitization" concept spread to other asset-backed securities, such as credit cards and other receivables like franchise fees and even royalties. This corporate financing tool was badly abused by the Enron Corporation before that company's spectacular failure in 2001. Enron used such structures to conceal debt and to increase its revenues improperly. That and other financial scandals led to corrective legislation in the form of the Sarbanes-Oxley Act of 2002.

The leveraged loan market became a popular source of funding for private equity acquisitions of public companies in this century. Those loans were syndicated by a lead bank and sold in pieces to other investors. The credit crunch that began in the summer of 2007 slowed the leveraged loan market and presaged the subprime crisis that shocked the nation between 2007 and 2009. The federal government invoked desperate measures in order to prevent a complete freeze in corporate finance. These government programs included the $700 billion Troubled Asset Relief Program (TARP), which injected billions of dollars of capital into financial services firms; the Asset-Backed Commercial Paper Money Market Fund Liquidity Facility (AMLF), which made nonrecourse loans on asset-backed commercial paper; the Commercial Paper Funding Facility (CPFF), which was created to purchase unsecured, asset-backed commercial paper from corporate issuers through a special-purpose vehicle (this program had purchased $334 billion in assets by December 31, 2008); and the $200 billion Term Asset-Backed Securities Loan Facility (TALF, expanded to $1 trillion in March 2009), which makes secured, nonrecourse loans available to banks and commercial firms, using as collateral such things as credit card debt, consumer loans, and student loans.

The subprime crisis gave rise to much concern

with, and criticism of, corporate finance. Many high-profile financial services firms, such as Lehman Brothers, Bear Stearns, Citigroup, AIG, and Merrill Lynch failed or had to be rescued. These firms were highly leveraged with high multiples of debt to equity, and were thought to have incurred excessive risk in order to increase the bonus pools of executives. This gave rise to efforts to reform compensation schemes in order to discourage undue risk taking in corporate finance. Although the economy seemed to be recovering as 2010 began, Congress was considering legislation that would put new constraints on corporate finance.

Jerry W. Markham

See also: Credit Rating Agencies; Debt Instruments; Fixed Business Investment; Inventory Investment; Leveraging and Deleveraging, Financial; Production Cycles; Savings and Investment; Stock and Bond Capitalization.

Further Reading

Markham, Jerry W. *A Financial History of the United States.* 3 vols. Armonk, NY: M.E. Sharpe, 2002.

Markham, Jerry W., and Thomas L. Hazen. *Corporate Finance, Cases and Materials.* 2nd ed. Rochester, MN: West Group, 2007.

Ross, Stephen A., Randolph W. Westerfield, and Bradford Jordan. *Fundamentals of Corporate Finance.* 9th ed. New York: McGraw-Hill, 2009.

Council of Economic Advisers, U.S.

Along with the Federal Reserve (Fed) and the Department of the Treasury, the Council of Economic Advisers plays a central role in understanding and managing American business cycles. It does so by helping identify, formulate, and implement policies that lead to economic growth and minimize contraction.

Created by the Employment Act of 1946, the Council of Economic Advisers (CEA) is an independent, three-member advisory body in the Executive Office of the President. In advising the president, the CEA represents the view of the economics profession on national economic policy. In fact, the CEA's only explicit mandate is to write the annual *Economic Report of the President*, which contains past economic performance data, projections of future macroeconomic performance, and discussion of relevant microeconomic and international issues.

Throughout its history, the CEA has focused primarily on maximizing long-term economic growth. In macroeconomic policy, this has meant trying to achieve full employment and price stability. In recent decades, the CEA has increased its scrutiny of microeconomic policy issues with the goal of realizing efficiency gains in government policy in both the short and long term.

Membership

The CEA consists of three members and their staffs. All three members are appointed by the president and confirmed by the U.S. Senate. The three members had equal status under the original legislation, but a chairperson—likewise designated by the president—was assigned special responsibilities in a 1953 reorganization. The chair is legally responsible for hiring staff and representing the CEA in dealings with the president and public. Since 1961, the chairperson has been a regularly attendee at cabinet meetings, albeit without formal cabinet status. All three members of the CEA oversee the professional staff, which comprises about thirty economists and statisticians.

According to the Employment Act, a qualified member of the CEA "shall be a person who, as a result of his training, experience, and attainments, is exceptionally qualified to analyze and interpret economic developments, to appraise programs and activities of the Government, and to formulate and recommend national economic policy. . . ." In practice, almost all CEA members have had doctorates in economics, have had significant academic experience, and have intended to return to academia once their service in Washington was over.

The same is true of professional staff, made up almost entirely of academic economists on one- or two-year leaves from their teaching positions. These nonformalized constraints mean that in comparison with other political appointments, the advice provided by the CEA is less biased and more consistent with the best practices of the economics profession as a whole. Because CEA members and staff typically come from academia and plan on returning to it, they are sometimes less willing to compromise their academic reputations by supporting policy to please the current administration. As another result of academic professionalism, Democratic economists have sometimes worked as members of Republican CEA staffs and vice versa.

Macroeconomic Efforts

Following the Employment Act of 1946 to "promote maximum employment," during the Harry S. Truman administration, the council was concerned primarily with maximizing aggregate output. Hence, during the late 1940s and early 1950s, the CEA focused on such issues as the supply of natural resources, the quality of the labor force, the development of new and improved technology, and government efforts to sustain investment.

During the administrations of John F. Kennedy, the council continued to focus on keeping unemployment low and investment high. Walter Heller, the CEA chairman from 1960 to 1964, promoted the adoption of a 4 percent unemployment target. Likewise, Heller set a targeted annual economic growth rate of 4 percent. These goals were to be achieved, in part, through discretionary fiscal policy as well as sharp cuts in marginal tax rates. Many scholars point to marginal income tax cuts in 1962 and 1964 as the fuel of that decade's economic expansion.

During the 1970s, the CEA stepped back from its advocacy of activist macromanagement, reflecting a shift in opinion across the economics profession. Among academic economists at the time, the idea of a fundamental trade-off between inflation and unemployment that could be used to maintain full employment was being discredited. At the same time, there was increasing recognition of the importance of monetary policy in dictating

aggregate demand. While the CEA did not stop advocating fiscal policy to stimulate aggregate demand, it attached greater importance to monetary policy and the Fed in determining aggregate economic growth.

Indeed, deference to the Fed and an appreciation of the role of monetary policy in minimizing economic fluctuations has only increased since the 1970s. In more recent decades, the macroeconomic efforts of the CEA have focused heavily on structural changes that promote long-term economic stability. Nonetheless, the council opposed a balanced budget amendment in the mid-1990s over concern about the amendment's effect on the stabilization of the macroeconomy, and the CEA approved several small fiscal stimuli in the first decade of the twenty-first century.

Microeconomic Policy

Since the 1960s, the CEA's growth-oriented advice to presidents has also addressed efficiency improvements in microeconomic policy. During the Kennedy administration, the CEA realized that it had the resources and expertise to give microeconomic policy advice that would promote long-term gains in overall economic efficiency. By calling attention to understated costs and overstated benefits of proposed policies and by emphasizing the importance of incentives to the outcome of spending, tax, and regulatory policies, the CEA has achieved several important improvements in microeconomic policy. If not always high-profile, such changes have yielded long-term benefits for the U.S. economy.

During the Richard M. Nixon administration, the CEA successfully advocated for the end of government subsidization of the politically popular but economically wasteful supersonic transport program. In addition, the 1970s also brought accelerated deregulation of the airline, railroad, and parcel service industries, in part due to the CEA's advice on the high cost of existing regulations. In the early 1990s, the CEA helped advance an early "cap-and-trade" energy program, a market-based approach to mitigating sulfur dioxide emissions from burning coal while realizing efficiency benefits over more burdensome Environmental Protection Agency regulations.

During the Bill Clinton administration later that decade, the CEA played an important role in two important policy initiatives: the North American Free Trade Agreement (NAFTA) and welfare reform. The passage of both of these initiatives required constant explanation to the public and Congress of the benefits, that, at least in theory, trade liberalization and social service reform would bring to the economy. As a relatively independent organization, the CEA had more credibility than other government agencies.

Among the first appointments made by incoming president Barack Obama in 2009 was Christina Romer as chair of the CEA. An adviser to Obama through much of the presidential campaign, Romer was a widely expected choice, not only because of her association with Obama but because of the economic troubles the new president inherited. Romer had made a name for herself among economists for her work on the Great Depression. Both as an adviser to the candidate and as chair of the CEA, Romer strongly advocated targeted tax cuts for middle- and working-class taxpayers. The advice was based on her analysis of President Herbert Hoover's tax hikes of the early 1930s, which, she maintained, helped prolong and deepen the depression.

Joshua C. Hall and Elliott McNamee

See also: Congressional Budget Office; Fiscal Balance; Fiscal Policy; Government Accountability Office; National Economic Council; Tax Policy.

Further Reading

Council of Economic Advisers Web site: www.whitehouse.gov/administration/eop/cea.

Feldstein, M. "The Council of Economic Advisers: From Stabilization to Resource Allocation." *American Economic Review* 87:2 (1997): 99–102.

———. "The Council of Economic Advisers and Economic Advising in the United States." *Economic Journal* 102:414 (1992): 1223–1234.

Norton, Hugh S. *The Employment Act and the Council of Economic Advisers, 1946–1976.* Columbia: University of South Carolina Press, 1977.

Porter, R. "Presidents and Economists: The Council of Economic Advisers." *American Economic Review* 87:2 (1997): 103–108.

Stiglitz, J. "Looking Out for the National Interest: The Principles of the Council of Economic Advisers." *American Economic Review* 87:2 (1997): 109–113.

Countrywide Financial

Once the largest mortgage lender in the United States—financing about one in five mortgages in the country in 2006—California-based Countrywide Financial Corporation was badly hit by the collapse of the subprime mortgage market beginning in 2007. Facing a myriad of problems—shrinking assets, plummeting stock prices, and a number of state investigations into allegedly deceptive lending practices—Countrywide Financial was absorbed by Bank of America in January 2008, whereupon its name changed to Bank of America Home Loans.

Founded in 1969 by business partners David Loeb and Angelo Mozilo, Countrywide went public that same year. Although the initial response from investors was lukewarm, Countrywide was a mortgage innovator—and a successful one—from early on. It opened its first branch office in 1974, and had more than forty before the decade was out. The company earned a listing on the New York Stock Exchange in 1985 and, within six years of that, had become the nation's largest mortgage lender.

Meanwhile, Countrywide was branching out into other businesses. In 1985, it created Countrywide Mortgage Investment (CMI), which bundled mortgages too large to meet the requirements of the quasi-government mortgage insurers Fannie Mae and Freddie Mac; it bundled them into collateralized debt obligation instruments that it sold to investors. In 1997, CMI was spun off as IndyMac. (Under the chairmanship of Loeb, IndyMac would become one of the nation's largest thrifts and mortgage originators—only to fail in 2008 and be placed under receivership by the Federal Deposit Insurance Corporation.)

Countrywide was well positioned to take advantage of the housing boom of the early to mid-2000s. Following the dot.com stock market collapse of 2000, the terrorist attacks of September 11, 2001, and the recession of 2001, the Federal Reserve moved to lower the interest rate it charged to member banks—a standard monetary policy for reviving the economy. Between 2000 and 2003, the rate was lowered from 6 percent to 1 percent. This historically low rate allowed lenders to charge much less for mortgages. Moreover, government policies to expand homeownership and loosen regulation encouraged many lenders to innovate with new kinds of mortgages and to pursue new customers, including those with little or bad credit history. Mortgage originators offered these customers subprime mortgages, which required little documentation of borrower eligibility. Between 2001 and 2007, subprime mortgages increased from 10 percent to 20 percent of the overall U.S. mortgage market. These mortgages carried an adjustable rate—after an initial period in which the borrower made monthly payments on the interest only, he or she was required to pay a higher interest rate and part of the principal as well. Such a dramatic increase in monthly payments normally would have overwhelmed many homeowners' budgets. But with home values rising dramatically—a result, in part, of low rates and aggressive mortgage financing—most borrowers were able to refinance at lower adjustable rates, using the rising equity in their homes as collateral.

No company was more aggressive or innovative than Countrywide Financial in exploiting this burgeoning home mortgage market. By 2006, the company had outstanding mortgages valued at $500 billion, assets of $200 billion, and some 62,000 employees working out of more than 900 offices nationwide. At the peak of operations in 2006, the company reported nearly $2.6 billion in profits.

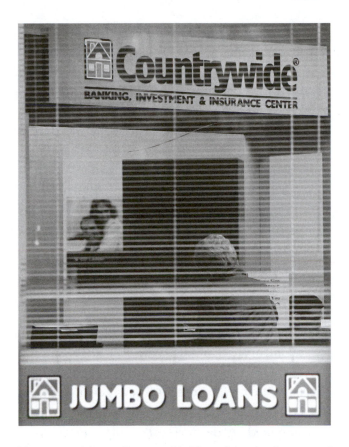

Mortgage originator Countrywide Financial took advantage of the housing boom of the early 2000s by aggressively marketing subprime loans. The collapse of real-estate prices spelled ruin for the firm, which was acquired by Bank of America in 2008. *(Bloomberg/Getty Images)*

By 2007, however, the U.S. housing bubble was bursting, a result of soaring home-price-to-income ratios—especially in hot markets such as Florida, the urban Northeast, and the Southwest—and a glut of newly developed properties. As housing prices declined, many of those with adjustable rates found it difficult to refinance, especially as the credit markets began to freeze up. Foreclosure rates soared, and housing starts plummeted.

Having risen so far and so fast, Countrywide was hit hard by the slump. With revenues declining rapidly, the company was forced to draw on its entire $11.5 billion credit line from a consortium of banks in August 2007. That same month, it sold a 16 percent equity stake for some $2 billion in stock from Bank of America. In September, it cut its workforce by roughly a fifth.

All of these measures proved insufficient. While chairman Mozilo (Loeb had died in 2003) maintained that the company would weather the crisis, rumors began to float through the financial markets that Countrywide was either about to be acquired by another institution or was on the verge of bankruptcy. In January 2008, the former proved true, as Bank of America paid $4 billion in stock to acquire the outstanding equity in the firm. Mozilo left the firm when the takeover was completed in July. For its part, Bank of America hoped to expand its presence in the home mortgage market.

Meanwhile, federal and state investigations into various lending and accounting practices were proceeding. Countrywide was accused by federal authorities of falsifying records before the takeover by Bank of America. More serious civil charges were filed by the attorneys general of California and Illinois, who charged that the company had engaged in deceptive lending practices by encouraging people to take out risky mortgages beyond their means, even when loan officers knew this to be the case. These allegations came in the wake of a 2006 case in which Countrywide settled with the New York State attorney general's office on charges of steering minority borrowers into higher-cost mortgages. In April 2009, Bank of America—eager to disassociate itself from a company with such a reputation—changed the name of Countrywide Financial to Bank of America Home Loans.

James Ciment

See also: Mortgage, Subprime; Recession and Finance Crisis (2007–); Shadow Banking System.

Further Reading

Michaelson, Adam. *The Foreclosure of America: The Inside Story of the Rise and Fall of Countrywide Home Loans, the Mortgage Crisis, and the Default of the American Dream.* New York: Berkley, 2009.

Muolo, Paul, and Mathew Padilla. *Chain of Blame: How Wall Street Caused the Mortgage and Credit Crisis.* Hoboken, NJ: John Wiley & Sons, 2008.

Creative Destruction

The term "creative destruction" refers to the process by which innovation creates new markets while inherently destroying old or existing ones. Thus, by the very act of creation, innovators are able to harness wealth for themselves by destroying the markets for established goods and services. Since the 1930s, economists have incorporated the concept of creative destruction within their understanding of how business cycles operate.

Origins

Early expressions of the concept can be traced to the writings of Mikhail Bakunin, a nineteenth-century Russian revolutionary, and Werner Sombart, a late nineteenth- and early twentieth-century German economist and sociologist. Bakunin stated in 1842 that "the passion for destruction is a creative passion." And in 1913, Sombart, in his book *Krieg and Kapitalismus* (War and Capitalism), wrote, "out of destruction a new spirit of creativity arises."

As commonly used and understood today, however, the term creative destruction was introduced into mainstream economic thinking and popularized by the famed Austrian-American economist Joseph Schumpeter. In his book *Capitalism, Socialism, and Democracy* (1942), Schumpeter characterized capitalism as a "perennial gale of creative destruction." In that work and others, Schumpeter examines capitalism as an expression of innovation in dynamic (unstable) business cycles. Specifically, creative destruction is used to describe the outcome of a particular kind of radical innovation.

In Schumpeter's words, "The opening up of new markets, foreign or domestic, and the organizational development from the craft shop to such concerns as U.S. Steel illustrate the same process of industrial mutation—if I may use that biological term—that incessantly revolutionizes the economic structure from within, incessantly destroying the old one, incessantly creating a new one. This process of creative destruction is the essential fact about capitalism." In other words, the constant churning of market forces leads to the destruction of the prevailing economic order and gives rise to a new one. Thus, the ups and downs of the business cycles are seen as part of an internal or endogenous (not external or exogenous) process that is driven primarily by innovation.

Creative Destruction and the Business Cycle

Schumpeter drew a vital connection between the concept of creative destruction and patterns of the business cycle. In particular, he saw radical new technologies competing and winning against existing products and, in the process, creating waves of economic expansion. In his own time (1882–1952), Schumpeter could look back on such breakthroughs as the steam engine, steel manufacturing, and the telegraph. In the current age, examples include the computer, the cell phone, and other information and communications technologies. Whatever the specific innovations, the cyclical process includes economic contraction when an existing technology matures, and expansion when—and only when—a new technology comes along to replace it. With the emergence of innovative new products, the old ones become obsolete and the marketplace stops buying them. Producers of outmoded products inevitably lose market share, and producers of new products shift consumer preference in their favor.

Schumpeter differentiates between two types of innovation—radical and incremental. Products characterized by radical innovation fundamentally transform the nature of the industry. Products with only incremental innovation (small modifications and minor improvements) do not radically transform an industry or affect the broader economy. Incremental innovations neither create new markets nor eliminate old ones.

The interpretation of economic reality employed in Schumpeter's explanation of creative destruction differs from that of mainstream macroeconomic theory. Schumpeter avoids the stylized conceptions of human rationality, competitive markets, and economies of scale, which have proven problematic for standard macroeconomic theory following the financial collapse of 2008. Schumpeter's alternative highlights instead the importance of small, innovative entrepreneurs, often idiosyncratic and quixotic, driven by a unique spirit of enterprise. Schumpeter uses the German term *Unternehmergeist* to refer to this entrepreneur-spirit.

Costs

Creative destruction is not without costs. Industry erosion, the demise of firms, and lost jobs are all a natural and essential part of the process. Radical innovation forces the rapid obsolescence of existing products and services as well as the workers and firms that produce them. During market turmoil, skills and knowledge also become outdated and lose value, leading to increases in unemployment. In the long run, even the largest and most powerful companies cannot prevail against innovative products and processes that meet market needs. Unless workers and firms actively seek to improve their skills and respond in a dynamic and proactive manner, the results may be bankruptcy and liquidation. All in all, however, evidence suggests that societies in which creative destruction is allowed to operate freely will eventually reap benefits in productivity, economic growth, and more jobs.

Manjula S. Salimath

See also: Austrian School; Schumpter, Joseph.

Further Reading

Foster, Richard, and Sarah Kaplan. *Creative Destruction: Turning Built-to-Last into Built-to-Perform.* New York: Currency, 2001.
Kirchoff, Bruce A. "Entrepreneurship's Contribution to Economics." *Entrepreneurship Theory and Practice* (Winter 1991): 93–112.

McCraw, Thomas K. *Prophet of Innovation: Joseph Schumpeter and Creative Destruction.* Cambridge, MA: Harvard University Press, 2007.

Schumpeter, Joseph A. *Capitalism, Socialism, and Democracy.* New York: Harper, 1942.

Credit Cycle

The term "credit cycle" is used today in reference to any economic process in which credit advances play a key role in business fluctuations. In particular, a credit cycle refers to how credit availability interacts with aggregate economic activity to generate business-cycle patterns over time. For instance, a shock to the system could generate dynamic endogenous, or internal, forces on the basis of the interaction between credit expansion and the prices of collateralized assets, which are then assumed to have ramifications for the course the real economy takes. These theories, which have been championed primarily by heterodox economists and followers of such well-known writers as Hyman P. Minsky, have evolved largely in opposition to traditional mainstream real business-cycle theories that deemphasize the credit-driven aspects of cyclical fluctuations.

Evolution: From the Banking School to Keynes

Despite its modern link with business-cycle theory, the concept of a credit cycle finds its origin in the recognition that credit (the provision of liquidity in a monetary economy for the purpose of financing the spending of economic agents) necessarily follows a sequential process, with credit coming into being when a bank makes a loan and advances funds to a creditworthy borrower on the basis of sufficient private collateral. Credit is destroyed when the borrowing unit extinguishes its double-entry bookkeeping counterpart—debt— at the moment of the reimbursement of the principal of the loan. This "life cycle" of credit was formally recognized by Thomas Tooke and the

disciples of the "banking school" in mid-nineteenth-century Great Britain. These theorists emphasized the circular nature of credit by espousing the flux-reflux principle, whereby the initial flow of credit is followed inevitably by a reflux of funds to the banking sector on a later date when the loan is extinguished. On the basis of this view, it was an easy step to formulate a theory of cyclical fluctuations that underlined the significance of credit availability and the tendency for the excessive leveraging of the borrowing unit.

In the nineteenth century, famous adherents of the banking principle, such as John Stuart Mill, developed theories of how exuberant expectations can feed recurrent waves of credit expansion, while such famous empiricists as Clément Juglar amassed enormous historical data on the anatomy of "commercial crises" and the bursting of speculative bubbles that had been fed by excessive credit advances. The periods of "prosperity, crisis, and liquidation" that characterized the credit cycle were defined and measured by the limited bank data series then available and, above all, by the course of prices over time. The empirical knowledge provided by the work of Juglar and such other famous institutionalist economists as Wesley C. Mitchell formed the basis of elaborate twentieth-century theories of the business cycle, especially during the interwar years.

While many economists of the early twentieth century had already elaborated credit-driven theories of business fluctuations based on the investment-saving relation, one of the most detailed attempts at developing a sophisticated theory of the credit cycle is found in John Maynard Keynes's two-volume work, *A Treatise on Money*, published in 1930. In the *Treatise*, Keynes presents a sophisticated model of the monetary system in which banks play an essential role in the financing of investment, with an elaborate analysis of the genesis and recurrent pattern of the credit cycle. Keynes's definition in volume I of the *Treatise* is most revealing of how he conceptualizes the cycle: "We now define the *Credit Cycle* to mean the alterations of excess and defect in the cost of investment over the volume of saving and the accompanying see-saw in the Purchasing Power of Money due to these alterations."

Influenced by the work of Knut Wicksell, Keynes describes how a shock to the system can generate a complete cyclical process of expansion and contraction in the flow of investment in relation to saving, which would explain the recurrent pattern of seesaw price movements that had been documented in the empirical studies of the Juglar variety. If *ex ante* investment can deviate from household saving, the gap would have to be filled by bank credit. For any initial shock that triggers a change in borrowing by business enterprise to finance investment, Keynes traces through period analysis how the economy moves from its initial primary phase of expansion. It is then accompanied by strong multiplier/accelerator effects characterizing its secondary phase, until the overinvestment leads to its collapse, debt liquidation, and subsequent recovery. While analytically different in some details from the broadly similar theories popularized by Friedrich von Hayek and Irving Fisher during the early 1930s, all of these writers bestowed on credit the vital role in the genesis, ultimate collapse, and liquidation of the accumulated credit advances.

Post Keynesian Views and Contemporary New Keynesian Analysis

Inspired by this Keynes-Fisher tradition of the credit cycle, late-twentieth-century Post Keynesian economist Hyman P. Minsky developed a more sophisticated model of cyclical fluctuation to describe how an economy evolves from a state of tranquility to one of instability and crisis. In the Minskian world, investment is propelled forward by the behavior of asset prices, which rise relative to the supply price of current investment goods when an economy begins to grow. This leads to increasing corporate indebtedness as credit demand expands during the upswing, thereby progressively pushing the borrowing unit into ever-higher leverage ratios. This financial fragility, characterized by higher debt ratios, will continue to deepen until some sudden event

leads to an unwinding of the credit-debt relation through stampede liquidation and a precipitous drop in asset prices, investment, and production. Accompanying this decline, there would be a concomitant drop in credit financing until asset prices reach bottom and begin to turn around.

The first decade of the twenty-first century brought growing interest in the behavior of credit and its cyclical character even among more mainstream neoclassical economists, spurred again by the financial crisis in the latter part of the decade. Some of the literature has moved forward largely because of the work of such New Keynesian economists as Nobuhiro Kiyotaki and John Moore, who developed an intricate nonlinear model of the behavior of various financial and macroeconomic variables to an initial shock affecting the value of collateralized assets.

Mario Seccareccia

See also: Bank Cycles; Capital Market; Corporate Finance; Financial Markets; Financial Modeling of the Business Cycle; Leveraging and Deleveraging, Financial.

Further Reading
Keynes, John Maynard. *A Treatise on Money.* 2 vols. New York: Harcourt, Brace, 1930.

Kiyotaki, Nobuhiro, and John Moore. "Credit Cycles." *Journal of Political Economy* 105:2 (April 1997): 211–248.

Minsky, Hyman P. *Stabilizing an Unstable Economy.* New Haven, CT: Yale University Press, 1986.

Niehans, Jürg. "Juglar's Credit Cycles." *History of Political Economy* 24:3 (Fall 1992): 545–569.

Seccareccia, Mario. "Aspects of a New Conceptual Integration of Keynes's *Treatise on Money* and the *General Theory:* Logical Time Units and Macroeconomic Price Formation." In *Money, Credit, and the Role of the State,* ed. Richard Arena and Neri Salvadori, 285–310. Aldershot, UK: Ashgate, 2004.

———. "Credit Money and Cyclical Crises: The Views of Hayek and Fisher Compared." In *Money and Business Cycles: The Economics of F.A. Hayek,* vol. 1, ed. Marina Colonna and Harold Hagemann, 53–73. Aldershot, UK: Edward Elgar, 1994.

Credit Default Swaps

Most privately issued financial securities carry some default risk—that is, the risk that the issuer will not pay the principal and interest on the security when it is due. A credit default swap is a contract that transfers the default risk from the purchaser of a financial security to a guarantor, who receives a fee for accepting the risk that the returns of the underlying security may fall below a certain amount. By hedging default risk, credit default swaps often are considered a form of insurance for the buyer and a tool used to manage risk. The buyer of the swap receives protection that a payment will be made by the seller if a credit "event," such as a default, occurs.

History of Credit Default Swaps

The first credit default swaps, created by J.P. Morgan and Company in 1997, were concentrated in corporate bonds. The underlying assets in swaps initially were bond funds that sought to insure their portfolios against default risk. The default risk is transferred to the seller of the swap in exchange for a premium. If the bonds are paid back in full, the seller retains the swap contract premium. The credit default swap market expanded in the early 2000s from corporate bonds to include a variety of other markets, including municipal securities, bank loans, and other financial assets.

Later, the credit default swap market expanded to include collateralized mortgage obligations (CMOs) and other collateralized debt obligations (CDOs) among the securities for which default insurance could be purchased. A CMO is a financial instrument (security) created from a pool of mortgages or mortgage-backed securities that redirects the cash flows (principal and interest) from the underlying mortgages to tranches (classes) with different risks. A CDO is a financial instrument created from pools of debt that are backed by the principal and interest payments made on the underlying securities, which are passed through to the owners of the CDO. Like CMOs, the payments made on CDOs are divided into tranches (classes) or slices with different risks. In essence, CMOs and CDOs are derivative instruments whose value is determined by the flows of cash in the underlying

Outstanding Credit Default Swaps, 2001–2008

Year	Credit Default Swaps Outstanding (billions of dollars)
2001	$918.87
2002	$2,191.57
2003	$3,779.40
2004	$8,422.26
2005	$17,096.14
2006	$34,422.80
2007	$62,173.20
2008	$38,563.82

Source: ISDA Market Survey, 1987–2008, International Swaps and Derivatives Association, Inc.

pools of securities. Thus, when a credit default swap is created from a CMO or a CDO, the buyer is literally purchasing a derivative of a derivative.

Another characteristic of credit default swaps is that an investor, such as a hedge fund, can buy or sell a swap without having any direct relationship to or ownership of the underlying securities. Thus, a speculator could purchase a swap based on a CMO if the speculator anticipated that defaults in the mortgage markets would lead to defaults on the CMOs. If there is a default, a payment would be made to the purchaser of the swap, even though the purchaser does not own the underlying CMO. This is basically wagering on an assumption. In 2007, credit default swaps peaked at approximately $62 trillion. The combined total of all U.S. corporate debt and mortgages was less than half of that amount. This demonstrates the extent to which these instruments were purchased by investors who did not own the underlying securities. Also, credit default swaps are bought and sold over and over in secondary markets, making it almost impossible for an investor in a credit default swap to evaluate the ability of the seller to make a payment if a credit event occurs. The outstanding amount of credit default swaps from 2001 to 2008 is shown in the table above.

Large banks also used credit default swaps to hedge against default risk. The table that follows was compiled in 2006, prior to the financial

Credit Default Swaps Used as Hedges, 2006

Date	Banks	Credit Exposure Before Hedging (billions)	Amount of Hedging Reported (billions)	Exposure Hedged (percent)
Year-end 2006	Bank of America	US$618	US$8	1
Year-end 2006	Citigroup	US$633	US$93	15
Year-end 2006	JPMorgan Chase	US$631	US$51	8
2006 Q1	Société Générale	€ 60	€ 15	25

Source: Michael S. Gibson, "Credit Derivatives and Risk Management." Finance and Economics Discussion Series, Division of Research and Statistics and Monetary Affairs, Federal Reserve Board, May 22, 2007.

crisis. It shows the amount of swaps used to hedge by the three largest U.S. commercial bank holding companies and one of the largest European banks. There are several reasons why commercial banks used swaps to hedge default risk: (1) credit spreads or costs were low, (2) accounting changes in Europe allowed banks to carry loans at fair value rather than book value, and (3) the Basel II Capital Accord allowed greater recognition of hedging.

Credit Default Swaps and the Financial Crisis of 2008–2009

Credit default swaps, which are largely unregulated and untraceable, played a key role in the financial crisis of 2008–2009. Because there is no regulation, there are no capital requirements for the seller of default protection and no standard way for a buyer of these instruments to assess the risks. Prior to the financial crisis, the Federal Reserve announced that credit derivatives were good strategies for hedging risk, and suggested that more banks use these credit derivatives. The explosion of credit default swaps created a ticking time bomb. If these exotic derivative-type instruments had not been created, the extent of the downturn caused by the subprime mortgage crisis would have been much less. This is an example of a situation in which the financial engineers who created these products were one step ahead of regulators—leading to disastrous results. Regulators and other market participants did not know the extent of these instruments until problems arose.

During the financial crisis of 2008–2009, the bankruptcy of Lehman Brothers and the bailout of AIG (American International Group) were caused by losses in swap markets in which these institutions had sold "default insurance" to speculators, including hedge funds. During AIG's bailout, Société Générale, one of the largest European commercial banks, was the largest recipient of both credit default swap collateral postings ($4.1 billion) and payments ($6.9 billion), which were paid in whole or in part by U.S. taxpayers.

It is apparent, say most experts, that greater global regulation of these markets is needed, including a standardized clearinghouse that could make sure that sellers of this protection have the ability to pay a mechanism to insure that the payment is made.

Maureen Burton and Jamie Shuk Ki Yuen

See also: Collateralized Debt Obligations; Collateralized Mortgage Obligations; Debt Instruments; Recession and Financial Crisis (2007–); Securitization; Troubled Asset Relief Program (2008–).

Further Reading

Fabozzi, Frank J., Franco Modigliani, and Frank J. Jones. *Foundations of Financial Markets and Institutions.* 4th ed. Upper Saddle River, NJ: Prentice Hall, 2009.

Gibson, Michael S. "Credit Derivatives and Risk Management." Finance and Economics Discussion Series, Divisions of Research and Statistics and Monetary Affairs, Federal

Reserve Board of Governors, May 22, 2007. Available at www.federalreserve.gov. Accessed February 2010.

Mengle, David. "Credit Derivatives: An Overview." *Economic Review* 92:4 (Fourth Quarter 2007): 1–24. Available at www.frbatlanta.org/filelegacydocs/erq407_mengle.pdf. Accessed March 2010.

Parkinson, Patrick M. "Over-the-Counter Derivatives." Testimony before the Subcommittee on Securities, Insurance, and Investment, Committee on Banking, Housing, and Urban Affairs, U.S. Senate, July 9, 2008. Available at www.federalreserve.gov. Accessed March 2010.

White, Patricia. "Over-the-Counter Derivatives." Testimony before the Subcommittee on Securities, Insurance, and Investment, Committee of Banking, Housing, and Urban Affairs, U.S. Senate, June 22, 2009. Available at www.federalreserve.gov. Accessed March 2010.

Credit Rating Agencies

Credit rating agencies are private companies that offer ratings on the risk associated with debt instruments, such as bonds, issued by private corporations and nonprofit organizations, as well as various government entities. Credit rating agencies also offer ratings on structured financial instruments—issued by special-purpose entities created for the task of issuing such instruments—such as mortgage-backed securities and other collateralized debt obligations. (Credit rating agencies should not be confused with the more familiar credit bureaus or credit reporting agencies, such as Experian, Equifax, and TransUnion, which provide information to lenders on the creditworthiness of consumers.)

Operations

High credit ratings indicate that the debt issuer has a low chance of default; low ratings indicate a relatively high level of risk. Ratings are determined by a number of factors. For corporations, this includes asset-to-debt ratios, earnings-to-debt ratios, revenues, past history of meeting debt obligations, and a host of other financial factors. For governments, a different set of factors come into play in the credit rating process, including public and private investment flows, foreign direct investment, foreign currency reserves, transparency, political stability, and history of meeting debt obligations.

Credit ratings serve a number of critical market functions. By offering a tested method for rating credit and providing simple, letter-based grades on debt, credit rating agencies make it easier for investors to purchase a range of debt securities, giving them an understanding of the risk they are taking on versus the returns they stand to make. Credit ratings also give smaller entities, including developing world countries, start-up companies, and nonprofit organizations, the opportunity to market debt to a wider array of investors.

Credit rating agencies, which make their money by charging fees to issuers of debt, operate in many large developed and developing countries. Among the most important are three U.S. firms—Moody's Investors Services (usually referred to as Moody's), Standard & Poor's (S&P), and Fitch Ratings. These agencies rate bonds with letter grades, much like in a classroom, though the exact methods differ slightly from agency to agency. The highest rating is "AAA" (Aaa for Moody's) and the lowest rating is "D." Any variation on a "D" rating indicates the instrument is already in default. (Moody's lowest rating is C, which is for securities that are predominantly speculative and that may be in default.) There are also variations in the ratings system depending on whether the debt instrument is short term or long term. In general, the higher the rating the lower the risk, meaning that the issuer can offer a lower interest rate on top-rated securities. Bonds above BBB– (or Baa3 by Moody's) are rated investment grade, meaning that they offer a very low chance of default, while those below that rating are considered low grade, or "junk bonds," meaning that the chance of default is high. The sellers of below-investment-grade junk bonds call these "high-yield" bonds. Historically, about one in fifty investment-grade corporate bonds has been defaulted on while the figure for noninvestment grade is about one in three. For municipal bonds, the figures are about 1 in 1,400 for investment grade and 1 in 23 for noninvestment grade.

History

Credit rating agencies in the United States date back to the nineteenth century when the forerunners of today's Dun & Bradstreet and Standard & Poor's began offering reports to investors and lenders, who paid fees for the service, about the creditworthiness of various companies and individuals, the latter even being examined for such nonbusiness-related things as whether too much was spent on entertainment by the company or individual. In 1860, Henry Varnum Poor, founder of the company that would eventually become Standard & Poor's, published his *History of the Railroads and Canals in the United States*, the forerunner of later securities analyses. By the early twentieth century, the two companies had been joined by the forerunners of Moody's and Fitch, which also began to rate bonds, stocks, and other securities. In 1924, Fitch introduced the grade ratings system still in use today.

Credit rating agencies grew along with the U.S. economy through much of the twentieth century, but underwent fundamental change in the 1970s. Prior to that period, credit rating companies made their profits by charging investors and lenders a fee to subscribe to their reports. But the main credit rating agencies came to the conclusion that their services increased the value of the securities being issued, making the issuing entities more profitable or, in the case of governments, more cost effective. In effect, the credit rating agencies were increasing the profits of the companies whose securities they rated with no return to the agencies. In addition, the growing complexity of the capital markets—along with the growing number of securities being offered—was raising the costs of providing rating services beyond what investors and lenders were willing to pay. And so, the credit rating agencies turned their fee system on its head, collecting fees from the issuers of securities.

Criticisms

This arrangement has led to the predictable criticism that requiring the issuers of securities to pay for their ratings undermines the impartiality of the rating. More generally, since rating agencies must learn everything they can about the companies whose securities they are rating, their agents, say critics, establish too-close relationships with the management of the companies being examined, which also undermines their impartiality. Other experts offer criticisms of the rating process itself, noting that it inevitably leads to an oligopolistic sector. That is, companies always seek out one of three leading agencies to rate their securities since only ratings from those businesses are valued by investors and lenders. Moreover, those agencies take on quasi-regulatory activities, since they influence how the credit markets work by allowing the investment divisions of banks to use reports from credit agencies in calculating reserve requirements, as per Securities and Exchange Commission regulations. In addition, the whole credit rating process can, say some analysts, devolve into a vicious cycle for entities issuing securities. A lower rating makes issuing securities more expensive, which undermines the creditworthiness of the company being rated, and so on.

Finally, both the corporate scandals of the early 2000s and the financial crisis in the latter years of the decade have pointed up new problems with the credit rating business. Some critics have noted that credit agencies have on occasion been too slow to react to fast-changing economic circumstances. For example, the various credit rating agencies were giving bonds issued by Enron investment-grade ratings just days before the troubled energy giant declared bankruptcy in 2001. Far more troubling, according some experts, were the high ratings that credit agencies gave to some of the riskiest structured financial instruments in the years leading up to the financial crisis of 2008–2009. Critics charged that this was the result of a cozy relationship between officials of credit rating agencies and officials of the special-purpose vehicles and financial institutions that created them.

In the wake of Enron's bankruptcy and other corporate scandals, Congress passed the Sarbanes-Oxley Act in 2002, calling for more transparency in corporate accounting, among other things. Included in the bill was the requirement for the Securities and Exchange Commission to investigate and correct abuses in the credit rating process. Subsequently, the collapse of the market in structured financial instruments has brought about new calls for reform. From the Left has come the idea of some kind of market authority—either a nonprofit entity, consisting of representative investors, or a public agency—that would manage conflicts of interest between the agencies and the companies they rate, assure transparency of the rating process, provide ratings information to the public, assign which agencies rated which securities, and handle the payments made by the companies offering the securities to the ratings agencies. From the Right, the criticism has focused on the fact that securities regulations are dependent on credit rating agencies. By getting rid of many of these regulations, the market could more effectively decide which credit rating agencies provided the best product to investors, thereby eliminating abuses. Given the scope of the recession and financial meltdown in the 2007–2009 period, it seems unlikely, however, that Congress will get rid of many of the regulations.

James Ciment

See also: Capital Market; Consumer and Investor Protection; Corporate Finance; Debt; Debt Instruments; Financial Markets; Indicators of Financial Vulnerability.

Further Reading

Fabié, Vincent. "A Rescue Plan for Rating Agencies." April 19, 2009. Available at http://ideas.berkeleylawblogs.org/2009/04/19/a-rescue-plan-for-rating-agencies. Accessed January 2010.

Sandage, Scott A. *Born Losers: A History of Failure in America.* Cambridge, MA: Harvard University Press, 2005.

Sinclair, Timothy J. *The New Masters of Capital: American Bond Rating Agencies and the Politics of Creditworthiness.* Ithaca, NY: Cornell University Press, 2005.

Current Account

The current account is that part of a nation's balance of payments that includes imports and exports of goods and services and transfer payments to and from foreigners. It is an important measure of a country's international economic relationships and one that is both a cause of and a response to economic booms and busts.

The current account (CA) is one element of the balance of payments, together with the capital and financial accounts. The balance of payments is the cumulative measure of how much net income has been coming into a country from abroad via international trade, foreign investments, and other sources. Often, economists examine only the trade part of the current account, looking at imports and exports of goods and services, or what is called the balance of trade. Including incomes such as corporate profits earned in other countries and transfers such as remittances from workers employed in other countries adds up to the total current account.

A CA surplus means that the sum of these four accounts is positive (greater than zero), while a CA deficit means that is negative. This does not mean that all four accounts are necessarily either positive or negative. For example, a country with an aggregate CA deficit may have a foreign trade deficit and a negative income account, while its services and current transfers accounts may be running surpluses. In 2009, the United States ran up a deficit in goods—that is, imports over exports—of roughly $517 billion, but a surplus in services of $136 billion, producing an overall imbalance of about $381 billion.

Goods and Services Account

The goods account pertains to income generated from international trade activity; it reflects a country's net income from exports and imports. This includes both national exports (goods sold abroad by the residents of a specific country) and imports for national consumption (goods purchased from abroad by the residents of a specific country). Exports, essentially the sale of goods for money, generate income for the exporting country while imports represent a loss of income for the importing country. Thus, a positive goods balance means that, in a given period, the country in question has exported more (in value) than it has imported. In other words, the country has generated more income from exporting than it has lost from importing. But a negative imbalance of trade does not necessarily mean an economy is in bad shape, as prosperous consumers buy up foreign goods. By all accounts, the U.S. economy in the late 1990s was doing extremely well, with low unemployment, high gains in productivity, low interests, and a shrinking U.S. budget deficit. Yet between 1995 and 2000, the overall trade imbalance rose from around $96 billion to just under $380 billion, a roughly 400 percent increase. At the same time, a sagging economy can depress imports, leading to a positive current account, as was the case during much of the late 1970s and early 1980s.

In addition to final and intermediate goods, the services account reflects international trade in services as well. Thus, the services account records revenues from the export of services and the cost of imported services. A positive balance means that a country is a net exporter of services. Services are considered exported if the residents of a specific country offer those services to the residents of other countries. (For example, if foreign tourists stay at a hotel in Country A, the latter is technically exporting travel services to the country from which the tourists came.) Services are counted as imports if residents of a foreign country offer those services to residents of the home country in question. (For example, if goods from Country B are shipped abroad by ships from Country C, Country B is said to be importing services and Country C exporting them). The United States has had a service account

surplus as a result of its dominance in banking and other financial services and in entertainment copyrights such as movies and TV shows. While not as large as the goods account deficit, it has helped to buffer this deficit. As a result, swings in the value of the U.S. dollar have not been as large as they would otherwise have been.

Income Account

The income account reflects the flow of income between residents of a country and nonresidents. It records two main categories of income: compensation of employees, including wages and benefits; and investments and income coming to citizens, businesses, and the government from all foreign investments. (Sometimes other primary income—rent, taxes, and subsidies on products and production—is included as a separate category). A positive income balance means that the country in question earns more income from abroad than its residents and businesses pay to citizens, businesses, and governments in other countries. If a country has attracted a lot of foreign capital but has not invested very much abroad, its income balance will be negative. In other words, it loses more income to foreigners investing in that country than it has gains from its own investments abroad.

Current Transfers Account

The current transfers account (sometimes called the secondary income account) records transactions related to the accumulation of residents' disposable income but not reflected in other parts of the CA. Current transfers include such categories as donations, fines, gifts, grants, indemnities, inheritance, insurance fees and premiums, membership fees, pensions, personal transfers (including worker remittances), social benefits and contributions, and taxes on income and wealth. A positive balance of current transfers means that a country is a net recipient of such transfers. The current accounts in many countries in Central America and Eastern Europe get a positive boost from the remittances sent back to families and friends by guest workers and immigrants—both legal and illegal—in North America and Western Europe respectively.

CA Deficits

A CA deficit, or negative CA, means that a country is a net debtor to the rest of the world. Because its income from exports is not large enough to cover its loss of income from imports, that country must borrow from abroad or attract foreign investments or foreign aid in order to maintain its consumption level. (The current account balance can also be caused by low productivity, high inflation, a decline in the world prices of the products the country exports heavily, an increase in the prices of those it imports heavily, natural disasters, armed conflicts, or an inappropriately strong domestic currency. In addition, a CA deficit may be caused by large foreign investment inflows or heavy imports of technology, though in these cases, large exports tend to follow in subsequent years.)

If a country has a large and persistent current account deficit that it is not able to finance itself, its currency may start to depreciate rapidly. This occurs because other countries—and currency speculators—begin to think that the country in question might not be able to pay back what it owes and that it might not have enough cash to pay for needed domestic projects. Other countries might respond by dumping the country's currency on the foreign exchange market. The increased supply of the currency on the world exchange—together with plummeting demand for it—leads to devaluation on international currency markets. To cope with their CA deficit and other balance-of-payments problems, countries may have to resort to borrowing funds from the International Monetary Fund. In doing so, they often have to agree to severe belt-tightening measures in order to improve their CA position.

Tiia Vissak

See also: Balance of Payments; Capital Account; Exchange Rates.

Further Reading

International Monetary Fund. *Balance of Payments and International Investment Position Manual.* 6th ed. Washington, DC: International Monetary Fund, 2010.

————. *Balance of Payments Statistics Yearbook.* Washington, DC: International Monetary Fund, 2008.

Debt

A debt is a liability to the borrower (debtor) and an asset to the lender (creditor) who purchases the debt instrument (loan, bond, etc.), issued by the borrower. The creditor has the expectation of full payback within a predetermined period of time, often in fixed, regular installments and with additional compensation (interest), calculated as a percentage of the debt instrument's value compounded over the time period. The terms of the debt, including interest, duration, and other considerations, are typically set forth in a written contract before the debt instrument is issued and made available to be purchased by the creditor. Debts can be accrued by individuals, households—who take out loans and mortgages, businesses, and governments, which may borrow or issue bonds.

When an individual, business, or, more rarely, government debtor finds itself unable to meet its obligation to its creditors, that individual or institution is said to be insolvent, usually requiring it to file for bankruptcy within the jurisdiction in which it operates. In the United States, all bankruptcies are handled by federal courts.

Borrowing and lending through debt markets are critical components in the functioning of a modern capitalist economy, allowing individuals to finance major purchases, businesses to conduct daily operations and expand, and governments to finance war, infrastructure projects, or other extraordinary expenses.

Types of Debt

Debts come in several overlapping categories. A secured debt guarantees the creditor the right to an asset held by the debtor should the latter fail to pay back the debt. Common secured debts include home mortgages and car loans, since the contract contains a proviso that the lender can seize the home or car should the debtor fail to pay back the full amount on a timely basis. An unsecured debt, by contrast, is one in which the borrower puts up no collateral to secure the loan. For individuals, the most common unsecured debt is credit card spending; the financial institution that issues the card cannot seize the assets that was purchased by the funds lent.

Debts can also be held by private individuals and entities or publicly owned corporations. A typical privately held debt is a loan offered directly by a financial institution to a borrower. Debts

The National Debt Clock in New York City stood at $11.5 trillion in July 2009 and exceeded $12 trillion by year's end. As a percentage of gross domestic product, a key economic indicator, the U.S. debt rose to an alarming 67 percent in 2010. *(Timothy A. Clary/ AFP/Getty Images)*

held by publicly owned companies, also known as bonds, represent IOUs issued by businesses to investors, with a fixed amount of interest and a fixed time in which they must be paid. (Public debts are not the same as "public debt," which refers to the amount owed to bondholders by a government.) Bonds, which are issued by businesses and governments, are typically sold as securities either directly to investors or through brokers. Bonds may be secured or unsecured, meaning that the bondholder has a higher priority for repayment should a business, or, more rarely, a government, be unable to pay all of its debt obligations and find itself in bankruptcy.

Finally, private loans may be syndicated or bilateral. A bilateral loan is a loan between one lender and one borrower. Syndicated loans are those offered by more than one lender to a single borrower. Typically, syndicated loans involve very large sums of money, either beyond the means of a single institution or individual to lend or, more typically, above the amount that an institution or individual cares to risk on a single borrower. Syndicated loans are usually tendered for large-scale building projects or for corporate mergers and acquisitions. In the case of a syndicated loan, the

lead lending institution often makes a guarantee (for a fee) that the full amount of money will be available, thus providing a kind of bridge loan to the borrower until other lending institutions or individuals can be brought on board. This service is known as underwriting and helps to expedite large-scale lending.

Debt is essential to the smooth functioning of a modern economy because it facilitates and encourages consumer spending, and consumer spending is the primary engine of developed-world economies. In the United States, for instance, roughly 70 percent of all economic activity is related to consumer spending. Just as importantly, companies often rely on short-term loans to meet payroll, fill stock, and cover other operational needs and on bilateral and syndicated long-term loans to make strategic investments, expand operations, and acquire property or raw materials—all critical for growth and modernization. In addition, without the ability to float bonds, businesses and governments would be denied a means of obtaining revenues to create new plants and infrastructure. Finally, debt is critical to the functioning of national and global financial systems, as financial institutions routinely acquire short-term debt to meet asset requirements against loans they themselves are making. Indeed, it was the freezing up of short-term, interbank lending and bank-to-business lending in the late summer and fall of 2008 that prompted the U.S. government and others around the world to inject hundreds of billions of dollars into leading financial institutions. Should this kind of lending stop, it was feared, the credit markets would freeze up and the global economy could grind to a halt, plunging the world into a new Great Depression.

Financial Crisis of 2008–2009

Indeed, debt was central to the crisis that gripped the world's financial markets in 2008—either directly, through nonperforming mortgages when the housing boom collapsed in 2007, or via derivatives, a financial instrument whose value is derived from some other asset. Because lending is an inherently risky business, creditor institutions seek ways to spread the risk around. Derivatives that are used to hedge, such as futures options, allow those most willing and able to bear a risk to do so and hence make financial markets more efficient. Other derivatives, such as securitizations, take relatively illiquid assets, package them together, and sell them off to investors as relatively liquid assets.

The idea behind all of these derivatives was that by diffusing risk, financial institutions were protecting themselves and making it possible to extend credit to more and more individuals. But by spreading risk around, the financial institutions that originated the mortgages had less incentive to ensure that borrowers were creditworthy, thus creating a moral hazard problem. When large numbers of high-risk borrowers began to default on their mortgages, the aggregate losses overwhelmed the system. Derivatives, then, created what economists call "systemic risk," in which so many large institutions become insolvent that the global financial system was threatened. Some economists came to fear a similar scenario with regard to collateralized credit card debt. If enough people default on their credit card bills, the strain

on the global financial system could be as great as that caused by the mortgage crisis.

Public Debt

Public, or government, debt operates somewhat differently from private debt, but can also produce systemic problems when it grows too large. The U.S. government, for example, has operated with large deficits for several decades, except for a brief period at the turn of the twenty-first century when it ran small surpluses. To reduce the debt, the government can raise revenues or cut spending, risky choices politically; it can increase the money supply and thereby inflate its way to a reduced debt, which risks undermining the credibility of the government to borrow in the future on favorable terms; or it can issue bonds, which only pushes debt repayment into the future. For domestic holders of U.S. Treasury bonds, there is little risk of losing money, since the U.S. government cannot default on its debt—barring a catastrophe of unimaginable proportions.

However, for foreign holders of U.S. public debt—or the public debt of any country other than their own—there is another risk factor, inflation, which can undermine the value of a bond, since a U.S. bond is denominated in dollars, and dollars may fall in value against the currency in the lender's country. With the U.S. government posting unprecedented deficits, which have contributed to a debt load hovering above $12 trillion at the end of 2009, many economists and politicians have come to fear that foreign lenders—notably, the Chinese, who hold roughly $1 trillion of that debt in bonds—might shy away from buying the Treasury bonds that help to service the debt. The huge debt to China is a result of the vast trade imbalance between the United States and that country, which the United States pays for by borrowing from outside sources, including China itself.

Thus far, China and other foreign holders of U.S. Treasury bonds have continued to invest in them for two reasons. First, despite the recession of 2007–2009 and the mounting public debt,

U.S. Treasury bonds are still seen as perhaps the most secure investment in the world, since the U.S. dollar remains the world's reserve currency; second, selling off the bonds or not buying more would undermine the value of the large quantity of U.S. Treasury bonds China and other countries already hold.

James Ciment

See also: Corporate Finance; Debt Instruments; Fiscal Balance; Minsky's Financial Instability Hypothesis.

Further Reading

Bonner, William, and Addison Wiggin. *Empire of Debt: The Rise and Fall of an Epic Financial Crisis.* Hoboken, NJ: John Wiley & Sons, 2006.

Burton, Dawn. *Credit and Consumer Society.* New York: Routledge, 2007.

Deacon, John. *Global Securitisation and CDOs.* Chichester, UK: John Wiley & Sons, 2004.

Foster, John Bellamy, and Fred Magdoff. *The Great Financial Crisis: Causes and Consequences.* New York: Monthly Review Press, 2009.

García, José, James Lardner, and Cindy Zeldin, with assistance from Myra Batchelder and Jennifer Wheary. *Up to Our Eyeballs: How Shady Lenders and Failed Economic Policies Are Drowning Americans in Debt.* New York: New Press, 2008.

Wiggin, Addison, and Kate Incontrera, with Dorianne Perrucci. *I.O.U.S.A.* Hoboken, NJ: John Wiley & Sons, 2008.

Debt Instruments

Debt instruments, which may play a central role in the dynamics of business cycles, enable the transfer of ownership of a debt obligation from one party to another (or to multiple parties). When a homeowner takes out a mortgage with a local bank, the bank can then sell the debt. Nothing changes for the homeowner—not the amount, terms, or interest rate of the loan. In that regard, the transfer of the mortgage is not analogous to a debtor selling off a debt to a collection agency, to which the balance is then owed. Nevertheless, such arrangements make the bank's debt-based assets more liquid. In addition to mortgage packages, debt instruments include any agreement between a lender and a borrower—including bonds, leases, and credit card agreements—and as well as financial arrangements derived from them.

Bonds

The most familiar form of debt instrument is the bond. The issuer of a bond assumes a debt to the purchaser that is collectible at maturity; the interest on the debt is called the "coupon." Bonds are used for long-term financing and are especially common as ways for governments to raise funds. Local or county governments, for instance, might issue municipal bonds to fund a large, one-time expense, such as the construction of a new building or new infrastructure. The federal government issued war bonds to raise funds for World War II. Corporate bonds are different from both government bonds and corporate stocks. A corporate bond is a debt owed by the company (rather than the government) to the bondholder, while a share of stock confers a portion of ownership of the company. The value of stock shares fluctuates according to market trends, whereas bonds are more stable.

Government and corporate bonds are issued for a specific principal or face amount. This is the amount repaid at maturity and upon which interest is calculated. The issue price is the amount paid when the bond is issued. The maturity date is the point in time at which the principal is paid (and interest stops accruing). The coupon is the interest rate; the term originated from the physical coupons originally given to purchasers, exchangeable at the bank for an interest payment.

Bonds are generally grouped into three categories based on the term, or duration, of the instrument: short-term (maturity of one year or less); medium-term (one to ten years); and long-term (more than ten years). Short-term bonds are often referred to as bills, medium-term bonds are called notes. Extremely long-term bonds remain a rarity, but the twenty-first century has seen a flourishing market for fifty-year bonds backed by euros.

Junk Bonds

Bonds, like other securities and instruments, are rated by credit rating agencies, such as Standard & Poor's. Government-issued bonds are often considered zero-risk because of the unlikelihood that the issuing government, at any level, would default (i.e., fail to pay off the principal and accrued interest at the time of maturity). Other bonds are rated according to the scale used by the particular rating agency. In the United States, the scale is often (from lowest to highest) C, CC, CCC, B, BB, BBB, A, AA, AAA. Bonds given a low rating (BB or lower) at the time of issuance are commonly referred to as "junk bonds," or, more formally, speculative-grade bonds. Junk bonds have a higher—sometimes significantly so—risk of defaulting, and investors who buy them should expect of a relatively high yield to make the gamble worthwhile.

Because of the high risk associated with them, junk bonds are generally excluded from mainstream financial portfolios; pension funds and other investment institutions are often required (by their own rules) to invest in only high-rated bonds. Junk bonds are especially popular in the United States, and only in the twenty-first century have they become common in the European and Asian markets. Michael Milken, the "Junk Bond King," made junk bonds a household term in the 1980s. Originally an investor in "fallen angels"—bonds that had been highly rated and lost their perceived value but had the potential to rise again, allowing the savvy investor to profit by buying them low and selling them high—Milken became attracted to "junks" as a way to quickly raise the large sums of money needed to finance the era's flurry of large-scale mergers and acquisitions. He was, in a sense, the financier of the corporate raider era. Milken's appetite for high-risk, high-yield ventures would prove his undoing, however, as he was indicted on nearly 100 charges of racketeering in 1989. His indictment marked one of the first times the federal Racketeer Influenced and Corrupt Organizations Act (RICO) was used against an alleged criminal with no organized crime ties. Milken's crimes were related primarily to insider trading, securities fraud, and evasion of taxes on the income he had earned illegally. Junk bonds, meanwhile, while they did not shed their unsavory reputation entirely, reached their peak in trading in 1998.

Collateralized Debt Obligations (CDOs)

CDOs are structured notes created from other debt instruments that are pooled together and treated as an asset that backs (acts as collateral for) the notes themselves, increasing liquidity. Mortgage obligations or credit card accounts, for instance, can be pooled together and used to issue a number of notes that are easier to trade on the market than the mortgages themselves. There is a wide variety of CDOs, including those backed by bank loans, by bonds, by credit derivatives, by insurance obligations, and even by pools of other CDOs. One of the advantages of creating a CDO is that its credit rating is often higher than that of the backing assets. This, in turn, can make the CDO available to investors, such as pension funds, that are required to stick to high-rated securities.

The term "toxic debt" became another household phrase during the 2008–2009 financial crisis, as subprime mortgage loans and other unstable assets were used to back collateralized debt obligations. This resulted in the extraordinarily widespread presence of such CDOs in the portfolios not only of individual investors, but also of banks, funds, and corporations. What the crisis revealed was that many CDOs had been overvalued—sometimes willfully, but often as a result of their sheer structural complexity.

Bill Kte'pi

See also: Collateralized Debt Obligations; Corporate Finance; Credit Default Swaps; Debt; Mortgage-Backed Securities.

Further Reading

Bookstaber, Richard. *A Demon of Our Own Design: Markets, Hedge Funds, and the Perils of Financial Innovation.* Hoboken, NJ: John Wiley & Sons, 2007.

Brigham, Eugene F., and Michael C. Ehrhardt. *Financial Management: Theory and Practice.* Mason, OH: South-Western, 2008.

Chancellor, Edward. *Devil Take the Hindmost: A History of Financial Speculation.* New York: Farrar, Straus and Giroux, 1999.

Madura, Jeff. *Financial Markets and Institutions.* Mason, OH: South-Western, 2008.

Shefrin, Hersh. *Beyond Greed and Fear: Understanding Behavioral Finance and the Psychology of Investing.* New York: Oxford University Press, 2007.

Deflation

The standard definition of inflation is a protracted period of generalized price increase, which can occur when too much money chases too few products. By the same token, deflation is defined as a protracted period in which the overall price level falls. Deflation may be due to too little demand for products, or to improvements in technology that allow for production costs to fall. In general, if output prices are falling due to less demand, wages, employment, and incomes will also tend to fall or to increase more slowly. Deflation is a problem for an economy because debts are denominated in dollars, and if there is deflation, there is a real increase in debt levels in the economy. Deflation should not be confused with disinflation, which refers to declining rates of inflation.

Changes in the supply of money in an economy are a normal part of the market process. For example, when one nation imports more goods than it exports, there will be a decrease in the money supply as monetary reserves are exported to pay for imports. As the supply of money decreases, domestic prices tend to decrease, or deflate. Then, however, lower domestic prices will discourage imports (because they become too expensive for the country undergoing deflation) and encourage exports (because they are now less expensive

for buyers from other countries). This process is known as the price-specie flow mechanism. Even though money and prices deflate in one country, strictly speaking this may not be deflation. The reason is that the international trade system corrects the price imbalance in a relatively short amount of time; thus there is no *protracted* period of price decline, and hence the definition of deflation is not satisfied.

Deflation and the Great Depression

The fear of deflation has been called "apoplithorismosphobia," based on the severe deflation of the Great Depression that led some economists to believe that deflation is the cause of severe economic downswings. According to this view, shocks to the banking and financial system can cause a sharp decrease in lending and bank failures, resulting in a decrease in the supply of money and credit. This reduction makes it difficult to finance production and to purchase goods. Lower prices and incomes place individuals, businesses, and banks in danger of bankruptcy. This, in turn, feeds back into the economy and creates a deflationary depression spiral. Such fears were particularly pronounced during the Japanese recession of the 1990s and again during the economic crisis and recession of 2007–2009, with the bursting of the housing bubble.

At the same time, some economists have reevaluated the economic phenomenon of deflation and found that it is not always the evil or threat that many believe it to be. Rather, in most instances, it is a normal market process and not a true cause of economic depression. Indeed, these economists maintain, the deflation associated with depression is best viewed as a consequence that facilitates correction and recovery. More generally, deflation is associated with prosperity, as when increases in the production of goods due to increases in productivity that exceed the increase in wages result in lower prices and higher real wages. The result for consumers is that it costs less to buy a car or a dishwasher or week's worth of food—hardly cause for fear. In addition, deflation may be offset by increases in the velocity of money. That is, as the money supply falls, each dollar circulates more rapidly through the economy, which can help stabilize spending and prices.

Four Types of Deflation

Deflation of prices implies that a unit of money has greater purchasing power than it did previously. This helps identify four different types of deflation, two of which operate on the demand for money and two on the supply of money: growth deflation, cash-building deflation, bank credit deflation, and confiscatory deflation. The first represents the general, beneficial case of deflation, the second and third are remedial (or corrective) processes that tend to reverse adverse economic conditions, and the fourth refers to extreme and harmful measures undertaken during emergencies.

On the demand side, the usual form of deflation is "growth deflation," which occurs in a market economy when the production of goods expands faster than the wages increase due to increases in productivity. If production expands faster than wages, per-unit costs fall, which puts downward pressure on prices and tends to increase the real wage. This is a process by which economic growth is transmitted into higher standards of living throughout the economy.

"Cash-building deflation" is another form of demand-based deflation, albeit more unusual. It typically occurs during economic emergencies in which difficult circumstances, such as the prospects of war or depression, threaten the standard of living. If the production of goods and money remain the same, but the demand for money increases to purchase goods in the future, this exerts downward pressure on the price of goods and on wages. This is pejoratively referred to as "hoarding," because the additional savings puts short-term pressure on the suppliers of goods. However, because money is so useful in emergency conditions, it is a perfectly logical strategy that

benefits even nonhoarders because their money also has greater purchasing power.

On the supply side of money, the common form of deflation is "bank credit deflation." When depositors perceive that banks have expanded lending for nonprofitable or risky projects, they will withdraw their money, forcing banks to curtail lending and causing insolvent banks to fail. This depositor-driven process results in an overall decrease in the supply of money in the economy, falling prices, and a greater purchasing power of money. The resulting contraction is merely a symptom of, but does not in itself cause, a depression. The actual cause of the Great Depression of the 1930s was the previous expansion of money and credit into unprofitable or risky investments. Bank credit deflation, once widely feared and maligned, is actually the correction process of the business cycle. Since the 1930s, in the United States, federal deposit insurance has greatly reduced fears caused by bank credit deflation.

The more unusual form of deflation on the supply side is "confiscatory deflation," in which the government prevents depositors from accessing their money. Such actions often take place after a bank credit deflation has revealed banks to be bankrupt. The government's policy response reduces money in circulation and puts further downward pressure on prices. It may force people to resort to barter, self-sufficiency, and other primitive means. Confiscatory deflation represents a transfer of wealth from depositors to bank owners and can lead to social chaos.

Perhaps deflation's greatest threat concerns debts. As the value of money increases, it makes the costs of paying back or servicing debt that much more expensive, pushing more businesses and consumers and other borrowers into insolvency and bankruptcy. In late-nineteenth-century America, for example, many indebted farmers pushed for inflationary measures—such as the monetization of silver—to help relieve their debt burden.

All changes in the supply and demand for money, and the subsequent changes in prices that ripple through the economy, result in winners and losers. The association of deflation and depression has resulted in an unwarranted phobia of deflation. In reality, with the exception of the confiscatory type, deflation should be seen as a positive force in an economy, either as a natural component of long-term economic growth or as a corrective process that addresses the root cause of depressions or economic emergencies such as war.

Mark Thornton

See also: Inflation; Price Stability.

Further Reading

Rothbard, Murray N. "Deflation: Free and Compulsory." In *Making Economic Sense.* Auburn, AL: Ludwig von Mises Institute, 2006.

Salerno, Joseph T. "An Austrian Taxonomy of Deflation—With Applications to the U.S." *Quarterly Journal of Austrian Economics* 6:4 (Winter 2003): 81–109.

Thornton, Mark. "Apoplithorismosphobia." *Quarterly Journal of Austrian Economics* 6:4 (Winter 2003): 5–18.

Demographic Cycle

Demographic cycles are the fluctuations in human population over time, or the continuities and changes in birth rates, mortality rates, composition, and overall size of a given population. Economists have long noted connections between demographic cycles and economic developments, with an extensive literature on the subject dating back to the eighteenth century.

Pre–Industrial Revolution

For most of human history—from the beginning of human civilization in about 3,000 BCE to the onset of the industrial revolution in the mid-eighteenth century—the demographic cycle was characterized by three basic trends: relatively high birth rates (about 40 per 1,000 persons annually, with adult females averaging six to eight live births in their lifetimes) and high mortality rates (25 to 38 per 1,000 persons per year); a steady, secular rise in world population over time,

from about 25 million at the dawn of civilization to 750 million on the eve of the industrial revolution; and periodic population catastrophes, usually the result of epidemic, war, or social chaos.

The high birth and death rates were due to a variety of factors. High birth rates resulted from a lack of contraception; high infant and child mortality rates, which motivated parents to have a lot of children; agricultural economies that required the labor of children; and social customs that grew out of these necessities. Meanwhile, the high death rates—which nearly canceled out the high birth rates—resulted from poor diet or periodic famine, primitive medical practices, and poor hygiene. The long-term secular gain in population was largely due to expanded agriculture, as humans moved into new areas of the globe, cut down forests and replaced them with farmland, or used irrigation and other ancient techniques to expand fertile lands. Increasing population densities were critical to the development of civilization and interregional trade, as they allowed for the creation of agricultural surpluses that could be consumed by artisans, merchants, and other urban dwellers.

Yet while the general trend in preindustrial human history had been gradually upward, periodic cataclysms have dramatically reduced the population in specific regions and periods of time. In the history of Western civilization, the most dramatic of these was the coming of the bubonic plague in the mid-fourteenth century, an episode known as the Black Death. The disease wiped out about one-third of the population of Europe in just a few years, ending two centuries of solid demographic growth.

While the suffering of victims was ghastly and the psychological impact on survivors was harrowing, economic historians cite significant benefits resulting from the Black Death. By substantially reducing the peasantry—the poor, as is often the case in pandemics, are the worst affected—it gave additional bargaining power to those who survived. Landlords desperate to retain laborers had to concede new freedoms and increased compensation, leading to the end of the feudal order that had dominated Europe for centuries and allowing for the rise of a more prosperous peasantry and an increase in urban populations, as newly freed serfs flocked to towns and cities. These developments, say historians, established the foundation for a modern capitalist Europe.

While the Black Death was a unique episode in European history, its effects were similar to admittedly less dramatic ones put forward by the first scholar to extensively study the relationship between demographic and economic cycles, Britain's Thomas Malthus. In his *Essay on the Principle of Population* (1798) and *The Principles of Political Economy* (1820), Malthus presented a model of population fluctuation based on agricultural output. As output grows, he hypothesized, so does population, but at a much faster pace. Rising population in turn puts upward pressure on agricultural prices even as it causes a drop in income, as more farmers try to make due on less land and more workers compete for existing jobs. Eventually, income drops by enough to cause hunger and starvation, thereby reducing the population and allowing survivors more land and the ability to negotiate for better wages. And the cycle continues.

Industrial Revolution

The industrial revolution, which ushered in the modern demographic cycle, eventually proved Malthus wrong, as it introduced new agricultural techniques and equipment and created a transportation infrastructure that allowed farm products to be shipped more efficiently. Population growth went from steady to spectacular. As industrialism took off, more and more people left the farm for the city, even as those who remained behind became more productive. Meanwhile, the increasing wealth created by industrialization, as well as new technological and scientific innovations, allowed for improved public health measures, which dramatically lowered mortality rates. However, it also allowed for lower-cost contraception.

All of this contributed to a period of dramatic population growth in the areas most directly af-

fected by the industrial revolution, particularly Europe. While that continent's population stood at about 160 million in 1750, it climbed to more than 400 million by 1900. In other words, while it had taken Europe 2,000 years to increase by 100 million people (from about 60 million at the beginning of the common era), it took just 150 years to climb another 240 million. The continent's population would rise to approximately 550 million by 1950 and to more 700 million by the year 2000.

Even as the population rose, however, other developments were slowing the rate. The rise from 160 million to 400 million represented an increase of 250 percent in 150 years, while the rise from 400 million to 700 million represented an increase of just 75 percent over 100 years. As mortality rates dropped—particularly for infants and young children—couples felt less compelled to produce as many children, lowering birth rates. In addition, as people left the land and went to work in factories and businesses, they no longer relied on their children's labor in the fields. Children, in a sense, became liabilities rather than assets, economically speaking, as they increasingly came to spend long years in school, a nonremunerated occupation but one critical to the child's future success in an urbanized, industrialized economy. Over time, as parents came to recognize these costs and the fact that their children were more likely to survive to adulthood, they reduced the number of children they had.

Thus, the modern demographic cycle is marked by dramatic population growth with the advent of industrialization and modern public health measures, and a tapering off as couples make the decision to have fewer children. And just as the economy has a profound impact on demography, so demography has a major impact on the economy. Increased populations allow for the creation of larger internal markets and economies of scale.

Post–World War II Era

Gradually, what happened in Europe spread to the rest of the world, though with a difference.

In much of the developing world, industrialization lagged behind dramatic population growth, as public health measures and modern medicine lowered the death rate before economic modernization could lower the birth rate. Thus, populations in the developed world exploded after World War II, as the new health measures—along with the more bounteous harvest the green revolution in agricultural crops produced—spread around the globe. From 1950 to 2000, Asia's population grew from 1.4 billion to 3.6 billion, Africa's from 220 million to 770 million, and Latin America's from 170 million to 510 million.

The relationship between dramatic population growth and economic performance is murky, however. In some instances, including various countries in Asia and Latin America, rapid population growth has not stunted economic development. At the same time, it is clear that overpopulation can produce economic ills, including unemployment and poverty. Such is the case in much of the Middle East and Africa, which continue to experience some of the highest population growth rates in the world. In addition, overpopulation can put enormous strains on the natural environment.

Meanwhile, the growing prosperity of East Asia has produced the same results as in Europe—though in a more truncated period of time, reflecting the region's much more rapid industrialization. As those societies become more prosperous and economies modernize, parents come to the realization that it makes more economic sense to have fewer children, who can then be educated more effectively. Indeed, across East Asia, rapid population increase is giving way to more gradual gains and in some cases, such as South Korea, declines. In China, the large decline in the population growth rate was also the result of draconian laws limiting most urban couples to a single child.

Indeed, population declines seem to be a hallmark of many countries in the industrialized world, the most notable exception being the United States. And just as dramatic population increases can place a burden on an economy to provide enough goods, jobs, and services for the rising numbers, so ebbing populations—which also mean aging populations—can create problems as well. Not only do they shrink internal markets and reduce the labor force, but they also require each worker to support more retirees, usually through taxes or public insurance schemes such as America's Social Security.

James Ciment

See also: Malthus, Thomas Robert.

Further Reading

Chesnais, Jean-Claude. *The Demographic Transition: Stages, Patterns, and Economic Implications: A Longitudinal Study of Sixty-Seven Countries Covering the Period 1720–1984.* New York: Oxford University Press, 1992.

Demeny, Paul, and Geoffrey McNicoll. *The Political Economy of Global Population Change, 1950–2050.* New York: Population Council, 2006.

Easterlin, Richard A. *Reluctant Economist: Perspectives on Economics, Economic History, and Demography.* New York: Cambridge University Press, 2004.

Malthus, Thomas Robert. *An Essay on the Principle of Population,* ed. Philip Appleman. New York: W.W. Norton, 2004.

Simon, Julian L., ed. *The Economics of Population: Classic Writings.* New Brunswick, NJ: Transaction, 1998.

Denmark

Denmark is a northern European country, made up of a peninsula and an archipelago of more than 400 islands. The population of Denmark is approximately 5.5 million people, one-fifth of whom reside in the capital of Copenhagen and surrounding regions. The country is governed by a constitutional monarchy with a unicameral parliament.

Denmark offers a high standard of living for its citizens through a well-developed social welfare system. In 2007, Denmark had the highest tax-to-gross domestic product (GDP) rate among the 30 Organisation for Economic Co-operation and Development (OECD) countries, at 48.9 percent. Despite this tax burden, Danes report a high level of contentment. Government expenditure in the economy for the years 1999 to 2008 constituted an average of 52.95 percent of the *nominal* GDP (the value of goods and services produced in the domestic economy during a given year, measured in current prices), compared with 42.54 percent for the euro area countries. Denmark has been a member of North Atlantic Treaty Organization (NATO) since its inception in 1949 and was the first of the Nordic countries to join the European Economic Community, now the European Union (EU), in 1973. However, along with two other EU members, Sweden and Great Britain, Denmark has not joined the eurozone, despite two domestic referendums on the question and a possible third in the offing.

The service sector makes up most of the economy, with finance and business accounting for the lion's share. These functions are enabled by the country's robust communications and technology infrastructure, which boasts the highest broadband penetration among OECD countries. In manufacturing, machinery and transport equipment account for over one-quarter of the exports. Denmark has a large fishery, a high-tech agricultural sector, and is a leading exporter of milk, dairy, and pork products. It is a net exporter of energy and has been self-sufficient in consumption since 1997, drawing on the North Sea for crude oil and natural gas, and on wind power for renewable energy.

Denmark has a long history of banking and entrepreneurship with significant periods of economic growth. Between 1995 and 2000 real GDP grew at an average rate of 2.9 percent. (Real GDP is the market value of all the goods and services produced within a country during a given year and measured in constant prices, so that the value is not affected by changes in the prices of goods and services.) With the onset of the recession in 2001, real GDP grew at an average rate of only 0.53 percent over 2001–2003, returning to a healthier average of 2.6 percent over 2004–2006, concomitant with the construction boom related to housing and domestic engineering projects. The rate of growth of real GDP slowed to 1.7 percent in 2007 and an anemic 0.2 percent in 2008. After years of expansion and maintaining a healthy surplus, growth is expected to slow and stagnate with the end of the construction boom and the slump in the housing market, which has been overvalued in recent years. Danish homeowners are among the most heavily indebted in the world. Denmark's real GDP was expected to decline in 2009, in step with the euro area. There was a tangible loss in consumer confidence beginning in the summer of 2008 as Danes experienced deterioration of personal financial circumstances, followed by a fourteen-year high rate in personal and business bankruptcies.

Banking Sector Vulnerable

In the banking sector, credit expanded greatly in the mid-2000s, with resulting overextension of credit, mainly to property developers. This, along with other factors, put a number of small banks at risk, most notably Roskilde, a regional bank, the tenth largest in Denmark, which experienced significant losses on property loans in summer 2008. By November, Roskilde and two other banks were taken over by the Nationalbank (Denmark's central bank). In early October 2008 the government passed the first bank rescue package in an attempt to build confidence in the financial markets, guaranteeing the claims of depositors and unsecured creditors. A second bank rescue package of DKK100 billion (5.5 percent of the GDP), in effect February 2009, is aimed at bank and mortgage lenders with a view to stimulate lending. This enables the government to buy up bank stocks and sell them when conditions are warranted, thus recapitalizing the financial system. In return, the government requires financial institutions to maintain lending. The package also places limits on banking executives' pay and dividends and aims to improve supervision and regulation of financial institutions. At the same time, the export industry was given a boost.

The Danish krone is pegged to the euro as the Nationalbank tends to follow rates set by the European Central Bank. As the world's major banks cut their interest rates, the Nationalbank initially raised its rates in an effort to support the krone, resulting in a significant difference in interest rates between Denmark and the eurozone. There since has been a downward adjustment in rates.

Demographically, Denmark is faced with a shrinking workforce as evidenced by record low unemployment in 2008, leading to upward pressure on wages. However, despite this and the global financial crisis, due to its receptivity to foreign investment and well-developed infrastructure, Denmark continues to be one of the best countries in the world for business, with its global ranking for business (among eighty-two countries) projected to slip from second place in 2004–2008 to third place during the 2009–2013 period.

Marisa Scigliano

See also: Finland; Iceland; Norway; Sweden.

Further Reading

Central Intelligence Agency. *The CIA World Factbook—Denmark.* Available at www.cia.gov/library/publications/the-world-factbook/geos/da.html. Accessed March 2009.
Economist Intelligence Unit (EIU). *Country Report—Denmark.* London: EIU, 2009.
———. *ViewsWire—Denmark.* London: EIU, 2009.
Statistical Office of the European Communities (Eurostat). *Eurostat Yearbook 2008.* Available at http://epp.eurostat.ec.europa.eu/. Accessed March 2009.
———. *Key Figures on Europe, 2007/08 edition.* Available at http://epp.eurostat.ec.europa.eu/. Accessed March 2009.
Organisation for Economic Co-operation and Development (OECD). *OECD Economic Outlook,* no. 84. Paris: OECD, 2008.

Depository Institutions

A depository institution is any financial intermediary that accepts customers' deposits and uses those deposits to fund loans and other investments. Nondepository intermediaries include insurance companies, pension funds, investment funds, and finance companies. Depository institutions include banks, savings associations, and credit unions. The vast majority of commercial banks and savings associations purchase insur-

ance from the Federal Deposit Insurance Corporation (FDIC). Credit unions can purchase deposit insurance from the National Credit Union Administration. Deposits are insured up to a current limit of $250,000. Not all accounts and funds held by a depository institution are insured by the FDIC—only checking accounts, negotiable order of withdrawal accounts, savings accounts, money market accounts, time deposit accounts (such as CDs), and negotiable accounts drawn on the bank's accounts. (The Securities Investor Protection Corporation does protect investors from loss in the case of brokerage failures but not for losses in investment accounts.) Until 1989, savings and loan institutions (S&Ls) were insured separately by the Federal Savings and Loan Insurance Corporation, but this agency was dissolved by the Financial Institutions Reform, Recovery, and Enforcement Act (passed in response to the S&L crisis) and its responsibilities transferred permanently to the FDIC.

Deposit Accounts

The defining characteristic of the depository institution is of course the deposit account, of which there are three main types: demand accounts, savings accounts, and time deposit accounts. Balances in deposit accounts are part of the nation's money supply. Different account types place different restrictions and fees (or interest rates) on the deposits, but the depositor remains the owner of the money held, while it becomes a liability for the bank. Typically, under the fractional-reserve banking system that characterizes modern banking, the institution holds reserve assets equal to a fraction of the deposit liabilities in reserve and loans the rest out to other customers, earning a profit on it. It is from that profit that banks are able to pay interest on some accounts (most savings and time deposit accounts, some checkable accounts), which protects the customer by negating the effects of inflation—without which there would be no incentive to save money, which would depreciate over time, perhaps faster than those things it might be spent on. With liquidity comes the loss of evaporation. Interest, safety, and the insurance of the FDIC are the primary incentives for using banks for long-term money storage, instead of stuffing it under the mattress. In addition, interest is the reward depositors receive for postponing present consumption in favor of future consumption.

Though they are not involved in monetary policy and do so incidentally rather than to enact macroeconomic effect, depository institutions have the power to increase the money supply. Most of the money supply, in fact, is held in accounts at depository institutions. Every time a bank grants a loan, it is increasing the money supply by a certain amount, essentially "creating money" by increasing the amount of money available to that customer without increasing, dollar for dollar, the amount of cash held by the bank.

Demand accounts are more typically known as checking accounts. While savings accounts earn interest and thus make a profit or protect against inflation, checking accounts held by members of the Federal Reserve System are prohibited from earning interest by Regulation Q. In some cases this prohibition is bypassed by banks that do not participate in the Federal Reserve System (interest-earning checking accounts are one of the selling points of the new wave of online-only bank accounts such as ING Electric Orange) or by offering negotiable order of withdrawal (NOW) accounts, which function similarly but are allowed to pay interest. NOW accounts were developed in the 1970s to circumvent Regulation Q by creating deposit accounts that included the ability to issue "withdrawals" that could be given to third parties—more or less a trick of semantics.

The main benefit of a checking account is the convenience. Most debit cards draw from checking accounts, so even customers who rarely write checks have come to rely heavily on checking accounts for easy access to funds. Many checking accounts charge fees—either flat or associated with usage (such as a cost per check)—unless a minimum balance is maintained.

Savings accounts are the simplest form of a bank account: money is deposited, and can be accessed only by dealing directly with the bank (through an in-person withdrawal, electronic balance transfer, or use of an ATM). A small amount of interest accrues on the account—less than would be expected to be earned from even risk-averse investing, but enough to offset inflation. Banking regulations limit the number of transfers and withdrawals that can be made on a savings account to six per month.

Time deposits function much like more restricted savings accounts: they earn interest but cannot be withdrawn from until a specific term has ended. The most common time deposit account in the United States is the certificate of deposit, which has a fixed term (typically three or six months, or one to five years) and a fixed interest rate. The interest rate is based, generally, on both the length of the term and the size of the principal (the deposit). Higher principal and longer terms mean higher interest rates. Typically, the highest interest rates are offered by smaller institutions in more need of liquid cash.

CDs can sometimes be closed early, but at a substantial penalty, in the form of loss of a certain amount of the interest that had so far accrued. Interest can be paid out as it accrues, and some customers prefer this option; however, it means they earn less over time, since the interest is not being "reinvested" through compounding.

Types of Depository Institutions

Commercial bank. This is the ordinary bank most people are familiar with, offering savings and checking accounts, mortgage and small business loans, and so on; the term distinguishes it from investment banks.

Savings and loan association. Also known as a thrift, an S&L operates primarily by accepting savings deposits and making mortgage loans. Although S&Ls were a prominent part of American banking in the early twentieth century, the advent of checking accounts offered by other types of banks saw their decline until the 1980s, when S&Ls were greatly deregulated. Suddenly they were allowed to do nearly anything other banks could do, but without being run by executives who had experience at doing it; the S&L crisis inevitably followed, resulting in the dissolution of the Federal Savings and Loan Insurance Corporation and the collapse of half the country's thrifts.

Mutual savings bank. Primarily located in the northeastern United States, mutual savings banks (MSBs) are designed to encourage savings and prioritize security over profit. They offer few of the bells and whistles of commercial banks, but because they are not chasing profit, they are risk averse and tend to survive most banking crises better than other depository institutions.

Credit union. A cooperative depository institution owned and operated by its members, a credit union is much like an MSB in risk aversion and promotion of savings. In addition, members of credit unions share a bond beyond being clients, as they often work at the same company or are members of the same union. Credit union fees are typically lower than those of commercial banks. Credit unions are "not for profit" but not "nonprofit" (a designation that applies to specific charities); they are, however, tax-exempt organizations. Federally chartered credit unions and most state-chartered credit unions are insured by the National Credit Union Administration, which actually often enjoys a higher ratio of insurance fund to capital insured than does the FDIC. Many credit unions serve members of the armed forces; the world's largest credit union, for instance, is the U.S. Navy Federal Credit Union.

Bill Kte'pi

See also: Banks, Commercial; Savings and Investment; Savings and Loan Crises (1980s–1990s).

Further Reading

Cottrell, Allin F., Michael S. Lawlor, and John H. Wood, eds. *The Causes and Costs of Depository Institution Failures.* New York: Springer, 1995.

Sicilia, David, and Jeffrey Cruikshank. *The Greenspan Effect.* New York: McGraw-Hill, 2000.

Dot.com Bubble (1990s–2000)

Tied to the early commercialization of the Internet, the dot.com bubble, which lasted from the mid-1990s through 2000, was one of the most exuberant speculative episodes in the history of American capitalism. During the peak years of the bubble at the end of the twentieth century, tens of billions of dollars were invested in thousands of start-up online and technology-oriented companies, a portion of which went public. When it became clear around the turn of the millennium that many of these companies were not only overvalued but poorly run—and when expectations about the revenues the early Internet was capable of generating proved overly optimistic—the bubble burst, with many of the start-up firms going bankrupt, taking hundreds of billions of dollars in market valuation with them.

Origins

Invented in 1969, the Internet—called the ARPANET in its early years—was originally a creation of the federal government, allowing for the transmission of digitized information from one defense-related computer to another. At first largely confined to government and university computers, the Internet was transformed into a commercial phenomenon by three developments. First was the personal computer revolution of the 1980s, in which small, inexpensive, easy-to-operate computers became ubiquitous in workplaces, schools, and homes. Second came the development in the late 1980s and early 1990s of graphical interface technology, culminating in the World Wide Web, which brought the intuitive point-and-click system familiar to many computer users to the Internet. The final piece came with the National Science Foundation's 1994 decision to open the Internet for commercial purposes.

In August 1995, an initial public offering (IPO) was tendered for Netscape Communications Corporation, the developer of the first commercial graphical interface browser. This was the first time the public could buy into an Internet-connected company, and they did so with gusto. Within fifteen months, the company was valued at more than $2 billion, making founder Marc Andreessen a billionaire almost overnight. The success of Netscape's IPO loosened the floodgates, as other companies with Internet connections went public, often reaping fortunes for the founders and their financial backers. While Netscape provided access to the Internet, other companies began to set themselves up to market products over the new medium. Perhaps the best known of these early Internet marketers was Amazon.com, which began as a bookselling outlet in 1994 and then branched out into other forms of retail. After its IPO in 1997, the company had a market valuation of nearly $500 million.

The Internet did offer clear advantages to retailers. A company such as Amazon.com could offer a far wider selection than even the biggest "brick-and-mortar" retailer, as dot.com advocates referred to traditional businesses operating out of actual stores. Not having to pay for the associated costs of retail space, Internet businesses could also operate in a leaner fashion, saving on rent, labor, and utility costs—"friction free commerce," as it was called. They could cut out the middleman, providing customers direct access to manufacturers and content originators—a process that came under the buzzword "disintermediation." And dot.com businesses had access to a far greater market, since customers could be located anyplace with Internet service.

Dot.com advocates, in both the business world and the many media outlets springing up to cover it, began to talk of a "new economy." Not only was Internet commerce destined to replace the traditional kind, but it appeared to be creating a whole new paradigm, freed from old notions of what made a business profitable. The slogan of the day was that you either "got it"—meaning,

understood that retail and even capitalism as a whole was undergoing a fundamental shift—or you did not and were doomed to be left behind economically. Proponents of Internet commerce grew breathless in their estimates of its marketing potential—hundreds of billions, they said, maybe even trillions, and all within a few years.

Despite what the more ebullient advocates of the dot.com business model believed, Internet commerce still required real world infrastructure—specifically, networks of powerful computers, known as "servers," to store the huge amounts of data contained on millions of Web pages and the high-speed telecommunication lines that kept the whole system connected. With expectations so high for dot.com commerce, various telecommunications companies—including some of America's most prestigious names—began to invest heavily in that infrastructure.

Venture Capitalists and IPOs

Venture capitalists, or those who wanted to invest directly in dot.com start-ups, rushed to take advantage of what was called "first-mover advantage." It was widely believed that the first company to take advantage of an Internet marketing niche was the most likely to succeed, as word of mouth spread ever more rapidly by yet another relatively new Internet phenomenon—email. All of the hype and sense of urgency drew in an estimated $120 billion in venture capital at the height of the boom between 1998 and early 2000, financing more than 12,000 dot.com start-ups. These businesses fell into several basic categories: "marketplace" sites such as eBay, which brought together buyers and sellers and took a fee on transactions; "portals" such as Yahoo!, which provided users a guide to Internet sites and earned money from online advertising; "aggregators"—Amazon.com being the best known early example—which put customers in contact with a number of different suppliers, in this case, publishers; "content providers" such as traditional media sources that wanted to place their written and visual materials online and charge a fee for looking at them; and Internet service providers (ISPs), such as America Online (AOL), which gave people access to the Internet and charged a periodic fee, as phone companies did for their services.

Roughly one in ten of the dot.com businesses went public, utilizing brokerage houses and investment banks to offer shares, most of which were bought and sold on the National Association of Securities Dealers Automated Quotations (NASDAQ), an exchange founded in 1971 and largely devoted to technology stocks. Between the end of 1995 and its peak in March 2000, the NASDAQ Composite Index quintupled, from just over 1,000 to 5,048.62. At the same time, Internet public company shares represented 20 percent of the trading volume of all shares on U.S. stock exchanges and 6 percent of capitalization, an enormous figure given the total capitalization of publicly trade companies. Investors also bought into the idea that vast amounts of new telecommunications infrastructure was needed; between 1997 and 2000, the Dow Jones Total Market subindex for the telecom sector more than doubled in value.

Bursting

The market was in a classic bubble phase during the last years of the twentieth century, as market valuations far outstripped the underlying values of companies. There were a host of reasons for this. First, many of the companies whose stock was rising the fastest—or which were garnering the large amounts of private venture capital—were operating deep in the red. Amazon.com, arguably the most successful of the aggregators, was bleeding money during the boom years of the dot.com bubble, some $750 million worth of capital from 1996 to 2000. And while Amazon.com kept its marketing costs down, other Internet start-ups did not. Many spent lavishly on advertising. OurBeginning.com, an online stationery vendor, took out ads during the 1999 Super Bowl alone worth four times its annual revenues. The idea was to jump-start the process of first-mover advantage. But combined with other expenses, such as lavish spending on company headquarters, the advertising put the companies deeper into red ink. Moreover, many firms lacked feasible business models and prospects for sustainable growth, as they were often run by young owners and managers who had great technological savvy but lacked business training or experience. To take perhaps the best-known example of such a company—Pets.com—market analysts began to question whether a firm devoted to selling pet supplies over the Internet, no matter how clever its advertising, was really worth the $300 million it had garnered in venture capital and through share sales following its early 2000 IPO.

Larger forces were also at work that helped deflate the dot.com bubble. In March 2000,

Jeff Bezos founded the online bookstore Amazon.com in 1994 and took it public three years later. Many other Internet start-ups of the mid-to-late 1990s shut down after spending millions in venture capital but not earning a penny. *(Paul Souders/Getty Images)*

when publicly traded companies published their data on revenues and profits, the picture they collectively presented was dismal. Predictions that the Christmas retail season of 1999 would demonstrate the viability of these companies and of Internet marketing generally were proved false. Meanwhile, to cool what was perceived as an overheated, potentially inflationary market—the much more substantive Dow Jones Industrial Average of more traditional companies was also hitting record highs—the U.S. Federal Reserve (Fed) posted no less than six interest rate increases between early 1999 and early 2000.

The bursting of the bubble began over the weekend of March 11–12, 2000, as major institutional shareholders put in automatic sell orders for key high-tech stocks—though not necessarily dot.com stocks—such as IBM, Cisco, and Dell. Many savvy market analysts had come to the conclusion that, even among these more solid firms, market valuations were too high. With preparations for the Y2K switchover done—in which millions of computer systems had to be adjusted to account for the change from the twentieth to twenty-first centuries—many investors came to believe that there would be a drop-off in the need for technology products and services. As is often the case, the fall in prices for the shares of high-profile companies dragged down the rest of the market sector they belonged to. Combined with the poor earnings reports and the growing sense that many of the dot.com start-ups were poorly run, the sell-off produced a panic in the market as investors desperately sought to unload shares and venture capitalists closed their wallets. Meanwhile, as the dot.com bubble burst so too did expectations about the need for the infrastructure to support it. Just as there was not enough consumer demand to sustain some of the more frivolous dot.com companies, so there was not enough Internet traffic to justify the huge amount of money invested in infrastructure.

The result of all of this was a dramatically deflated NASDAQ index—which fell by more than half by the end of 2000—and a wave of bankruptcies. By late 2002, with heavy ongoing declines in the telecom sector, the total loss in market valuation was estimated at an astonishing $5 trillion, or more than 10 percent of total U.S. wealth. Total online sales amounted to just $36 billion, a tiny fraction of what people had projected back at the height of the boom in the late 1990s. The bursting of the dot.com bubble helped trigger the recession of the early 2000s.

Legacy

Economists and analysts who study the dot.com boom—and the bust that followed—point to a more long-lasting legacy. While predictions that dot.com marketing would quickly outstrip traditional retailing were grossly overstated, online sales in the years since 2002 have garnered an increasing market share, and companies that survived the crash—including eBay and Amazon.com—became well positioned to take advantage of that growth. Moreover, both the technological and marketing innovations of the dot.com boom laid the foundations for an Internet marketplace that many experts agree may, in the long run, fulfill some of the more expansive predictions made for it in the late 1990s.

On the negative side, some economists lay blame for the housing bubble of the mid-2000s—which led to a market correction and recession in the late 2000s far worse than those of the early 2000s—at least in part on the dot.com bust. With stock prices falling by some 80 percent on the NASDAQ, and a smaller but still significant percentage on other major exchanges—the Dow Jones Industrial Average dropped by about 25 percent between 2000 and 2003—venture and speculative capital that had gone into corporate securities may have found its way into the housing sector. In addition, in responding to the dot.com-induced recession, the Fed lowered interest rates to record lows of just 1 percent in 2004, bringing down the cost of home mortgages and thereby encouraging home purchases among many people who otherwise (or in other times) could not have afforded them. In a sense, then, echoes of the dot.com bubble and burst continue to reverberate through the American economy.

James Ciment

See also: Asset-Price Bubble; Information Technology; Technological Innovation; Venture Capital.

Further Reading

Cassidy, John. *Dot.con: The Greatest Story Ever Sold.* New York: HarperCollins, 2002.

Henwood, Doug. *After the New Economy.* New York: New Press, 2003.

Marcus, James. *Amazonia.* New York: New Press, 2004.

Stross, Randall E. *eBoys: The First Inside Account of Venture Capitalists at Work.* New York: Crown Business, 2000.

Dow Jones Industrial Average

The Dow Jones Industrial Average (DJIA) is one of the most widely reported and monitored stock market indicators in the world. An index of the stock value of thirty major U.S. corporations, its goal is to broadly represent the performance of the stock market by measuring the performance of companies with established track records that are dominant players in their respective industries. As of July 2009, a majority of the DJIA 30 were companies that manufactured and sold industrial or consumer goods ranging from construction equipment to household goods and pharmaceuticals, with the rest in industries including financial services, information technology, and entertainment. Although other indexes are better measures of the stock market, the DJIA is influential simply because it is so widely reported and closely watched. While economists dismiss fluctuations in the DJIA in assessing the overall health of the economy, broad trends in the index may indicate future corporate profitability.

The ancestor of the modern Dow Jones index was first published in 1884 by *Wall Street Journal* founder Charles H. Dow and consisted of eleven companies, nine of which were railroads. In 1896, the first version of what is now known as the Dow Jones Industrial Average debuted with twelve companies listed by Charles Dow and statistician Edward Jones. It grew to twenty companies in 1916 and expanded to thirty in 1928. To pursue its objective of measuring the average performance of the domestic stock market, the list has undergone more than two dozen revisions since 1928 (not counting company name changes) in response to shifts in the national economy or the ranks of corporate giants. Indeed, of the original twelve companies listed on the 1896 DJIA, only General Electric is still included today. Changes to the index are made by the editors of the *Wall Street Journal* when something happens to one of the component companies (if it is acquired by another company, for example) or when the change would reflect a shift in the nontransportation, nonutility profile of the

Component Companies of the Dow Jones Industrial Average, July 2009

Company	Ticker Symbol
3M	MMM
Alcoa	AA
American Express	AXP
AT&T	T
Bank of America	BAC
Boeing	BA
Caterpillar	CAT
Chevron Corporation	CVX
Cisco Systems	CSCO
Coca-Cola	KO
DuPont	DD
Exxon Mobil	XOM
General Electric	GE
Hewlett-Packard	HPQ
The Home Depot	HD
IBM	IBM
Intel	INTC
Johnson & Johnson	JNJ
JPMorgan Chase	JPM
Kraft Foods	KFT
McDonald's	MCD
Merck	MRK
Microsoft	MSFT
Pfizer	PFE
Procter & Gamble	PG
Travelers	TRV
United Technologies	UTX
Verizon Communications	VZ
Wal-Mart	WMT
Walt Disney	DIS

economy. Recent changes include the removal of troubled financial services company Citigroup and bankrupt automobile manufacturer General Motors, both in 2009, and their replacement by the computer networking and services provider Cisco Systems and the insurance giant Travelers.

Other stock indices such as the Standard & Poor's 500 and the New York Stock Exchange index track more stocks than the thirty in the DJIA. In addition, these and other stock indices take into account the relative size of corporations rather than simply measuring the value of one share as in the DJIA. Thus, based on February 2009 figures, components Kraft Foods and JPMorgan Chase would have roughly the same weight in the DJIA (both share prices were in the low $20s) even though Kraft's market cap ($34 billion) was less than half of JPMorgan's ($75 billion). As a result, most financial studies do not rely on the DJIA—even though it remains the most widely watched indicator of stock market performance.

One of the reasons for its ongoing status is that adjustments to the calculations underlying the DJIA have remained consistent and can be interpreted over more than a century of existence. When a new company replaces an old one, the price differential between the two would cause the overall index to fluctuate, even though no market changes had occurred. Adjustments to the denominator have also been made when company stock prices change because of stock splits, mergers and acquisitions, large dividends, or other events that change share price but do not reflect market valuation of those shares.

Over the years, the DJIA has provided a useful if imprecise reflection of the overall health or weakness of U.S. corporations, though its fluctuations tend to be greater than those of overall corporate well-being. This is because the share price of a specific stock reflects less the underlying value of a company than perceptions of that value, which are subject to speculation. In addition, stock prices tend to reflect investor predictions about a company's future prospects, which by definition is a

Greatest One-Day Gains and Losses, Dow Jones Industrial Average

Measure/Date	Percentage Change	Point Change
Gain by percentage		
1. March 15, 1933	15.34	8.26
2. October 6, 1933	14.87	12.86
3. October 31, 1929	12.34	28.40
Gain in points		
1. October 13, 2008	11.80	936.42
2. October 28, 2008	10.88	889.35
3. November 13, 2008	6.67	552.59
Loss by percentage		
1. October 19, 1987	22.61	508.00
2. October 28, 1929	12.82	38.33
3. October 29, 1929	11.73	30.57
Loss in points		
1. September 29, 2008	6.98	777.68
2. October 15, 2008	7.87	733.08
3. September 17, 2001	7.13	684.81

more speculative enterprise. Thus, for example, while overall U.S. industrial output fell by roughly 50 percent between its peak in mid-1929 and its trough in mid-1932, the DJIA fell by nearly 90 percent. Or, to take a more recent example, the 13.3 percent decline in U.S. industrial output from the beginning of the most recent recession in December 2007 to April 2009 was accompanied by a nearly 50 percent drop in the DJIA.

John J. Neumann and James Ciment

See also: New York Stock Exchange.

Further Reading

Bodie, Z., A. Kane, and A. Marcus. *Essentials of Investments.* Boston: McGraw-Hill/Irwin, 2008.

Dow Jones Indexes Web site: www.djaverages.com.

Shiller, Robert J. *Irrational Exuberance.* Princeton, NJ: Princeton University Press, 2005.

Duesenberry, James (1918–2009)

James Stemble Duesenberry was a professor of economics at Harvard University from 1955 to

1989 whose most significant contribution to economics was the relative income hypothesis, with which many economists were uncomfortable. He served on President Lyndon Johnson's Council of Economic Advisers, and subsequently was chairman of the Federal Reserve Bank of Boston.

Duesenberry was born on July 18, 1918, in West Virginia. He earned bachelor's (1939), master's (1941), and—after serving in the Air Force during World War II—doctorate (1948) degrees from the University of Michigan. His doctoral thesis, published as *Income, Saving, and the Theory of Consumer Behavior* (1949), was an important contribution to the Keynesian analysis of income and employment. Duesenberry taught at MIT (1946) and at Harvard (1955–1989). While at Harvard, he chaired the Department of Economics from 1972 to 1977. He served on the President's Council of Economic Advisers from 1966 to 1968, along with Otto Eckstien, with whom he had collaborated on a 1960 article in *Econometrica* about recession; and, from 1969 to 1974 he was chairman of the board of the Boston Fed. Following his retirement from Harvard, he continued to serve as a consultant at the Harvard Institute for International Development.

While such economists as Milton Friedman and John Maynard Keynes became familiar to many people in the twentieth century, Duesenberry was known mainly among other economists for his writings on economic concepts and theories. The field of economics since the 1920s, and especially since the Great Depression, had aspired to be the hardest, or most scientific, of the social sciences. It was the first field to integrate game theory, and it aimed to remain distinct from such "soft" sciences as psychology and sociology, which examine motive and other intangible forces to explain behavior. Even John Maynard Keynes's theories were modified by more scientific principles as his followers deemphasized what Keynes viewed as irrational "animal spirits" that caused consumers and investors to make decisions based on emotional, rather than purely rational, impulses.

But Duesenberry's relative income hypothesis deals specifically with motivation. In the 1960s—a decade during which the "Other America" and the Great Society gained prominence and the issues of poverty and the disenfranchisement of minorities were the focus of much public attention—sociologists examined the effects of income inequality. Rises in crime, for instance, were predicted to occur when the economically disadvantaged were socialized to desire the same material things and lifestyles as those with more money, and this socialization was seen to be encouraged partly by television and the national media.

Similarly, in Duesenberry's view, attitudes toward purchasing and saving were influenced by decision makers' perceptions of others'—and their own recent—standards of living. He believed that even when individuals' needs could be met by spending less, they continued to spend more than necessary—even buying on credit—because they aspired to a more affluent lifestyle. Duesenberry sought to explain why spending habits tended not to react "rationally" to recessions, and why the affluent were more likely to save money than the less affluent (who would benefit more from saving).

The similarity of Duesenberry's relative income hypothesis to sociological approaches is apparent in his language; he refers to a "demonstration effect" (a term common in sociology and political science) in the relationship between the consumption behavior of the wealthy and the awareness of such behavior by the less affluent and their subsequent attempts to emulate it. (There is a similar effect when children mimic adult behavior through such make-believe play as "house" or "doctor," or by setting up "businesses" such as lemonade stands.) Such observations seem to place Duesenberry more in the annals of sociology than economics.

Friedman's permanent income hypothesis became the canonical theory of consumption, displacing, although not entirely replacing, Duesenberry's. Extensions of Duesenberry's theory have been used in the globalist era to describe intangible economic relationships between developed (economically advantaged) and developing (economically disadvantaged) nations, and the macroeconomic behavior of both.

Bill Kte'pi

See also: Eckstein, Otto; Friedman, Milton.

Further Reading

Duesenberry, James S. *Income, Saving, and the Theory of Consumer Behavior.* Cambridge, MA: Harvard University Press, 1962.

Frank, Robert H. "The Mysterious Disappearance of James Duesenberry." *New York Times*, June 9, 2005.

Gilpin, Robert. *Global Political Economy: Understanding the International Economic Order.* Princeton, NJ: Princeton University Press, 2001.

Mayer, Thomas, James S. Duesenberry, and Robert Z. Aliber. *Money, Banking, and the Economy.* New York: W.W. Norton, 1996.

Eastern Europe

Eastern Europe is a region composed of countries that were, for much of the post–World War II period, organized under communist-type economic and political systems. These include Albania, Bulgaria, the Czech Republic, Hungary, Poland, Romania, Slovakia, and the states of the former Yugoslavia (Bosnia, Croatia, Macedonia, Montenegro, Serbia, and Slovenia). The former eastern half of Germany, once known as the German Democratic Republic, or East Germany, was also part of this region. (East Germany is discussed in the article "Germany.") In addition, the three former Soviet Baltic states of Estonia, Latvia, and Lithuania are also usually included (although in this encyclopedia they are discussed separately in the article "Baltic Tigers.") More debatable is the inclusion of the other former Soviet republics located on the eastern fringes of Europe: Belarus, Moldova, and Ukraine, though they are included in the discussion here.

With the collapse of both the Soviet Union and Soviet-backed regimes in the late 1980s and early 1990s, all of these countries, with the exception of several former Yugoslavian republics, transitioned peacefully from communist to free-market systems in the early 1990s, though in most cases with enormous economic dislocations. While levels of economic development vary widely among the different Eastern European states, the region as a whole lags significantly behind Western Europe in terms of gross domestic product (GDP) per capita and other key economic indicators to the present day.

Origins of Eastern Europe's Economic Lag

While virtually all economists agree that the communist-inspired, command-style economic systems stunted economic development in the region—especially when compared to the mixed market, capitalist-socialist hybrid systems of Western Europe—the origins of Eastern Europe's relative economic backwardness go back to at least the Middle Ages, when instead of gradually winning new freedoms, as in Western Europe, peasants in Eastern Europe found themselves under new landlord-driven restrictions that resulted in serfdom or near-serfdom in much of the region. The enhanced power of the landlords stunted the growth of an innovative merchant class while slowing the development of cities, both keys to industrialization. While several Eastern Europe countries had thrown off many of the restrictions by the nineteenth century and begun to industrialize, the damage, say historians, was already done. As late as the 1930s, on the eve of World War II and the subsequent subjugation to Soviet power after the war, the economies of Eastern Europe lagged significantly behind those of Western Europe.

World War II inflicted further blows on the region in several critical ways. First, the war heavily damaged the economic infrastructure of Eastern Europe, particularly in the Soviet Union, while the Nazi occupying forces rounded up hundreds of thousands of Eastern Europeans, most notably Jews, for slave labor and for extermination in death camps. Besides being crimes against humanity, such practices resulted in an incalculable loss in economic productivity, as much factory production went to servicing the German war machine rather than creating economic growth in the region.

Causing longer-term economic damage, say economists, was the legacy of the war. As the Soviet Red Army marched into the region, pushing the German army out, it imposed pro-Soviet, communist governments across the region. Only in Yugoslavia (and Albania), which had large and well-organized anti-Nazi resistance forces during the war, were the Soviets unable to impose their will. Still, both countries chose to adopt the same centrally controlled, command-style economic systems, though Yugoslavia's did allow for a modicum of market forces to operate.

Communist Era

But whether under Soviet-controlled regimes or independent communist ones, the economic development of Eastern European countries followed similar trajectories, as various forms of the Soviet prewar economic system were imported into the region. Economic planning was instituted, usually through adoption of what were often known as Five Year Plans. Economic experts and political appointees, working for the central government, developed long-term blueprints for where investment was to be made. The emphasis was on heavy industry, which, in itself, was not a bad idea, given how Eastern Europe had often lagged in this sector, and given the enormous destruction to what infrastructure it did have during World War II.

Meanwhile, agriculture was collectivized, though in some countries, such as Poland, much land remained in private hands. But whatever the case, relatively few resources were allocated to the agricultural sector. Similarly, there was little emphasis on consumer goods, particularly in the early postwar decades.

As most noncommunist economists point out—particularly those of the Austrian school—such command-style economics fail because they dispense with normal market forces in the allocation of resources. That is, economic authorities set goals for final output, then try to find the economic resources to meet those goals. But such centralized planning and direction is not an effective substitute for such market forces as profits and prices in allocating resources and motivating firms to become more efficient or meet the needs of consumers. And with few consumer goods available, workers lack the motivation to be particularly productive. Eventually, economic planners in various Eastern European countries tried to make adjustments, by allocating more resources to consumer goods. But again, the command-style system did not find a particularly efficient means for making sure the right goods to meet demand were being made in sufficient quantities, or at all.

Also setting back postwar Eastern European economic development were geopolitical factors. Fearing that too much economic integration with Western Europe would undermine their control, the Soviet Union and pro-Soviet regimes in much of Eastern Europe severed traditional trade ties between the two halves of the continent. In addition, the Soviet Union spurned any cooperation with the U.S. Marshall Plan of the late 1940s, a massive injection of U.S. capital that did much to lay the foundations for Western Europe's economic "miracle" of the 1950s and 1960s.

Thus, by the end of the communist era in the late 1980s, Eastern European economies consistently lagged behind those of the West, though some, particularly in Central Europe and the Baltic republics of the Soviet Union, did achieve a certain degree of economic prosperity. In general, GDP per capita in communist Eastern Europe was roughly one-fourth that of Western Europe, though with much variation on both sides of what was then known as the "Iron Curtain."

Fall of Communism and Market Reforms

While some Eastern European countries were beginning to experiment with the introduction of market forces before the fall of communism, the collapse of communist regimes in Eastern Europe and the Soviet Union between 1989 and 1991 greatly accelerated the process. Meanwhile, the fall of communism in Eastern Europe coincided with a move toward more market forces among the stagnating hybrid economies of Western Europe and a new consensus in the West that less government interference in the economy was best for economic growth.

To varying degrees of speed and thoroughness, every postcommunist Eastern European regime began freeing prices from centralized control, turning over state enterprises to private owners, and attempting to strengthen their currencies and balance their budgets, often taking advice from strongly pro–free-market advisers from the United States and other countries in the West.

The impact of these market reforms on the lives of ordinary Eastern Europeans was often harsh. While a few well-connected individuals—often members of the old communist leadership—were able to buy up state enterprises at fire sale prices, most citizens faced unemployment, rising prices, and a deteriorating social safety network. With access to superior Western-made goods for the first time, many Eastern Europeans spurned local products,

leading to the closing of factories, many of which were inefficient and technologically backward after years of operating in a command-style economy.

By the late 1990s to early 2000s, however, many of the more advanced Eastern European economies had recovered from the shock of transitioning to free-market mechanisms of resource allocation. Meanwhile, Western European companies began investing heavily in existing Eastern European firms or in setting up their own operations in Eastern Europe, both to gain access to consumers with rising incomes and to take advantage of relatively low-cost yet highly educated workers. Indeed, during this period, real GDP growth in Eastern Europe usually outpaced that of Western Europe by a significant margin. Between 2002 and 2006, for example, the more advanced Eastern European economies experienced real GDP growth rates averaging roughly 5 percent while the core countries of the European Union (that is, not including those Eastern European countries that had joined during this period) averaged less than 2 percent GDP growth per annum.

Meanwhile, as the accession of many of these countries to the European Union and World Trade Organization indicated, Eastern European countries had turned away from the former Soviet economic orbit and joined the globalized economy. But while market reforms produced substantive growth and the new openness to global trade improved standards of living, it also exposed the region to fluctuations in the global financial system.

During the boom years of the late 1990s through mid-2000s, many Eastern European countries borrowed heavily from Western banks to help develop their economies and provide a rising standard of living for their citizens. In doing so, they were aided by the loose credit policies of Western financial institutions eager to earn profits in rapidly growing emerging markets. This inflow of capital prompted much speculation in stocks, particularly in the housing sector, leading to price bubbles.

When the credit crisis in the global financial markets emerged and intensified between 2007 and 2009, many Eastern European banks and

Members of the Hungarian Trade Union Association gather in front of parliament in downtown Budapest to protest government economic policy in 2009. Hungary and other Eastern European nations were among the hardest hit by the global financial crisis. (*Attila Kisbenedek/AFP/Getty Images*)

companies found themselves unable to obtain new loans to service their existing debts to Western financial institutions. The liquidity crisis sent the value of local currencies plunging against the euro. Many homeowners, having taken out mortgages with Western financial institutions in order to get lower interest rates, were forced into foreclosure.

The problems in Eastern Europe's liquidity crisis were not confined to that region, of course, since Western European—and some U.S.—financial institutions found themselves exposed to massive amounts of bad loans and toxic securities assets originating in Eastern Europe. Meanwhile, the European Central Bank decided in early 2009 not to provide a massive bailout to troubled Eastern European financial institutions, as had the Treasury Department to institutions in the United States, but instead to analyze each institution's need on a case-by-case basis.

James Ciment

See also: Baltic Tigers; Emerging Markets; Russia and the Soviet Union; Transition Economies.

Further Reading

Aligica, Paul Dragos, and Anthony J. Evans. *The Neoliberal Revolution in Eastern Europe: Economic Ideas in the Transition from Communism.* New York: Edward Elgar, 2009.

Gros, Daniel, and Alfred Steinherr. *Economic Transition in Central and Eastern Europe: Planting the Seeds.* 2nd ed. New York: Cambridge University Press, 2004.

Lane, David, ed. *The Transformation of State Socialism: System Change, Capitalism or Something Else?* New York: Palgrave Macmillan, 2007.

Roche, David. "Eastern Europe and the Financial Crisis." *Wall Street Journal*, March 28, 2009. Available at http://online.wsj.com/article/SB1238199323316462089.html. Accessed September 21, 2009.

Wagener, Hans-Jürgen. *Economic Thought in Communist and Post-Communist Europe.* New York: Routledge, 1998.

Echo Bubble

An echo, or secondary, bubble is a smaller speculative bubble that follows a major financial bubble that has burst. These secondary bubbles behave as aftershocks within the same financial markets. Echo bubbles often result from the conditions that created the original bubble, such as excessive speculation in real estate, new issues of stock, or derivatives. However, an echo bubble also may be stimulated by the policies used to counter the effects of the original bubble. For example, a central bank might increase the supply of money and credit or maintain a low interest-rate policy in order to stabilize financial markets after a bubble bursts. Such policies, however, might increase liquidity in financial markets, spurring a new speculative surge in the same markets. This secondary bubble "echoes" the original bubble, but often with a lower volume of speculation.

The most famous example of an echo bubble occurred in 1930. Between 1927 and 1929, corporate securities in the United States experienced one of the greatest speculative bubbles in history, with the Dow Jones Industrial Average soaring from roughly 160 to more than 380. This rapid growth came to an end in October 1929 when the stock market crashed, and the Dow Jones fell below 200 in a matter of days. A variety of factors, including bullish talk by leading financial experts, along with a cut in the Federal Reserve's interest rate, touched off a new speculative rally, driving the Dow Jones back up 50 percent to nearly 300 in the first two quarters of 1930. But the rally proved short-lived. Ultimately, the Dow Jones would hit bottom at just over 40 in mid-1932.

The discovery of echo bubbles resulted from the laboratory work in economics of Nobel laureate Vernon Smith. He conducted experiments that simulated financial market decision making as early as the 1960s. Smith's original experiments were conducted in the classroom, but then were extended to groups of financial market professionals. Based on his experiments, Smith was able to identify the existence of echo bubble patterns. An echo bubble expands before it bursts. Financial professionals analyze the recovery periods in stock markets after a crash or a bust in terms of major adjustments that occur within financial markets. During some recoveries, stock markets experience "corrections." If the markets are moving toward a secondary bubble, the correction stops the echo bubble. In this context, stock market corrections indicate that the recovery is unsustainable. There is a direct connection between stock market corrections and the end of an echo bubble.

The existence of an echo bubble indicates that the experience from a major speculative bubble's failure has not changed the behavior of financial market participants. Thus, during an echo bubble, investors follow the same patterns of behavior as in the original bubble. In other words, the experience of the original bubble does not alter the speculative motivations in financial markets; as a result, a correction will take place, causing the echo bubble to burst. It is as if a second round of irrational exuberance must take place before the speculative drive in financial markets can come to an end. In experimental economics, these secondary bubbles show up about half of the time in the aftermath of a major speculative bubble. Empirical evidence from financial markets to support the theory of echo bubbles is more limited, but professional observations regarding the need for "market corrections" after a major bubble support the existence of echo bubbles.

The speculative behavior reflected in echo bubbles suggests that efficient market theory, the standard model of finance, is flawed. This model assumes that individuals behave rationally, and that they use all available information to form expectations about financial prices. Thus, financial prices reflect all available information. However, echo bubbles indicate that speculative behavior is driven by overly optimistic expectations of future prices of specific financial assets. The historical experience of major speculative bubbles and their collapse does not necessarily change the speculative motivation in financial markets. Instead of a readjustment of expectations, the underlying pattern of speculation carries over into a new bubble period. This supports the observation made by John Maynard Keynes that there are extended periods of time when "animal instincts"—that is, emotions—overwhelm rational calculation in investment decisions. This is also consistent with Hyman Minsky's theory that financial bubbles—and the underlying behaviors that create them—are an inherent part of financial markets.

William Ganley

See also: Asset-Price Bubble.

Further Reading

Ball, Sheryl, and Charles Holt. "Speculation and Bubbles in an Asset Market." *Journal of Economic Perspectives* 12:1 (Winter 1998): 207–218.

Durlauf, Steven N., and Lawrence E. Blume. *Behavioural and Experimental Economics.* Hampshire, UK: Palgrave Macmillan, 2010.

Foster, John Bellamy, and Fred Magdoff. *The Great Financial Crisis: Causes and Consequences.* New York: Monthly Review, 2009.

Galbraith, John Kenneth. *A Short History of Financial Euphoria.* New York: Penguin, 1990.

Garber, Peter M. *Famous First Bubbles: The Fundamentals of Early Manias.* Cambridge, MA: MIT Press, 2000.

Kindleberger, Charles P. *Manias, Panics and Crashes: A History of Financial Crises.* 3rd ed. Hoboken, NJ: John Wiley & Sons, 1996.

Magdoff, Fred, and Michael Yates. *The ABCs of the Financial Crisis.* New York: Monthly Review, 2009.

Smith, Vernon. "The Effect of Market Organization on Competitive Equilibrium." *Quarterly Journal of Economics* 78:2 (Fall 1964): 181–201.

———. "Experimental Methods in Economics." In *Behavioural and Experimental Economics,* ed. Steven M. Durlauf and Lawrence E. Blume. Hampshire, UK: Palgrave Macmillan, 2010.

Smith, Vernon, Gerry Suchanek, and Arlington Williams. "Bubbles, Crashes and Endogenous Expectations in Experimental Spot Asset Markets." *Econometrica* 56:5 (September 1988): 1119–1151.

Eckstein, Otto (1927–1984)

Harvard economist and professor Otto Eckstein introduced the concept of core inflation and developed large-scale macroeconometric models, or measurements of macroeconomic data. He was a member of the President's Council of Economic Advisers during Lyndon Johnson's first full term (1964–1968) and, in 1969, a cofounder with businessman Donald Marron of Data Resources Inc. (DRI), which became the world's largest nongovernmental supplier of economic data.

Eckstein was born on August 1, 1927, in Ulm, Germany. His family fled Germany in 1938 and settled in the United States. Eckstein graduated in 1946 from Stuyvesant High School in New York City, received a bachelor of arts degree in economics from Princeton University in 1951, and master's (1952) and PhD (1955) degrees from Harvard University, where he served as a professor from 1955 to 1984 (he died on March 22 of that year). From 1957 to 1966, he was a consultant to the Rand Corporation, a think tank.

Eckstein's work focused principally on macroeconometrics. His concept of "core inflation" became especially important in American economics in the 1960s and 1970s, when inflation was a serious concern. Core inflation is an inflation metric that excludes from consideration those items that are especially volatile, such as food and energy. Energy prices—particularly that of oil—are subject to volatility independent of the factors that drive the inflation of other prices, and can often go up or down even when the prices of other goods are moving in the opposite direction. Seasonal food prices are subject to volatility as a result of climate issues, and usually go up when energy prices do because of transportation costs. The official measure of core inflation used by the Federal Reserve since 2000 is based on the core personal consumption expenditures price index (PCEPI, which includes data from the consumer price index and the producer price index), a switch from the previously used consumer price index (CPI). Unlike the CPI, the PCEPI accounts for substitution; in other words when the price of a particular good goes up, consumers often buy a different good instead. Thus the PCEPI is less affected than the CPI by volatile price shocks. The switch from CPI to PCEPI, occurring sixteen years after Eckstein's death, reflected the issues he worked on. Although inflation may seem simple to understand, the question of how to measure it, what to measure, what data to consider, and what time period to measure, is complicated and subject to frequent revision.

Bill Kte'pi

See also: Council of Economic Advisers, U.S.; Deflation; Inflation.

Further Reading

Eckstein, Otto. *The Great Recession*. Amsterdam, NY: North-Holland, 1978.

———. *Industry Price Equations*. Cambridge, MA: Harvard Institute of Economic Research, 1971.

Wilson, Thomas A. "Otto Eckstein: Applied Economist Par Excellence." *Review of Economics and Statistics* 66:4 (1984): 531–536.

Effective Demand

During the first half of the twentieth century, the concept of effective demand was invoked by economic theorists—in particular the great John Maynard Keynes—as an explanation of the extended economic depression of the 1930s.

The term "effective demand" has two different meanings, one related to microeconomics (the study of economic decision making at the level of individual households, firms, and markets), and the other to macroeconomics (the study of the performance of the economy as a whole). The concept of effective demand in microeconomics is concerned with two ideas: (1) the consumer's or producer's willingness to pay; and (2) the consumer's or producer's ability to pay for a good or service at various prices, with all other factors affecting demand held constant.

Effective demand starts with the consumer's willingness to pay, and then identifies potential demand that cannot be realized due to insufficient income. The term is widely used in development economics to describe the inability of households, small businesses, and farmers in less developed economies to grow because of constraints on demand by low earning potential.

The macroeconomic concept of effective demand has its origins in classical economic literature, most notably Thomas Malthus's *Principles of Political Economy* (1820). Although Malthus is more known for his theories of population, his writings in *Principles of Political Economy* about the lack of "effectual demand" laid groundwork for Keynes's pathbreaking work, *The General Theory of Employment, Interest and Money*, more than a century later, in 1935.

Malthus was concerned about the long-term implications for individuals and families in a capitalist society. His analysis demonstrated that a capitalist economy can indeed grow due to improved access to resources and the application of improved technology. However, Malthus noted, the lack of "effectual" or sufficient demand—now referred to as effective demand—places limits on economic growth. Malthus argued that the purchasing power of the "large body of very poor workmen" and the luxury spending of "a comparable small body of very rich proprietors" would be insufficient to employ the expanding workforce, thus creating unemployment and misery.

Malthus's ideas were in direct opposition to those of the classical economic school, led by David Ricardo, which held that unemployment is impossible in a properly functioning, nonregulated economy. Following the work of Jean-Baptiste Say, the classical economists believed that the act of production generated an equal amount of spending on consumption and investment. This basic principle—that supply creates its own demand—became known as Say's law or Say's identity. According to that proposition, only workers who are unwilling to work at the going wage will be unemployed.

Keynes criticized classical Ricardian theory as overly "optimistic" and not in tune with reality. Confirmation, at least in Keynes's view, came in the form of the Great Depression of the 1930s, in the midst of which he wrote his *General Theory*. Classical economists, meanwhile, continued to maintain that the capitalist economies of the Western world would "self-correct" and eventually return to full employment.

According to Keynes, the essential fact that was not being considered by the classical adherents to Ricardo was that a capitalist economy can in fact remain at a stagnant equilibrium with a high rate of unemployment for a substantial period of time. Thus, Keynes's key theoretical innovation can be understood as a deepening of Malthus's concept of effective demand. According to the model developed by Keynes, the plans of business enterprises to produce and invest—which, according to classical economic rules, should lead to a correspondingly higher level of consumption—may in fact be insufficient to employ all workers who wish to be employed at the going wage. In considering the full impact of effective demand, Keynes maintained that market forces in this situation do not necessarily budge the economy from an underemployed state. "[T]he paradox of poverty in the midst of plenty," he wrote, is a consequence of "the mere existence of an insufficiency of effective demand [that] may, and often will, bring the increase of employment to a standstill *before* a level of full employment has been reached."

Keynes's work led to the adoption of discretionary fiscal policy by Western governments during the Great Depression to make up for the deficiency of aggregate (or effective) demand; this resulted in the creation of public works spending in economic downturns and social safety nets such as social security systems and unemployment insurance. The success of these economic and social policies, the expansion of economic activity, and the improving living standards for the balance of the twentieth century has largely muted the interest in insufficient effective demand. The recession and economic crisis of 2007–2009, however, sparked new interest in some circles as debt-ridden and unemployed consumers cut back on spending, reducing demand and employment in the process.

Derek Bjonback

See also: Confidence, Consumer and Business; Consumption; Keynesian Business Model.

Further Reading

Hartwig, Jochen. "Keynes Versus the Post Keynesians on the Principle of Effective Demand." *Journal of the History of Economic Thought* 14:4 (December 2007): 725–739.

Keynes, John Maynard. *The General Theory of Employment, Interest and Money.* New York: Harcourt, Brace, and World, 1935.

Malthus, Robert. *The Principles of Political Economy.* 2 vols., reprint. Cambridge and New York: Cambridge University Press, 2008.

Schumpeter, Joseph. *History of Economic Analysis.* New York: Oxford University Press, 1954.

Efficient Market Theory

Efficient market theory holds that in an efficient stock market, prices reflect all available information. In other words, price changes occur only as a result of new information entering the market. This theory classifies markets into three levels of efficiency: strong-form efficiency, semi-efficiency, and weak-form efficiency. In the strong-form efficient market, prices reflect all information, including public and nonpublic information. In the semi-efficient market, prices reflect all available public information. In a weak-form efficient market, prices reflect only past security prices.

Origins of the Theory

Efficient market theory first was expressed in the doctoral dissertation of French mathematician Louis Bachelier, written in 1900. Bachelier concluded that stock market prices are unpredictable, but his thesis went largely unnoticed until the 1960s, when the "random walk" theory of stock market prices became popular. This theory posits that stock prices are random and that past prices cannot be used to predict future prices. Efficient market theory evolved from this concept. Economists associated with the efficient market theory school of thought include Milton Friedman, Eugene Fama, and George Stigler.

Classical economics turned on the belief that encouraging the pursuit of economic self-interest was the most favorable approach to government economic policy, allowing the so-called invisible hand of the market to work unimpeded by regulation. Neoclassical economists sought to make the invisible hand visible in the form of efficient market theory. In academia, the difference between the school of thought advanced by the neoclassicists and that of the classical economists was referred to as the "freshwater versus saltwater" debate. This was a reference to the fact that many efficient market theorists were concentrated inland—most notably at the University of Chicago—while the classic economists were concentrated on the coasts.

Legal Implications for Corporate Governance

Neoclassical economics spread deep into law faculties, especially at the University of Chicago, giving this school of thought the moniker "Chicago school of law and economics." The professors who were attracted to this movement sought to induce a paradigm shift that would use efficient market theory to guide the regulation of financial markets. They believed this theory provided a sound basis to support their argument that markets are largely self-policing, thus reducing the need for government regulation.

Efficient market theory also was applied to corporate governance. Neoclassical economists argued that corporate managers should have incentives to align their interests with those of stockholders. This resulted in the widespread use of stock options as compensation for managers. These professors argued that the corporation was really a "nexus of contracts" that could be negotiated with each party's best interests in mind. Leaders in the Chicago school on matters involving corporate governance included Richard A. Posner and Frank H. Easterbrook, both of whom are now federal appellate court judges, and the former dean of the University of Chicago Law School, Daniel R. Fischel.

These legal theorists argued that market forces ensure that managers do not overreach in negotiating their contracts with shareholders—otherwise, no one would buy the company's stock. Under the contractual theory, shareholders are assured only of the rights they might have under a contract with the corporation. The courts would not be called on to create rights that the parties themselves did not establish by contract. This theory of corporate governance proved to be highly controversial. Traditional legal theorists applied fiduciary duties (borrowed from trust law) that required corporate managers to act in good faith, use due care in mak-

ing decisions, and avoid conflicts of interest that would undermine their duty of loyalty to the firm. The neoclassicists believed that the application of fiduciary duties to managers was just an "off the rack" guess by judges about what the parties would have agreed to had they thought to contract over the matter at issue. Instead, they argued that the focus should be the presumed intentions of the parties to any particular dispute.

Supporters of the Chicago school contended that fiduciary duties are created and applied by judges with no knowledge or experience in business. They pointed out that bondholders are protected only by contract terms, and not by fiduciary duties. Why should shareholders have any greater rights or fare any better than creditors? Critics of fiduciary duties also pointed to what they considered a particularly egregious decision, in which the Delaware Supreme Court (*Smith v. Van Gorkom,* 488 A.2d 858 [1985]) ruled that a board of directors had breached its fiduciary duty of care in too hastily approving the sale of a public company. However, the board members were highly experienced, they had been considering selling the company for some time, and the sale price was at a substantial premium. The Delaware legislature responded to that decision by passing a statute allowing Delaware corporations to waive the duty of care. Delaware is the favorite place of incorporation for large corporations, and most of those businesses obtained shareholder approval for such a waiver.

Efficient market theory reached its apex when the U.S. Supreme Court adopted a "fraud-on-the-market" theory (*Basic Inc. v. Levinson,* 485 U.S. 224 [1988]) that relieved plaintiffs of the burden of showing reliance on false statements in company press releases. Now, plaintiffs need not have read or heard the information claimed to be false. Rather, reliance is presumed because, in an efficient market, the price of a stock reflects all available information, including the information that is alleged to be false. The effect of the false information is transmitted through changes in the price of the stock.

The fraud-on-the-market theory presumes that the market is efficient and that the market does not discount false statements. That presumption was challenged by Justice Byron White, who pointed out that, "while the economists' theories which underpin the fraud-on-the-market presumption may have appeal of mathematical exactitude and scientific certainty, they are, in the end, nothing more than theories which may or may not prove accurate on further consideration" (485 U.S. at 254). He noted that the fraud-on-the-market theory is at odds with federal policy because it seeks market discipline instead of government regulation and that "some of the same voices calling for acceptance of the fraud-on-the-market theory also favor dismantling the federal scheme which mandates disclosure" (485 U.S. at 259).

Justice White was right to be concerned. The efficient market hypothesis was undermined by the market breakdown during the stock market crash of 1987. That market event did not appear to be the result of any new information that would have justified such a sharp market contraction. Instead, economists identified something called "noise trading"—a concession that some trading in the market is irrational and uninformed, reducing market efficiency and creating unpredictable volatility. By the mid-1990s, efficient market theory was being attacked from all quarters as overly simplistic and even wrong. Even its strongest proponents acknowledged that the theory was riven with flaws. Eugene Fama, the leading proponent of the efficient market hypothesis, was among those who conceded its shortcomings.

One example of its failings was the movement to align the interests of corporate managers with those of shareholders through stock options. This effort turned into a disaster after the Enron Corporation, WorldCom, and numerous other public companies were found to have manipulated their accounts in order to boost stock prices and garner massive bonuses through exercisings. Market efficiency was further called into question during the financial crisis of 2008–2009, when markets worldwide proved to be remarkably inefficient.

A new school of "behavioral economics" led by Richard Thaler attacked the efficient market theory. This school of thought argues that human behavior affects market prices, that such behavior is not always rational, and that humans make systematic errors in judgment that affect prices. In 1999, economists Jon D. Hanson and Douglas A. Kysar noted that although many jurists subscribed to a view of economic actors as purely logical and analytical, scholars in other social science disciplines were coming to a very different conclusion. "Those scientists—cognitive psychologists, behavioral researchers, probability theorists, and others—were discovering powerful evidence that the rational actor model, upon which the law and economics project depends, is significantly flawed," Hanson and Kysar wrote. "In place of the rational actor model, those scientists were developing a human decision maker model replete with heuristics and biases, unwarranted self-confidence, a notable ineptitude for probability, and a host of other nonrational cognitive features."

Jerry W. Markham

See also: Consumer and Investor Protection; Information Technology; Neoclassical Theories and Models.

Further Reading

Cunningham, Lawrence A. "From Random Walks to Chaotic Crashes: The Linear Genealogy of the Efficient Capital Market Hypothesis." *George Washington Law Review* 62 (1994): 547–608.

De Long, J. Bradford, Andrei Schleifer, Lawrence H. Summers, and Robert J. Waldman. "Noise Trader Risk in Financial Markets." *Journal of Political Economy* 98:4 (August 1990): 703–738.

Hanson, Jon D., and Douglas A. Kysar. "Taking Behavioralism Seriously: The Problem of Market Manipulation." *New York University Law Review* 74 (1999): 630–749.

Malkiel, Burton G. *A Random Walk Down Wall Street.* New York: W.W. Norton, 1973.

Emerging Markets

A term coined by World Bank economist Antoine van Agtmael in the 1980s, "emerging markets"—or emerging economies—refers to developing world countries notable for their high economic growth rates in recent decades, which places them in a kind of economic limbo between the developing and developed worlds. Most emerging markets are located in Asia, Latin America, and the former communist bloc of Eastern Europe and the Soviet Union, with a few cases in Africa and the Middle East as well. Large and high-profile members of the emerging markets group include Brazil, Russia, India, and China—the so-called BRIC nations—but there are numerous smaller ones as well. In addition, the grouping has changed over time, with most economists now placing the emerging markets of the 1980s—such as the Asian Tigers (Hong Kong, Singapore, South Korea, and Taiwan)—on the list of developed-world countries.

Developing world nations face a host of problems, from low educational attainment to widespread poverty to lack of infrastructure. Many find themselves trapped in a vicious economic cycle—little education and few skills keep income levels low, which results in an inadequate savings rate, which means low investment. With little investment in capital goods, productivity also remains low, which in turn keeps income levels down—and the cycle repeats.

From Underdevelopment to Emerging Market Status

A country's shift from underdevelopment to emerging market status can result from a host of factors, though all emerging markets have one thing in common—they have managed to lift the rate of investment substantially and have made sure to put a lot of resources into improving education and skill levels, as well as the overall health of the populace. Poor health often impedes growth because it lowers productivity. In addition, emerging markets have emphasized basic macroeconomic fundamentals, making sure domestic savings rates stay high and inflation is kept in check, as the latter can undermine sav-

ings by forcing people to spend now rather than risk higher prices later. In many cases, emerging markets have had the advantage of being able to adopt and imitate technologies pioneered in the developed world.

Beyond these fundamentals, however, the path from underdevelopment to emerging market status can vary greatly. In some countries, a valuable resource base is key, as in the case of hydrocarbons in the Persian Gulf states. Of course, simply having a lot of oil is not enough to guarantee emerging market conditions. Nigeria has long been one of the world's largest producers of oil and yet its economy remains mired in underdevelopment.

In other cases, economic liberalization has helped achieve emerging market status. In the late 1970s and 1980s, for example, Chile privatized much of its industry, lowered tariffs and other barriers to foreign investment, and saw economic growth take off at one of the fastest rates in the world. The Asian Tigers followed a very different path to rapid economic growth, maintaining punitive tariffs and other restrictions on imports and a high level of government direction of the economy, though the free market was generally left on its own to create wealth. The example of China presents yet another means of attaining emerging market status, taking a mixed economic approach to development—government ownership of key industries, with local managers setting production and marketing policies to meet demand.

Foreign Investment

Whatever path they take, emerging markets are generally successful at luring foreign investment and capital, critical in low-income countries. This is nothing new, of course. A key element in the emergence of the United States as an industrial powerhouse in the nineteenth century was the high level of foreign—often British—capital. In the case of the Persian Gulf states, bringing in foreign capital was often simply a function of selling the oil beneath their feet. But in cases where natural resources are not enough to lift countries out of

Leaders of the world's top emerging economies—Brazil, Russia, India, and China (BRIC)—held their first official summit in June 2009 in Yekaterinburg, Russia. Discussions focused on ways to increase their influence during the global economic crisis. *(Vladimir Rodionov/Stringer/AFP/Getty Images)*

the vicious cycle of underdevelopment, the key element in attracting foreign capital is the lure of high returns for overseas investment. One important factor here is keeping corruption under control. If foreign investors believe the benefits of investment are monopolized or stolen by insiders, they are unlikely to put their money into a country.

Even more important is the investment a country makes in a healthy and highly educated workforce and adherence to macroeconomic fundamentals, since inflation can destroy the value of foreign investment. If all of these things come together at once, the vicious cycle of underdevelopment turns into a virtuous cycle of rapid economic growth. As investment levels increase, so, too, does productivity. And since wages often lag behind productivity growth, profits increase, which lures in more foreign investment. As a country grows richer, it can invest more in education and infra-

structure, thereby increasing productivity, and the cycle repeats.

But foreign investment can also subject emerging markets to the vagaries of international finance. With improvements in communications and technology from the 1980s onward, it became easier for investors in the developed world to put their money into developing world economies as they were lured by the possibility of profit levels unattainable in more mature economies. Poor countries, of course, were eager for such investment and lowered barriers to it. From the late 1980s onward, for example, vast amounts of foreign capital were invested in the emerging markets of East Asia, creating a speculative bubble in everything from housing to commercial property to manufacturing capacity to stock market securities.

The presence of all of this foreign capital was premised on high growth rates, which assured high profits and financial market stability. But foreign investors can be fickle. Any perception of instability or slowing growth rate will cause them to pull their money out of high-risk emerging markets. This is exactly what happened in Thailand and then much of East Asia during the so-called Asian financial crisis of 1997–1998. As foreign capital pulled out, governments tried to bolster their own currencies—many were on fixed-rate exchange systems to attract foreign capital in the first place—which further depleted their foreign currency reserves. Desperate, the governments then turned to the International Monetary Fund (IMF) for loans. But the IMF required the various governments to impose fiscal policies that led to economic contraction, causing more foreign capital to flee. Depending on the country, it took several years for many of these emerging markets to return to positive economic growth.

The social and political ramifications of emerging market status tend to be more similar than dissimilar among countries. The key outcome is the growth of an urban middle class, and in cases as diverse as Chile and South Korea, the authoritarian governments that created the conditions for economic takeoff are pushed to cede increasing political power to an educated and prosperous middle-class electorate. Whether or not emerging market status always guarantees such an outcome, however, is being tested by the largest emerging market of all—China.

James Ciment

See also: Africa, Sub-Saharan; Argentina; Asian Financial Crisis (1997); Baltic Tigers; Brazil; BRIC (Brazil, Russia, India, China); Central America; Chile; China; Colombia; Eastern Europe; India; Latin America; Mexico; Middle East and North Africa; Russia and the Soviet Union; South Africa; Southeast Asia; Transition Economies; Turkey.

Further Reading

Emerging Markets Monitor Web site: www.emergingmarkets monitor.com.

Enderwick, Peter. *Understanding Emerging Markets: China and India.* New York: Routledge, 2007.

Manzetti, Luigi. *Neoliberalism, Accountability, and Reform Failures in Emerging Markets: Eastern Europe, Russia, Argentina, and Chile in Comparative Perspective.* University Park: Pennsylvania State University Press, 2009.

Mavrotas, George, and Anthony Shorrocks, eds. *Advancing Development: Core Themes in Global Economics.* New York: Palgrave Macmillan, 2007.

Motamen-Samadian, Sima, ed. *Capital Flows and Foreign Direct Investments in Emerging Markets.* New York: Palgrave Macmillan, 2005.

Employment and Unemployment

Employment and unemployment are two distinct labor market states in which individuals of working age can find themselves. In the case of the former, an individual holds a job and is said to be employed. In the case of the latter, a person does not hold a job but is available for work and is actively looking for work. The sum of these two measures of labor market participation constitutes the total labor force.

How Employment and Unemployment Are Measured

Labor market variables are measured by a household survey that national statistical agencies conduct monthly in most industrialized countries based on a representative sample of the civilian noninstitutional working-age population. In the United States, the Current Population Survey, which is conducted by the Census Bureau (on behalf of the Bureau of Labor Statistics), surveys approximately 50,000 households each month to generate estimates of labor market variables such as employment, unemployment, and labor force participation. The survey covers a sample of the population that is sixteen years of age and older, excluding members of the armed forces and inmates of institutions.

While the specifics of the sample and the definition of "working-age population" vary from country to country (e.g., in Canada, the survey samples about 50,000 households from a working-age population of individuals fifteen years of age and older), most industrialized nations rely on household surveys rather than statistical information based on records from unemployment insurance offices and employment centers to calculate their estimates of monthly labor force statistics. This is because of possible statistical bias—for instance, an individual may have exhausted his or her unemployment insurance benefits, and yet still would be considered unemployed according to the household survey by virtue of his or her continued job search. This suggests that unemployed individuals receiving assistance constitute only a portion of the actual total unemployed.

Definition of Employment and Unemployment

The U.S. Bureau of Labor Statistics defines the number of employed as including all individuals who, during the reference week in which the statistical survey was conducted,

1. Held a job and worked at least one hour for pay or profit, or were unpaid and contributed at least fifteen hours in a family business;

2. Did not work, as a result of nonlabor market reasons such as vacation, illness, bad weather, strike or lockout, or other family or personal reasons that temporarily kept the individual off the job.

Hence, regardless of the skill requirements for a particular occupation, the number of hours an individual works (part-time or full-time), or the number of jobs held by an individual participant in the labor market (single versus a multiple job holder), everyone counts as one employed person in the official employment statistics. According to the Organisation for Economic Co-operation and Development (OECD), about 538 million people were employed in the OECD countries out of a civilian labor force of 572 million individuals in 2008. This indicates that the vast majority of individuals who were actively participating in the labor market were employed, regardless of whether they worked part-time or held multiple jobs. On the other hand, the employment rate, also referred to as the employment/population ratio, is defined as the number of employed persons as a percentage of the civilian noninstitutional working-age population—that is, the number of employed persons as a share of the total number of individuals in an economy who *potentially* could offer their labor services. In 2008, the employment rate in the United States was 62.2 percent, which was down from 63.0 percent in 2007.

According to the Bureau of Labor Statistics, unemployment is a particular labor market state that encompasses all individuals in the working-age population who, during the reference week, held no job, were available for work, and actively engaged in a job search during the preceding four weeks. According to this definition, in 2008, approximately 34 million people in the OECD countries were without work and were actively seeking work out of a civilian labor force of 572 million. In contrast to the employment rate, the unemployment rate is defined as the percentage of the *actual* labor force that is unemployed. For all of the OECD countries together, the weighted average unemployment rate in 2008 was 5.9 percent, ranging from a low of 2.5 percent in Norway to a high of 11.4 percent in Spain.

Patterns of Unemployment and Underemployment

Both employment and unemployment show strong seasonal, cyclical, and long-term patterns. Depending on climate and the structure of industry, in some countries, the magnitude of the seasonal difference could far exceed the cyclical variations because of the booms and busts that regularly afflict advanced market economies. However, the long-term behavior of unemployment differs somewhat among these countries. The figure on the next page illustrates the trend in the unemployment rate in the major industrialized countries between 1970 and 2008, adjusted to the U.S. statistical measure. Each of the three panels depicts the U.S. unemployment rate series (the continuous line, as compared to the broken lines for other countries).

The top panel of the figure shows the unemployment rate of the largely English-speaking members of the G-7 countries from 1970 to 2008. It depicts a relatively stationary trend with local spikes during major recessions, as occurred in the mid-1970s, early 1980s, early 1990s, and early 2000s. Unemployment rates converge at less than 6 percent by the end of the period, before the deep recession that originated in the United States in late 2008 and spread internationally throughout 2009. In contrast, in the middle and lower panels, one can compare the historical trend in the U.S. unemployment rate to that of continental Europe and Japan, respectively. In the early 1980s, the major countries of the eurozone departed significantly from the U.S. pattern, experiencing rates far surpassing those in the United States since the 1980s; in the case of Japan, unemployment rates trended upward throughout the period, especially during the 1990s and the first half of the 2000s, rising from levels of less than 2 percent in the

International Comparison of the Unemployment Rate Experience of the United States in Relation to Its G-7 Partners, 1970–2008 (adjusted to U.S. statistical measure)

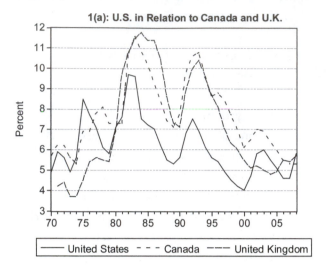

1(a): U.S. in Relation to Canada and U.K.

United States - - - Canada --- United Kingdom

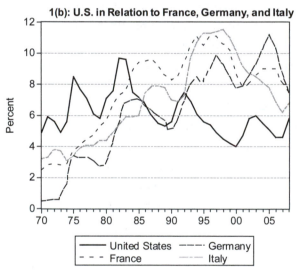

1(b): U.S. in Relation to France, Germany, and Italy

United States ----- Germany
- - - France -·-·- Italy

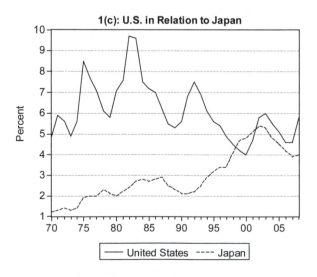

1(c): U.S. in Relation to Japan

United States ---- Japan

Source: U.S. Bureau of Labor Statistics.

early 1970s to converge on U.S. rates during the last decade.

Although labor market variables such as the employment and unemployment rates display strong cyclical patterns, they generally are known to be lagging indicators of the business cycle compared to, say, real gross domestic product (GDP), which roughly coincides with the reference cycle. This is because in times of recession, as firms cut production, they do not shed employment proportionally, but first choose to utilize their skilled personnel and supervisory staff less intensively in order to retain essential human capital within the enterprise. This is why we often witness real GDP declining well before unemployment begins to rise in a recession, with the ratio of output per employed person falling sharply. On the other hand, during a period of recovery, firms will choose to employ their underutilized workforce more intensively before hiring more workers, resulting in what observers refer to as a "jobless" recovery, with output per employed person rising.

Other Measures of Underutilization of the Labor Force

While the unemployment rate is the most widely used measure of the underutilization of human resources in an economy, there are other useful measures of labor market performance that add dimension to the problems of underemployment and underutilization of labor. Because firms choose to employ their workforce less intensively during a recession, this suggests that work hours should decline during recessions and the incidence of part-time employment should rise. While many part-time workers choose part-time jobs and thus are voluntarily underemployed, the number of *involuntary* part-time employed could be especially high during recessions. For instance, in any given month in 2009, close to half of all part-time workers (i.e., those who were employed for fewer than thirty-five hours per week) in the United States worked on a part-time basis for "economic reasons"—that is, they could not find full-time jobs because of slack labor market conditions resulting from cyclical (or even seasonal) factors affecting labor demand. The importance of involuntary underemployment, which persists even during periods of growth and prosperity, points to a bias toward focusing only on the official employment and unemployment rates as appropriate indicators of labor market performance.

The behavior of firms in hiring involuntary part-time workers also can lead to a substantial underestimation of the magnitude of the underutilization of labor in an economy. Another type of underestimation could occur as a result of the cyclical behavior of participation in the labor market. Out of the total civilian working-age population (i.e., the potential labor force), there are a significant number of individuals who are not counted as part of the current labor force because they are not searching for a job, but who are available for a work and have looked for work in the past twelve months. The Bureau of Labor Statistics classifies these individuals as "persons marginally attached to the labor force." Officially, they are classified as not in the labor force because of they are not searching for a job; however, some argue that these individuals constitute a "disguised" or "hidden" form of unemployment. Indeed, a subset of these marginally attached individuals who give a strictly job-related reason for not looking for work are described as "discouraged workers." These are individuals who stopped looking for work because of their negative expectations of finding a job vacancy, became discouraged, and officially dropped out of the labor force. The proportion of marginally attached labor market participants displays a strong cyclical pattern, rising during times of increasing unemployment and falling during periods of high growth in employment.

To understand the magnitude of involuntary part-time employment and marginal attachment to the labor force, it is useful to compare the official unemployment rate with an expanded labor underutilization rate that adds these two groups to the estimate of the measured unemployed. For

Job seekers scan the listings at an employment office in San Francisco in November 2009. The U.S. unemployment rate reached 10.2 percent that month, the highest since 1983. *(Justin Sullivan/Getty Images)*

instance, in January 2010, the official seasonally adjusted unemployment rate was estimated at 9.7 percent, according to the Bureau of Labor Statistics. When estimates of the total unemployed, plus all persons marginally attached to the labor force, plus the total involuntary part-time employed are added together and calculated as a percentage of an expanded denominator (which includes the official labor force as well as all persons marginally attached), we get a broad, seasonally adjusted estimate of underutilization of labor of 16.5 percent in January 2010. This means that as many as one out of every six individuals was directly affected by the recession. Like the unemployment rate, the gap between this broad estimate of underutilization of labor and the official unemployment rate widens during recessions and narrows during periods of strong growth in labor market demand.

Economic Concepts of Unemployment

There exists a whole typology of unemployment concepts referring both to the characteristics and the underlying mechanisms of unemployment in an economy. Economists normally classify unemployment into four main categories:

1. Seasonal unemployment is the least controversial concept. This type of unemployment is becoming less significant, both because of the relative decline in primary activities such as agriculture and because of changing technology, which allows many building activities to be carried out during the winter months in regions where seasonality is important. It is because of seasonal variations that the raw monthly labor force statistics normally are seasonally adjusted.

2. Frictional unemployment recognizes that in a dynamic labor market, there is continual turnover as individual labor market participants voluntarily engage in job searches. Mainstream economists emphasize this voluntary search activity to explain patterns of unemployment using a choice theoretic framework of analysis.

3. Structural unemployment refers to the constant churning between the structure of demand and the structure of labor supply that leads to a mismatch between people and jobs. This mismatch between the skills required and those supplied by labor force participants can be the result of technological change (often referred to as technological unemployment) or other factors that lead to changing industrial, occupational, and/or regional patterns of demand.

4. Cyclical unemployment relates to changes in aggregate demand that reflect the general pattern of booms and busts in an economy; this also is referred to as deficient-demand unemployment. Although economists recognize that both frictional and structural unemployment are sensitive to overall business fluctuations, traditionally, they have sought to identify cyclical unemployment as charac-

teristically different from other categories of unemployment. Indeed, much debate in macroeconomics centers on the existence and nature of cyclical unemployment.

Classical/Neoclassical Versus Keynesian/Post Keynesian Concepts of Unemployment

Because it uses an individualist methodology, traditional mainstream economic analysis, which is referred to in modern macroeconomics textbooks as "classical" or "neoclassical" economics (which dominated economic thinking both immediately before the publication of John Maynard Keynes's *General Theory of Employment, Interest and Money* in 1936 and since the rise of monetarism and the new classical school in the 1970s and 1980s), historically has had difficulty grappling with the category of cyclical unemployment. This is a type of unemployment that Keynes originally described as "involuntary" unemployment.

To modern mainstream neoclassical economists, who analyze economic behavior within a purely choice theoretic framework of analysis, demand-deficient unemployment is an aberration. In times of recession, unemployment rises, not because of a shortfall in demand, but because of an inadequate supply-side response to the decline in labor demand. As long as wages are sufficiently downward flexible, this should preclude the existence of any demand-deficient unemployment. If cyclical unemployment exists, it can be attributed to an insufficient cut in wages as a result of workers' bargaining strength, or to institutional impediments such as minimum wage legislation or the generosity of unemployment insurance benefits. Although not all unemployment is "voluntary," the existence of involuntary unemployment is attributable to institutional imperfections in the labor market that prevent the competitive downward bidding of wages.

Keynes and Post Keynesians reject this neoclassical conception of the labor market as a self-correcting mechanism. Keynes argued that the existence of involuntary unemployment was not attributable to wage rigidity, but to the incapacity of the labor market to clear on its own because of the negative aggregate demand-side feedback effect that a decrease in wages would have on the demand for labor, and thus on the equilibrium level of employment. Hence, even if wages were downward flexible, the economy would not necessarily return to a state of full employment—that is, a level of unemployment consistent with the existence of frictional unemployment. This is because wages are not just an element of cost to business enterprises, but they are also an element of aggregate demand arising from workers' consumption spending, with the latter depending on household employment income. A cut in wages would make it less expensive to hire labor, thereby putting *upward* pressure on employment, as the economy moves along a downward-sloping demand curve for labor. However, the negative feedback effect of the wage cut through the demand side also could shift the demand curve for labor inward, thereby putting *downward* pressure on employment at the lower level of wages because of the shrinking aggregate consumption demand resulting from lower overall labor income. Depending on the strength of the downward shift in labor demand, falling wages could exacerbate the overall state of cyclical unemployment.

These Keynesian ideas about the determination of employment and unemployment, which are reflected in the threefold classification of frictional, structural, and cyclical unemployment, became popular in the decades following World War II. In this framework, full employment means the absence of cyclical unemployment, or unemployment attributable to the business cycle. However, by the 1970s, some neoclassical economists were seeking to revive the classical theory of employment by fusing the established concept of frictional unemployment with what they dubbed the "natural rate" of unemployment, a concept this is associated with economist Milton Friedman.

Frictional unemployment can be described as a desired or "equilibrium" state in which, at any give time, some labor market participants may find themselves temporarily moving "between jobs." Friedman accepted the notion of equilibrium turnover. However, he appended an important condition pertaining to wages and prices to the concept of frictional unemployment. He concluded that, when wages and prices are not accelerating in an economy and when expectations about the future course of wages and prices are being fully realized by individual participants, the economy rests at its natural rate of unemployment (also often referred to as the nonaccelerating inflation rate of unemployment, or NAIRU). Cyclical deviations from this steady-state rate of unemployment occur when expectations regarding the future course of wages and prices are not being realized because of short-term, unanticipated fluctuations in demand. Later, new classical macroeconomists such as Robert Lucas ruled out even short-term fluctuations in involuntary unemployment, on the strict assumption of continuous market clearance and strong information about the future course of the economy. However, if this is so—if cyclical unemployment really is of little importance—is this natural rate of unemployment a constant, or does it vary cyclically over time?

Most mainstream economists who subscribe to the concept of a natural rate of unemployment argue that as long as the underlying structural characteristics of the labor market in terms of labor mobility and labor turnover remain unchanged, so will the natural rate of unemployment.

However, a new literature that has emerged during the last two decades among New Keynesians and Post Keynesians sought to restore the concept of involuntary unemployment by showing that the natural rate of unemployment closely tracks the actual rate of unemployment. This often is referred to as a "hysteresis" model of the labor market, and it points to the permanent effects that cyclical changes in actual unemployment have on the natural rate of unemployment because of phenomena such as skill deterioration resulting from long spells of unemployment. It may be argued that the endogenization of the natural rate of unemployment to the behavior of the actual rate of unemployment revived the Keynesian notion of deficient demand, or involuntary unemployment, that had been eclipsed in the economics literature since the 1970s.

Mario Seccareccia

See also: Unemployment, Natural Rate of; Wages.

Further Reading

Bean, Charles R. "European Unemployment: A Survey." *Journal of Economic Literature* 32:2 (June 1994): 573–619.

Freeman, Richard B. *America Works: Critical Thoughts on the Exceptional U.S. Labor Market.* New York: Russell Sage Foundation, 2007.

Galbraith, James K. "Time to Ditch the NAIRU." *Journal of Economic Perspectives* 11:1 (Winter 1997): 93–108.

Organisation of Economic Co-operation and Development (OECD). *Employment Outlook: Tackling the Jobs Crisis.* Paris: OECD, 2009. Available at www.oecd.org. Accessed March 2010.

Osberg, Lars. "The 'Disappearance' of Involuntary Unemployment." *Journal of Economic Issues* 22:3 (September 1988): 707–727.

Solow, Robert M. *The Labor Market as a Social Institution.* Oxford, UK: Basil Blackwell, 1990.

U.S. Bureau of Labor Statistics Web site: www.bls.gov.

Endogenous Growth Models

Endogenous growth models are a class of economic growth theories, and those associated with them, that emerged in the 1980s. The main premise of these models is that economic growth is an endogenous outcome of an economic system, a result of forces operating within the economy. Simply put, the main idea behind endogenous growth models is that knowledge—as embodied in greater productivity—drives economic growth. Because the emphasis on productivity connects endogenous growth models to real-world circumstances, endogenous growth models have gained widespread popularity and acceptance in the economic profession.

Underlying Concepts

If one could synthesize hundreds of years of research on economic growth, especially in the post–industrial revolution period, three fundamental ingredients would dominate the discussion: the capital-to-labor ratio, the concept of diminishing returns, and the growth in productivity or knowledge. Beginning with Adam Smith's *Wealth of Nations* (1776), in which Smith identified an increase in the well-being of the population as the true wealth of a nation, particular importance has been attached to capital accumulation and the capital-to-labor ratio for an economy's growth. The concept of diminishing returns is more closely associated with the English economist David Ricardo, who argued that an increase in output diminishes as more capital is put into the production process—to the point that it will ultimately come to a standstill. Finally, the neoclassical growth model, which dominated the growth literature after its introduction by the American economist Robert Solow in 1956, added a third key ingredient to the growth equation: technological progress. According to this view, as long as the growth in productivity resulting from technological change is greater than diminishing returns to physical capital, an economy will experience long-term growth.

Endogenous growth models were introduced in the 1980s in an attempt to reconcile theory with a more statistically based analysis of the economic growth process. Two main assumptions of the neoclassical model were that technology was exogenously determined—that is, arising from forces that arose independent of economic forces, such as genius—and that all countries have the same level of technology available to them. Given these two assumptions, along with the assumption of perfect competition, one of the main implications of the neoclassical growth model was that of convergence. Convergence implies that poorer countries will grow faster than wealthier countries and, over time, will catch up with wealthier countries. Even though initial estimates gave empirical support to this theory, it did not hold up when the economic researchers broadened their sample of countries outside the West and the time period was lengthened. Attempts to compare incomes across countries found evidence of divergence rather than convergence—in other words, that poorer countries do not necessarily catch up with wealthier ones but often lag further and further behind.

To explain the apparent contradiction between the neoclassical theory and empirical evidence, American economist Paul Romer, considered one of the pioneers of endogenous growth theory, suggested that technological progress is determined internally by positive knowledge spillovers. Positive spillovers (also known as positive externalities) are benefits accruing to all firms due to knowledge accumulation—that is, productivity gains—within one firm. Endogenous growth models were so named because of the endogenous nature of technology—it is driven by economic decision making. Additionally, given the nature of knowledge creation, there are increasing returns associated with new knowledge or new technology. Thus, it is possible to show that investment in knowledge creation allows for growth in productivity that can offset the effects of diminishing returns as originally conceived by Ricardo.

The reason behind increasing returns to knowledge is the nonrival nature of knowledge. Knowledge and ideas, once produced, can be shared free of cost or very cheaply. It is this nonrival nature of knowledge that drives growth. This quality implies that knowledge may be path-dependent in the sense that it may be possible to develop new technologies based on what is learned from existing ones. In other words, decisions made for any given circumstance are limited by decisions made in the next, so that economic practices become self-reinforcing. This may explain why certain technologies prevail longer than others. Another implication of the nonrival nature of knowledge is that it is relatively easy and cheap to replicate a new technology once it has been produced. However, even though knowledge is nonrival, it is also what economists call "excludable

or partially excludable," given socially and legally determined property rights. Licenses, patents, and trademarks allow the creator of new knowledge to exclude others from the ideas or allow others to share such ideas (after an initial time period) at an additional cost. Without this protection, private or public entities would not have the incentive for new knowledge creation.

The nonrival nature of knowledge implies that countries can continue to grow prosperous by augmenting their knowledge of how to increase output with ever-decreasing inputs. However, given the unique characteristic of knowledge, markets may tend to underinvest in knowledge. It is much cheaper for a firm to duplicate an idea after it has been produced rather than invest in research and development of such knowledge, which may or may not bear results. Thus, given the initial high cost of investing in knowledge creation, the larger the market share, the greater the profits. This is because a greater market share lowers the average cost of producing such knowledge. Additionally, given the excludable nature of knowledge and the exclusive monetary gains from creating such knowledge, there is a tendency for monopolies to be formed in the market. This is why countries introduce and execute antitrust laws to prevent the creation of such monopolies.

Categories

Endogenous growth models can be grouped into four categories, depending on their emphasis. The first type of model emphasizes the size and productivity of the research sector. In this view, economic growth depends on the ability of this sector to provide new ideas to the other sectors that produce goods and services.

The second group of endogenous growth models emphasizes new products that make older ones obsolete. These models are similar in concept to Austrian school economist Joseph Schumpeter's concept of "creative destruction," according to which new technologies lead to overall economic growth even as they produce specific winners and losers in the economy. Here, too, there are spillovers from the research sector, which lead to new innovations and products.

A third group of endogenous growth models recognizes the difference between fundamental or theoretical research and the application of such research to the real economy. According to these models, theoretical research does not add value unless it can be applied to secondary innovations that lead to the production of new goods. These models highlight the importance of learning by doing. They are also known as two-stage innovation models.

The fourth category attempts to explain why most economic growth occurs at intervals rather than evenly over time. Fluctuations in growth are related to vertical innovations whereby the possibility of new innovations dampens current research efforts, as researchers fear that existing technologies and products will soon become obsolete, making it less than worthwhile to improve them. Another explanation of uneven growth lies in the positive externality effects of general-purpose technologies in one sector, which can lead to improved technologies in many sectors. These may be due to the learning-by-doing nature of innovations. A good example would be the invention of the steam engine or the invention of computers and how they have revolutionized production and technology in many sectors of the economy.

Not all innovation is positive, however. As noted earlier, innovation can lead to economic instability. And as the financial crisis of 2008–2009 has demonstrated, innovations in the financial sector can be especially destabilizing. As finance is the lubricant and energy source for all economic activity, innovation in this sector has an impact on virtually all economic activity. Given that, it is not surprising that the worst financial crisis since the Great Depression—a crisis brought on, in part, by innovation in the financial sector—produced the worst overall economic downturn since the Great Depression.

Sharmistha Self

See also: Growth Cycles; Growth, Economic.

Further Reading

Aghion, Philippe, and Peter Howitt. *Endogenous Growth Theory.* Cambridge, MA: MIT Press, 1998.

———. "A Model of Growth Through Creative Destruction." *Econometrica* 60:2 (1992): 323–351.

Grossman, Gene, and Elhanan Helpman. "Technology and Trade." NBER Working Paper no. W4926. Washington, DC: National Bureau of Economic Research, 1994.

Rivera-Batiz, Luis A., and Paul M. Romer. "Economic Integration and Endogenous Growth." *Quarterly Journal of Economics* 106:2 (1991): 531–555.

Romer, Paul M. "Endogenous Technological Change." *Journal of Political Economy* 98:5 (1990): S71–S102.

———. "The Origins of Endogenous Growth." *Journal of Economic Perspectives* 8:1 (1994): 3–22.

Schumpeter, Joseph. "The Creative Responses in Economic History." *Journal of Economic History* 7:2 (1947): 149–159.

Solow, Robert M. "A Contribution to the Theory of Economic Growth." *Quarterly Journal of Economics* 70 (1956): 65–94.

Enron

Once one of the largest and apparently most innovative corporations in America, Houston-based Enron was originally an energy company that had diversified from the 1980s through the early 2000s into a number of businesses, the most lucrative of which was the supply and trading of natural gas and electricity. Hailed as an innovator, Enron also engaged in a number of illegal activities, including falsification of its accounting records for the purposes of driving up its stock price and manipulation of the California electricity market. As revelations of these practices became public in 2001, the company was forced into bankruptcy, decimating the assets of thousands of investors, including many of the company's own employees. Several high-level executives were charged and found guilty of various forms of fraud. The scandal also destroyed the venerable accounting firm of Arthur Andersen, which had been tasked with overseeing Enron's books, and led to far-reaching reforms for corporate responsibility.

Origins and Growth

The origins of Enron date to 1985, when Inter-North, an Omaha-based natural gas pipeline operator, merged with Houston Natural Gas. The resulting company was soon renamed Enron by its chief executive officer (CEO), Kenneth Lay, formerly head of Houston Natural Gas. The merger came during a period of deregulation of the natural gas industry. In 1978, Congress passed the Natural Gas Policy Act, which created a national market for natural gas. This was followed by other laws and regulatory changes that allowed pipeline operators to get into the business of buying and selling natural gas. The idea behind natural gas deregulation was that market forces, rather than government regulators, would be better able to ensure that consumers—both individuals and industries—got the most competitive price for their energy supplies.

In 1989, Enron began trading in natural gas futures, soon diversifying into a variety of other forms of energy, including electricity, an industry that was also undergoing deregulation in many states. In 1990, Lay hired an energy consultant named Jeffrey Skilling to head Enron's commodities trading department. By 1994, the company had become the largest seller of electricity both in the United States and the United Kingdom, which had also deregulated much of its energy markets.

By the late 1990s, the company—now consistently rated "America's Most Innovative Company" by *Fortune* magazine—was building and operating power plants and gas pipelines across North America and in many other parts of the world. At the same time, Enron was developing new derivative commodities products that investors could buy and sell, including those based on weather. That is, people could bet on how weather conditions would affect the price of commodities, including energy, and purchase derivatives—a form of insurance—against those conditions. Always technically savvy, the company opened what would become the largest Web-based commodities trading market in the world in 1999. By that same year, the company had become so large and influential that it had a hand in roughly one-fourth of all major energy deals in the world. In August

2000, its share price reached its all-time high of roughly $90 a share; the company reported revenues of $100 billion that year and employed more than 20,000 people in over thirty countries.

Questionable Business Practices

At the same, however, Enron was engaging in dodgy business activities. It began to set up a web of subsidiaries and partnerships, with interlocking ownership, with which it engaged in all kinds of business and trading activity. All of this was perfectly legal except for the fact that Enron was using the subsidiaries to hide losses and debt, allowing it to maintain the illusion of ever-increasing revenues and profits. Enron was also engaged in rigging markets, most notably in the California electricity market, which had been deregulated in 1996, permitting energy wholesalers more leeway in the prices they charged and allowing California utilities to sell their electricity to other states. Although the facts only came out later, by 2000, Enron and other electricity suppliers were gaming the system, either holding off supplies or diverting them elsewhere to create false shortages that would send prices spiking. Enron and other wholesalers made huge windfall profits as a result.

But the revenues were not enough to save the company. By 2001, Enron was sustaining large losses in its various business endeavors, including broadband provision, and through its partnerships, saddling the company with unsustainable debt. This was never divulged to investors, however, including employees whose retirement accounts often consisted largely of Enron stock. Previously, the company had hidden much of this debt with its subsidiaries, but by the summer of 2001 the losses and debt had become so large that this was no longer possible.

As rumors circulated through the financial markets that Enron was in serious trouble, Skilling, now CEO, resigned, replaced by former CEO Lay. In October, the company reported a $638 million loss for the third quarter and a $1.2 billion reduction in shareholder equity, much of the losses caused by the various partnerships and subsidiaries set up by Andrew Fastow, a Skilling protégé and the company's chief financial officer. That same month, the Securities and Exchange Commission launched an investigation into Enron's accounting practices as the company fired Fastow.

With its finances collapsing, and its share price falling below $10, Enron began borrowing from banks, to the tune of several billion dollars. In November, Enron made public the extent of its debt, and the company's bonds were downgraded by the rating agency Standard & Poor's to that of no-investment grade, or "junk bond" status, the latter a popular term for the highest-risk bond. Then, after a contentious takeover bid by a small rival named Dynegy fell through, Enron filed for bankruptcy protection under Chapter 11 of U.S. bankruptcy laws on December 2, 2001. It was the largest such filing to date in U.S. history.

Meanwhile, revelations soon emerged—some by the company itself—that huge bonuses had been paid to executives even as the company was becoming insolvent. Later, it would be learned that executives and their families had sold off huge blocks of stock as they were telling investors and their own employees that the company was still profitable.

Prosecutions and Legacy

With the company in bankruptcy, Lay resigned as CEO in February 2002 while various lower-level executives at Enron and its accounting firm, Arthur Andersen, pleaded guilty to charges of obstructing justice, for destroying crucial documents, as well as money laundering and conspiracy. In late 2002, Fastow was indicted on seventy-eight charges of conspiracy, fraud, money laundering, and other crimes, pleading guilty to two counts of conspiracy in January 2004. He received a ten-year prison sentence. A month later, Skilling—indicted on multiple counts of insider trading, fraud, and conspiracy—would plead innocent. In

July, the FBI indicted Lay for participating in a conspiracy to falsify the company's financial statements. He, too, would plead innocent. Both men, however, would be found guilty. In May, Skilling was convicted on nineteen counts of security and wire fraud and sentenced to more than twenty-four years in prison while Lay was convicted on six similar counts and faced up to forty-five years in prison. However, Lay died of a heart attack in July, before sentencing could proceed.

In the end, some twenty-one individuals were found guilty of various forms of securities malfeasance and fraud, including four at the brokerage firm of Merrill Lynch, which had marketed some of Enron's equity. While the firm of Arthur Andersen was found guilty of obstructing justice by destroying documents, the conviction was later overturned. Nevertheless, the bad publicity surrounding the scandal led most of the accounting firm's clients to abandon it, forcing it to close down operations, though it never dissolved or declared bankruptcy.

Aside from the nearly $75 billion lost by investors, nearly two-thirds of which investigators said was attributable to fraud, the main outcome of the Enron scandal were twofold: it invigorated calls to re-regulate energy markets in a number of states, including California, and it led to tougher federal corporate accounting and financial reporting standards with congressional passage of the Public Company Accounting Reform and Investor Protection Act of 2002, better known as Sarbanes-Oxley, after its co-sponsors, Senator Paul Sarbanes (D-MD) and Representative Michael Oxley (R-OH).

James Ciment

See also: Corporate Corruption.

Further Reading
Bryce, Robert. *Pipe Dreams: Greed, Ego, and the Death of Enron.* New York: PublicAffairs, 2003.

Fox, Loren. *Enron: The Rise and Fall.* Hoboken, NJ: John Wiley & Sons, 2003.

McLean, Bethany, and Peter Elkind. *The Smartest Guys in the Room: The Amazing Rise and Scandalous Fall of Enron.* New York: Portfolio, 2004.

European Central Bank

Established in June 1998, several months ahead of the launch of Europe's common currency, the euro, the European Central Bank (ECB) conducts monetary policy for the countries of the eurozone (officially the euro area), which encompasses those European Union (EU) member states that have adopted the euro as their currency, forming the European Monetary Union (EMU). As of late 2009, sixteen of the twenty-seven EU countries have adopted the euro. The sixteen countries that participate in the EMU are Austria, Belgium, Cyprus, Finland, France, Germany, Greece, Ireland, Italy, Luxembourg, Malta, Netherlands, Portugal, Slovakia, Slovenia, and Spain. The eleven that have not adopted the single currency either do not want to or do not meet the requirements set by the EU to join. They are Bulgaria, Czech Republic, Denmark, Estonia, Hungary, Latvia, Lithuania, Poland, Romania, Sweden, and the United Kingdom.

The ECB has played an increasingly important role in monitoring and attempting to adjust for economic fluctuations within the business cycles in the eurozone. The ECB is one of the world's most important central banks as the euro area is the world's largest economy after the United States. The euro has become the second most important international currency after the U.S. dollar. The adoption of the euro by the EMU member countries has promoted foreign trade and foreign investment flows, enhanced competition, and as a result, also contributed to higher economic growth. The euro area is expanding as several other EU member states plan to adopt the euro in the near future.

The headquarters of the ECB is located in Frankfurt am Main, Germany, continental Europe's leading banking center. The current president of the ECB is Jean-Claude Trichet. He is the second holder of this position: until November 2003, Willem (Wim) Duisenberg held this post. The main decision-making body of the ECB is the Governing Council, consisting of the six members of its Executive Board—including the president, the vice president, and four other members—and the governors of the national central banks of the sixteen euro area countries. The Governing Council usually meets twice a month.

The primary objective of the ECB is maintaining price stability (keeping inflation below 2

A sculpture of the euro symbol stands outside the headquarters of the European Central Bank in Frankfurt, Germany. The ECB administers monetary policy for the sixteen European Union nations that have adopted the euro. *(Bloomberg/Getty Images)*

percent or close to it) over the medium term and, through that, achieving sustainable economic growth and prosperity in Europe. The ECB also has several other important tasks. It is responsible for defining and implementing the monetary policy for the euro area, conducting foreign exchange operations, holding and managing the euro area countries' official foreign reserves, ensuring the smooth operation of payment systems, and monitoring progress in financial integration. The ECB has the exclusive right to authorize the issuance of banknotes within the euro area (member states can issue euro coins, but they have to inform the ECB beforehand and get its approval). The ECB also cooperates with relevant EU and international institutions, bodies, and forums. In addition, the ECB collects monetary and financial statistical information from national authorities or economic agents. Every year, the ECB has to give an overview of its monetary policy and other activities to the European Parliament, the EU Commission, and the European Council. The ECB publishes monthly bulletins, statistics pocket books, annual reports, financial stability reviews, research, and occasional and legal papers. Thus, the ECB is quite active in knowledge creation and dissemination.

The ECB is politically independent. It and its member national central banks are not allowed to take instructions from any national governments, EU institutions, or anyone else. This independence is critical; otherwise, politicians might be tempted to increase output and decrease unemployment for the short-run election cycle, for example, by printing more money, despite creating higher inflation in the longer run. This helps the ECB to maintain price stability and retain the credibility of the single monetary policy. To ensure its political independence, the ECB has its own budget. It gets its capital from the national central banks of the euro area.

One of the ongoing issues surrounding the ECB is whether its policies and regulations are, or can ever be, optimal for all of the European countries that have adopted the euro. Critics point out that Europe is not what economists refer to as an "optimal economic area," meaning that what policies may work well for some countries may not work well in others with different types of economies, and may in fact prove economically destructive to them. A second controversy is whether the ECB and the U.S. Federal Reserve can coordinate responses to crises, such as in dealing with the global financial meltdown of 2007–2008. In the early months of the crisis, Germany—as the dominant player in the ECB—resisted U.S. calls for decisive monetary stimulus action to fight the growing recession. But as the economic downturn deepened, the ECB began to loosen credit more, as the United States had urged.

Tiia Vissak

See also: Banks, Central; Monetary Policy.

Further Reading

Dutzler, Barbara. *The European System of Central Banks: An Autonomous Actor? The Quest for an Institutional Balance in EMU.* New York: Springer, 2003.

European Central Bank Web site: www.ecb.int.

Issing, Otmar, Vitor Gaspar, and Oreste Tristani. *Monetary Policy in the Euro Area: Strategy and Decision Making at the European Central Bank.* New York: Cambridge University Press, 2001.

Kaltenthaler, Karl. *Policymaking in the European Central Bank: The Masters of Europe's Money.* Lanham, MD: Rowman & Littlefield, 2006.

Exchange Rates

Exchange rates—the values of individual currencies in terms of others—are a critical element in the international transmission of business cycles and in modern international financial crises. The exchange rate system that exists between international currencies lies at the heart of the economic crises experienced since the 1980s in Latin America, Eastern Europe, and Asia, since the exchange rate affects the capital flows, imports, exports, and terms of trade among countries in those regions.

Exchange rates play a major role in international business. If, for example, an American-made washing machine costs US$500, while a similar Mexican-made appliance costs 6,000 pesos, the Mexican product will be cheaper for an American to purchase if the exchange rate is 25 pesos per dollar (or 4 cents per peso), while the American machine will be cheaper for the American to buy if the exchange rate is 10 pesos per dollar (10 cents per peso). In the first case, if the exchange rate were 25 pesos per dollar, the American would have to pay only US$240 for the 6,000 pesos to purchase a Mexican appliance. If the exchange rate were 10 pesos per dollar or 10 cents per peso, the American would have to pay US$600 for the 6,000 pesos to purchase the machine. Hence in this case, the American would not purchase the machine made in Mexico. Thus, which machine is cheaper (the best buy) depends on the exchange rate at the time of the purchase.

Fluctuations in the exchange rate thus play a major role in determining the profitability of international trade, the direction of foreign investment, and the attractiveness of foreign tourism. Economists cite three major categories of exchange rates: nominal, real, and effective.

Nominal Exchange Rates

Exchange rates as described above—between the currencies of two countries without regard to inflation—are known as nominal exchange rates. Nominal rates between the U.S. dollar and major foreign currencies are reported daily by financial publications such as the *Wall Street Journal* and the *Financial Times*.

Exchange rates are set in a number of different ways. Some countries, like the United States, Canada, and Great Britain, let their currencies float freely, with the rate being determined entirely by supply and demand. Under such a system, if Americans want more British pounds—to buy British goods, to invest in Britain, or to travel in Britain—the increased demand will raise the price of the pound. Since demand and supply change from day to day, exchange rates also fluctuate

on a daily basis in a freely floating system. For a floating currency, a rise in the currency's value is called appreciation, while a fall in value is called depreciation. For example, if the yen/dollar exchange rate rises from 140 to 150, then the dollar has appreciated, since after the rise it is worth more yen (150 versus 140). Likewise, the yen has depreciated, because after the change it takes 150 yen to get US$1 while before the change it took only 140 yen to get US$1.

On the other hand, some countries adopt a fixed or pegged exchange rate mechanism, tying the value of their currency to another currency. Saudi Arabia, for example, has pegged its currency to the U.S. dollar at 3.75 riyals per dollar, a level it has maintained since the mid-1990s; similarly, the Lithuanian currency has been fixed at 3.5 litas per euro since 2002. A country with a fixed exchange rate maintains that rate artificially no matter what changes take place in the demand and supply of that currency by using its reserves of foreign currency. If, on a given day, demand for the Saudi riyal falls, leading to downward pressure on the price of the currency, the Saudi government sells some of its foreign currency reserves (U.S. dollars) and buys riyals. This puts more foreign (non-Saudi) currency into the foreign exchange market, thereby increasing the supply of those currencies; it also reduces the supply of riyals in the foreign exchange market. The result is an increase in the value of the riyal relative to the U.S. dollar, thus making up for the previous fall in price and maintaining the relationship between the two currencies, as required by the fixed relationship between the two.

Similarly, if demand for the riyal rises, creating upward pressure on its price, the government sells riyals and buys foreign currency. To maintain a fixed exchange rate, the government must have adequate reserves of foreign currency. If reserves are depleted as a result of supporting the value of the domestic currency, it may have to be pegged at a lower level. This kind of adjustment is known as devaluation, while repegging at a higher value is called a revaluation.

The euro is the second most traded currency in the world after the U.S. dollar. A relatively strong exchange rate has yielded increased foreign investments for many eurozone countries, but acute economic problems have persisted for some. *(Michel Porro/Stringer/ Getty Images)*

A country can also follow an exchange rate system known as a managed float. This has elements of both floating and fixed rate regimes. Many emerging economies, such as Brazil, China, and Singapore, follow a managed float. In this system, the currency does not have an official value that the government is committed to maintain, but it is not allowed to fluctuate freely in response to demand and supply, as the government tries to steer the value in a particular direction by buying and selling it in the foreign exchange market (using reserves). Thus, for example, China, which switched from a pegged system to a managed float in July 2005, allowed the yuan to rise gradually, from 12.3 U.S. cents to 14.6 cents in July 2008, before intervening to prevent a further rise over the next six months.

In all three of the above systems, the exchange rate is determined by market forces. In a freely floating system, only market forces come into play, while in a pegged rate or a managed float, governments intervene by buying or selling currencies to maintain the pegged rate. In some countries, however, market forces have little or no role, as the government sets a value for its currency and declares all other rates to be illegal. This typically leads to the rationing of foreign currencies, and often to black markets. In the past, many countries, such as China, India, and Russia, had such controlled exchange rates, but today they are relatively rare; Iran and Venezuela are among the few countries that maintain such a system.

Recent research shows that, under the flexible exchange rate system, business cycles are more synchronized, especially among the industrial countries.

Real Exchange Rates

Real exchange rates are used by economists to analyze the competitiveness of a country's products, based on changes in the nominal exchange rate as well as inflation in the country and its trading partners. Referring to the example of the American-made washing machine costing US$500 and a similar Mexican washing machine costing 6,000 pesos, one can see that the two products cost the same at an exchange rate of 12 pesos per dollar (or 8.3333 cents per peso). If the peso appreciates to 10 cents (one peso is now worth more—10 cents versus 8.3333 cents), the Mexican machine now costs the equivalent of US$600, or 20 percent more than its American counterpart. Mexican products thus become less competitive.

If, with the exchange rate unchanged, inflation in Mexico is higher than in the United States, the effect is the same. If inflation in the United States is zero, the American machine will cost the same (US$500) a year later. If inflation in Mexico is 20 percent, the Mexican machine will cost 7,200 pesos a year later—6,000 pesos plus (6,000 pesos times 20 percent)—or the equivalent of US$600 if the exchange rate remains unchanged at 12 pesos per dollar. Since the Mexican product is now less competitive by 20 percent, the peso is said to have undergone a real appreciation of 20 percent. Similarly, if the Mexican inflation of 20 percent is accompanied by U.S. inflation of 2 percent, Mexican products become less competitive by 18 percent—or there has been a real appreciation of 18 percent of the peso.

If there are changes in the nominal exchange rate and differences in inflation rates, the real exchange rate is especially useful for tracking competitiveness. In the situation where there is 20 percent inflation in Mexico and 2 percent inflation in the United States, a 10 percent nominal depreciation of the peso against the dollar—from 8.3333 cents to 7.5 cents, say—will reduce the price disadvantage faced by Mexican products by 10 percent. Specifically, the disadvantage will decrease from 18 percent to approximately 8 percent; the peso will have experienced a real appreciation of 8 percent.

Real exchange rates are closely monitored by international economists and organizations like the International Monetary Fund, since a country whose currency has undergone a strong real appreciation is going to find its products becoming less competitive on the international market. This is likely to lead to decreased exports and increased imports, and may ultimately generate a balance-of-payments crisis. Several transition economies in Eastern Europe, which tried to keep their currencies stable against the euro while undergoing higher inflation, found themselves in this predicament in the 1990s.

Effective Exchange Rates

An effective exchange rate is an index used to determine how a currency's value has changed against (or compared to) a group of currencies, usually those of major trading partners. In 2008, for example, the U.S. dollar rose by 24 percent against the Canadian dollar and by 4 percent against the Malaysian ringgit. If Canada and Malaysia had been the only trading partners of the United States, and if each accounted for half of U.S. trade, they would have been assigned equal weights and the effective value of the dollar would have risen by half of 28 percent, or 14 percent.

In practice, of course, effective exchange rates are calculated against a much larger number of currencies, with different weights. The Federal Reserve System, for example, publishes a trade-weighted index of the effective exchange rate of the U.S. dollar against a basket of twenty-six currencies, with weights varying from 17 percent for the euro to 0.5 percent for the Colombian peso. Similarly, the European Central Bank compiles an index showing the effective exchange rate of the euro against a basket of twenty-one currencies, with weights varying between 24 percent for the United States to 0.1 percent for Latvia.

Exchange Rates and Financial Crises

Exchange rates pose enormous risks for national economies, as well as for international businesses. Speculators can intensify—or even cause—a financial crisis by buying and selling currencies in anticipation of a specific event. Even if the expected event, such as political upheaval in a particular in a country, does not take place, the damage is done. Speculators have already bought and sold currencies on the foreign exchange market and have thereby weakened the value of that country's currency relative to other currencies. Moreover, less developed countries that borrow money from lenders in a more developed economy run the risk that foreign exchange movements will go in the wrong direction for them, making it harder to repay the loans and sending them deeper into debt and financial crisis. Note that the development of foreign exchange forward and options markets has been in response to the need of market participants in international trade to be able to reduce or hedge the risk of changes in the exchange rate eliminating their profits. However, these markets can also be used for speculation.

Just such developments occurred in the Asian financial crisis of 1997–1998. Massive overdevelopment of commercial real estate throughout Asia in the 1990s led to anticipation by currency speculators of large-scale foreclosures as developers could not repay loans to Asian banks. As a result, speculators started getting rid of Asian currencies by selling them onto the foreign exchange market. This led to rapid devaluation of Asian currencies, beginning with the Thai baht. The situation was made even worse by the so-called spillover or contagion effect. Asian banks, which had borrowed dollars from the United States and converted them into their own local currencies, now had to pay back the U.S. lenders in dollars—which proved more difficult as the value of their own currencies continued to plunge. As a result, the Asian economies, one by one, spun out of control. The disaster continued to resonate a decade later as the global financial crisis of 2008–2009 began heating up.

Animesh Ghoshal

See also: Balance of Payments; Capital Account; Current Account.

Further Reading

Ho, Lok-Sang, and Chi-Wa Yuen. *Exchange Rate Regimes and Macroeconomic Stability.* Boston: Kluwer Academic, 2003.

Krugman, Paul R., and Maurice Obstfeld. *International Economics: Theory and Policy.* Boston: Pearson Addison Wesley, 2009.

OANDA, The Currency Site Web site: www.oanda.com.

Rajan, Ramkishen, and Reza Siregar. "Choice of Exchange Rate Regime." *Australian Economic Papers* 41:4 (2002): 538–556.

Yarbrough, Beth V., and Robert M. Yarbrough. *The World Economy: Trade and Finance.* Mason, OH: South-Western, 2006.

Fannie Mae and Freddie Mac

Freddie Mac and Fannie Mae are two housing-related government-sponsored enterprises (GSEs) listed on the New York Stock Exchange. Both have the same charters, and both purchase and securitize home mortgages to ensure that private institutions that lend money to homebuyers have the funds to do so. At one time, Fannie Mae bought mortgages primarily from savings and loans (S&Ls), while Freddie Mac bought them from commercial banks. Today, the difference no longer holds. Both GSEs were implicated in the mortgage crisis of the late 2000s. According to some critics, their practices had encouraged too many aspiring homebuyers—including those with poor credit histories or inadequate incomes—to take out mortgages. Even so, backing about half of all mortgages issued in the United States inevitably left both institutions vulnerable to the wave of defaults that followed the bursting of the housing bubble beginning in 2007. In both cases, the federal government was forced to step in to avert financial catastrophe. Fannie Mae and Freddie Mac were placed under the conservatorship of the Federal Housing Finance Agency (FHFA) in September 2008.

Fannie Mae

The first of the two institutions, Fannie Mae (the Federal National Mortgage Association), was established as a federal agency in 1938 to support housing by increasing the supply of mortgage credit. In 1968, it was chartered by Congress as a private, shareholder–owned, government-sponsored company and split into two parts: Ginnie Mae (Government National Mortgage Association, which continued as a federal agency and concentrated on special assistance programs) and Fannie Mae. Until 1968, Fannie Mae could only buy mortgages insured by the Federal Housing Administration (FHA); after that it was also allowed to buy other mortgages.

Fannie Mae does not offer loans directly to homebuyers. Thus, even if Fannie Mae has bought a homeowner's mortgage, the borrower still sends his or her monthly mortgage payments to the loan servicers, who then forward them to Fannie Mae, which in turn passes them on to the holders of mortgage-backed securities, minus service fees. Fannie Mae also operates in the secondary mortgage market by packaging home loans into mortgage-backed securities, which make them easier to sell to investors. Selling the securities provides additional capital to lenders, which allows them in turn to lend money to new low-, moderate-, and middle-income customers. For better or for worse, mortgages become more available and affordable to prospective homebuyers.

The activities of Fannie Mae were modernized in 1992, providing a variety of financial services, products, and solutions to lenders and housing partners. It securitizes both single- and multifamily mortgage loans into Fannie Mae mortgage-backed securities funded by issuing debt securities in domestic and foreign capital markets. As the events of 2007–2008 made painfully clear, securitizing home mortgages puts the securities holder at greater risk should too many borrowers default. In addition to making homeownership possible for more Americans, Fannie Mae has also supported rental, workforce, and supportive housing for homeless people.

Washington, D.C.–based Fannie Mae and its sister organization, Freddie Mac, backed more than half of all mortgages in the United States before the housing bust of the late 2000s. The government assumed control of both institutions to avoid further turmoil. *(Karen Bleier/AFP/Getty Images)*

Freddie Mac

Freddie Mac (originally the Federal Home Loan Mortgage Corporation, but officially doing business as Freddie Mac since 1994) was founded by Congress in 1970 to support homeownership and rental housing, ending Fannie Mae's monopoly. Freddie Mac reduces the costs of housing finance, increases stability in the secondary market for residential mortgages and the liquidity of mortgage investments, improves the distribution of investment capital for residential mortgage financing, and thus helps more families (including those with low and moderate income) to buy, rent, and keep their homes if they have undertaken mortgage obligations. Freddie Mac is one of the biggest buyers of home mortgages in the United States. To raise funds, it issues debt securities.

The customers of Freddie Mac are predominantly mortgage lenders in the primary mortgage market, including mortgage bankers, commercial banks, savings institutions, credit unions, and state and local housing finance agencies. Freddie Mac buys mortgage loans from lenders, packages the mortgages into securities, holds some in its retained portfolio for investment purposes, and sells the rest to investors, including banks, pension funds, and others. Moreover, it guarantees that investors will receive payment of principal and interest on time. The lenders can then use the received funds for lending to other customers. In this way, Freddie Mac helps finance one out of six American homes—not only single-family houses, but buildings with rental housing as well.

Freddie Mac's role is not directly visible to homebuyers because, like Fannie Mae, it does not offer loans directly. Nevertheless, its activities result in more readily available home mortgage credit, lower mortgage interest rates, a broader selection of mortgage products, and reduced origination costs. Thanks to Freddie Mac, economists estimate that homebuyers save up to 0.5 percent on their mortgage rate, helping them collectively to save at least $23.5 billion every year.

Although Freddie Mac does not prescribe to

lenders how much they should lend and to whom, it does offer guidelines and has developed a system called Loan Prospector to help lenders make sound financial decisions. The system helps lenders determine whether a borrower will be able to repay the mortgage on time and if the property value is sufficient to pay off the mortgage if the borrower is not able to continue regular payments.

Mortgage Crisis

In the late 1990s and early 2000s, several developments encouraged Fannie Mae and Freddie Mac to begin purchasing and securitizing riskier home mortgages. Under pressure from both the Bill Clinton and George W. Bush administrations to expand homeownership, the two GSEs began to ease credit requirements on the mortgages they would buy from lending institutions, allowing the same institutions to offer mortgages to riskier clients at higher interest rates. With housing prices rising steadily, this seemed safe to Fannie Mae and Freddie Mac investors, who drove up the price of the GSEs' stock.

Although one of the goals was to provide safe standards for subprime mortgages, the opposite occurred. The lending industry began offering all kinds of adjustable mortgages not backed by Fannie Mae and Freddie Mac that could hit borrowers with huge increases in their monthly payments once the low initial "teaser" rates expired. When housing prices began to deflate beginning in 2007, many of these borrowers found that they lacked the equity needed to refinance and went into default.

While Fannie Mae and Freddie Mac were not exposed to the worst of the subprime mortgage business, the sheer volume of loans they purchased proved devastating when the wave of foreclosures began to affect lower-risk mortgages in 2008. By July, the situation had become so perilous for the two GSEs that the federal government announced plans for a possible takeover, sending the share prices of Fannie Mae and Freddie Mac plunging.

Meanwhile, the government restructured its regulatory and supervisory oversight of the GSEs, shifting responsibility from the Office of Federal Housing Enterprise Oversight (OFHEO) in the Department of Housing and Urban Development (HUD), where it had resided since 1992, to the new Federal Housing Finance Agency (FHFA). The latter agency was created by the Housing and Economic Recovery Act of 2008, taking over the functions of OFHEO and the Federal Housing Finance Board. FHFA was granted the authority to set minimum limits on Fannie Mae and Freddie Mac capital, to regulate the size and content of their portfolios, and to approve or disallow new mortgage products.

In February 2009, Freddie Mac and Fannie Mae began participating in President Barack Obama's Homeowner Affordability and Stability Plan, designed to help 4 million to 5 million solvent homeowners refinance their mortgages and reduce monthly payments through the two institutions, and to help another 3 million to 4 million at-risk homeowners avoid losing their properties. To help reach these goals and to reassure investors that the two GSEs have the full backing of the federal government, the Treasury Department increased its funding commitment to Freddie Mac and Fannie Mae.

Tiia Vissak and James Ciment

See also: Housing Booms and Busts; Mortgage Lending Standards; Mortgage Markets and Mortgage Rates; Mortgage, Subprime; Recession and Financial Crisis (2007–).

Further Reading

Fannie Mae Web site: www.fanniemae.com.

Federal Housing Finance Agency Web site: www.fhfa.gov.

Freddie Mac Web site: www.freddiemac.com.

Ginnie Mae Web site: www.ginnaemae.gov.

Leonnig, Carol D. "How HUD Mortgage Policy Fed the Crisis." *Washington Post*, June 10, 2008.

Office of Federal Housing Enterprise Oversight Web site: www.ofheo.gov.

Federal Deposit Insurance Corporation

Created at the height of the banking crisis in 1933, the Federal Deposit Insurance Corporation

(FDIC) is an independent government agency responsible for maintaining public confidence by providing deposit insurance for banks and thrifts, monitoring and dealing with risks to depositor funds, and ensuring that bank or thrift failures have minimal impact on the economy and financial system. The FDIC is self-supporting, funding its activities through premiums paid by banks and thrifts for insurance on their deposits. The FDIC also invests in U.S. Treasury securities. During the financial crisis of 2007–2009, the FDIC was forced to assume control of several troubled banks, though no depositor lost any money in the process.

The FDIC has approximately 5,000 employees, six regional offices, and multiple field offices. Its five-member board of directors is appointed by the president and confirmed by the Senate. The FDIC supervises more than half of all U.S. banking institutions; it also acts as a backup overseer of other thrifts and banks and as a regulator of state-chartered banks that are not members of the Federal Reserve. When a chartering authority—state regulator, Office of Thrift Supervision, or comptroller of the currency—closes a bank or thrift, the FDIC commonly sells deposits and loans to another institution and transfers customers automatically to the new bank.

The origins of the FDIC go back to the depression of the 1890s, when several leading politicians began to talk about federal protection for depositors of failed banks. Democratic presidential standard-bearer William Jennings Bryan, for one, proposed that funds be set aside by the federal government to help banks withstand financial panic-induced runs by depositors. At about the same time, states began establishing deposit security programs. With the creation of the Federal Reserve System in 1913, the United States created a central bank that would become a lender of last resort to member banks, though these were larger and usually safer institutions.

The state–Federal Reserve combination worked well until the Great Depression. Between the stock market crash of 1929 and the bank holi-

day of 1933, when newly inaugurated president Franklin Roosevelt closed the nation's banks to stop panic withdrawals, more than 9,000 banks across America shut down. The federal government responded by merging failed banks with stronger ones and, after months of delay, paid depositors about 85 percent of their deposits.

While Roosevelt himself remained skeptical of a federal protection on bank deposits, many in his administration and in Congress believed it was necessary. In 1933, Congress passed the Glass-Steagall Act, which established the FDIC to restore public confidence in the financial system by insuring deposits. Although many bankers opposed the concept of an insurance fund, the FDIC quickly covered 19,000 banking offices, guaranteeing deposits up to $2,500 per depositor. With the establishment of the FDIC, the nation's banking system stabilized and only nine insured banks failed in 1934. Moreover, since the FDIC opened for business on January 1, 1934, no depositor has ever lost any deposit in an insured banking account.

The FDIC became permanent under the Banking Act of 1935. The FDIC's initial funding was $289 million, lent by the U.S. Treasury and Federal Reserve, which it repaid in 1948. By the early 2000s, the insurance fund exceeded $45 billion, covering more than $5 trillion in deposits.

The insurance ceiling guaranteed by the FDIC has risen periodically over time. Under the Banking Act of 1935, it was raised to $5,000. The Federal Deposit Insurance Act of 1950 raised the limit to $10,000 and authorized FDIC lending to a member bank in danger of closing if it were deemed essential to its community. Additional insurance limit increases came in 1966, 1969, and 1974, with the $100,000 limit set by the Depository Institutions Deregulation and Monetary Control Act of 1980. The current insurance limit was set at $250,000 per depositor on October 3, 2008, as a temporary measure in response to the financial crisis.

The limit covers all accounts of a single depositor, but a depositor who owns multiple types of accounts—single or joint accounts or retirement IRAs and Keoghs, for instance—is covered to the maximum for each type. Accounts in separate banks are insured separately, but accounts in separate branches of the same bank are treated as one account. FDIC insurance does not cover securities, mutual funds, or other bank and thrift investment vehicles.

The FDIC's protections were utilized relatively infrequently during the economic boom of the post–World War II era. Commercial banks, heavily regulated, were conservative in their lending practices and barred from engaging in other potentially riskier businesses, such as investment banking. The savings and loan (S&L) crisis of the late 1980s and early 1990s was the first major postwar test of the FDIC. While thrifts are protected by their own federal insurance program—Federal Savings and Loan Insurance Corporation (FSLIC)—the FDIC was forced to step in to protect depositors when its sister agency ran out of funds. During the S&L crisis, lax regulation opened the way to a glut of bad loans that cost the industry hundreds of billions of dollars.

The FDIC has also played a key role in the financial crisis of the late 2000s. Under its widely respected director, Sheila Blair, the agency, in the spring of 2008, became one of the first to warn that the U.S. banking industry was facing unprecedented stress due to the collapse of the subprime mortgage market. By the summer, the crisis was full blown and the FDIC was forced to step in and cover the deposits of a number of failing banks. The best-known case was that of IndyMac, a California bank with some $19 billion in deposits. The FDIC took over the institution, creating what was known as a "bridge bank" to manage its assets and liabilities, before transferring its assets to the newly created OneWest Bank.

By mid-2009, the FDIC had taken over more than seventy banks during the financial crisis. Although this was a historically high number, it was well below the total for the early 1990s, during the aftermath of the S&L crisis. Nevertheless, the failures left the agency's Deposit Insurance Fund

nearly depleted, down from more than $45 billion in mid-2008 to just over $13 billion in mid-2009. In response, the FDIC imposed an emergency fee on member banks to shore up the fund.

James Ciment and John Barnhill

See also: Banks, Commercial; Great Depression (1929–1933); New Deal; Regulation, Financial.

Further Reading

FDIC Web site: www.fdic.gov.

Seidman, L. William. *Full Faith and Credit: The Great S&L Debacle and Other Washington Sagas.* New York: Times Books, 1993.

Federal Housing Administration

An agency of the U.S. Department of Housing and Urban Development (HUD), the Federal Housing Administration (FHA) insures mortgages on homes, multifamily dwellings, manufactured (or mobile) homes, and hospitals. By doing so, the FHA allows lenders to offer mortgages at more competitive rates for homebuyers with low incomes or limited credit histories.

Lenders whose loans meet FHA standards enjoy several benefits. They are insured against default by mortgagors, which allows lenders to be more flexible in calculating payment ratios and household income. For their part, buyers can qualify more easily because the government, not the lender, assumes the risk. The mortgagor pays the monthly insurance premium as part of the mortgage.

As of 2009, the FHA required less than a 3.5 percent down payment, compared to a conventional down payment of 5 percent or more. Mortgagors can also borrow the costs of mortgage insurance and closing fees, whereas conventional loans require payment of these costs with the down payment. The FHA also allows a larger percentage of personal income to be spent on housing than would normally be the case with private lenders.

Since its creation in 1934, to help jump-start a housing industry crippled by the Great Depression, the FHA has insured some 35 million mortgages, with nearly 5 million currently on its books. Because the agency maintained strict standards regarding the types of mortgages it would insure, the FHA was not overly exposed to the subprime mortgage crisis that began in 2007. Yet with the recession that followed, especially high unemployment rates, many economic analysts fear a wave of foreclosures on FHA-insured properties, which might subject the agency to tens of billions of dollars in losses. Typically, FHA-backed loans require a very small down payment, leaving many homebuyers in upside-down mortgages—those in which the homeowner ends up owing more than the house is worth, which lead many to abandon their properties rather than struggle to pay a mortgage they can no longer afford.

Prior to the creation of the FHA, home mortgages were difficult to finance for most working- and lower-middle-class Americans. Lenders often required a down payment of 50 percent or more, followed by several years of interest-only payments, with a large balloon payment at the end. Thus, when the Great Depression began in the 1930s, just 40 percent of Americans owned the homes they lived in. With the credit markets frozen during the early years of the Great Depression, the housing market collapsed as homebuyers found it difficult to get financing to make their balloon payments. Foreclosure rates soared, dampening lender interest in financing new construction. Annual housing starts fell from about 700,000 in the late 1920s to just 93,000 in 1933. Millions of construction workers were laid off in the slump, adding to an unemployment rate that topped 25 percent.

The FHA offered a revolutionary new approach to mortgage financing. By backing loans 100 percent, it reassured lenders that they would not be stuck with foreclosed properties. The agency also helped promote a new form of mortgage, which became standard—one with a relatively small

down payment, followed by principal and interest payments that would amortize over a longer period, typically twenty or thirty years.

The FHA has helped promote homebuying ever since. In the late 1940s and early 1950s, it provided the insurance for mortgages taken out by hundreds of thousands of returning World War II veterans. Beginning in the 1950s, it was active in helping marginalized groups, including minorities and the elderly, secure mortgages. Today, African-Americans and Latinos generate about one-fourth of FHA business, compared to less than one-tenth of conforming conventional mortgages. Through the decades, FHA standards have fluctuated. When standards are high, the number of loans drops; when standards are low the number of loans rises. In addition, during slumps in the housing market, such as those in states hit hard by the oil price slump of the 1980s, the FHA has stepped in to replace private mortgage insurers, thereby steadying housing markets.

While the FHA has backed millions of mortgages over the years, this figure is small compared to the overall mortgage market. But by helping to foster easier mortgage terms for those who are eligible, the FHA has played an outsized role in the U.S. housing boom of the post–World War II era, which has seen homeownership rates (the percentage of occupied housing units being occupied by the owner) climb to more than two-thirds. But as private lenders began to market mortgages to more and more homebuyers, conservative politicians and commentators began to wonder why the federal government was in the business of insuring home mortgages, and there were calls in Congress to abolish the FHA in the 1990s and early 2000s.

The subprime mortgage crisis largely ended such talk, as it became clear that the FHA's twin role as a setter of lending standards and as a backer of mortgages to financially less secure homebuyers were more crucial than ever. Indeed, in 2008, the FHA came forward with two new programs to help troubled mortgagors. One allowed the agency to refinance adjustable rate mortgages—whose monthly payments could soar once the initial "teaser" rate expired—to fixed-rate thirty-year mortgages. The applicants, however, had to have at least 3 percent equity in their homes and had to meet standard income qualifications. These requirements left many of the most vulnerable unable to qualify.

For homeowners in difficult circumstances—specifically, those whose mortgage balance exceeded the market value of the home and whose monthly mortgage payments exceeded 31 percent of gross income—a second program was initiated. If the mortgagee could get the lender to agree to a 90 percent settlement on the principal, the homeowner could refinance with an FHA-guaranteed mortgage at a thirty-year fixed rate. However, housing experts worried that because lenders were not mandated to accept the partial write-down on the principal, few would participate in the program.

Meanwhile, the FHA was facing operational problems that made its job even more difficult and its programs less effective. Short of adequate staff, the agency was unable to properly police the mortgages it guaranteed, meaning that many were offered by private lenders to persons who did not meet FHA standards for potential solvency. This, say economic analysts, means that the FHA could be exposed to up to $100 billion in losses by 2015, as many of the mortgage holders go into default and the agency is left to foot the bill to private lenders.

John Barnhill and James Ciment

See also: Mortgage Lending Standards; Mortgage Markets and Mortgage Rates; New Deal.

Further Reading

Federal Housing Administration Web site: www.fha.com.

Federal Housing Administration. "The History of FHA." Available at www.hud.gov/offices/hsg/fhahistory.cfm. Accessed May 2010.

Hays, R. Allen. *The Federal Government and Urban Housing.* Albany: State University of New York Press, 1995.

Wright, Gwendolyn. *Building the Dream: A Social History of Housing in America.* Cambridge, MA: MIT Press, 1983.

Federal Housing Enterprise Oversight, Office of

In operation from 1992 through 2008, the Office of Federal Housing Enterprise Oversight (OFHEO) was responsible for maintaining a stable housing sector, largely by collecting data and through oversight of the quasi-governmental mortgage insurers the Federal National Mortgage Association (Fannie Mae) and the Federal Home Loan Mortgage Corporation (Freddie Mac). Lacking enough funding and the power to impose changes on the insurers, OFHEO, say many experts, was unable to prevent the excesses of the subprime mortgage market in the mid-2000s—excesses that helped lead to the financial crisis of 2008–2009.

OFHEO was established by the Federal Housing Enterprises Financial Safety and Soundness Act in 1992 as an agency within the Department of Housing and Urban Development (HUD), with the broad mission of supporting a stable housing sector. To that end, it promoted more available and affordable home financing, meeting affordable housing and homeownership goals set every year by the secretary of HUD and, most importantly, ensuring that Fannie Mae and Freddie Mac, which owned or guaranteed more than 40 percent of residential mortgages in the United States, remained financially safe and sound. OFHEO did not receive taxpayer dollars but instead was funded through assessments on Fannie Mae and Freddie Mac. (Note that Fannie Mae and Freddie Mac were put into conservatorship by the U.S. government on September 7, 2008.)

After 1996, OFHEO also published the quarterly (later, monthly) house price index, measuring average seasonally adjusted price changes in repeat sales or refinancing on the same single-family properties in different geographic areas. The index was based on purchase prices of houses backed by mortgages that had been sold to or guaranteed by Freddie Mac or Fannie Mae since 1975. Between

1975 and 1995, there were 6.9 million of these repeat transactions. The sole use of these repeat transactions in the house price index minimized the problem of quality differences and thus, the index also has been called a "constant quality" house price index.

To fulfill its goals, OFHEO had to examine Fannie Mae and Freddie Mac regularly and provide an annual report of the results of these examinations to Congress. In addition, OFHEO had to adjust Fannie Mae and Freddie Mac loan limits every year, develop new risk-based capital standards, calculate capital adequacy, simulate stressful interest rate and credit risk scenarios, prohibit excessive executive compensation, issue regulations concerning capital and enforcement standards, oversee the reporting of suspected or actual mortgage fraud (in cooperation with the Financial Crimes Enforcement Network), and take necessary enforcement actions.

According to its strategic plan for 2006–2011, OFHEO initiated a special examination of Fannie Mae and Freddie Mac in 2003 and identified serious accounting, internal control, and management weaknesses. Misstated earnings were estimated to be $16 billion, resulting in fines of $500 million and lawsuits totaling over $1 billion, while remedial costs exceeded $2 billion. Moreover, their portfolios of mortgage assets grew at annual rates that considerably exceeded residential mortgage market growth. As a result of these findings, OFHEO strengthened its efforts to address these problems and to check that Freddie Mac and Fannie Mae were making required improvements. However, it lacked independent funding authority and bank regulator–like powers to reduce the possibility of a systemic disruption in the financial sector. This limited its capacity to implement long-term planning and negated its ability to react quickly if serious problems emerged with the two enterprises—for instance, if they needed assistance during an exceptional economic crisis.

With the Housing and Economic Recovery Act of 2008 (signed by President George W. Bush

on July 30, 2008), Congress abolished OFHEO and combined its functions with those of the Federal Housing Finance Board (FHFB) and HUD's mission group to form the new Federal Housing Finance Agency (FHFA). All regulations, orders, and determinations of these agencies continued to be incorporated into the new agency while its authority was expanded to increase its ability to oversee the country's secondary mortgage markets.

FHFA started regulating the activities of the Office of Finance and fourteen housing-related, government-sponsored enterprises (GSEs): Fannie Mae, Freddie Mac, and the twelve Federal Home Loan Banks (in Atlanta, Boston, Chicago, Cincinnati, Dallas, Des Moines, Indianapolis, New York, Pittsburgh, San Francisco, Seattle, and Topeka). These banks were created in 1932 for providing additional funds to local lenders for financing loans for home mortgages. They provide liquidity for more than 8,000 member lenders, mainly through two key housing programs—the Affordable Housing Program and the Community Investment Program—and this allows those lenders to continue financing the purchase, construction, or rehabilitation of affordable owner-occupied or rental housing and the economic development of low- to moderate-income neighborhoods during economic crises. In June 2008, the combined debt and obligations of these fourteen GSEs was $6.6 trillion. They also purchased or guaranteed 84 percent of new mortgages. The regulation of twelve Federal Home Loan Banks was previously performed by FHFB.

The Federal Housing Finance Agency also began publishing the FHFA monthly index (the former OFHEO monthly house price index) for nine census divisions, the fifty states and the District of Columbia and all 363 metropolitan statistical areas (11 of the metropolitan statistical areas are further divided into 29 metropolitan divisions). Index values are only provided for periods where at least 1,000 transactions have been made.

Tiia Vissak

See also: Fannie Mae and Freddie Mac; Housing Booms and Busts.

Further Reading

Calhoun, Charles A. "OFHEO House Price Indexes: HPI Technical Description." Available at www.ofheo.gov/Media/Archive/house/hpi_tech.pdf. Accessed February 2009.

Federal Housing Finance Agency Web site: www.fhfa.gov.

Federal Housing Finance Board Web site: www.fhfb.gov.

"Housing and Economic Recovery Act of 2008." Available at www.ofheo.gov/media/pdf/HR3221FINAL.pdf. Accessed February 2009.

Smith, John, ed. *The Rescue and Repair of Fannie Mae and Freddie Mac.* Hauppauge, NY: Nova Science, 2009.

Federal Reserve System

The Federal Reserve System—often referred to as the "Fed"—is the American approximation of a central bank. Like the central banks of many other countries, the Fed regulates banks and other financial institutions and sets the federal government's monetary policy, with the goals of maintaining a stable financial sector, reining in inflation, and assuring sustained economic growth. The Fed differs from most other central banks in that it has a decentralized structure with twelve regional banks, but its most important decision making remains with the central board of governors.

Operations

Founded in 1913, the Federal Reserve System consists of a board of governors seated in Washington, D.C., and twelve regional Federal Reserve banks. The Fed is the primary institution for setting monetary policy in the United States. It has several tools at its disposal to achieve this, the most important being its purchase and sale of U.S. Treasury and other federal agency securities. The Fed also establishes the minimum capital requirements its member banks must maintain against outstanding obligations and it sets the discount rate—the rate it charges thousands of private member banks to borrow money. (All federally chartered banks must be members of the Fed, while state-chartered banks can apply for membership.) The discount rate—which is nominally set by the Reserve banks but is in fact controlled by the board of governors—is more of a symbol, signifying the Fed's open market actions of buying and selling federal securities. In addition, since the 2008 financial crisis, the Fed has also supported bank liquidity by directly buying bank assets, a new policy whose future is unclear.

Regulating the expansion of the nation's money supply, a key tool in fighting inflation or spurring economic growth, is the responsibility of the Federal Open Market Committee (FOMC), which consists of the board of governors, the president of the Federal Reserve Bank of New York—the most important of the regional banks—and, on a rotating basis, the presidents of the other eleven regional banks.

The board of governors oversees the operations, reviews the budgets, and otherwise controls the activities of the twelve regional banks. At the same time, those regional banks act as the operating arm of the Fed. The regional banks resemble private corporations—and are often confused as such—issuing stock to member banks. However, the stock is not issued for the purposes of making a profit but because member banks by law must hold a specific amount of Fed stock. Dividends are set at 6 percent per annum, and the stock cannot be sold, traded, or used as security. The Fed is both a not-for-profit and a nonprivate entity.

The Fed enjoys a great deal of independence, sometimes attributed to the goal of political independence, preventing, for example, a situation in which politicians might want to expand the money supply and produce economic expansion in pre-election periods, thereby jeopardizing long-term stability. Members of the board of governors are appointed by the president—and confirmed by the Senate—for a single fourteen-year term, with the seven members' appointments staggered every two years. The president also chooses—and the Senate also confirms—the chair and vice chair from the board for a renewable four-year term. Along with these relatively long terms of office, the board's freedom of action is assured by its independent source of funding. Rather than relying on tax dollars—and, hence, Congress—the board pays for its operations through interest on federal securities, interest on foreign currency holdings, and loans to member banks, investments, and fees for services, such as check clearing and transfer of funds. Any excess of income beyond the Fed's own needs goes to the U.S. Treasury.

Critics of the Fed point out that independence gives the Fed wide latitude to follow economic policies in line with its primary constituency, the banking system, thus perhaps paying less attention to consumer interests and worrying more about banks' fears of inflation than concerns about unemployment. There is potential oversight of the Fed, including most importantly, twice-annual reports to Congress and occasional congressional debate when a new governor is under consideration or new responsibilities are considered for the Fed. In addition, the Fed banks and board are reviewed annually by an outside auditor. Other watchdogs include the Government Accountability Office and the board's own inspector general.

History

Antecedents of the Fed go back to 1791 and the creation of the First Bank of the United States. Modeled after the Bank of England, it was part of Secretary of the Treasury Alexander Hamilton's efforts to secure a sound financial footing for the nascent republic. Funded largely by government capital, along with some from private investors, the bank issued notes, or currency, and lent money to the government. In 1811, the bank's charter lapsed and it took five more years for the Second Bank of the United States—which was also given a twenty-year charter—to begin operation. Like the First Bank of the United States, the second was not popular with those who felt it gave the federal government too much control over the nation's economy. In 1836, President Andrew

Jackson vetoed its rechartering, ending America's first attempts at maintaining a central bank.

For the next twenty-seven years, the U.S. banking system remained a hodgepodge of state-chartered or privately owned banks, each issuing its own banknotes, and all competing to keep their money at face value. The diverse types of money and highly variable reliability of the different banks made interstate economic activity difficult. In 1863, Congress established a system of "national" banks, with standard operations, minimum capitalization, and rules for lending and administering loans. A 10 percent tax on nonfederal currency effectively removed all but the federal currency from circulation.

Still, many economists argued then and since that the lack of a central bank exacerbated the volatility of the U.S. economy in the nineteenth and early twentieth centuries, since it denied the federal government any effective means for setting a monetary policy that might smooth out the business cycle.

While private bankers, led by J.P. Morgan, were able to rescue the nation's financial sector from the effects of the Panic of 1907, many financiers and economists concluded that it was time America—now the world's leading industrialized country—had a central bank. But the politics were tricky. While easterners wanted the economic stability a central bank would provide, with its power to regulate the money supply, westerners and southerners feared that the bank would choke off the easy credit they needed to expand their relatively underdeveloped economies. In 1913, Congress compromised by creating the noncentralized central bank known as the Federal Reserve.

But if stabilizing the economy via the money supply was the intended goal of the Fed, it did not do such a good job in its first decades of operation. Many economic historians say its rapid expansion of the money supply fueled the real-estate and stock market bubbles of the 1920s, while its rapid contraction of the money supply deepened the effects of the Great Depression.

The Federal Reserve System—consisting of twelve regional banks—was established in 1913 to serve as the central bank of the United States. The board of governors meets at the Marriner S. Eccles Federal Reserve Board Building in Washington, D.C. *(Bloomberg/Getty Images)*

After World War II, the Fed adopted the dominant Keynesian economic paradigm of countercyclical monetary policy. That is, it lowered interest rates during recessions, hence expanding the money supply, and it raised the rates during times of expansion. But the paradigm was tested in the 1970s, when such countercyclical actions failed to control an economic phenomenon known as "stagflation," a combination of slow or negative growth and high inflation.

The monetary school rose up in the postwar era in response to the Keynesians. Led by University of Chicago economist Milton Friedman, the monetarists argued that economic growth was best assured by creating a stable monetary supply, expanding only to meet the needs of a growing economy rather than trying to control economic expansion. Such thinking came to be incorporated into Fed decision making during the late 1970s and early 1980s, but this was short-lived.

Under the chairmanship of Paul Volcker, which began in 1979, the Fed imposed a dramatic tightening of credit—and the money supply—as a way to wring inflation out of the economy. It was effective, though at a cost—the 1981–1982 recession that many economists agree was triggered by the Fed's action was the worst since the Great Depression.

During the 1980s, the focus gradually shifted toward attaining a specified level of the federal funds rate, a process that was largely complete by the end of the decade. Beginning in 1994, the FOMC began announcing changes in its policy stance, and in 1995 it began to explicitly state its target level for the federal funds rate. Since February 2000, the statement issued by the FOMC shortly after each of its meetings usually has included the committee's assessment of the risks to the attainment of its long-run goals of price stability and sustainable economic growth.

2007–2009 Financial Crisis

Many also blame the Fed for the dot.com stock market bubble of the late 1990s and early 2000s and the housing bubble of the early and mid-2000s that triggered the worst financial crisis since the Great Depression. Eager to lift the economy out of the recession of 2001–2002, Chairman Alan Greenspan dramatically lowered the prime interest rate the Fed charged member banks, from 6 percent in 2000 to just 1 percent in 2003. Moreover, the Fed was very slow to raise the rate again, despite growing evidence that the low rates were fueling an unsustainable run-up in housing prices. (Since most people borrow money to buy homes, interest rates are a key factor in housing prices.)

When the housing bubble burst, setting off the financial crisis of 2007–2009, the Fed, which had been gradually raising rates, reversed itself again. In 2002, before becoming Fed chairman, Ben Bernanke, a student of the Great Depression, indicated that he supported the theory Milton Friedman and Anna Schwartz set forth in their *Monetary History of the United States, 1867–1960*, which said that rather than keeping the downturn from taking banks under, as was its mandate, the Fed exacerbated the Great Depression by contracting the money supply by one-third and letting one-third of U.S. banks, generally smaller ones, fail under a philosophy of weeding out the unfit.

Bernanke indicated that he did not intend the Fed to be the culprit when the next cycle turned downward. In 2007 he got his chance. The Fed has historically intervened aggressively in America's financial crises, and the bust of 2007–2009 was no exception. In December 2008 the board cut the key interest rate to what it called a "target range" of zero to 0.25 percent. The cut was the ninth in fourteen months. The FOMC cited deteriorating labor markets and slowed consumer spending, business investment, and industrial production, as well as stressed credit and financial markets. At the same time it indicated that it did not intend to raise rates anytime soon.

But the Fed did more than merely lower interest rates. In November 2008, it began buying the mortgage-backed securities at the heart of the crisis in an attempt to shore up the housing market. The November purchases were a partial realization of the Fed's decision to spend $500 billion on mortgage-backed securities backed by Fannie Mae and Freddie Mac, the quasi-governmental mortgage insurers, and to spend another $100 billion buying mortgages held by Fannie Mae, Freddie Mac, and the Federal Home Loan Banks directly. The loans were reported as investment grade, not the subprime packages that had sparked the crisis in 2007. The intent was

to lower the cost of mortgages and make loans more readily available.

Announcement of the plan cut rates about half a percentage point and produced a noticeable increase in mortgage refinancing. However, while many economists believe the Fed's moves helped slow the rapid decline in housing prices, it was unable, as of late 2009, to lift that key sector of the economy out of its worst slump of the post–World War II era.

John Barnhill and James Ciment

See also: Banks, Central; Banks, Commercial; Bernanke, Ben; Burns, Arthur; Greenspan, Alan; Monetary Policy; Regulation, Financial; Volcker, Paul.

Further Reading

Federal Reserve System Web site: www.federalreserve.gov.

Greider, William. *Secrets of the Temple: How the Federal Reserve Runs the Country.* New York: Simon & Schuster, 1989.

Hetzel, Robert L. *The Monetary Policy of the Federal Reserve.* New York: Cambridge University Press, 2008.

Fellner, William John (1905–1983)

William John Fellner earned a doctorate in economics from the University of Berlin in 1929, joined the faculty of the University of California–Berkeley, in 1939, became a U.S. citizen in 1944, and became a full professor at Berkeley in 1947. He left Berkeley for Yale University, becoming a professor of economics there in 1952, and retiring in 1973.

Beginning in 1964, Fellner chaired, with Princeton University professor Fritz Machlup, a series of conferences that drew thirty-two economists from academic institutions around the world for the purpose of discussing alternative exchange rate regimes to replace the gold standard that had been established by the Bretton Woods Agreement in 1944. The group, known as the Princeton-Bellagio Study Group on International Monetary Reform, met eighteen times between 1964 and

1977 in Bellagio, Italy, Washington, D.C., and Princeton, New Jersey, as well as in eight other European centers.

In 1969, Fellner became president of the American Economic Association. He was appointed in 1973 to the Council of Economic Advisers, taking on the assignment in the same year that Richard M. Nixon resigned the U.S. presidency, and concluding his tenure in 1975. Thereafter, he consulted for the Congressional Budget Office on issues of taxation and inflation and returned to a life of scholarship with the American Enterprise Institute.

Competition Among the Few

Fellner's book *Competition Among the Few* (1949) describes the tacit collusion of big firms within the same industry to protect their common interests, control competition, and avoid conflict, taking their prices from the most dominant firm in the industry without any direct contact. Fellner's work made a significant contribution to our understanding of industry concentration and isomorphism (sameness), and of the impact of large firms on wages, prices, and inflation.

Wage and Price Controls in a Full Employment Strategy

Fellner believed that the pursuit of a full employment strategy—a condition in which every individual who is willing and able to work at the prevailing wages and working conditions does so—led monopolistic groups of industrialists and workers to consistently raise wages and prices, thereby accelerating inflation and resulting in a government policy of wage and price controls. In Fellner's view, unemployed individuals holding out for higher wages should not be included among measures of the involuntarily unemployed. He advised raising the target unemployment rate from 4 percent to 5 percent to deal with the inevitable frictions in the employment market. Fellner advocated implementing a fed-erally subsidized employment program to offset the hardship of the 5 percent target and government spending aimed at avoiding big recessions while letting small ones run their course.

Rational Expectations and Credibility: Impact on Inflation

Fellner is associated with the rational expectations theory, which asserts that economic outcomes do not differ regularly or predictably from what people expect them to be, and with the concept of "credibility" as it is applied to policy makers. In his book *Towards a Reconstruction of Macroeconomics* (1976), Fellner argued that there is a game of strategy going on between policy makers and the public: each anticipates and acts on assumptions about the other's future responses. Further, the public attaches probability judgments to the way in which the behavior of the authorities may be influenced by the behavior of the public. Hence, expectations based on presumed future behavior underscore the importance of credibility. For example, government policy to combat inflation will be effective only if businesses and workers are convinced that the rising unemployment and declining real output brought on by demand-management strategies will not be followed by a reversal of policy. If government policy lacks credibility, then wages and prices will be rolled back, and a reduction in real output will be required to control inflation.

Although Fellner had reservations about some of the propositions of rational expectations theory and the emerging monetarist view, he felt that both offered policy guidance that was superior to the mix of policy solutions known as "neo-Keynesian fine-tuning" because monetarism focused on a single policy variable—namely, the money supply.

Carol M. Connell

See also: Council of Economic Advisers, U.S.; Deflation; Fisher's Debt-Deflation Theory; Inflation; Price Stability; Wages.

Further Reading

Fellner, William J. *Competition Among the Few: Oligopoly and Similar Market Structures.* New York: Alfred A. Knopf, 1949.

———. *Towards a Reconstruction of Macroeconomics: Problems of Theory and Policy.* Washington, DC: American Enterprise Institute for Public Policy Research, 1976.

Sobel, Robert, and Bernard S. Katz, eds. *Biographical Directory of the Council of Economic Advisors.* New York: Greenwood, 1988.

Spulber, Nicolas. *Managing the American Economy, from Roosevelt to Reagan.* Bloomington: Indiana University Press, 1989.

Financial Development/ Deepening

The concept of financial development/deepening has two defining aspects. First, financial development/deepening represents growth in the quantity of financial assets relative to gross domestic product. The higher this ratio, the greater the opportunity for individuals to use their savings productively and for investors to obtain financing for their investment plans. Second, financial development/deepening yields an increase in the variety of assets available to savers and investors, thus allowing for risk diversification. In short, financial development/deepening involves an increase in both the quantity and the variety of assets that the financial system offers to savers and investors.

The role of the financial system in any market economy is to serve as an intermediary between those who wish to save (consume less than their income) and those who wish to invest. Many individuals who save are not prepared to invest because they lack the skill, knowledge, or inclination to incur risk. Those who are willing to invest may not be able to finance their ventures with their own savings, as the investment may require levels of funding that are beyond any individual's saving capability. Thus, the financial system collects the resources of the savers and makes them available to investors. A return is paid to those who save, and interest is charged to those who borrow (investors).

The interest rate charged to borrowers (investors) exceeds that paid to savers—this is how the financial system profits by acting as an intermediary.

The financial system offers savers a variety of assets or forms in which to hold their savings. These include simple savings accounts offered by banks; accounts at nonbank intermediaries, such as brokerage firms, credit unions, and savings and loan institutions; and accounts at stock and bond exchanges. These assets vary in the degree of risk that is borne by the purchaser of the asset. This makes possible the diversification of individual wealth holdings, which, in turn, reduces the overall risk borne by savers and investors.

Economic Impact: Long Run

The economic impact of financial development/deepening is best understood by distinguishing between short-run and long-run impacts. Analysis of the short-run impact focuses on the role of financial development/deepening in the business cycle. The long-run impact refers to the cyclical rise and fall to which all market-based economic systems are subject. That is, market-based systems go through periods of expansion, in which unemployment falls, followed by periods of contraction, in which unemployment rises. These cyclical episodes typically last three to ten years, depending on a diverse set of factors including credit markets and levels of inventory. Analysis of the long-run impact of financial development/deepening focuses on the growth of gross domestic product over periods of ten years or more. One can view the economy as cycling up and down around, it is hoped, a steadily rising standard of living (in both the short and long run).

What is the impact of financial development/deepening on long-run growth? There are two broad schools of thought on this question. The first view sees financial development/deepening as a result of economic growth. In this view, as the real economy (production and distribution) grows and develops, businesses and individuals find themselves in need of more and a greater variety of financial assets. This creates a profitable opportunity for the financial system to expand and diversify to meet the growing demand. According to this explanation, growth of the real economy causes the development/deepening of the financial sector, not the other way around. An economist would say that causality runs from the growth of the real economy to the development/deepening of the financial sector.

The second school of thought argues the opposite view. That is, financial development/deepening enhances the rate of growth in the real economy. More explicitly, financial development/deepening causes economic growth, rather than the reverse. The financial sector enhances the efficiency of the economy by making it easier to match savings with investment opportunities. In addition, saving and investment depend on the amount of financial assets available and their diversity—more of the latter creates more of the former. Finally, financial development/deepening is likely to increase the rate of technical innovation in an economy. Investors not only build more factories, shops, and so on, they also build better ones. Investment usually brings new technology as well as expanded facilities. The easier it is for investors to tap into a pool of savings, the faster new innovations will be introduced. Thus, financial development/deepening leads to more savings, greater efficiency, and more rapid innovation—enhancing long-run growth.

These opposing schools of thought set off a series of experiments to empirically test which hypothesis is correct. Does growth cause financial development/deepening, or does financial development/deepening cause growth? The consensus is that causality runs in both directions, but the evidence remains inconclusive as to which direction is more important. Nevertheless, economists agree that financial development/deepening is a critical component of long-term economic growth.

Economic Impact: Short Run

While financial development/deepening has a positive role in the long-term growth of the econ-

omy, in the short run, it is thought to increase the fragility of the economic system. That is, as the quantity and variety of assets expand, this results in a greater likelihood of increased financial volatility or instability, a greater likelihood of booms (expansions) and busts (contractions), and intensified levels of booms and busts. The following discussion will focus on a bank-centered financial system.

Banking systems operate on the "fractional reserve" principle. That is, individuals deposit money into a bank, in return for which they hold some sort of account. The bank, in turn, keeps reserve assets—such as cash in its vault—in an amount equal to a fraction of the deposit liabilities on reserve at the bank, and it loans out the rest of the money. When banks make loans, they create money. All banks operate in this manner. Because the proceeds of the loans made by banks often are deposited at other banks, those banks can use the new deposits to make more loans. The result is that an initial deposit into the banking system creates a multiple expansion of loans (credit). In addition, banks within the system are linked by a web of financial relationships—the loans of Bank A may serve as the reserves for Bank B, and so on.

At any point in time, no bank has enough reserves on hand to pay all of its depositors should they demand their money. But under normal circumstances, people leave most of their money in the financial system. There may be some withdrawals, but these generally are offset by new deposits.

During periods of expansion, the economy is growing, profits for businesses are rising rapidly, and the prospects for future investment look bright. In these periods, banks seek to minimize their reserves in order to expand lending and credit. The information that is available to the financial system tends to reinforce views of a continued expansion, leading to further lending. The deeper and more developed the financial system becomes, the more extensive this process will be. The quality of the loans made by banks for investment tends to decline as information becomes less reliable.

The turning point in the foregoing process can occur in several ways. If some of the investments financed through bank lending fail, the depositors of these banks may seek to withdraw their money, fearing a collapse. The threatened banks may call in their loans (or stop making new loans) in order to generate funds to pay depositors. Other firms in the economy will find their position threatened as well. As credit becomes scarcer, some of these firms will default on loans to other banks. Those banks, in turn, will recall loans and cut back on credit. As one can see, a self-reinforcing contraction begins.

This process may unfold in different ways. The expansion of credit may cause a general inflation in prices, or it may cause the prices of particular assets, such as real estate, to rise. As the latter occurs, the owners of this asset (real estate) find that the increased value can be used as collateral for additional borrowing, and banks, in an expansionary phase, are likely to increase lending. As the value of real estate continues to increase, an asset bubble begins to form—that is, the asset's value rises above its long-term value, as determined by its income/earning prospects.

When the bubble bursts—that is, when real-estate values begin to fall back toward their long-run equilibrium levels—the collateral behind the loans extended by the financial system begins to shrink. Once again, a number of banks will find their situation deteriorating, and depositors will begin to withdraw their deposits, leading to further financial contraction.

In an attempt to keep financial systems stable, most governments act as guarantors. When credit begins to contract, depositors, fearful for the value of their deposits, often will run to draw their money out, thus exacerbating the contraction. Most central governments in developed countries promise to step in and provide the funding so that depositors always will be able to get their money, no matter what (this is known as deposit insurance). Assured by the government's guarantee, depositors have no reason to rush to the financial system to withdraw their money. This tends to stabilize the system.

However, the problem with this system is that it creates "moral hazard." Banks and other financial institutions know that the government will step in and solve the problem. As a result, they have an incentive to increase the riskiness of their investments. If things work out, they will make extremely high profits. If they do not, the government will step in and provide the necessary resources in times of financial difficulty. In addition, depositors have no incentive to verify the financial viability of their bank, because the state has insured them against default by the lending institution. Thus, the entire financial system becomes subject to even greater probability of failure.

The implication is that the stability of the financial system depends critically on its regulatory institutions. This institutional structure must act as a watchdog to restrain banks and other financial institutions from engaging in increasingly risky investments. This is difficult, as the financial system is constantly developing new types of assets for diffusing risk and mobilizing savings. In the long run, this will enhance overall growth, but if regulatory institutions are unable to adjust (keep up), then the riskiness of the financial system will increase, thus raising the probability of collapse. Thus, it is essential that regulatory institutions be given the resources necessary to keep up with technical innovations in the financial sector.

Ultimately, however, the stabilization of the financial system depends on the ability to restrain credit expansion so as to prevent a rapid expansion of credit (which ultimately will lead to a contraction). In many countries, the central bank plays this role. Using monetary policy tools, the central bank can drain reserves from the financial system, reducing the extent of credit expansions. In turn, during contractions, the central bank can inject reserves into the system, giving banks additional means for extending loans. The problem, of course, is determining when it is the right time to restrain a credit expansion. If the central bank acts too soon, it will restrain normal growth processes, reducing the future standard of living. If it acts too late, the likelihood of financial collapse increases dramatically, as does the severity of the collapse.

Implications

Financial development/deepening occurs as the quantity of financial assets grows and as the variety of such assets expands. In the long run, this increases economic growth by matching savings with investment, stimulating increased saving (and investment), and promoting investment in new technology. In the short run, however, financial development/deepening tends to increase financial instability. More assets and a greater variety of assets lead to greater credit expansions and contractions. In order to dampen this instability, say many experts, the state must invest sufficient resources in financial regulatory institutions. Central banks also must become more adept at dampening excess credit expansion.

Richard Grabowski

See also: Financial Markets; Savings and Investment.

Further Reading

Cooper, George. *The Origin of Financial Crises: Central Banks, Credit Bubbles and the Efficient Market Fallacy.* New York: Vintage, 2008.

King, Robert. "Finance and Growth: Schumpeter Might Be Right." *Quarterly Journal of Economics* 108:3 (August 1993): 717–737.

Rajan, Raghuram G., and Luigi Zingales. "Financial Dependence and Growth." *American Economic Review* 88:3 (June 1998): 559–586.

Shaw, Edward S. *Financial Deepening in Economic Development.* New York: Oxford University Press, 1973.

Valderrama, Diego. "Financial Development, Productivity, and Economic Growth." *Federal Reserve Bank of San Francisco Economic Letter* 2003:18 (June 2007): 1–3.

Financial Markets

Financial markets are the figurative space in which financial instruments—such as corporate equities and bonds—are bought and sold. Highly regulated in the aftermath of the financial crisis that led to the Great Depression in the 1930s, financial markets in the United States and in much of the world were liberated from government constraints beginning in the 1970s. That deregulation, along with the introduction of new technologies and new financial instruments, allowed for much innovation and rapid growth in financial markets, but also increased instability, as the financial crisis of 2008–2009 demonstrated.

Four Types of Finance

Finance means different things in different contexts. Consider the following four types of finance: corporate, personal, public, and international.

Corporate finance concerns the means by which firms raise capital to make investments. It examines the relative efficacy of issuing bonds (debt) or stock (equity) and the impact of the method of finance on firm performance and investor returns. It also concerns the use and valuation of other financial claims such as options, convertible bonds, and preferred stock. Personal finance looks at the way in which individuals or families save money and insure themselves. It deals with matters such as pension plans, deferred savings plans, insurance, and income taxes. Public finance pertains to government's use of taxes to raise revenues and its expenditure of these funds. It deals with deficits and debt, as well as the connection between the timing of benefits from government projects and the collection of funds for their financing. International finance focuses on exchange rates and international financial flows. It considers the relationship between capital flows and trade in goods and services, as well as interest rate differentials across countries. All four types of finance are interrelated and deal with the same fundamental issues: time, risk, and uncertainty.

Financial Prices

The most common financial price is the interest rate, or "rate of return." This rate may be viewed as a contingent claim. For example, if the interest rate is 25 percent, the price of 100 current dollars is equal to 125 future dollars—$(1 + 0.25) \times 100$—and the price of 100 future dollars is equal to 80 current dollars—$[1 / (1 + 0.25)] \times 100$. Economists typically consider the pure interest on risk-free assets, independent of any default risk. For a lender buying a contingent claim for future payment, uncertainty regarding the future payment (default risk) will increase the interest rate that the lender requires. In this case, the interest rate includes two components: a risk-free return and a risk premium.

In insurance markets, a premium is the price charged for monetary payments in the event of a bad outcome. Consider a policy for which the customer pays a $1,000 premium in exchange for an $8,000 claim to be paid in the event of a bad outcome. Suppose the probability of a bad outcome is 10 percent. The insurance company (insurer) sells a contingent claim of $8,000 to the customer (insured) with an expected payout of $800 ($8,000 × 10 percent = $800) for a price of $1,000 with certainty. Although the bad outcome, if it occurs, will take place in the future, this time dimension typically is not considered in an insurance context. With perfect information, the insured is willing to pay $1,000 for a contingent claim with an expected value of $800 in order to reduce his or her risk of an $8,000 loss if the contingency (bad) outcome occurs.

Micro/Macro, Real/Nominal Distinctions

The purchase or sale of insurance, and the saving and lending behaviors of individual decision makers, may be analyzed in detail in a microeconomic context. In this case, preferences, present value calculations, and expectations of the probabilities of different outcomes are the focus. Transactions that are based on differences in preferences, a desire to pool or diversify risk, or different productive real investment opportunities benefit both parties to the transaction, even if they possess the same information. Such transactions represent a positive-sum game because both parties benefit. However, some financial transactions may be based on differences in beliefs regarding changes in future conditions or the probabilities of particular outcomes. Trades based on such differences generally represent a zero-sum game—that is, the better-informed party will benefit at the expense of the other.

As is true in nonfinancial markets, when aggregated, individual decisions and transactions by individuals, firms, governments, and foreigners will have broader macroeconomic effects. Because financial assets may be "moved" across locations at virtually no cost, financial prices such as interest rates are nearly identical across national markets. Thus, the macroeconomic and microeconomic views of finance are particularly intertwined. Moreover, financial markets greatly affect other markets throughout an economy. For example, if equity prices on the New York Stock Exchange increase, high-tech firms in Silicon Valley will find it easier to raise investment funds through initial public offerings. This may influence their decision to expand production. In addition, if potential customers are stockholders who experience an increase in wealth, they may increase their demand for the high-tech firms' output.

Some classical economists speak of a dichotomy between real and nominal factors, in which real values are not affected by monetary values. For example, if the money supply doubles, and all prices (including wages and nominal wealth) double, in theory, there need not be any real effect. However, real-world experience is filled with cases in which monetary or, more generally, financial problems have had a significant, measurable impact on "real" values such as output and employment. Simple analogies may be instructive in conceptualizing the relation between monetary and nominal factors.

An automobile engine needs an appropriate amount of oil for lubrication in order to operate properly. Although the physical engine parts, when combined with gasoline, provide the power, if there is too little oil, the engine will experience increased friction. This could impair its performance and cause permanent damage. Similarly, too much oil may adversely impact the real workings of the engine as well. Just as an engine needs an appropriate amount of oil to operate efficiently, an economy needs an appropriate amount of money, or "financial liquidity."

By this analogy, the real effects of money become visible when there is too much or too little.

Another analogy might be considered, this time with "liquidity" representing the availability of credit in an economy. Visualize a real economic landscape comprising productive farmland and some arid, nonproductive wasteland. The proper amount of liquidity (credit) channeled toward the farmland (truly productive sectors of the economy) could lead to a more verdant landscape (vibrant real economy with rapid growth). Too little credit channeled toward productive sectors could spur a drought, with dry and unproductive but fertile farmland. Excessive credit, however, could flood the farmland. And liquidity funneled toward the arid land could cause erosion and flash floods—analogous to harmful speculative bubbles.

Financial Intermediaries as "Middlemen"

In a well-functioning economy, financial intermediaries channel investment funds from savers toward borrowers with productive real investment projects. They act as "middlemen," not directly producing goods and services, but enhancing the real productivity of other economic agents. They provide real benefits to savers, reducing individual risks or transferring risk to parties who are better able and willing to assume it. A middleman earns a profit by buying at a low (wholesale) price and selling at a higher (retail) price. In a competitive market, a successful middleman must provide truly valuable services, such as moving products geographically or repackaging them. Similarly, although financial intermediaries do not produce physical goods themselves, they provide very real benefits to market participants.

Banks, savings and loan institutions, and credit unions all accept deposits, make loans, and facilitate payments by customers. They reduce transaction costs by providing checking and credit services, and by reducing the risk faced by individual investors or depositors. Although the funds provided to a bank by depositors may be loaned out, each individual depositor faces virtually no default risk, as the bank pools the funds of many depositors together (in addition, most developed countries offer deposit insurance). Moreover, a bank's experience and expertise in lending allows it to better evaluate the likelihood that any one borrower will default. Financial conglomerates, securities firms, and mutual funds accept investment funds, pool them, and channel them toward truly productive investments. Their expertise should enable them to "pick the winners" and reduce transactions costs. Investors may be individuals or other intermediaries such as insurance companies or pension funds. By pooling the risk of individual policyholders, insurance companies aim to reduce risk for their customers.

It is useful to conceptualize financial intermediaries as simplified balance sheets. Variation in the types of assets and liabilities distinguishes the different types of financial intermediaries. A difficulty may arise from a mismatch between the maturities of assets and liabilities. In the past, banks held shorter-term liabilities (customer deposits) and longer-term assets (loans), and so were hurt by unanticipated increases in interest rates.

Financial intermediaries face two fundamental, interrelated problems: insolvency and illiquidity. Insolvency occurs when a firm's assets are worth less than its liabilities; in this case, its "capital" (net worth or owner's equity) is negative. Technically, it is bankrupt. Illiquidity occurs when a firm's assets are worth more than its liabilities, but the assets cannot be liquidated quickly without severe losses. One reason that the Federal Reserve was established in the early twentieth century was to provide liquidity to solvent firms with illiquid assets.

Markets, Financial and Nonfinancial

In modeling markets for goods and services, economists typically consider private goods, for which ownership and property rights are clear and well defined. When buyers know exactly what they are getting and sellers know exactly what they are giving up (i.e., all participants are rational and well informed), each voluntary trade benefits both parties. Competitive auction markets are the standard benchmark, in which buyers and sellers periodically transact at prices that no one party can affect individually. With the "market-clearing" assumption that all transactions occur at equilibrium prices, markets instantaneously move from one equilibrium to another as conditions change, with no shortages or surpluses. A complication arises for goods that last more than one "period," as the future expected prices of both buyers and sellers will influence the current equilibrium. If the current equilibrium price changes, this may alter future expected prices.

Financial markets involve trade in contingent claims—for example, the delivery of a dollar "tomorrow" or in a particular "state of nature" (e.g., one's car is damaged in an accident). Thus, uncertainty and expectations of future conditions play central roles. If the supply of a financial asset increases and its equilibrium price falls, this may cause a shift in current demand if investors revise their future expected prices downward as a result. This tends to amplify the decline that is required to reach a new equilibrium. Thus, the current prices of "storable," "nonperishable" financial assets are particularly sensitive to expected future prices.

Financial assets generally are not demanded for their intrinsic value, but for their associated financial flow. Their demand is "derived" from the anticipated value of associated future payments. A change in the rate of discount will affect all assets providing future payments. Financial claims are highly substitutable in a way that is qualitatively different than claims in nonfinancial markets. A future dollar provided by one financial asset does not differ from that provided by another—thus, the prices of these assets tend to move together. Differences in maturity and risk across assets affect the magnitude of price changes.

Markets for nonfinancial assets usually are conceptualized in terms of "flows"—the amount of the good or service that is bought and sold per period. In financial markets, long-lived "stocks" of assets are transacted, further increasing the connection between the expectations of future conditions and

the current market equilibrium. This issue exists in nonfinancial markets for durable goods as well. For example, an increase in car sales in one period may reduce the demand for cars in the next. In the housing market, one may consider only those homes potentially bought or sold, so the equilibrium quantity is the number transacted, not the stock of homes in existence. Similarly, one may consider the "market for loanable funds" as a flow of financial assets transacted rather than the stock of assets in existence. The relation between the stocks and flows of durable assets is one aspect of financial markets not typically seen in most nonfinancial markets for goods and services.

Deregulation, Leverage, and the 2008–2009 Financial Crisis

In the aftermath of the stock market crash of 1929 and subsequent Great Depression, regulations were put in place to stabilize the financial system and the economy. These included deposit insurance (to stop bank runs), separation of investment and commercial banking (to minimize risk for depository institutions), increased auditing and oversight (to prevent fraudulent bookkeeping), restrictions on the types of assets that financial intermediaries could own (again to reduce risk), increased reserve requirements (to protect against illiquidity), increased capital requirements (to protect against insolvency), and interest rate ceilings and segmentation of financial markets (to reduce competition and increase stability).

By the end of the 1970s, however, these regulations were coming under attack on two fronts. First, firms were using new technology and mounting legal challenges to circumvent the intent of the regulations. Second, the belief that financial markets require regulation to remain stable was declining in popularity. Policy errors of the 1960s and 1970s—such as excessive deficit spending associated with the Vietnam War, rapid monetary growth before President Richard M. Nixon's re-election bid, and wage and price controls to fight inflation—had convinced many that government was the problem and that unregulated markets were the solution. The trend toward deregulation moved forward, with a slight break in the late 1980s, until the financial crisis of 2008–2009.

Deregulation, advances in technology, huge flows of financial capital from abroad, an increasing belief that major recessions and financial crises were a thing of the past, and perhaps an exaggerated belief in the Federal Reserve's ability stabilize the economy all created an environment in which financial intermediaries, particularly investment banks and hedge funds, were taking on excessive risks in search of ever-higher returns.

Increased leverage—more borrowing and expansion of assets for a fixed amount of capital—can increase the return to capital for a given return on assets. One factor that mitigates the excessive use of leverage is a fear that this amplification is working in reverse, so when asset values fall, bank capital becomes negative and the firm becomes bankrupt (insolvent). By the early 2000s, the fear of bankruptcy seemed to have diminished, and deregulation allowed financial intermediaries to take on greater leverage and assume greater risk.

A general fall in home prices, which spurred a decline in the value of assets backed by home mortgages, led to the forced sale of investment bank Bear Stearns to JPMorgan Chase in March 2008 and the outright failure of Lehman Brothers in September 2008. In the ensuing panic, asset prices unrelated to home mortgages began to fall as well. The Federal Reserve and the Treasury Department stepped in to loan against otherwise illiquid assets in an effort to forestall a greater financial collapse. This event illustrated that the basic fragility of financial markets had not been conquered, and that financial crises still have a significant impact on the overall economy.

Bruce Brown

See also: Asian Financial Crisis (1997); Bank Cycles; Banks, Central; Banks, Commercial; Banks, Investment; Credit Cycle; Efficient Market Theory; Fragility, Financial; Investment, Financial; Liberalization, Financial; Money Markets; Panics and Runs, Bank; Regulation, Financial; Stock Markets, Global; Systemic Financial Crises.

Further Reading

Bagehot, Walter. *Lombard Street: A Description of the Money Market.* New York: Scribner, 1912.

Burton, Maureen, Reynold Nesiba, and Bruce Brown. *An Introduction to Financial Markets and Institutions.* 2nd ed. Armonk, NY: M.E. Sharpe, 2010.

Eatwell, John, Murray Milgate, and Peter Newman, eds. *Finance: The New Palgrave.* New York: W.W. Norton, 1989.

"A Short History of Modern Finance." *The Economist,* October 16, 2008.

"Why Is Finance So Unstable?" *The Economist,* January 22, 2009.

Financial Modeling of the Business Cycle

Financial data models of the business cycle combine mathematical techniques and data from the financial markets to illustrate and predict expansions and contractions. Such models are useful because financial market activity is intimately connected to larger economic and business indicators, which themselves are the key components for measuring business cycle stages. This is especially the case in economies where the financial sector plays an outsized role, such as that of the United States in recent years. According to experts who utilize mathematical models to understand the business cycle, the huge growth of the U.S. financial sector—from 16 to 40 percent of overall domestic corporate profits between the late 1990s and the late 2000s, to take just one measure—helps explain why the crisis in the financial markets triggered such a deep recession in the United States starting in late 2007.

Financial models of the business cycle are analogous to experiments in the natural sciences. That is, they study the relationship between a dependent variable and its related independent variables. In economics, however, it is impossible to fully isolate a single variable as in a scientific experiment. Usually, historical data are utilized to form and develop a model in order to reach a conclusive and axiomatic statement about a given economic phenomenon.

Among the most important of the economic and business indicators studied through financial modeling are investment, consumer credit, and the indices of economic indicators. Investment activities, which are essential factors of a nation's gross domestic product and closely related to business cycles, occur largely in the capital or financial markets. Technically speaking, investments are savings or unconsumed incomes reallocated for higher returns. Since the reallocation of past income is usually associated with such capital market products as bonds, stocks, and other financial instruments, investments provide a critical link between financial market performance and fluctuations in the business cycle. Thus, models generated from financial market performance data provide useful tools for predicting business cycles and offer guidance to governments in their fiscal and monetary decision making.

Consumer credit, both a key financial resource and an engine of economic activity, is made up of two components: secured debt, such as mortgages and home equity lines of credit, and unsecured debt, such as credit card balances. Outstanding credit balances and variables derived from them, such as consumer credit usage or payment patterns, represent various types of consumption and default-risk behavior patterns. The latter can take the form of defaults on home mortgages or car loans, and missed payments on credit card balances. Major banks and financial research institutions utilize such proprietary information in their financial modeling to forecast phases of the business cycle; lending and investment institutions often use it to determine their own investment activity. In addition, the Conference Board—a nonprofit, nongovernmental business research organization—combines aggregations of consumer credit data with leading economic indicators to create financial models that can anticipate movement in the domestic and international capital markets.

Economic Indicators

Indices, which combine several economic indicators, are critical both for and to financial modeling. They consist of leading indicators, coincident indicators, and lagging indicators—each measuring data in relation to business cycle fluctuations. Leading indicators—bond yields and stock market valuations are good examples—anticipate and often predict near-term changes in the economy. The Index of Leading Economic Indicators, a widely followed and much-respected measure calculated and published monthly by the Conference Board, is based on ten variables: the S&P 500 Index of major stock prices, the money supply, the spread between long- and short-term interest rates, unemployment insurance claims, consumer sentiment, new building permits, manufacturers' new orders for consumer goods, delivery of new merchandise from suppliers to vendors, new orders for capital goods, and manufacturing working hours. The index is closely monitored by the government to determine fiscal, monetary, and other economic policies, such as changes in the interest rate the Federal Reserve charges to member banks, the tax code, unemployment insurance compensation and, during recessionary periods, various forms of economic stimulus. While generally a reliable indicator, the Index of Leading Economic Indicators is not perfect and has failed at times to provide policy makers with sufficient warning of economic downturns and upturns.

Coincident indicators provide a picture of the economy in the current state. The Conference Board's Index of Coincident Indicators includes data on nonfarm payroll workers, personal income (minus government transfer payments such as welfare, Social Security, unemployment compensation, and disability), industrial production, and trade sales. High figures in these categories, especially personal income, indicate that an economy is in an expansion stage of the business cycle.

Lagging indicators measure past performance and help economists predict what will occur later on during the business cycle. For example, unemployment rates can be expected to remain high even as the overall economy recovers. The components of lagging indicators include employment, outstanding commercial and industrial loans, the consumer price index for services, labor cost per unit of output, ratio of manufacturing and trade inventories to sales, ratio of consumer credit outstanding to personal income, and the prime lending rate, which is based on the federal funds rate and the interest rates banks charge for home equity lines of credit and some credit cards.

Indicators are also divided into two other categories: procyclical and countercyclical—that is, whether upticks reflect economic expansion or not. Good examples of the former include manufacturers' new orders for consumer goods, industrial production, and the ratio of consumer installment credit to personal income. Key countercyclical indicators are unemployment claims, outstanding commercial and industrial loans, and changes in labor cost per unit of output.

While many people watch stock prices vigilantly and the financial media often assumes that changes in stock market indices offer signs of future economic performance, economists are more skeptical of share prices as a reliable leading indicator. Some believe that falling indices do increase the likelihood of a recession, especially in the U.S. economy, where stock prices play a more important role in predicting changes in the business cycle. Internationally, however, near-term fluctuations in stock prices are less telling, since the global financial system is much more deeply affected by changes in the interest rate.

In the United States, for example, interest rates or interest rate term structure (the difference between short- and long-term rates), do have an important predictive value, as adjustments in the interest rate can reduce business cycle volatility. In the 2008–2009 financial crisis, the Federal Reserve Bank dropped the interest rate it charged member banks to near zero in order to ease the recession. However, lowering interest rates risks flooding the economy with money, increasing the possibility of inflation. The net benefit of the trade-off between interest rate smoothing and inflation instability therefore depends on the timing and level of interest rate–adjustment policies from the Federal Reserve Bank.

The interest rate spread—that is, the difference between low-risk and high-risk loan rates—is also a useful predictor of future business cycle phases because it measures the fluctuation of real output or investment, which is contingent on innovations in the financial markets. For example, an increase in high-risk loan generation increases the likelihood of default risk; this, in turn, causes a decrease in investment or output, as investors are unable to adjust their investment decisions without the assistance of external risk–reducing mechanisms. In recent years, the securitization of subprime mortgages—whereby such mortgages were bundled and sold to investors to help spread the financial risk of default—led investors to increase their investments, which produced a boom in the housing market. Nevertheless, the absolute amount of risk—the aggregate risk of all subprime mortgages—remained the same. Thus, when homeowners began to default on their mortgage payments, investors pulled back, producing the financial shock of 2008.

2008–2009 Financial Crisis

The financial shock of 2008 and its role in the recession that followed revived interest in the role that financial markets play in the business cycle. As American economist Hyman Minsky argued in the mid-twentieth century, during prosperous times corporations tended to overinvest in productive capacity, saddling themselves with debt that they had a hard time repaying when revenues sank during economic downturns. The result was a financial crisis that saw banks and other lenders shutting off credit.

Earlier, in the first half of the twentieth century, Austrian-American economist Joseph Schumpeter highlighted the importance of innovation—including financial innovation—in economic development. The point was dramatized in the early to mid-2000s, as rapid-fire innovations in the financial markets produced an economic boom. As subsequent events proved, however, it was a shaky expansion since some of the new financial instruments—such as mortgage-backed securities—increased risk dramatically. Because of the importance of these financial innovations to the boom of the early to mid-2000s, some economists argued, better financial modeling—or more attention to such financial modeling by policy makers—could have predicted that the boom would not last and that it would inevitably lead to a collapse in the financial markets. Indeed, an economic strategy group at IBM created a financial model that predicted just such a collapse, though their warnings were largely ignored by the Federal Reserve Bank, which maintained the low interest rates that had fueled the mortgage securitization boom.

Traditionally, risk aversion in the investment decisions by firms during a recession phase is seen as having a major influence on business indicators, such as employment or new durable goods orders. During economic contractions, investors require higher returns—that is, higher interest rates or dividends—to account for the greater risk of investing at a time when borrowers have a greater likelihood of financial loss or outright failure. Such risk aversion heightens the cost of borrowing, leading businesses to forego projects they would have undertaken when credit was cheaper, as during periods of economic expansion. This, then, leads to declines in such indicators as employment or durable goods orders. In short, the higher cost of financing during a recession has important consequences for the business cycle.

As recent economic history indicates, fluctuations in the financial markets have become an increasingly important factor in determining trends in the business cycle. Indeed, some economists have argued that the economic boom of the early to mid-2000s was largely a creation of the financial markets. As Schumpeter and others students of the business cycle have contended, technology innovation leads to economic expansion, while maturation of a given technology and investment saturation in that technology lead to economic contractions. Nothing illustrates this phenomenon better than the dot.com boom and bust of the 1990s and early 2000s. Yet the boom-and-bust cycle that followed depended not on new technology but on new financial instruments, as well as government interest rate policies that made them possible and profitable. The heightened role of the financial sector has made the need for financial modeling even more imperative.

Beryl Y. Chang and James Ciment

See also: Financial Markets.

Further Reading

Buch, Claudia M., and Christian Pierdzioch. "The Integration of Imperfect Financial Markets: Implications for Business Cycle Volatility." *Journal of Policy Modeling* 27 (2005): 789–804.

Faia, Ester. "Finance and International Business Cycles." *Journal of Monetary Economics* 54:4 (2007): 1018–1034.

Fuerst, Michael E. "Investor Risk Premia and Real Macroeconomic Fluctuations." *Journal of Macroeconomics* 28:3 (2006): 540–563.

Kato, Ryo. "Liquidity, Infinite Horizons and Macroeconomic Fluctuations." *European Economic Review* 50:5 (2006): 1105–1130.

Kwark, Noh-Sun. "Default Risk, Interest Rate Spreads, and Business Cycles: Explaining the Interest Rate Spread as a Leading Indicator." *Journal of Economic Dynamics & Control* 26:2 (2002): 271–302.

Schumpeter, Joseph A. *The Theory of Economic Development.* New Brunswick, NJ: Transaction, 1983.

Sensier, Marianne. "The Prediction of Business Cycle Phases: Financial Variables and International Linkages." *National Institute Economic Review*, October 1, 2002.

Tallarini, Thomas D., Jr. "Risk-Sensitive Real Business Cycles." *Journal of Monetary Economics* 45:3 (2000): 507–532.

Vercelli, Alessandro. "Structural Financial Instability and Cyclical Fluctuations." *Structural Change and Economic Dynamics* 11:1 (2000): 139–156.

Finland

Finland is a northern European country surrounded by the Baltic Sea and the gulfs of Finland and Bothnia. Its shares borders with Sweden to the west, Norway to the north, and Russia to the east. The population of Finland is approximately 5.3 million, one-fifth of whom live in the capital of Helsinki and the surrounding region. Finland is a parliamentary republic. Government expenditure in the economy for the years 1999 to 2008 constituted an average of 49.09 percent of the *nominal* gross domestic product (the value of goods and services produced in the domestic economy during a given year measured in current prices), compared with 42.54 percent for the euro area countries.

Finland joined the European Union (EU) in 1995 and, unlike the other Nordic countries in that body, chose to adopt the euro as its currency in 1999. Finland has been offered membership in NATO a number of times, most recently in January 2009, but has declined to join in deference to its neighbor to the east.

Finland is heavily forested, with little arable land. Its economy depends on forestry to a large extent, with exports of forestry-related products per capita almost three times greater than those of Canada. In fact, Finland's forestry exports in 2007 accounted for almost 10 percent of global exports in this sector. Finland is an energy-poor country with no reserves of gas or oil, a fact that poses a major challenge for a country that has one-third of its land above the Arctic Circle and experiences prolonged periods of darkness and cold. The latter factors account for Finland's high energy consumption—one of the highest in the world, in fact, and nearly two-thirds higher than the EU average. To minimize dependency on a specific energy source, usage is spread across a variety of resources, including oil, wood fuel, natural gas, coal, and peat, as well as nuclear energy. Mining and related processing also contribute to the national economy.

In recent years, the economic hegemony of natural resources in Finland finally has been eclipsed by the information and communications technology sector. Along with a significant output of radio and television equipment, Finland is also home to Nokia Corporation, the world's largest mobile-telephone handset producer. Until the recession of 2008–2009, Finland recorded large trade surpluses. Government plays a significant role in the economy and, despite a broad privatization program launched in 1991, state ownership remains substantial.

After prospering in the 1980s, Finland in the early 1990s suffered one of the worst recessions of any Organisation for Economic Co-operation and Development (OECD) country since the end of World War II, largely because of the collapse of the Soviet Union, one of its major trading partners. That loss was compounded by the banking crisis that swept Scandinavia during the same period. The Finnish economy rebounded in 1994, and over the next five years (1995–2000), real GDP grew at an average rate of 4.62 percent. This was the strongest expansion among the Nordic countries and especially favorable compared to the euro area and OECD, where the average growth rates were 2.68 percent and 3.23 percent, respectively, for the same period. (Real GDP is the market value of all goods and services produced in a country during a given year, measured in constant prices so the value is not affected by changes in price.)

With the onset of the recession in 2001, real GDP grew at an average rate of 2.00 percent for 2001–2003, then returned to a healthier 3.83 percent. The rate of real GDP growth was 4.4 percent in 2007 but started a downward trend in 2008. Although the forecasts for Finland at the beginning of the global financial crisis were relatively optimistic, the tide began to turn for this country as well. Both imports and exports fell by more than one-third in 2008, compared to the previous year. The global crisis situation put Finland's economy at greater risk than that of other countries, given its new reliance on the vulnerable information, communications, and technology sectors. The country officially entered a recession at the end of 2008, after two consecutive quarterly declines in GDP. The silver lining was an easing of inflation, which had been significantly higher in Finland than in the euro area.

Demographically, Finland faces the economic challenges of an aging population, which is maturing sooner and more quickly than the populations of other Western European countries. In response, the government has promoted a number of measures to keep individuals working longer and postponing retirement.

Despite the economic crisis, government finances remained relatively balanced, and the banking sector was relatively immune from the crises faced in other countries, largely because of reforms instituted after the banking crisis of the early 1990s. Nevertheless, in 2009, the Finnish government introduced tax cuts and announced a stimulus package of 3 billion euros to encourage construction, among other initiatives. The nation's banking sector emerged relatively unscathed, as it did not invest heavily in the Baltic States. In fact, at least one Finnish bank turned misfortune into opportunity with the acquisition of the Swedish subsidiary of Iceland's bankrupt Kaupthing Bank.

Marisa Scigliano

See also: Denmark; Iceland; Norway; Sweden.

Further Reading

Central Intelligence Agency. *The CIA World Factbook–Finland.* Available at https://www.cia.gov/library/publications/the-world-factbook/geos/fi.html. Accessed May 2010.

Economist Intelligence Unit (EIU). *Country Report—Finland.* London: EIU, 2009.

———. *ViewsWire: Finland.* London: EIU, 2009.

Organisation for Economic Co-operation and Development (OECD). *OECD Economic Outlook*, no. 84. Paris: OECD, 2008.

Statistical Office of the European Communities (Eurostat). *Eurostat Yearbook 2008.* Available at http://epp.eurostat.ec.europa.eu/. Accessed March 2009.

———. *Key Figures on Europe, 2007/08 Edition.* Available at http://epp.eurostat.ec.europa.eu/. Accessed March 2009.

Fiscal Balance

"Fiscal balance" is a phrase usually used to refer to the net spending of the federal government, but it can also be applied to the finances of lower levels of governments. As such, it is the difference between the government's receipts and disbursements; thus, it can be either positive or negative. When a government's outlays exceed what it collects in taxes, it is said to be running a deficit, in which case it will have to find other sources of financing such as borrowing and/or creating new money. Accumulated deficits lead to what is called the "public debt." Some economists regard the public debt as a burden on society and actively lobby for its reduction or even elimination. Others argue that budget deficits (and therefore the public debt) serve an important function by allowing for the continuation of capital projects and expansionary fiscal policy during economic downturns. The ultimate impact of deficits and debt on the economy depends on two issues: Will public investment hinder or help the economic growth? And is the debt a drag on economic growth, by crowding out private borrowing or driving up interest rates, or a necessary stimulant for economic growth, by easing the tax burden on households and businesses and spurring employment and economic activity through government spending?

Sound Finance

The idea that "responsible" governments should not spend more than they are able to receive in the form of taxes is not new and can be traced back to classical economists such as David Ricardo, who argued back in the early nineteenth century that any government disbursements, including reimbursement of debt and payment of interest, must ultimately be paid for by taxes. More recently, economists—sometimes known as "deficit hawks" and including people like Stephen Friedman and N. Gregory Mankiw—have elaborated on this idea, arguing that taxes are the only legitimate source of government revenue; such economists are therefore opposed to any deficits at all. For instance, in the United States, although unsuccessful, many attempts have been made (such as the Balanced Budget Act of 1997) to impose binding constraints on federal spending. In Europe, the 1992 Maastricht Treaty creating the European Union requires that budget deficits in member countries participating in the monetary union not exceed

3 percent of gross domestic product (GDP) and that public debt not exceed 60 percent of GDP. In reality, however, such legal limits are largely irrelevant because governments often find it necessary to increase their spending (and incur deficits) in order to stabilize or stimulate the economy—as they did during the 2008–2009 financial crisis.

More conservative proponents of sound finance put forward two major arguments to justify their opposition to public deficits and debt. First, they argue, when the government borrows on financial markets, it competes with private investors and forces the rate of interest to rise. In this view, higher interest rates discourage private investment and lower aggregate demand, which leads to a fall in total production (GDP), an idea known as "crowding out." The second argument is that if the government finances its deficit by printing more money, the increase in monetary circulation leads to inflation. Since domestic products will consequently be more expensive than foreign ones, producers will suffer a loss of competitiveness and sell less both domestically and abroad. As a result, they produce less, and aggregate output (GDP) will fall again. Thus, it is concluded, if governments want to avoid these negative effects, they must follow a policy based on balanced budgets or budget surpluses.

Alternate View

Other economists, generally on the more liberal end of the political spectrum, view the crowding-out hypothesis as one of the more misleading conceptions in modern economic thought. For instance, some argue, because government expenditures generate income for the private sector and taxes reduce the disposable income, there will necessarily be a net addition to incomes whenever government spending exceeds tax revenue (a budget deficit). Higher income will increase consumption and have further positive effects as households spend more on goods and services. For this reason, as the history of the United States suggests, many economists maintain that deficits stimulate the economy whereas surpluses are harmful. Indeed, as economist Randall Wray wrote in *Surplus Mania* (1999), "since 1776 there have been six periods of substantial budget surpluses and significant reduction of the debt. . . . Every significant reduction of the outstanding debt has been followed by a depression, and every depression has been preceded by significant debt reduction."

In a similar way, some empirical evidence also shows that budget deficits have been followed by periods of economic expansion. The theoretical explanation for the association between public deficits and private sector performance is easer when one takes a closer look at what happens in reality. For example, public infrastructure projects such as the construction or improvement of roads, schools, and public transportation require the creation of millions of new jobs. In addition to reducing unemployment, government spending in general—and public investment in particular—stimulates private investment. Consider, for example, the construction of an airport. By the time the facility opens, private investors will build hotels, open restaurants, introduce a taxi service, and launch other related businesses. These companies, in turn, will hire workers and pay them wages, which helps expand the local economy. Furthermore, the new money created by the government to pay for all these expenditures will increase the amount of available liquidity in the system, which helps lower interest rates. This makes the cost of borrowing cheaper and encourages both investors and households to acquire assets and build wealth. It is important to note that the money supplied in this process is exactly equal to the amount that was demanded as wages, salaries, and other payments. Therefore, it is impossible to have an excess supply of money and, as has been documented, the fear of inflation appears to be unfounded.

Hassan Bougrine

See also: Fiscal Policy; Tax Policy.

Further Reading

Bougrine, Hassan. "The Stabilizing Role of Public Spending." In *Introducing Macroeconomic Analysis: Issues, Questions and Competing Views*, ed. Hassan Bougrine and Mario Seccareccia, 165–175. Toronto: Emond Montgomery, 2009.

Ricardo, David. "Essay on the Funding System." In *The Works of David Ricardo*, ed. J.R. McCulloch [1846]. London: John Murray, 1888.

Seccareccia, Mario. "Keynesianism and Public Investment: A Left-Keynesian Perspective on the Role of Government Expenditures and Debt." *Studies in Political Economy* 46 (Spring 1995): 43–78.

Wray, L. Randall. *Understanding Modern Money: The Key to Full Employment and Price Stability.* Aldershot, UK: Edward Elgar, 1998.

Fiscal Policy

Fiscal policy is viewed by economists as one-half of macroeconomic policy, the other half being monetary policy. Fiscal policy concerns how a government raises revenue—such as through taxes—and how it spends that revenue on services and other expenditures. Putting together a government budget thus constitutes a major step in fiscal policy making. Despite their fundamental differences, fiscal policy and monetary policy go hand in hand because a country's currency will lose its value if its fiscal policy is not seen as sustainable, especially over the long term.

Fiscal policy is seen as sustainable or rational when the general public and those buying government debt instruments perceive that the policy is predictable and that the government will continue to make payments on its debt. Under the most rational fiscal policy, a government's revenue sources (taxes, tariffs, user fees) will roughly equal its expenditures on government programs—in other words, the budget will be balanced. Under a rational fiscal policy, the government will also make its budgets—and the process by which the budgets are formulated—open to public scrutiny. In addition, it is common practice and rational fiscal policy for governments to prepare financial statements and to have these statements audited.

The business cycle can have a major effect on fiscal policy. During economic contractions, taxes and other sources of government revenue typically go down as people become unemployed and corporate profits shrink and disappear. At the same time, such periods often see heightened demand for government services, such as unemployment compensation. In addition, many governments seek to enhance aggregate demand during slumps by increasing spending on things like infrastructure, which creates investment and jobs, and by cutting taxes. An expansive fiscal policy can help to lift an economy out of recession but it can also exacerbate a downturn if the government is forced to borrow too much, making it more expensive for businesses to obtain the credit they need to operate, invest, expand, and hire.

Keynesian Fiscal Policy

Keynesian economists—those who adhere to the principles of John Maynard Keynes—believe that fiscal policy can help governments manage the economy to ensure full employment. Keynesians believe that when private economic activity is not creating enough demand to allow for full employment, fiscal policy can be used to increase demand, stimulate production, and create more jobs. The idea of active economic management by the government was articulated in Keynes's landmark work, *The General Theory of Employment, Interest and Money*, published in 1936 during the Great Depression. The prolonged high unemployment rates of that period prompted Keynes to recommend that governments take action to create jobs. The *General Theory* marked the first time that a comprehensive theoretical framework described how fiscal policy can be used to create full employment. The book is also regarded among economists as the beginning of macroeconomics as a subdiscipline of the field.

An active fiscal policy, then, is the use of government taxing and spending policy to stimulate economic demand. In political discourse, the use of government fiscal policy to increase demand came to be known as "fiscal stimulus." If the private sector is not investing enough in productive assets and not spending enough to increase output, including the hiring of employees, Keynesians believe that a fiscal stimulus on the part of government will trigger an upward cycle of economic activity.

As government spending increases through fiscal stimulus, the argument goes, private individuals will see an increase in income and spend more on consumer goods. The increase in consumer spending and demand, in turn, will encourage private companies to spend more on output—including the hiring of more people. The newly hired employees will then spend more themselves, boosting demand even higher and feeding the upward cycle of economic activity. The principle underlying active fiscal policy is also known as "demand management," as it is predicated on boosting consumer demand and the necessary production to meet it.

Keynesian economists believe that a fiscal stimulus is created when the government spends more than it receives in taxes and other revenue sources—a practice called "deficit spending." A government can use deficit spending to create a fiscal stimulus in several ways. The differences between these strategies are often the subject of political debate in the formulation of government policy. Economists who believe that government programs help people urge more spending on such programs. Aside from the help to ordinary people, they maintain, the increased government spending also fuels greater demand. Other economists recommend fiscal stimulus through a reduction in taxes, because taxes are seen as a drain on private economic activity. Thus, deficit spending can be created in any of three ways: (1) increasing government spending while keeping taxes the same; (2) reducing taxes while keeping spending the same; or (3) reducing taxes and increasing government spending simultaneously.

Deficit spending is also widely referred to as "priming the pump" of economic activity. The term implies a process analogous to the flow of water through a closed system, the priming of

which starts an upward cycle and restores the flow of water (or money). The first overt use of active fiscal policy in the United States—when, say some economic historians, Keynesian economics first became institutionalized in American policy—was the Pump Priming Act of 1938, which increased the federal government budget by 5 percent over the previous year. In hindsight, a spending increase of this magnitude does not seem substantial enough to pump-prime an economy facing above-average levels of unemployment—indeed it is not much greater than the general increase in government spending from year to year—but it marked a significant departure at the time.

Criticisms

Fiscal policy as a tool for managing the economy has been criticized on a variety of grounds. Perhaps the most cogent argument against Keynesian economics is that political reality does not allow it to work in practice as it is proposed in theory. The purpose of a fiscal stimulus—running a deficit in the short term to boost economic activity in the short term—is to create a temporary increase in private sector demand, fueling production, job creation, and broad-scale economic growth. However, history has repeatedly shown that once increased government spending has been put in place, deficit spending generally does not decrease once full employment is achieved. The "public choice" school of economics explains why it is difficult to reduce spending on any government program due to the special-interest groups created by it.

Many economists argue that the private sector, rather than government, can best create long-term productivity increases (which is what supports higher standards of living) through the natural profit incentives of the marketplace. Thus, it is argued, when governments continue to run budget deficits, increasing their debt levels from year to year, society's resources are diverted from vital private sector activity (including investment) to paying the interest on government borrowing. In the United States, for example, the federal debt prior to the adoption of Keynesian economics (except during times of war) averaged less than 10 percent of national income. After the 1930s (again excepting periods of war), the national debt as a percentage of national income has averaged more than 35 percent.

Another common criticism of demand management as fiscal policy is what is known as the "lag time" involved in implementing public policy. In order for a fiscal stimulus to be effective, the deficit spending must take place when the economy is performing poorly. However, given the months or even years that it often takes for fiscal policy to have an effect, the period of greatest potential benefit has already passed. Whatever the causes of booms and busts in the economic cycle, the periods of growth and contraction are extremely difficult to forecast. It is all but impossible to time a fiscal stimulus so that it will take effect at the precise moment of downturn—or even close to it. In the first place, it takes time for the government to gather the economic data required to determine when unemployment is increasing. Then it takes time to put together a budget proposal recommending the stimulus, more time for the legislative body to approve the budget, and even more time for the government to spend the additional funds so as to increase demand.

In short, the lag times in public policy make it exceedingly difficult for the government to manage the economy purely through fiscal policy. It is often the case that fiscal stimulus spending on a government program flows through the economy at the same time that the private sector is already increasing its economic activity. When this occurs, both the government and the private sector are competing for the scarce economic resources of a society at the same time. Deficit spending on the part of the government may therefore be counterproductive, worsening the effects of the boom-and-bust cycle because productivity gains in the up-cycle are not as great as they could be due to government using scarce economic resources at the wrong time. In economic thinking this is known as a negative "unintended consequence" of public policy.

Every government by definition creates fiscal policy—the management of government revenues and expenditures—as part of its budget formulation process. Specifically, it is the use of fiscal policy to manage demand that is still under debate in economic circles, even after being common political practice for more than seventy years.

Cameron M. Weber

See also: Fiscal Balance; Monetary Policy; Public Works Policy; Stimulus Package, U.S. (2008); Stimulus Package, U.S. (2009); Tax Policy.

Further Reading

Borcherding, Thomas E., ed. *Budgets and Bureaucrats: The Sources of Government Growth.* Durham, NC: Duke University Press, 1977.

Keynes, John Maynard. *The General Theory of Employment, Interest and Money.* New York: Harcourt Brace, 1936.

Mankiw, N. Gregory. *Principles of Macroeconomics.* 5th ed. Mason, OH: South-Western, 2009.

Fisher, Irving (1867–1947)

Irving Fisher was an American economist and monetary reformer who developed the modern quantity theory of money and made contributions to the study of the relationship between money, inflation, interest rates, and economic activity. He was also an early exponent of the application of mathematics to economic theory and a world-renowned expert on the theoretical and statistical properties of index numbers. An early neoclassical economist, he is credited with having laid much of the groundwork for modern monetary economics.

Irving Fisher was born on February 27, 1867, in Saugerties, New York. He received a bachelor's degree from Yale University in 1888 and was awarded the school's first PhD in economics in 1891. He spent his entire teaching career at Yale, as an instructor, tutor, assistant professor,

Monetary theorist Irving Fisher, a pioneer of modern quantitative economics, explained fluctuations in the economy as a function of avoidable disturbances in monetary policy and of debt-deflation theory. *(The Granger Collection, New York)*

professor of political economy (1898–1935), and professor emeritus (1935–1947). Fisher was elected president of the American Economic Association in 1918, and in 1930 became a founder and the first president of the Econometric Society. In addition to economics, he had a keen interest in such areas as eugenics, nutrition, pacifism, and the environment.

Among his most important contributions to mathematical economics is the so-called Fisher equation of exchange. According to the equation, $MV = PQ$, the money supply (M) multiplied by the velocity of circulation (V, or the number of times a unit of currency purchases goods and services within a specified period of time) is equal to the total output of goods and services (P, the average price level, multiplied by Q, quantity—measured by real gross domestic product). Put more simply, the Fisher equation states that the amount of money spent over a given period of time must equal the amount of money used during the same period. For example, if the U.S. money supply is $1 trillion and each dollar is used twelve times per year to purchase goods and services, then $12 trillion worth of goods and services must have been purchased. The Fisher equation is the cornerstone of the modern quantity theory of money and provides an explanation for the causes of inflation. If V and Q remain constant over a period of time, any increase in the money supply will lead to an increase in the price level.

A second element of Fisher's work was the discovery of "money illusion." This refers to the confusion that arises from changes in monetary terms and changes in real terms. For example, if a worker's salary increases by 8 percent but inflation increases by 16 percent over the same period, the worker would be suffering from "money illusion" to believe that he is better off; in reality, his new salary will buy him less than his old salary did before the inflation.

An important example of Fisher's contribution to macroeconomics is his debt-deflation theory of economic fluctuations. Fisher initially attributed the onset of the Great Depression to the actions of the Federal Reserve, which unnecessarily contracted the money supply (a view later reaffirmed by Milton Friedman and Ben Bernanke). The severity of the Depression, however, eventually led Fisher to develop his debt-deflation theory. The central element of this theory is that the downswing of the cycle (leading to possible depression) results from the discovery of overindebtedness throughout the economy. Given that overindebtedness is unanticipated when debts are incurred, the discovery of the problem is followed by rapid attempts at correction through liquidation and possible bankruptcies. Since debts are commonly denominated in nominal terms, a massive sale of assets, leading to a broad-based drop in the price level, would only place greater emphasis on the real value of the debt burden. A vicious downward spiral would therefore be generated by a combination of excessive real-debt burden and deflation.

Fisher's reputation was damaged by his misjudgment of the stock market in 1929 and his insistence during the course of the Great Depression that recovery was imminent. In 1913, Fisher made a fortune with his patented index-card system (the forerunner of the Rolodex), but lost half of it through speculation in the stock market. Adamant that stock prices would quickly rebound after the crash of October 1929, he borrowed heavily to invest further, but lost his entire fortune as prices continued to slide. Following the collapse of Fisher's personal fortune, Yale University was forced to purchase his house in order to save him from eviction. Fisher, who died on April 19, 1947, in New Haven, Connecticut, remained heavily in debt for the rest of his life. It is only in recent years that he has received proper recognition, not only as the father of modern monetary economics but as one of America's most important economists.

Christopher Godden

See also: Debt; Deflation; Fisher's Debt-Deflation Theory.

Further Reading

Dimand, Robert W., and John Geanakopolos, eds. *Celebrating Irving Fisher: The Legacy of a Great Economist.* Oxford, UK: Blackwell, 2005.

Fisher, Irving. "The Debt-Deflation Theory of Great Depressions." *Econometrica* 1:4 (1933): 337–357.

Thaler, Richard. "Irving Fisher: Modern Behavioral Economist." *American Economic Review* 87:2 (1997): 439–441.

Fisher's Debt-Deflation Theory

Developed by American economist Irving Fisher in the Great Depression of the early 1930s, Fisher's debt-deflation theory examines how a high level of indebtedness in an economy can, when hit by a shock such as the stock market crash of 1929, enter a vicious cycle in which the indebtedness triggers crippling deflation, which, in turn, leads to additional indebtedness. That is because as deflation sets in, money becomes more valuable, making it more expensive for borrowers to pay off their debts.

Because debts are denominated in dollars, when the price level falls (deflation), there is a real increase in debt levels, making the debts much more difficult to service. The result can be massive defaults and a prolonged downturn, like that of the period in which Fisher developed his theory.

A successful businessman and one of the most highly respected economists of the 1920s, Fisher had a gift for rendering complex theory into terms understood by the lay reader. He was especially hard hit by the Wall Street crash of 1929 and the Great Depression that followed, losing both his fortune and his reputation as an economist in the downturn. In an article titled "The Debt-Deflation Theory of Great Depressions," published in 1933 in *Econometrica*, the journal of the Econometric Society, he critiqued the prevailing classical paradigm of economic equilibrium, according to which the normal push and pull of supply and demand inevitably leads to a balance, or equilibrium, of high output and low unemployment. The period of equilibrium cannot be maintained for any length of time, Fisher contended, since the economy is usually at a point where there is over- or underconsumption, over- or undersavings, over- or underproduction, and so forth. Normally, such unstable states do not lead to recession, even when the economy is buffeted by the normal flux of the short-term business cycle.

But, Fisher argued, should the economy be burdened with a lot of indebtedness, then any shock to the system that undermines the confidence of creditors and debtors—such as the stock market crash of 1929—can set off a deflationary cycle that can plunge an economy into a prolonged downturn like the Great Depression. Fisher laid out nine cascading steps in the process:

1. Debt liquidation leads to distress selling.
2. As bank loans are paid back, the deposit currency contracts and the circulation velocity of money slows.
3. Decreasing velocity and contraction of deposits create a falling price level and a swelling in the value of money.

4. The net worth of businesses declines, leading to bankruptcies.

5. Losses in profits create greater anxieties about future losses.

6. Such anxiety reduces output, trade, and employment.

7. People lose confidence about their economic futures.

8. People tend to hoard their money, further reducing the velocity of circulation.

9. Disturbances in interest rates follow, such as a fall in the nominal rate or a rise in real rates.

On the basis of this analysis, Fisher urged that the government should take action to stop the deflationary cycle as quickly as possible. The credit system has to be restarted, he insisted, because deflation can lead to its complete collapse. Alternatively, the collapse in the credit system is not reversed until deflation is under control.

Fisher's remedies for policy makers of the 1930s included taking the United States off the gold standard and getting rid of fractional banking reserves—requirements that banks hold on to a certain amount of assets against which they lend money. Fisher opposed the fiscal stimulus policies of the Franklin Roosevelt administration—in which the federal government pumped money directly into the economy to put people to work—arguing instead that the government should restrict itself to controlling the money supply and coordinating the reform of the financial system.

Just as Roosevelt largely ignored Fisher's recommendations, so the economic community generally disregarded his debt-deflation theory. According to at least some economic historians, this was because Fisher's theory raised uncomfortable questions about the role the Federal Reserve and Wall Street had played in creating excess debt in the 1920s and thereby triggering debt deflation in the 1930s.

Long overlooked by economists who adhered to British theorist John Maynard Keynes's theories of countercyclical spending (even though Keynes

himself described Fisher as the "great-grandparent" of some of his own ideas), Fisher's theory has been resurrected by a number of economists in more recent years, including James Tobin and Hyman Minsky in their work on financial instability. In addition, the financial crisis of 2008–2009 has led some to reexamine Fisher's analysis of how high debt levels in an economy—as was the case with rising mortgage levels—can lead to debt deflation and a prolonged economic downturn.

Bill Kte'pi and James Ciment

See also: Debt; Deflation; Fisher, Irving; Great Depression (1929–1933).

Further Reading

Allen, W.R. "Irving Fisher, F.D.R., and the Great Depression." *History of Political Economy* 9:4 (1977): 560–587.

Fisher, Irving. "The Debt-Deflation Theory of Great Depressions." *Econometrica* 1:4 (1933): 337–357.

"Irving Fisher: Out of Keynes's Shadow." *The Economist*, February 12, 2009.

King, Mervyn. "Debt-Deflation: Theory and Evidence." *European Economic Review* 38:3–4 (1994): 419–445.

Wolfson, Martin A. "Irving Fisher's Debt-Deflation Theory: Its Relevance to Current Conditions." *Cambridge Journal of Economics* 20:3 (1996): 315–333.

Fixed Business Investment

Fixed business investment (FBI) is, as the name implies, the investment that businesses make in fixed assets, primarily buildings and equipment (the latter including transportation and computing equipment) that have a useful life span of more than one year. Gross FBI is defined as the purchase of new fixed assets and the depreciated cost of used fixed assets. Net FBI is gross FBI minus the depreciated cost of used fixed assets. Net FBI represents the net addition to the capital stock. FBI, along with residential investment, is defined as total fixed investment in the national economic accounts. Residential investment includes new construction of residential single and multifamily dwellings.

The other component of gross private domestic investment in the economic accounts is inventory investment, which is not "fixed" within the business sector but a product destined for sale to other business, consumers, government, or exports. In summary, gross private domestic investment includes FBI, residential investment, and changes in inventories, the first two of which are considered fixed.

FBI is broken down into two basic categories—buildings and equipment. Nonresidential building investment includes new structures (including own-account production); improvements to existing structures; expenditures on new mobile structures; net purchases of used structures by private businesses and by nonprofit institutions from government agencies; and broker fees and sales commissions connected to all of the above. Nonresidential structures also include equipment considered an integral part of a structure, such as plumbing, heating, and electrical systems.

Investment in equipment and software consists of capital account purchases of new machinery, equipment, furniture, vehicles, and computer software; dealers' margins on sales of used equipment; and net purchases of used equipment from government agencies, persons, and the rest of the world. Own-account production of computer software is also included. Information-processing equipment and software includes computer equipment and software, medical equipment, and office and accounting equipment. Industrial equipment includes fabricated metal products, engines, metalworking machinery, materials-handling equipment, and electrical transmission equipment. Trucks, buses, truck trailers, automobiles (purchased by businesses rather than households), aircraft, ships and boats, and railroad equipment are included in transportation equipment. The "other equipment" category includes furniture, fixtures, and household appliances (purchased by businesses), and agricultural, construction, mining, and service industry equipment.

FBI accounts are useful for a wide variety of purposes. For the business owner and investment analyst, the elements in such accounts are often leading indicators of future economic activity. For example, if the accounts detect the decision to postpone capital spending on new equipment, this is commonly perceived as a signal that economic and business conditions will slow in the near-term future. Likewise, if economic conditions have been slow, an uptick in fixed business investment suggests increased optimism by business and improved conditions in the short-term future.

At the macroeconomic level (i.e., regarding the national economy as a whole), the data on investment are vital to the study of productivity improvements in the economy. The quantity and quality of FBI is a forerunner of improved productivity growth, output per worker, and future economic growth in terms of gross domestic product (GDP) and per capita GDP. The exact mechanisms of these processes are under continuous scrutiny. The performance of business investment as a source of macroeconomic instability is also an important area of research. In the late 1990s, for example, investment in computing equipment and software was a leading cause of the overheating of the economy and the subsequent decline when the dot.com bubble burst.

At the microeconomic level, economists study the effect of business investments on economic growth for a particular metropolitan area, state, group of states, or region. In particular, economists search for models that link the investment performance of firms and their influence on overall regional productivity and growth. Development policies by states and communities have been crafted that provide financial incentives for firms to invest in new plant and equipment as a means of creating higher-paying jobs and generating higher rates of income growth.

In short, trends in fixed business investment are often important indicators of economic expansions or contractions to come. As such, they are of considerable interest to economists who study the timing and intensity of business cycles. During the economic expansion of 2005–2007, for example,

FBI constituted about 25 percent of net growth in the GDP, the key measure of national economic output. As real (inflation-adjusted) GDP grew at a pace of 2 to 3 percent per year, about 0.5 to 0.8 percentage points of this growth was accounted for by FBI.

As the economy cooled during 2008, however, FBI also declined (with the exception of the second quarter), contributing directly to the contraction. This was especially the case as the recession intensified following the financial crisis of late 2008. Still, the decline in FBI played a relatively minor role in the fall in GDP that quarter, compared to the much greater downturn in personal consumption expenditures.

Derek Bjonback

See also: Mortgage, Commercial/Industrial; Savings and Investment.

Further Reading

Bondonio, Daniele, and Robert T. Greenbaum. "Do Business Investment Incentives Promote Employment in Declining Areas? Evidence From EU Objective 2 Regions." *European Urban and Regional Studies* 13:3 (2006): 225–244.

Doms, Mark. "The Boom and Bust in Information Technology Investment." *Economic Review, Federal Reserve Bank of San Francisco*, January 1, 2004.

Khan, Aubhik. "Understanding Changes in Aggregate Business Fixed Investment." *Business Review, Federal Reserve Bank of Philadelphia*, second quarter, 2001.

Kopche, Richard W., and Richard S. Brauman. "The Performance of Traditional Macroeconomic Models of Business Investment Spending." *New England Economic Review*, no. 2 (March/April 2001): 3–40.

U.S. Department of Commerce, Bureau of Economic Analysis. *A Primer on GDP and the National Income and Product Accounts.* Washington, DC: U.S. Government Printing Office, 2007.

Fleetwood Enterprises

Formerly based in Riverside, California, Fleetwood Enterprises was, until its 2009 bankruptcy, the largest producer of recreational vehicles (RVs) and manufactured (mobile) homes in the United States. Fleetwood experienced great swings of fortune through much of its history, and its fate il-

lustrates the impact volatile fuel prices and tight credit can have on business.

Founded in 1950 under the name Coach Specialties Company, the firm specialized in the manufacture of window blinds for travel trailers. After its owner John Crean built his own travel trailer in the early 1950s, the company won a contract to build the vehicle for a local dealer. Crean did well, but the seasonal nature of the business led him to expand into the production of manufactured homes, a growth industry during the early baby boom years. Cheaper to build and not reliant on weather conditions to construct, manufactured homes grew in popularity in the first decades after World War II.

In 1957, the firm reincorporated as Fleetwood Enterprises and began to buy up other travel trailer firms. In 1965, the firm went public. These were boom years for both the recreational vehicle and manufactured home industries. But the oil shocks of the 1970s and early 1980s—which sent gas prices soaring—hit the RV industry hard, as did the harsh recession of the early 1980s. For the first time in its history, Fleetwood had to cut back on production, closing nine of its manufacturing plants.

While low oil prices and a booming economy allowed Fleetwood to prosper through much of the 1980s, it also faced growing government scrutiny. In 1988, the company paid a multimillion-dollar fine after investigations by the U.S. Justice Department and the Housing and Urban Development Department led to charges that its manufactured homes were defective. In addition, several company subsidiaries were fined after pleading guilty to overcharging veterans for financing.

By the boom years of 1990s, Fleetwood was once again prospering, with a 21.6 percent share of the manufactured home business and a 34.6 percent share of the motor home market, the most lucrative market in the RV sector. At its peak, it employed some 21,000 workers. But it was also facing increased competition in both sectors. In response, the company teamed up with the Michigan-based Pulte Corporation to set up a nationwide network of retail centers as a way to counter competition. It also bought out competitors. But the rapid expansion saddled the company with a significant debt load that it was never able to get out from under.

By 2001, the increased competition and the servicing of Fleetwood's debt sent the company permanently into the red. Two events in 2008 sealed the company's fate. In the summer peak season for RV sales, gas prices soared to more than $4 per gallon nationally, crippling demand for the fuel-hungry RVs the company manufactured. Then, in the fall, credit markets collapsed. As with standard homes, most manufactured homes and RVs are largely purchased on credit. When that became much harder to obtain—particularly for the typically lower-income buyers of manufactured homes—the bottom fell out of that market as well.

By November 2008, Fleetwood's shipments of RVs had fallen to their lowest level since 1978 and it was forced to shut down its RV division, closing plants and laying off 2,500 workers. This was not enough. By March 2009, when the company filed for protection under Chapter 11 of U.S. bankruptcy law, it had assets of $558.3 million and debts of $518 million. In June, the bankruptcy court approved the sale of the company's shutdown RV operations to a New York private equity firm for $53 million, which reopened several of the company's former plants in Decatur, Indiana, while the manufactured housing division was sold to Cavco Industries of Phoenix.

James Ciment

See also: Manufacturing; Recession and Financial Crisis (2007–).

Further Reading

"As Fleetwood Enterprises Fades from Inland Area, It Leaves Trail of Prosperous Times." *The Press Enterprise*, August 18, 2009. Available at www.pe.com/localnews/inland/stories/PE_BIZ_20090818_fleetwood.ee0e6687.html. Accessed August 19, 2009.

Funding Universe. "Fleetwood Enterprises, Inc." Available at www.fundinguniverse.com/company-histories/Fleetwood-Enterprises-Inc-Company-History.html. Accessed August 18, 2009.

Florida Real-Estate Boom (1920s)

One of the greatest land-sale booms in twentieth-century America, the Florida real-estate frenzy of the early 1920s saw a huge run-up in land prices in Miami and other parts of South Florida—much of it fueled by canny developers—before crashing in 1925. Although the boom was short-lived, it increased public awareness of Florida as an attractive place to live and left behind a number of new towns that would grow into major population centers after World War II.

Underlying Factors

The Florida real-estate boom was a direct outgrowth of the economic prosperity and easy money culture of the United States in the 1920s. Between 1921 and 1929, the U.S. gross national product rose from $74.1 billion to $103.1 billion, an increase of 40 percent, one of the fastest expansions in history. Meanwhile, per capita income rose from $640 to $850, a nearly one-third increase. In the low tax, pro-business environment of the day, most of the gains accrued to the wealthy, but the middle class and skilled members of the working class saw significant gains as well.

Moreover, following the sharp but brief recession of 1921–1922, the newly created Federal Reserve Board rapidly increased the money supply by lowering the interest rate it charged member banks to borrow money. This produced a flood of cheap credit for borrowers throughout the country, as banks became more amenable to loaning money for real-estate purchases and, in the case of Florida, speculation.

For much of its history since joining the Union in 1845, Florida had been a relatively small and insignificant state, with most of the population residing in its northern half, where they engaged in agriculture. Hot, humid, and swampy, the southern half of the state was seen as disease ridden and unsuitable for settlement. In 1900, Florida still had the smallest population of any state east of the Mississippi and, as late as 1910, its population had yet to reach 1 million.

Among the residents at the time, however, were a number of wealthy and socially prominent individuals, drawn to the state as a winter home by its subtropical climate and transported there on a new railroad line that, by the mid-1890s, had reached Palm Beach and Biscayne Bay, where Miami was located. Over the course of the early twentieth century, the Atlantic Coast of Florida began to gain a reputation as a warm-weather paradise.

Beyond the railroad and a few luxury hotels, there was little infrastructure. In 1910, an automotive parts millionaire named Carl Fisher bought a winter home in Miami. Eyeing a barrier island several miles across Biscayne Bay, Fisher decided it would make an ideal beachside resort. With developer John Collins, Fisher built a bridge and began dredging swampland, planting trees and other plants to stabilize the expanded island.

While Collins undertook much of the civil engineering, Fisher focused on promotion, utilizing newly developed advertising and public relations techniques to sell Miami Beach—the island had been incorporated in 1915—to northerners looking for a warm winter home. Celebrities were encouraged to visit, and pictures of bathing beauties were placed in newspapers. All kinds of stunts were tried, including the use of baby elephants as golf caddies to promote South Florida as the ideal place for those interested in the sport. In general, Miami was sold as an exotic tropical outpost that one could reach by train from the Northeast in a little over one day.

Boom

At first, conditions were not conducive to Fisher's campaign, particularly after the United States entered World War I. He even offered free lots to anyone who would build on the island, but got few takers. Things changed when the war came to an end, and especially when the recession of 1921–1922 gave way to the "Coolidge prosperity" of the mid-1920s. By the end of 1922, the boom was in full tilt.

Over the next two years, Florida's population increased by 300,000, with most of the increase coming in the southern part of the state. Yet while the population increase contributed directly to the land boom, what really drove up prices was speculation. Investors large and small began to see Miami real estate not as a place to build a home but as an opportunity to make money. Lax regulation meant that banks—some of them founded specifically to cash in on the boom—could offer easy-term loans of 10 percent down (an almost unheard-of deal in 1920s America) with little capital in their vaults to safeguard depositors against default. Indeed, default seemed a distant possibility in the early 1920s, as investors bought property for just months or even weeks at a time before selling it for a profit and investing in more. So contagious was Florida land fever that most of the investors bought property sight unseen: fully two-thirds of sales were done by mail.

Bust and Aftermath

By 1925, signs began to appear that the market was overheated. Land prices had risen so high—into the hundreds of thousands of dollars for some parcels (or millions in 2009 dollars)—that the middle class was priced out of the market. Adding to inflation was a shortage of building materials. So overburdened was the railroad connecting Miami with points north that, at one point, it refused to transport any freight other than essential goods. The situation was made worse by the sinking of a large ship at the entrance to Miami Harbor, blocking sea access to the city, in January 1926. Meanwhile, Miami Beach was not the only new resort municipality in South Florida. Other developments along the Atlantic Coast, such as Boca Raton and Hollywood, along with Tampa and Marco Island on

High-rise construction fills the Miami skyline during the Florida real-estate boom of the 1920s. Easy credit, rampant speculation, and rapidly escalating property values ended abruptly in 1925, but the growth and development had lasting effects on the state. *(The Granger Collection, New York)*

the Gulf Coast, were increasingly competing for investor dollars.

By late 1925, the bubble was beginning to deflate, as financial advisers began to warn investors that rising land prices were not based on the actual value of the property but on the prospect of that land being quickly resold. As prices began to deflate and people were unable to sell the land, they could not service their loans. This forced much property into foreclosure and put further downward pressure on prices. Local banks, already hurt by a slump in agriculture, which had been hit by a series of devastating freezes, began to go under. At the same time, a slump in the bond markets made it difficult for new municipalities to borrow money to pay for the improvements all the newcomers demanded and needed, further rubbing the shine off Florida as a place to winter or live year-round.

According to many accounts, a devastating hurricane that struck Miami in September 1926 caused the bursting of the bubble. In reality it was only the last pinprick. Prices had already deflated

significantly in Miami and many of the other South Florida developments when the storm laid waste to the east coast and panhandle of Florida, causing some $14 billion in damage statewide (about $170 billion in 2008 dollars).

While the Florida real-estate boom was short-lived, it left a lasting legacy in the form of new counties, new towns, and, most importantly, an image of the southern half of the state as a carefree getaway or living destination with a warm year-round climate. With the national economic boom and the development of low-cost air-conditioning after World War II, that image would pay great dividends in an expanding population and economy that would make Florida the fourth-largest state in the Union by the early 2000s.

James Ciment

See also: Asset-Price Bubble; Boom, Economic (1920s); Housing Booms and Busts; Real-Estate Speculation.

Further Reading

Foster, Mark S. *Castles in the Sand: The Life and Times of Carl Graham Fisher.* Gainesville: University Press of Florida, 2000.

Frazer, William Johnson, and John J. Guthrie, Jr. *The Florida Land Boom: Speculation, Money, and the Banks.* Westport, CT: Quorum, 1995.

Nolan, David. *Fifty Feet in Paradise: The Booming of Florida.* New York: Harcourt Brace Jovanovich, 1984.

Foreclosure

A foreclosure occurs when a lender (bank or secured creditor/investor) regains control over, or repossesses, property used as collateral for a loan. The lender's objective is to resell the property in an attempt to recover the amount owed against it. Foreclosure begins after a borrower defaults on a loan payment and the lender gives public notice to the borrower that his or her right to redeem the mortgage has been severed.

The Role of Foreclosures in the 2008–2009 Recession

A fall in residential real-estate prices and a sharp rise in home mortgage foreclosures played an important role in causing and perpetuating the recession that began in the United States in December 2007. In a modern economy characterized by well-developed capital markets, ample liquidity, and widespread access to credit, consumption expenditures are a function not only of income, but also of wealth and consumer confidence. Income matters, but consumption growth can rise above income growth for long periods of time. Prior to the recession, rising housing values were tapped through home equity lines of credit to finance household expenditures. These credit-fueled expenditures were used to maintain standards of living during a period of flat or declining wage growth. As long as housing prices continued to increase, consumer expenditures could rise, and they did. In the United States, consumption has risen from 63 percent of gross domestic product (GDP) in the 1950s to 70 percent today. Thus, over the last several decades, economic growth has been largely driven by consumption expenditures. These in turn have been driven by rising consumer confidence and the home equity credit made available from the upward trend in home prices. Both came to an end in 2007.

Between 2007 and early 2010, median U.S. real-estate values fell by over 20 percent. According to Federal Reserve estimates using Mortgage Bankers Association data, in the first half of 2007, 650,000 foreclosures were initiated. By the first half of 2008 this nearly doubled to 1.2 million. The share of total mortgages in foreclosure increased from 1 percent in 2005 to 3.3 percent in 2008. Among subprime mortgages, the share in foreclosure increased from 3.3 percent in 2005 to 13.7 percent in 2008. These trends led to a recessionary cascade of decreasing consumption, falling GDP, growing unemployment, falling incomes, and many households owning more against their homes than what the homes were worth. The result was a further increase in foreclosures. To stop a downward spiral such as this, housing prices must stabilize to prevent further erosion in wealth. In addition, household expenditures must be buoyed by increases in wage income rather than by further increases in household debt.

The Foreclosure Process

The foreclosure process varies depending on state laws as well as lenders' specific policies. However, there is a typical process that applies to most. Generally, after the first two months of missed payments, the borrower will receive letters and phone calls from the lender. Late fees will apply and begin to accrue. After the third month of nonpayment, the borrower will likely receive a demand letter from the lender requesting that the borrower make his or her loan current within thirty days. If the borrower fails to do this, then the lender sends out a foreclosure package and gives public notice that the loan is being called. The full amount is now due, and the foreclosure process has been initiated.

Types of Foreclosure

There are three primary types of foreclosures: judicial, power-of-sale, and strict foreclosure. Judicial foreclosure takes place through the use of the court system. The lender (or lender acting on behalf of a secured creditor/investor) initiates the foreclosure by filing a claim with the court. After the claim has been filed, the borrower will receive a notice from the court requesting payment. If the borrower does not make a monthly mortgage payment within thirty days, the house can be auctioned by the sheriff's office. When the house is sold, the individuals living in house will receive an eviction notice from the sheriff's office and will be forced to leave the property. Typically, the borrower has a 180-day redemption period following the sheriff's sale. During this period the borrower can pay off the loan in full and would then be allowed to reclaim the property. This rarely occurs.

A power-of-sale foreclosure can take place when there is a clause included in the deed of trust or mortgage that grants the lender the right to sell the property without judicial proceedings in case of default. This is similar to a judicial foreclosure, but the lender demands payment directly from the borrower rather than working through the court. The lender, rather than the sheriff, is also the one to carry out the auction of the property after the borrower has failed to make payments within the specified time. This type of foreclosure generally takes place more quickly than judicial foreclosures.

A strict foreclosure occurs when the lender itself takes possession of the property after the borrower fails to make a payment within the court-ordered time period. This differs from judicial foreclosure in that there is no auction of the house, but the lender, instead, takes direct possession of the property. Although strict foreclosure was the original form of foreclosure, it is now limited to a few northeastern states. It is also typically limited to situations in which the mortgagee owes more on the property than it is worth. Despite the differ-

ences in process, each of these forms of foreclosure requires a public notice of foreclosure. These public records provide the basis for the widely reported numbers and trends in foreclosures.

If the amount of money made on the sale of the property exceeds what is needed to cover the amount of the mortgage and costs of foreclosure—which rarely occurs—the borrower will receive the surplus. If there is not enough money to compensate for the foreclosure costs and mortgage, then the lender can try to receive additional funds through a deficiency judgment in most states. The deficiency judgment is a separate legal action, and it gives the lender the right to take other property from the borrower in order to satisfy the remaining debt. In most cases this is not pursued because the borrower could and would claim bankruptcy, making the deficiency judgment moot. In some states, first mortgages are nonrecourse loans, meaning that if the original mortgage has not been refinanced, then the only recourse for the lender is to seize the home; in this case, the lender is not able to "go after" the personal assets or income of the borrower.

The borrower's final option to retain his or her home can occur during a redemption period. After the sale has been made, some states refrain from transferring the title of the house until after the specified redemption period is complete. If the borrower can repay the full amount of the mortgage as well as the foreclosure costs, he can reclaim the house.

Recent Trends and Areas of Contention

As of this writing, the number of foreclosures has continued to rise since the beginning of the housing crisis in 2007. According to the *Economist*, over 5 million homes in the United States have entered the foreclosure process between 2006 and 2008. The *International Business Times* reported that the total number of foreclosures in 2009 reached 2.8 million, which was 21 percent higher than the number of foreclosures in 2008, and 120 percent higher than 2007. Certain areas of the country have been far more affected by foreclosures than others. Nevada, Arizona, Florida, California, and Utah are the states with the highest foreclosure rates. Coupled with the increasing number of foreclosures was a decrease in home prices. From 1999 to the summer of 2006, home prices doubled, making housing a valuable investment. However, according to the *New York Times*, housing prices fell by about 27 percent between the summer of 2006 and the end of 2009.

The reason for the decrease in housing prices and increase in the number of foreclosed homes stems in part from lending practices. Subprime loans were one area of contention. "Subprime" refers to the perceived lower quality of the loan. Many subprime loans had low initial "teaser" rates to entice borrowers; these loans were usually characterized by higher fees and interest rates. Furthermore, interest rates on loans with the teaser rates usually escalated to very high rates in two to three years. As a result, many borrowers who would not traditionally have been approved for a mortgage were able to purchase homes. An ongoing question is what share of these borrowers could have qualified for traditional, prime mortgages had they been steered in that direction.

Adjustable rate mortgages were also utilized. These are loans with low initial rates that increase after a few years or in response to changes in overall interest rates. Additionally, a number of "liar" and/or "NINJA" loans were also originated. Liar loans are mortgages granted to borrowers who gave information on their income and assets without providing documentation. Similarly, NINJA loans were mortgages obtained by individuals with no proof of income, job, or assets. These loans were given to borrowers who then purchased homes that they were unable to afford. When the owners of these homes began to default, it led to problems for the buyer, the bank, and the businesses and individuals who had invested in mortgages or securities backed by those mortgages. Since housing prices had decreased, many borrowers were now "under-

water," owing more on their house than it was worth. Selling or refinancing the home was not a realistic option because the borrower would still not be able to pay the mortgage. Thus, many of these loans resulted in foreclosure, which further depressed housing prices.

Proposed Policy Solutions

In order to rectify this downward spiral of decreasing housing prices and increased foreclosures, several government programs have been proposed. Hope for Homeowners and FHASecure were two initiatives developed during the Bush administration. Both of these programs provided avenues for borrowers to refinance their loans to government-secured, fixed-rate, thirty- to forty-year mortgages administered through the Federal Housing Administration (FHA). Both of these programs were severely underutilized, and the FHASecure program was terminated in 2008. The Hope Now Alliance has been more successful, as the coalition of mortgage industry executives, counseling agencies, investors, trade groups, and mortgage companies provided a hotline for borrowers to call and be connected with a mortgage counselor. Representative John Conyers, Jr., supported the Homeowners Protection Act of 2008, which would have allowed bankruptcy judges to modify mortgages by reducing the amount owed, extending the life of the loan, or adjusting the interest rate. This practice is also known as the "cram-down," meaning the lender would be forced to accept treatment of a loan that it did not agree to. By allowing judges to modify mortgages, homeowners could remain in their homes while they worked to pay off the modified mortgage. This proposal did not become law.

President Barack Obama has also proposed a plan for keeping people in their homes. One part of his plan was to allow Fannie Mae and Freddie Mac loans that are underwater to be refinanced. Another component of his plan was to decrease monthly payments for individuals who were near foreclosure. With the help of Fannie Mae, lenders are now routinely doing loan modifications before the foreclosure process commences. Interest rates are lowered, terms extended, and in some cases principal amounts are reduced in an attempt to reduce mortgage payments to 31 percent of a borrower's gross monthly income. Unfortunately, many borrowers seeking loan modifications are also burdened by credit card, auto, and other personal loans. Thus, the hope that modifications would greatly reduce foreclosures has not been realized.

Homeowners were not the only ones who received assistance through government programs. Banks were also lent funds to help with the losses they suffered during the housing crisis. Former Treasury secretary Henry Paulson initiated the Troubled Asset Relief Program, also known as TARP. The original plan for TARP consisted of banks auctioning their bad loans and other struggling assets at a price that would benefit the bank in the short term and the government in the long run. Additionally, the TARP Capital Purchase Program allowed the government to infuse capital into banks through purchases of senior preferred stock, which became the main focus of TARP. TARP led to the government owning preferred stock in hundreds of banks as well as providing funding to insurance giant AIG, General Motors, and Chrysler. Another step taken was to place Fannie Mae and Freddie Mac under government conservatorship in September 2008. This conservatorship resulted in the replacing of the board of directors and chief executive officers with individuals appointed by the Federal Housing Finance Agency, and quarterly capital investments by the government. President Obama's plan also provided some assistance for banks. His plan of reducing monthly payments for mortgage holders came with incentive payments for each modified loan the lender completed. The plan was estimated to provide relief for 3 million to 4 million people. As of December 2009, there have only been 66,465 permanent modifications and 787,231 active trial modifications.

Andrea Krogstad and Reynold F. Nesiba

See also: Housing Booms and Busts; Mortgage Lending Standards; Mortgage, Subprime; Recession and Financial Crisis (2007–).

Further Reading

Burton, Maureen, Reynold Nesiba, and Bruce Brown. *An Introduction to Financial Markets and Institutions.* 2nd ed. Armonk, NY: M.E. Sharpe, 2010.

Mortgage Bankers Association Web site: www.mortgagebankers.org.

The U.S. Department of Housing and Urban Development (HUD) Web site: http://portal.hud.gov/portal/page/portal/HUD/topics/avoiding_foreclosure.

Fragility, Financial

The term "financial fragility" refers to the degree to which a nation's financial system—made up of stock markets, currency markets, banks, and the like—is vulnerable to collapse. Some economists believe that financial fragility lies at the heart of the "bust" phase of the boom-and-bust cycle. While not all explanations of booms and busts support the superiority of financial causes, almost everyone agrees that the collapse of a large bank, for example, can make a bad economic situation worse.

Among the most prominent of recent theorists to explore financial fragility in depth was the American economist Hyman Minsky (1919–1996). In his financial instability hypothesis (FIH), Minsky describes how a prolonged economic expansion encourages investors to replace their expectations of a normal business cycle (incorporating an expected recession) with the expectation of ongoing expansion. The expectations of continuing profits in turn encourage businesses to take on greater debt, which, over time, leads to higher outflows relative to inflows, and hence greater financial instability. Where initially investors and businesses are cautious about the amount of funds they borrow and on what terms, borrowers become much less wary as the expansion continues. More and more funds are borrowed for shorter and shorter periods, with shorter loans rolled over and the loan payments becoming much more dependent on the delivery of capital gains. Over time, a given economic slowdown that eliminates capital gains and lowers business profits becomes that much more threatening to the overall system. "Thus," wrote Minsky, "after an expansion has been in progress for some time, an event that is not of unusual size or duration can trigger a sharp financial reaction."

A second source of fragility stems from the liquidity of marketable financial assets such as stocks, currencies, and derivatives (futures, option contracts, and the like). While the ease with which one can buy and sell part ownership of a company, for example, makes it considerably easier to raise funds to finance business operations and expansion (since with each investor committing only a fraction of his or her wealth to owning part of the business, the risk is reduced for each person), the greater liquidity also makes it much easier to sell the shares if one is dissatisfied with the company's performance and the return on one's investment. If profits are weak, dividends are low and the stock price increases that generate capital gains for the investor will be minimal or nonexistent. Facing low profits and minimal capital gains or even capital losses, shareowners are much more likely to sell their shares than they are to step in and try to help improve company performance. Although the company is itself a longer-term venture, there are, in a system of finance capitalism, fewer longer-term individual stakeholders in its success. The result is a greater impatience and movement of capital of the type stressed by British economist John Maynard Keynes in the 1920s. In this way, following George Edwards and other early writers on finance capitalism, the conversion from real to financial equity alone introduces an independent source of fragility.

The possibility that one can borrow to purchase liquid financial assets introduces a third source of financial instability. Borrowing to buy financial assets raises asset prices in a boom and lowers them in a bust. Suppose, for example, that stock in a company costs $100 per share to buy and that

it is purchased on a 60 percent down payment or margin—that is, with $40 of borrowed money. If the stock price rises to $150, the investor still owes only $40 but now has $110 of equity or margin collateral in the stock. The investor may use the $50 capital gain to leverage the purchase of an additional share in the company. Many investors acting to leverage their purchase of more shares in this way will drive up stock prices even further. But there is symmetry in this pyramiding process. When the trend is reversed, a fall in the market price of shares eliminates margin collateral. If the original stock price drops instead from $100 to $65, say, the investor still owes $40 but on a much devalued asset. Based on a value of $65, the maximum margin loan would be 40 percent of $65, or $26. In liquid-asset markets (stocks, currencies, options), lenders will demand that the investor pay off at least $14 of the $40 debt. If many investors sell off the stock to pay for such debt, stock prices will fall even further.

It is well known that financial liabilities incurred by a margin investor are fixed in nominal terms ($40 in the above example), but market prices are used to value the collateral asset. By forcing sales when asset prices are low or falling (which drives down asset prices even further), the market creates the paradoxical result that "the more debtors pay, the more they owe"—the Irving Fisher paradox (1932). A debt-deflation spiral of this type will bring distress both on lenders, who do not recoup the total amounts owed through sales of collateral assets, and on other asset holders, whose real value of outstanding debt (nominal debt divided by the value of the collateral asset) rises with each fall in asset prices.

Increasingly optimistic expectations, liquidity, and pyramiding all serve to drive the expansion into an area of increasing fragility. Where the changes in the underlying real economy are new (as when a technological innovation causes restructuring in large parts of the economy), the fragility is further enhanced by the intrusion of emotion and the increasing importance of the opinion of others. Economists Benjamin Graham, David

Dodd, and Sidney Cottle noted in their influential analysis of securities values of the early 1960s the effect emotion can have on asset values, while Brenda Spotton Visano has demonstrated how a social dimension of investing serves to augment a Minsky-type analysis of fragility when investors are facing a radically new—and unpredictable—economic environment.

In short, financial fragility is an aspect of the boom-and-bust phenomenon that attributes the fluctuations in output, employment, and prices to an inherently unstable financial system. It is a perspective that suggests the economy under finance capitalism is essentially more fragile than the underlying real economy alone.

Brenda Spotton Visano

See also: Minsky's Financial Instability Hypothesis.

Further Reading

Edwards, George. *The Evolution of Finance Capitalism.* New York: Augustus M. Kelley, 1938; reprint 1967.

Fisher, Irving. *Booms and Depressions: Some First Principles.* New York: Adelphi, 1932.

Graham, Benjamin, David L. Dodd, and Sidney Cottle. *Security Analysis: Principles and Techniques.* 4th ed. New York: McGraw-Hill, 1962.

Keynes, John Maynard. *A Treatise on Probability.* Vol. 8, *The Collected Writings of John Maynard Keynes*, ed. D. Moggeridge and E. Johnson. London: Macmillan, 1973, 1921.

Minsky, Hyman. *Can "It" Happen Again? Essays on Instability and Finance.* Armonk, NY: M.E. Sharpe, 1982.

Visano, Brenda Spotton. *Financial Crises: Socio-economic Causes and Institutional Context.* New York and London: Routledge, 2006.

France

France has been one of Europe's and the world's great economic and political powers since the end of the Middle Ages and its consolidation as a nation-state. However, from monarchy to republic, and through devastating wars, the French economy has experienced marked periods of both economic growth and stagnation. Perhaps Europe's greatest power in the sixteenth century, France fell behind Great Britain and Germany industrially in the nineteenth century, only to experience remarkable economic growth from World War II to the 1970s. Although it lagged behind the United States, Germany, Japan, and smaller nations in the late twentieth century and, like other developed countries, was challenged by the rise of China and East Asia by the turn of the twenty-first century, contemporary France remains one of the world's wealthiest, most productive economies, a global leader in many economic sectors.

Middle Ages to Napoleonic Rule

During the sixteenth, seventeenth, and eighteenth centuries, France moved from feudalism to a powerful, centralized monarchy, epitomized by the reign of Louis XIV (ruled 1643–1715). Economically, France was guided by mercantilism, a philosophy put into practice by Louis's long-serving finance minister, Jean-Baptiste Colbert. Mercantilism brought strict controls over the national economy, an influence that continues to the present day, but also sought to discourage imports and maximize exports. Colbert instituted protectionist policies, the state issued directives to guide production, industries were organized into guilds, and internal trade was encouraged with the reduction of tariffs, creation of ports, and the building of roads and canals. New or newly state-controlled industries included the royal tapestry works at Beauvais, the Gobelins tapestry works, marble quarries, and purveyors of luxury goods. As the French Empire began to grow, the French East India Company was established in 1664 and opened trade with West Africa. While France arguably was at the apogee of its power, Colbert's policies were a mixed blessing, encouraging industry but also incurring significant debt. The expulsion of the Huguenots in 1685 and war drained France of talent and expanded its debt.

The early eighteenth century brought the introduction of the *taille*, or tax, and a system of monetary stability based on conversion to gold and silver. However, the French economy did not begin to expand until the end of the 1730s, as agriculture, mines, metallurgy, and textiles became profitable industries. Technological development from abroad, such as John Kay's flying shuttle and James Watt's steam engine brought the first signs of the industrial revolution to France. Joseph-Marie Jacquard's loom for weaving figured fabrics sparked a burst of early development in the textile industry, and the first machines were introduced into production. Cities such as Lyons, an early home to textile mills, as well as Marseille, Bordeaux, and Nantes, became important commercial centers. Trade with North America and the Antilles grew significantly, with France importing sugar, coffee, cotton, and slaves. Paris became a center of international banking by the 1780s. France and Britain were the world's two richest countries in the mid-1700s, but France was slower to move to industrial production than its rival across the English Channel.

Economic reversals dominated the mid-to-late eighteenth century, as the Seven Years' War (1756–1763) resulted in the loss of most of France's North American colonies and a huge increase in public debt. Financial support for the American Revolution, together with several agricultural crashes and harsh winters in the 1770s and 1780s, brought the French to the verge of economic crisis. Louis XVI's ministers Anne-Robert-Jacques Turgot and Jacques Necker introduced reforms, paper money, and increased taxes through a program known as the *vingtième.* This combination of factors, together with an increase in poverty and the spread of Enlightenment ideas about liberty and democracy, led to the beginning of the French Revolution in 1789 and the fall of the monarchy.

The twenty-six years of revolution and Napoleonic rule brought French industrial development to a standstill, leaving France even farther behind Britain in economic development. The radical, early years of the revolution had sought to bring economic equality, but the Reign of Terror attacked merchants and other "enemies of the revolution," imposed wage and price controls,

and brought anarchy, looting, and plundering to much of France. The manorial system was ended, giving peasants ownership of their land. The military buildup under Napoleon after 1795 briefly stimulated the economy, but the success of British blockades, high inflation, and military defeat in 1815 left France in a shambles.

From Laggard to Leader: Since 1815

The Restoration of the monarchy and the early nineteenth century saw a time of economic stability. France remained largely an agricultural economy, with peasants living much as they had for hundreds of years. France was Europe's second most populous nation, after Russia, with about 30 million people, but barely 7 percent lived in towns of 20,000 or more. Yet canal- and road-building proceeded apace under the restored Bourbon monarchy of Louis-Philippe as well as during Napoleon III's Third Empire. However, the years from the 1840s to 1870 ushered in significant industrialization as roads and railroads were built, factories opened, and educational reforms were designed to raise students' knowledge and skills. The cotton and textile industries flourished, with a well-developed domestic supply of manufactured wool, yet French metallurgy and shipbuilding fell behind those of Britain and Germany.

Indeed, by the time of the Franco-Prussian War (1870–1871), France had fallen significantly behind these industrial powers, and people lamented *le retard français,* or French backwardness. While coal output increased, France lagged behind other European powers in power generation, including hydroelectric, and its steel and iron industries were laggards compared to its two major European rivals. The same was true in the new chemical and electronics industries, despite earlier French inventiveness. By the turn of the twentieth century, most French machinery was imported. In short, as large-scale industrialization proceeded apace in Britain, Germany, and the United States, France remained a country of *ateliers,* or small workshops, with few employees.

Although Germany, the superior economic power on the eve of World War I, was defeated, the Great War was catastrophic for France. More than 1.3 million Frenchmen died and 3 million were injured during the war, and the country lost 27 percent of its eighteen- to twenty-seven-year-olds, leaving the labor force in decline into the 1930s. The reparations extracted from Germany in the Treaty of Versailles failed to boost France's economic recovery, while ravaging Germany, a potentially peaceful trading partner. Industrial production did increase in the late 1920s, but France's combination of demographic stagnation, a huge and inefficient agricultural sector, and many poorly equipped industries was indicative of the economy's continuing structural weaknesses. France's colonial empire—in Africa, Asia, the Pacific, and the Caribbean—was as much a burden as a boon to the French economy, although it reached its peak just before the rise of Adolf Hitler. The French Empire, second in size only to the British, covered nearly 5 million square miles (13 million square kilometers), or 9 percent of the earth's land area.

The Great Depression hit France later and with less severity than the United States or Britain, as the franc was undervalued and its economy relied less on trade. Nonetheless, between 1931 and 1939, the French economy was in decline, as the country's production index declined roughly 10 percent and hundreds of thousands lost their jobs, though fewer than in other countries. German reparations, a prop to the economy, ended, small and medium-sized businesses suffered, and France's relatively backward economy led it to emerge from the Depression more slowly.

In the 1930s, the government nationalized industries such as railways, coal, banking, electricity, and natural gas. The leftist Popular Front government, elected in 1936, introduced the forty-hour workweek and vacations with pay, and responded to strikes by backing pay raises, but there was widespread civil unrest.

French occupation by the Nazis during World War II, the destruction of one-quarter of the nation's wealth, and immediate postwar privation gave way to one of the great miracles of economic development. In the late 1940s, Keynesian ideas of state intervention to promote growth, the development of successful national planning by civil servant and economic planner Jean Monnet (best known for leading the cause of post–World War II European unity), a baby boom, and U.S. aid through the Marshall Plan jump-started what the French economist Jean Fourastié was to call *"les trentes glorieuses"* (the glorious thirty years). During these three decades, the French economy grew faster than that of the United States, Britain, and, for much of the period, even West Germany. Anticapitalist sentiment, together with the heritage of Colbertism, made France ripe for state intervention. Monnet's "Plans" came to be known as "indicative planning," in concert with industry and labor, and in contrast to authoritarian Soviet-style planning. The Plans defined economic priorities, collected and disseminated a massive array of economic statistics, did extensive economic forecasting, and brought together big business, labor unions, and government to create an encouraging climate for business.

Although many industries and banks were nationalized, France achieved financial stability during the Fourth Republic and was increasingly integrated into the European and global economies. The European Coal and Steel Community, also devised by Monnet to unite Western Europe in peace and prosperity, led to the 1957 Treaty of Rome, creating the European Economic Community (now, the European Union). Tariffs were eliminated, French export industries blossomed, and the country's sacred agricultural sector was protected by massive subsidies. Although the state's share of investment fell from 38 percent to 28 percent between the early 1950s and early 1970s, the government accounted for about half of the French economy by the latter third of the twentieth century. The government invested heavily in prestigious projects and "national champions" such as Airbus, nuclear power, transportation, information technology, and armaments.

With the most rapid economic growth between the early 1950s and 1973, and per capita income doubling in the fifteen years after 1960, French average income grew from about one-half that of the average American in the early 1950s to four-fifths by the 1970s, and France passed Britain to become the world's fourth-largest economy. Technological innovation, government planning, pent-up demand, and the growth of huge multinational French industries contributed to the growth. By the beginning of the twenty-first century, France was a world leader in industries such as aerospace, rail, luxury goods, tourism, nuclear power, automobile production, telecommunications, pharmaceuticals, engineering, retail, capital goods, and banking, and its financial markets grew dramatically. About a dozen of the world's 100 largest companies and four of the top twenty-five were French in 2009, ranging from oil giant Total, retailer Carrefour, automaker Peugeot, and banks such as BNP Paribas and Société Générale. Other French giants include Saint-Gobain, Renault, Air France, Alstom, Christian Dior, Alcatel, Michelin, L'Oréal, EDF, LVMH, and Sodexo. While supporting business and investing in research, the government has helped maintain French education, health, and infrastructure among the world's best. The "French model" of balancing the dynamism of capitalism with a strong sense of social "solidarity" was supported across the political spectrum. France has traditionally also been one of the strongest supporters of the European Union and has benefited greatly by the increased access the union has given it to markets in other parts of Europe—today some 60 percent of the country's trade is with other EU members—and the subsidies the EU has lavished on the French agricultural sector, the largest in the union.

Despite such benefits, since the 1980s French economic growth has slowed, as policy makers began to reform labor markets and privatize many companies in the face of rapid global competition. High unemployment and a sense of economic "malaise" gripped France by the early twenty-first century. During the global financial crisis that began in late 2007, the French economy suffered, yet, as during the Depression, less than those of the United States and Britain. Significantly lower household debt and higher savings, together with a $40 billion stimulus that left government deficits at half the U.S. level, helped the economy emerge from recession, albeit with sluggish growth. Despite long-term structural weaknesses in the French economy and the need for economic re-

French president Nicolas Sarkozy announces a 35 billion euro ($52 billion) government investment plan in 2009 to boost the nation's economic growth in the medium term. The program targeted sectors of declining competitiveness, such as universities. *(Eric Feferberg/ AFP/Getty Images)*

form, French productivity is the world's highest and the average worker enjoys considerably more leisure and state benefits than their counterparts in other large, rich countries; income statistics thus understated the strength of the French economy and its people's high standard of living.

Andrew L. Yarrow

See also: Germany; Italy; United Kingdom.

Further Reading

Ardagh, John. *France in the New Century: Portrait of a Changing Society.* London: Penguin, 2000.

Cameron, Rondo, ed., with Franklin F. Mendels and Judith P. Ward. *Essays in French Economic History.* Homewood, IL: R.D. Irwin for the American Economic Association, 1970.

Dormois, Jean-Pierre. *The French Economy in the Twentieth Century.* New York: Cambridge University Press, 2004.

Hough, J.R. *The French Economy.* New York: Holmes & Meier, 1982.

Melitz, Jacques, and Charles Wyplosz. *The French Economy.* Boulder, CO: Westview, 1985.

Friction, Financial

In economics, the term "friction" refers to anything that slows or hampers trade, business, or exchange. It can be related to cost, time, or any number of other factors. Capital gains taxes, a long line at a store, a new business's lack of reputation, or a student's lack of access to loans are all forms of friction.

Financial friction, then, is any cost or other obstacle that causes a person or institution to not invest in something or hold onto an asset that they would normally sell. As such, financial friction can either heighten or lower a market participant's level of risk. In short, financial frictions generate costs—loosely defined—that interfere with an economic activity that a person would make in the absence of such friction.

When investors decide what to buy and sell, they normally balance risk against return. Riskier investments promise potentially higher returns

and vice versa. Financial frictions distort this decision-making process. For example, in a theoretically frictionless world, there is nothing to stop an investor from shifting money from corporate equities to bonds during a downturn in the stock market. But that investor might hesitate to do so if selling the stocks triggers a broker's fee or a capital gains tax.

Financial frictions have both direct and indirect costs. The former include the capital gains tax, while the latter include the losses incurred by making less-than-optimal financial decisions. At the same time, financial frictions can also bring direct and indirect gains. For every investor who pays a broker's fee, say, there is a broker collecting that fee. That would be a direct gain. In addition, a mutual fund that can lower what it charges to investors in fees can increase its competitiveness, all other things being equal, vis-à-vis other mutual funds, thereby heightening its profitability.

Moreover, over time, financial frictions change. Not only does Congress pass and repeal, and raise and lower taxes but new technologies and new financial instruments also come into play. For example, computers have made it cheaper to compare investment strategies, thereby lowering the costs charged by financial analysts. At the same time, the growing complexity of financial instruments raises those costs.

Financial frictions fall into five basic categories: transaction costs; taxes and regulations; asset indivisibility; nontraded assets; and agency and information problems. Transaction costs, the cost in money and time of making a transaction, are generally relatively low, and new technology is bringing down those costs even further. Taxes and regulations are self-evident; the capital gains tax, for example, might discourage an investor from selling an asset in a given year to avoid having to pay it.

The financial friction arising from asset indivisibility arises because some assets simply cannot be divided into portions small enough for every investor to own one—for example, a parcel of commercial real estate in Manhattan. Thus, while an optimal investment strategy would dictate that investors own such an asset, the latter's indivisibility makes that difficult or impossible. Mutual funds and other collective investment schemes, such as real-estate investment trusts (REITs), can overcome this friction since, by pooling investors' money, they can buy a large, indivisible asset and then divvy up returns on a pro rata basis.

Nontraded assets are those assets that simply cannot be traded or cannot be traded easily. For example, a person invests tens of thousands of dollars in gaining education and skills but cannot sell that "human capital," at least, not since Abraham Lincoln signed the Emancipation Proclamation. However, constant financial market innovation is ever expanding what can and cannot be traded. The explosion in debt-backed securities—whereby people invest in the revenue streams arising from mortgages or credit card debts—shows the ingenuity of financial institutions and their employees in overcoming the friction inherent in nontraded assets. Indeed, even human capital has become a tradable commodity, as musicians such as David Bowie and James Brown have shown by creating bonds to be paid off by the future earnings their skills and talents are expected to bring in.

Agency and information problems deal with the issue of incentive. It is a long held truism in the financial markets—and life itself—that people are more likely to make wise decisions when it comes to their own money than when it comes to the money of others. While it may make rational sense to purchase an asset controlled by another, investors may hesitate to do so and give up direct control of their money, or they may worry that the seller knows more about the liabilities that come with a particular asset and thus may hesitate to invest in it.

Financial frictions can also play a role in the business cycle, as the dot.com and housing booms and busts of the 1990s and 2000s make clear. The former boom and bust involved the dramatic run-up in the value of Internet and other technology-related stocks in the mid-1990s, followed by their dramatic crash in the early 2000s. One of the reasons for the sudden crash in share prices was due to the fact that little financial friction was involved in selling off shares—transaction costs were minimal and people taking losses were not subject to capital gains taxes (indeed, they could write off their losses against gains made elsewhere in their portfolio). Thus, when stock prices began to decline, people rushed to sell off their shares.

As housing prices took off in the mid-2000s, some economists feared that this sector too was experiencing an unsustainable bubble. They called for the Federal Reserve to raise interest rates so as to cool the inflation. But defenders of the low interest rates, including, for a time, Federal Reserve chairman Alan Greenspan, argued that housing prices were unlikely to experience the same dramatic swing as dot.com shares. They based their argument on the steep transaction costs involved in buying and selling a home—broker commissions, taxes, inspection fees, and so on. In other words, fears of housing market speculation were grossly exaggerated, they said, because financial frictions in that sector limited them. But as subsequent events illustrated, when potential returns are great enough—or when losses are substantial enough—investors will decide that the costs inherent in financial frictions are not substantial enough to alter their investment behavior.

James Ciment

See also: Financial Markets; Savings and Investment; Tax Policy.

Further Reading

DeGennaro, Ramon P. "Market Imperfections." *Journal of Financial Transformation* 14 (August 2005): 107–117.

DeGennaro, Ramon P., and Cesare Robotti. "Financial Market Frictions." In *Economic Review* of the Federal Reserve Bank of Atlanta (third quarter 2007). Available at www.google.com /#hl=en&q=financial+friction+degennaro&aq=f&aql=&aqi =&oq=&fp=435311d5ec9ae78f. Accessed January 2010.

Luttmer, Erzo G.J. "Asset Pricing in Economies with Frictions." *Econometrica* 64:6 (1996): 1439–1467.

Friedman, Milton (1912–2006)

One of the most influential economists of the late twentieth century, the Nobel Prize–winning Milton Friedman is best known in the profession for his monetarist theories, which emphasized a gradual expansion of the money supply as the best way to control inflation and create sustained economic growth. Outside of academia, Friedman was a controversial figure, both an outspoken opponent of government intervention in the economy and the intellectual mentor for conservative free-market politicians such as British prime minister Margaret Thatcher and President Ronald Reagan.

The son of Jewish immigrants, Friedman was born in Brooklyn, New York, in 1912, and grew up in suburban New Jersey. A mathematics major at Rutgers University, he earned his master's degree in economics at the University of Chicago in 1933 and, after a number of years working for the federal government in a variety of economics-related posts, he received his PhD in economics from Columbia University in 1946. That same year, he took a teaching post at the University of Chicago, where he would remain for the next thirty years, helping to turn the economics department there into a powerhouse of monetarist, free-market theory.

By his own admission, Friedman started out as a supporter of Keynesian ideas about the need for government to stimulate demand as a way to lift economies out of downturns. As part of New Deal Washington in the 1930s, he recalled later, he supported the job creation programs of President Franklin Roosevelt but questioned the administration's efforts to fix prices and wages, saying that it distorted more efficient market mechanisms for allocating resources where they were needed.

Even as Friedman was beginning his teaching career, he was recruited by National Bureau of Economic Research (NBER) head—and future Federal Reserve chairman—Arthur Burns. At the

NBER, Friedman began in earnest his study of the role the money supply played in the business cycle, research that would culminate in his pathbreaking 1963 book, *A Monetary History of the United States, 1867–1960*, cowritten with his longtime collaborator, economist Anna Schwartz. While, as the title indicates, the work covered the history of money and monetary policy for the previous century, its most important findings concerned the Great Depression. Conventional economic wisdom of the day had it that monetary forces played a minimal role in the economic downturn of the 1930s. Friedman and Schwartz brought those forces to the forefront and blamed the Federal Reserve (Fed) for making things worse by not keeping the money supply steady and not taking on the role of lender of last resort.

Few books on economics have been more in-

The conservative, free-enterprise views of Milton Friedman, associated with the Chicago school of economics, helped shape U.S. and international policy during the 1980s. His monetary approach provided a counterpoint to the fiscal policy of the Keynesians. *(George Rose/Getty Images)*

fluential. Not only did it revive monetary theory as a key component of economic thinking but it also influenced many future policy makers in times of economic crisis. Current Fed chairman Ben Bernanke—himself a student of the Great Depression—has said that the book and Friedman's work generally helped lead him to embrace the activist role the Fed assumed during the financial crisis of the late 2000s.

Important as the book was in economic circles, it had little effect on economic policy makers of the day. The Keynesian paradigm of activist government held sway for the first several decades after World War II, as both Republican and Democratic administrations sought to stimulate demand during times of economic contraction by direct spending, tax-cutting, and expansion of the money supply. But the "stagflation" of the 1970s—in which, contrary to Keynesian theory, high unemployment was accompanied by high inflation—undermined the prevailing liberal consensus and led to the triumph of conservatism at the ballot box.

Both Thatcher and Reagan adopted Friedman's ideas. In the United States, the Fed raised interest rates—thereby limiting the money supply—as a way to wring inflation out of the system. While this produced record postwar high unemployment in the short term, it did tame inflation. In general, Friedman's conservative argument that government efforts to stimulate demand were counterproductive held sway in policy-making circles during the 1980s. Outside of the Anglo-American world, Friedman and the Chicago school of economics had great influence over the Chilean government under dictator Augusto Pinochet in the 1970s and 1980s, which dismantled many social programs, privatized industries, and emphasized free-market forces.

Friedman also did important research into economic questions beyond monetary policy, developing his "permanent income hypothesis," which stated that most consumers saved rather than spent windfall gains, such as those provided by tax cuts, and that government could not reduce

long-term unemployment through inflationary fiscal policies.

In 1976, Friedman was awarded the Nobel Prize in Economic Sciences "for his achievements in the fields of consumption analysis, monetary history and theory and for his demonstration of the complexity of stabilization policy." He retired the following year and became affiliated with the Hoover Institution, a conservative think tank at Stanford University in California.

Aside from continuing his economic work, he became a public intellectual from the late 1970s onward. His 1980 book *Free to Choose*, cowritten with his wife Rose Friedman, was a paean to the efficacy of free-market economics and became the basis for a much-watched documentary series on PBS. Friedman also became well known for his espousal of libertarian ideas, not only advocating limited government in the economy but in the social sphere as well, calling for the legalization of prostitution and drugs. He died in San Francisco in 2006.

James Ciment

See also: Monetary Policy; Monetary Stability; Monetary Theories and Models; Schwartz, Anna.

Further Reading
Butler, Eamonn. *Milton Friedman: A Guide to His Economic Thought.* New York: Universe, 1985.

Ebenstein, Lanny. *Milton Friedman: A Biography.* New York: Palgrave Macmillan, 2007.

Friedman, Milton, and Rose Friedman. *Free to Choose: A Personal Statement.* New York: Harcourt Brace Jovanovich, 1980.

Friedman, Milton, and Anna Jacobson Schwartz. *A Monetary History of the United States, 1867–1960.* Princeton, NJ: Princeton University Press, 1963.

Frisch, Ragnar (1895–1973)

Norwegian economist Ragnar Frisch is among those credited with introducing the use of mathematical formulas and a scientific approach to the study of economics. He is responsible for coining the terms "macroeconomics," "econometrics" (which he defined as a scientific methodology and approach to studying economics, not as a subdiscipline of the field), and "macroeconometrics," as well as for making significant contributions in each of these areas. In 1969, he was a co-recipient with Jan Tinbergen of the first Nobel Prize in Economic Sciences for their work in macroeconometrics, in which they explored variations in business cycles largely as a response to the worldwide economic problems of the Great Depression. Frisch is proud of the Antonio Feltrinelli Prize awarded to him in 1961 by the Accademia Nazionale dei Lincei, the famous Italian society of which Galileo Galilei was a member.

Ragnar Anton Kittil Frisch was born in Oslo, Norway, on March 13, 1895. He graduated from Oslo University in 1926, spent a year as a visiting professor at Yale University in New Haven, Connecticut, and then was named professor of social economy and statistics at Oslo University, a position he held until his retirement in 1965; he also served as director of the Institute for Social Economy at the university.

Frisch was a pioneer in using mathematical tools in the study of economic problems. Although others had explored that approach since the nineteenth century, Frisch was able to achieve substantive breakthroughs using mathematics. Underlying his approach was a belief that economics could be an exact, quantitative science, much like physics. The field of econometrics was a direct result of his scientific, empirical, and quantitative approach, with the critical benefits of providing statistical data that could be used as a reliable basis for testing economic theories and rigorous models capable of predicting changes in an economy.

Among the specific areas that Frisch explored was demand theory, centering on consumer behavior. Additionally, he developed a comprehensive theory that explained production from the perspective of the processes themselves. In collaboration with economists Frederick Waugh and Michael Lovell, he developed a complex and influential econometric formulation called the Frisch-Waugh-Lovell theorem.

Frisch made important contributions to the study of business cycles. His interest stemmed from concerns that fluctuations in prosperity and depression could not be controlled and thus had a dramatic impact on employment. To address this issue, he developed a novel method of analyzing time-series data and used it to analyze business cycles so as to explain why prosperity or recession began or ended. He published his theory of business cycles in a 1933 article in *Econometrica* titled "Propagation and Impulse." Frisch served as editor of *Econometrica*, a leading journal in the field, for more than twenty years.

In the years following World War II, Frisch focused his efforts on ways to modernize the economies of other countries, particularly such developing nations as India and Egypt. In his later years, he opposed Norway's participation in the European Common Market. Frisch died in Oslo on January 31, 1973.

Robert N. Stacy

See also: Akerman, Johan Henryk; Babson, Roger.

Further Reading

Andvig, Jens Christopher. *Ragnar Frisch and the Great Depression: A Study in the Interwar History of Macroeconomic Theory and Policy.* Oslo: Norsk Utenrikspolitisk Institutt, 1984.

Bjerkholt, Olav. "Ragnar Frisch's Business Cycle Approach: The Genesis of the Propagation and Impulse Model." *European Journal of the History of Economic Thought* 14:3 (September 2007): 449–486.

Johansen, Leif. "Ragnar Frisch's Contributions to Economics." *Swedish Journal of Economics* 71:4 (December 1969): 302–324.

Strøm, Steinar. *Econometrics and Economic Theory in the 20th Century: The Ragnar Frisch Centennial Symposium.* New York: Cambridge University Press, 1998.